Flowers for Northern Gardens

FLOWERS
FOR NORTHERN GARDENS

LEON C. SNYDER

Professor Emeritus of Horticultural Science
University of Minnesota

University of Minnesota Press • Minneapolis

Copyright © 1983 by the University of Minnesota.
All rights reserved.
Published by the University of Minnesota Press,
2037 University Avenue Southeast, Minneapolis, MN 55414
Printed in the United States of America.

Library of Congress Cataloging in Publication Data

Snyder, Leon C.
  Flowers for northern gardens.

  Includes index.
    1. Flowers—Northwestern States. 2. Flowers—
Northeastern States. 3. Flowers—Canada. I. Title.
II. Title: Northern gardens.
SB407.S656 1983   635.9'51'7   83-3605
ISBN 0-8166-0943-8

The University of Minnesota
is an equal opportunity
educator and employer.

ACKNOWLEDGMENTS

The author wishes to acknowledge and thank the following people for their assistance in preparing this book: June Rogier, Minnesota Landscape Arboretum librarian, and her staff; Linda Sanford, naturalist at Missouri Botanic Garden, for the line drawings; Mary Hartung for typing the manuscript; Dr. Francis de Vos, Mervin C. Eisel, Michael L. Heger, Laurie Mainquist, Jane P. McKinnon, Glenn H. Ray of the Minnesota State Horticultural Society, and Grace Stokes for color photographs; and Dale E. Herman, Professor of Horticulture, North Dakota State University and F. A. Giles, Professor of Ornamental Horticulture, University of Illinois, for their helpful suggestions on the manuscript.

CONTENTS

Flowers for Northern Gardens

INTRODUCTION

The climate of the northern states and adjoining parts of Canada is characterized by marked seasonal changes. The annual rainfall varies greatly, from 10 inches or less in parts of the Rocky Mountain states and western prairies to 50 inches or more in the eastern states. Temperature changes can be sudden and severe. Winter temperatures as low as −50° F (−46° C) are not uncommon in the north and summer temperatures of 100° F (38° C) occur. In spite of these climatic conditions, many garden flowers thrive and some, like the garden peony, do better than in any other part of the United States.

This book provides information on those garden flowers that do well in our climate and offers suggestions for making a wise selection and suggestions for cultivation that will help you grow healthier, more attractive flowers. Only those species and cultivars that are commercially available are included.

ORGANIZATION OF THE BOOK

The greater part of this volume is an alphabetical guide to over 800 species of herbaceous plants and their botanical varieties and about 1100 named cultivars (horticultural varieties). Entries are organized by scientific names, with common names in parentheses. Cross references to scientific names are provided in the alphabetical list of common names included in the index. The scientific names are those used in *Hortus Third*, an accepted reference on cultivated plants. Since many nursery and seed catalogs are not up to date on their scientific names, the names that they use are included in the text with reference to the proper name.

For each entry, information is given on plant structure, size, time of bloom, and culture. This information is followed by a listing of botanical varieties and named cultivars, including brief descriptions. Accompanying the entries are 48 pages of colored illustrations, alphabetically arranged, to aid in identification and plant selection. A glossary of botanical terms and an index of common names are included at the end of the book.

To make an informed decision when plants are selected and to increase one's chances of growing healthy and beautiful plants, it is necessary to have some basic knowledge of plant nomenclature, morphology (i.e., structure and form), culture, and landscape use. Those readers requiring such information are advised to study the first three chapters of this book before turning to the plant entries; skilled gardeners may prefer to skim through these chapters for new information. The remainder of this chapter deals with plant names, morphological characteristics, plant hardiness and hardiness zones, and the metric system. The second chapter covers plant culture, and the third chapter includes plant lists for selecting plants for special purposes.

HOW PLANTS GET THEIR NAMES

All plants have a scientific name and usually one or more common names. The scientific name consists of the genus and species and is the same in all parts of the world. The common name can differ in various countries of the world and even in the same country. A plant may even have several common names in the same locality. The word lily can be found in the common name of species in 24 genera and nine plant families in this book alone. It would be most convenient if each genus had but one common name and each species had a descriptive common name. An example is Baneberry, which is the common name for *Actaea*. Red Baneberry is the common name for *Actaea rubra* and the White Baneberry is the common name for *Actaea pachypoda*, a species with white fruits. Unfortunately, this simplicity is not characteristic for most common names. The use of the genus name as part of the common name may be a step in the right direction. Ageratum, Alyssum, Anemone, Aster, Begonia, Caladium, Chrysanthemum, Clematis, Cosmos, Crocus, Cyclamen, Dahlia, Delphinium, Iris, Geranium, Lobelia, Narcissus, Phlox, Verbena, and Zinnia are well familiar common names used as the generic name for the same plant. Often the common name is the English translation of the genus name, as Aconite for *Aconitum*, Amaranth for *Amaranthus*, Gentian for *Gentiana*, Hyacinth for *Hyacinthus*, Lily for *Lilium*, Primrose for *Primula*, Thyme for *Thymus*, Tulip for *Tulipa*, and Violet for *Viola*.

Not all the plants within a species are identical. Sometimes plants of a certain species growing in a particular geographic area will differ from plants of the same species in other parts of its natural range. Occasionally, flower and fruit color and size may differ from the typical species. Where these differences are reproduced naturally, a third name is added to the scientific binomial name. These names are prefixed by var. (for botanical variety), f. (for forma), or subsp. (for subspecies). Examples are *Clematis recta* var. *mandshurica* for a geographic variant with larger flowers than the species; *Geranium maculatum* f. *albiflorum*, a variant with white flowers; and *Heliopsis helianthoides* subsp. *scabra*, a variant with pubescent or scabrous stems and leaves. When to use the prefix var., f., or subsp. is not always clear to the layman. This decision is best left to a trained plant taxonomist.

Those differences that do not reproduce themselves in nature, whether they initially occur in nature or are induced by plant breeders, are given cultivar names. Most cultivars in perennial flowers can be reproduced only by vegetative means. In annual flowers, some cultivars can be seed propagated but only when the breeding lines are isolated or in the case of F_1 hybrids, when the breeding lines are kept true to type. Cultivar names are designated by single quotes or by the prefix cv. Examples are *Ageratum houstonianum* 'Blue Mink', or *Ageratum houstonianum* cv. Blue Mink. When cultivars are the result of crossing two or more species, it is no longer practical to use a species designation. The cultivar name then follows the genus or the common name. Examples are: *Lilium* x 'Enchantment' or Lily 'Enchantment'. In this book cultivar names are indicated by single quotes.

Plant families consist of groups of genera having similar flower structures. In the RANUNCULACEAE (Buttercup Family), the flowers consist of a whorl of sepals, many stamens, and numerous carpels. Petals may or may not be present. When the petals are lacking, the sepals are usually petal-like. The stamens are attached to the receptacle. The rose family has a similar flower structure, except that the stamens are attached to the base of the sepals. Petals are usually present and the number of carpels tends to be a fixed number. With a little practice, one can learn to recognize certain plant families. This is a real aid in plant identification. It also helps in providing the proper growing conditions, since most plants in a family have similar cultural requirements.

In this book, a brief description of each family is given along with a list of genera. These are described in Chapter 4.

Before a cultivar is named, the name must be cleared by the proper registering authority. Usually this authority is the National or International Plant Society for the genus, such as the American Hosta Society for all Hostas. The name, a herbarium specimen, a color photograph, and a description are sent to the registering authority. If the name has not been used previously for plants in that genus and if the name meets the credentials set for cultivar names, it is accepted. If not, the name is rejected and another name must be submitted.

Nurseries and garden centers often list their plants by common names only. The same plant may be sold under a different common name by different companies. When scientific names are used, often only the genus name is given. Quite often the scientific name used is obsolete. An attempt is made in this book to list all common names currently being used in the trade in an index to common names, with proper reference to the correct scientific name as used in *Hortus Third*. Scientific names are listed alphabetically in the text with reference to the correct name. Over 100 nursery and seed catalogs were reviewed in the preparation of this book. This is by no means an exhaustive survey of plant and seed sources; however, most of the garden flowers that will grow in the north are included.

MORPHOLOGICAL CHARACTERISTICS

Plant Habit and Kinds of Stems and Roots

Plants grown for their flowers vary greatly in plant habit. Some are low and creeping, others are upright. Some develop a single flowering stem whereas others form clumps; several are mound-shaped.

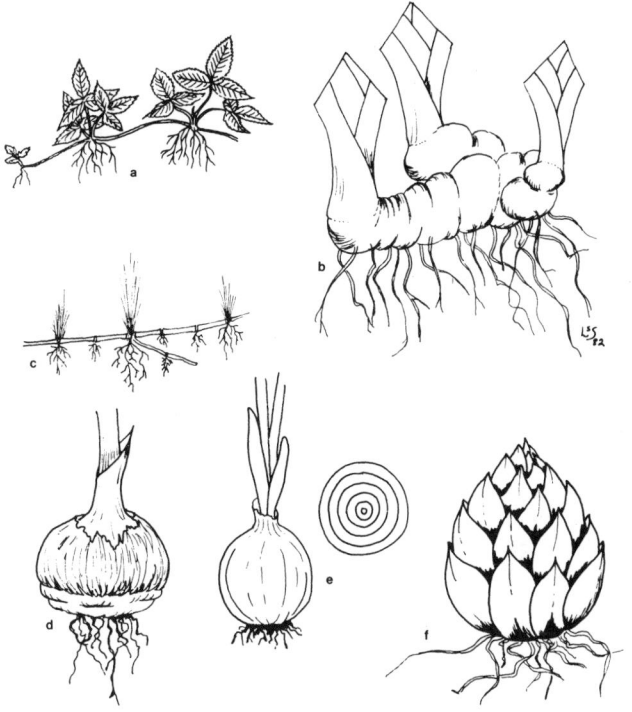

Modified stems: *a*. runner or stolon, *b*. fleshy rhizome, *c*. slender rhizome, *d*. corm, *e*. tunicate bulb, *f*. scaly bulb.

Stems are usually formed above ground. Stems that creep along the surface are called runners or stolons. Some plants, however, develop elongated underground stems called rhizomes. Some rhizomes, iris for example, are fleshy; others are slender. Corms and bulbs are also modified underground stems. Corms contain solid stored food in the center with papery, scalelike leaves on the surface. The gladiolus corm is a familiar example. Bulbs consist of fleshy leaf bases attached to a triangular basal stem plate. In the onion and hyacinth, the leaf bases form concentric rings. In the lily, the leaf bases form separate scales.

Roots are mostly formed underground and are either fibrous or fleshy. Fleshy roots are usually taproots that grow straight down or they are fascicled as in dahlias or peonies. The fleshy roots in such plants as bleeding hearts, dahlias, and peonies are used to propagate new plants.

Leaf Morphology

A typical leaf is made up of an expanded portion (the blade) and a stalk portion (the petiole). In some leaves, a pair of leaflike bracts (stipules) is found at the base of the petiole. In some herbaceous plants the leaf base attaches directly to the stem with no differentiated petiole. In others the leaf base forms a sheath around the stem.

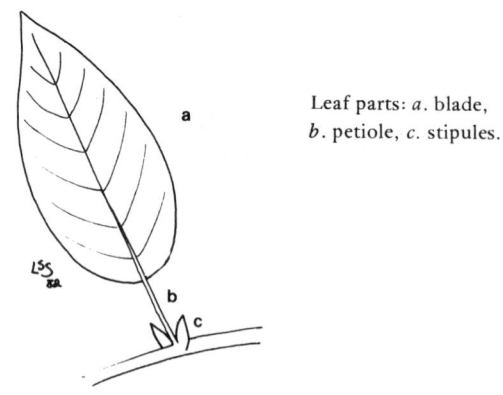

Leaf parts: *a*. blade,
b. petiole, *c*. stipules.

The leaf arrangement may be alternate, opposite, or whorled. When the leaves are alternate, they are usually arranged in a spiral fashion with one leaf at a node. When the leaves are opposite, two leaves are at a node and when they are whorled, three or more.

Leaf venation refers to the arrangement of the main veins. In pinnate venation, there is a central midrib and the lateral veins spread out from this midrib like a feather. In palmate venation, three or more prominent veins radiate from near the attachment of the petiole. Lateral veins spread out from these main veins. In both the pinnate and palmate types of venation, the vein branches form

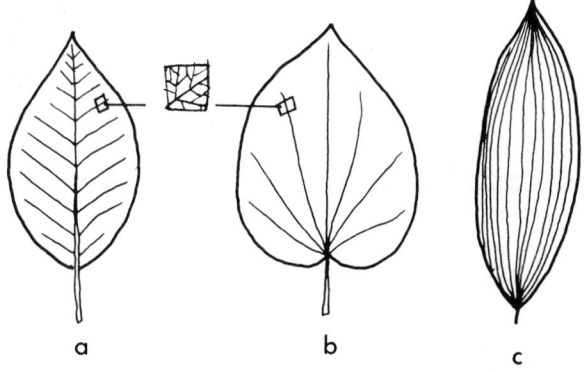

Leaf venation: *a*. pinnately netted, *b*. palmately netted, *c*. parallel.

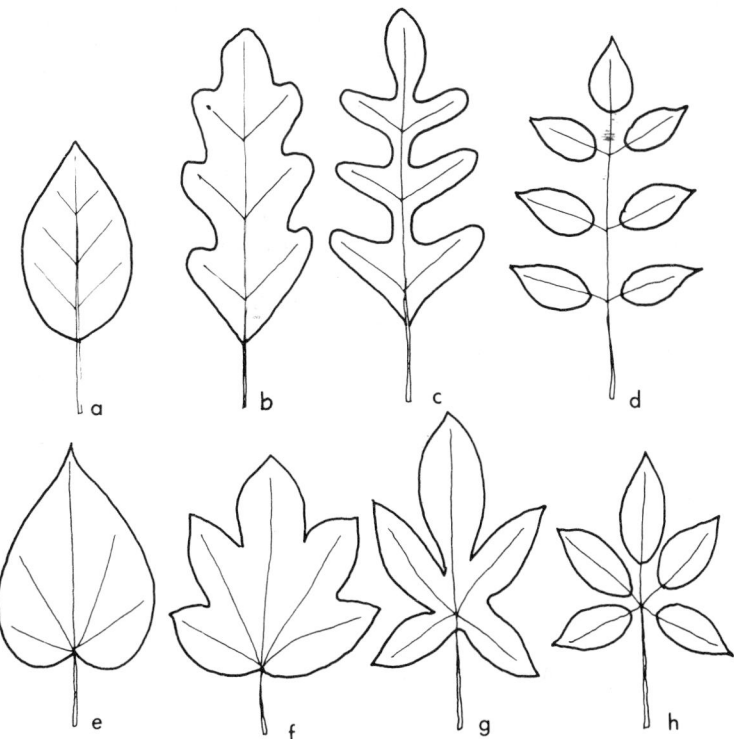

Stages in leaf compounding: *a*. simple pinnately veined leaf, *b*. pinnately lobed leaf, *c*. pinnately divided leaf, *d*. pinnately compound leaf, *e*. simple palmately veined leaf, *f*. palmately lobed leaf, *g*. palmately divided leaf, *h*. palmately compound leaf.

a distinct network that can be seen when the leaf is held up to the light. This type of venation is found in the dicotyledonous plants. In parallel venation, the main veins run parallel to each other. Parallel venation is found in monocots such as grasses and lilies.

Leaves may be simple or compound. A simple leaf has a blade all in one piece. In a compound leaf, the leaf blade is divided into separate leaflets. The accompanying illustrations show how pinnately compound leaves are derived from pinnately lobed leaves and how palmately compound leaves are derived from palmately lobed ones. To distinguish a leaflet of a compound leaf from a simple leaf, look for the bud that occurs in the axil formed where the leaf petiole attaches to the stem. No buds will be found in the axil of the leaflet.

Leaves can vary greatly in size. Some compound leaves may be several feet long and as wide. At the other extreme, leaves may be very small and scalelike. Leaves are usually flat and quite thin, but in some plants, they can be quite succulent. Such leaves usually store water and are adapted to dry situations.

Leaves have various shapes, which are quite uniform for each species and useful in recognizing plants. Some of the common shapes are illustrated.

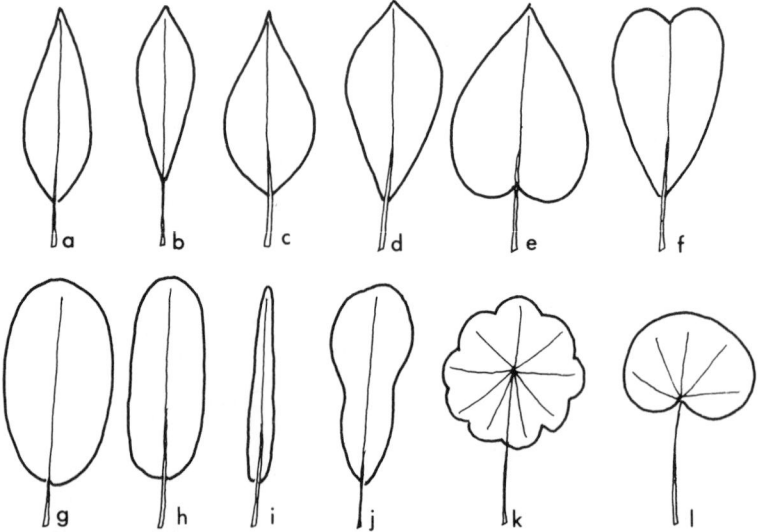

Leaf shapes: *a*. lanceolate, *b*. oblanceolate, *c*. ovate, *d*. obovate, *e*. cordate, *f*. obcordate, *g*. elliptical, *h*. oblong, *i*. linear, *j*. spatulate, *k*. peltate, *l*. reniform.

Leaf margins are also uniform for a given species and useful in plant identification. The variations in leaf margins are illustrated.

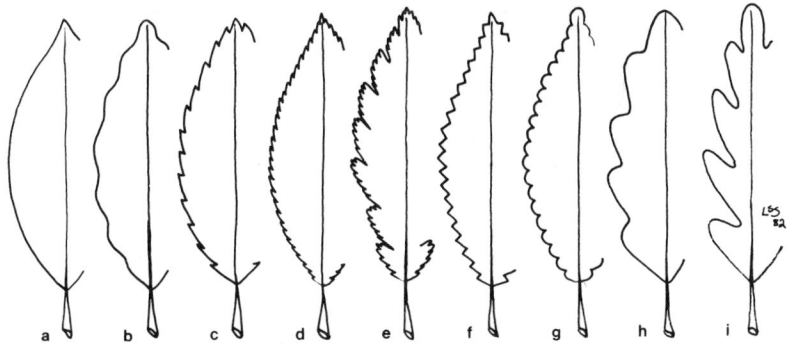

Leaf margins: *a*. entire, *b*. undulate, *c*. serrate, *d*. serrulate, *e*. doubly serrate, *f*. dentate, *g*. crenate, *h*. pinnately lobed, *i*. pinnatifid.

Leaf apices and leaf bases are also characteristic for each species, as illustrated in the following line drawings.

Leaf apices: *a*. caudate, *b*. acuminate, *c*. cuspidate, *d*. mucromate, *e*. acute, *f*. obtuse, *g*. truncate, *h*. emarginate.

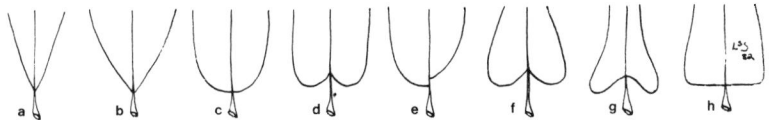

Leaf bases: *a*. cuneate, *b*. acute, *c*. obtuse, *d*. cordate, *e*. oblique, *f*. sagitate, *g*. hastate, *h*. truncate.

Flower Morphology

The flower is the least variable of the morphological characteristics and is used in most keys to identify plants. The typical flower has four sets of modified leaves, either spirally arranged or in whorls and attached to a short terminal swelling of the stem called a receptacle. The four sets of leaves are as follows:

Sepals. Lowest set of leaves, usually green. Collectively called the calyx.

Petals. Attached above the sepals, usually brightly colored. Collectively called the corolla.

Stamens. Located above the petals. Each stamen consists of a stalk portion (the filament) and pollen-producing sacs (the anthers). The number of stamens per flower varies from a few to as many as a hundred or more. Collectively called the androecium.

Carpels. Produced in the center of the flower. May be separate or fused to form a compound pistil. The pistil is made up of the swollen base (ovary), the neck portion (style), and the terminal portion, usually sticky (stigma). Carpels in a single flower are collectively called the gynoecium.

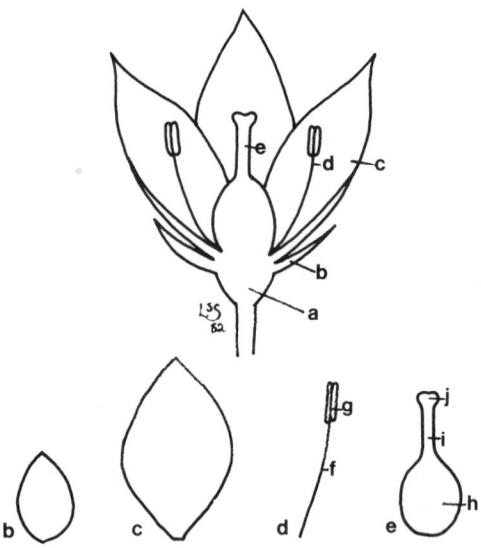

Parts of a typical flower: *a*. receptacle, *b*. sepal, *c*. petal, *d*. stamen, *e*. pistil, *f*. filament, *g*. anther, *h*. ovary, *i*. style, *j*. stigma.

The stamens and carpels are the reproductive organs of the flower. Pollen grains alight on the stigma and germinate to form a pollen tube that digests its way down through the style into the ovary chamber. Each pollen tube finds its way to an ovule where sperm cells are discharged to fertilize the egg and endosperm nuclei. The ovule then develops into a seed, and the fertilized egg divides to become the embryo.

The floral parts may remain separate or they may fuse. The fused calyx and corolla may be tubular or funnel-like with spreading lobes. Fused stamens are less common but in the pea and mallow families the filaments are fused to form a tube. The fusion of carpels to form a compound ovary is common.

Petal fusion in regular flowers: *a*. corolla of separate petals, *b*. corolla rotate, *c*. corolla campanulate, *d*. corolla funnelform, *e*. corolla salverform.

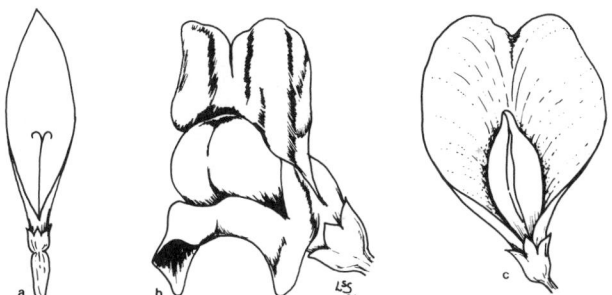

Petal fusion in irregular flowers: *a*. ligulate, *b*. bilabiate, *c*. papilionaceous.

Types of Flowers

Flowers differ in the placement of floral parts and in the presence or absence of parts. The following terms describe these differences.

Regular flower. Has radial symmetry. That is, any line cut vertically through the flower will divide it into two symmetrical halves.

Irregular flower. Asymmetrical in structure, so that only one vertical line will divide it into two symmetrical halves.

Complete flower. Has all four floral parts, sepals, petals, stamens, and carpels.

Incomplete flower. Lacks one or more floral parts. For example, in certain genera in the buttercup family, the petals may be lacking and the sepals are petal-like. In some plants the stamens and carpels may be produced in separate flowers, either on the same plant or on different plants.

Perfect flower. Has both stamens and carpels and may or may not have a calyx or corolla.

Imperfect flower. Has either stamens or carpels but not both in the same flower. Calyx and/or corolla may or may not be present. If staminate and pistillate flowers occur on the same plant, it is said to be monoecious; if on separate plants, it is dioecious.

Hypogynous flower. The ovary (gynoecium) is above (hypo) the attachment of the other flower parts. Thus the ovary is said to be superior.

Perigynous flower. The calyx cup, called the hypanthium, grows up around the ovary but is not attached to it. Sepal lobes, petals, and stamens are attached to the rim of the hypanthium.

Epigynous flower. The hypanthium fuses with the ovary, and sepal lobes, petals, and stamens appear to arise above the ovary, which is said to be inferior. This is the situation in genera belonging to the evening primrose family.

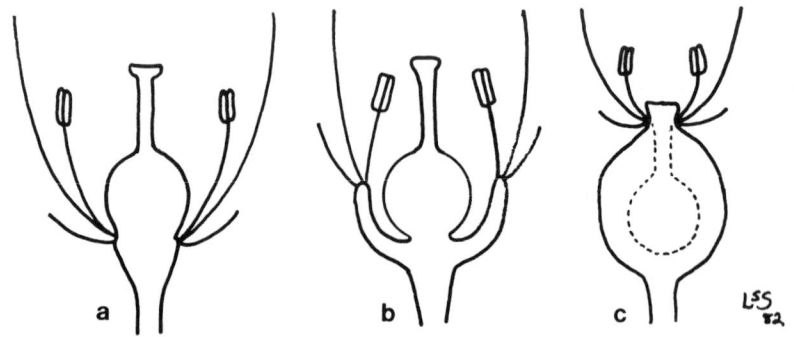

Placement of flower parts: *a*. hypogynous, *b*. perigynous, *c*. epigynous.

Types of Inflorescences

The inflorescence is the grouping of the flowers in a flower cluster. See illustrations on p. 15.

Spike. Flowers are borne sessile on a vertical axis.

Raceme. Flowers on short pedicels along a vertical axis. Snapdragon.

Corymb. Flowers on pedicels of varying length on a vertical axis. The lower pedicels are longer, giving the cluster a flat-topped appearance.

Panicle. A branched inflorescence with the oldest flowers near the base. Garden phlox.

Cyme. A branched inflorescence with the oldest flower at the tip of main stem and lateral branches.

Solitary. A single flower on a stalk. Pasqueflower, trillium.

Head. Many sessile flowers on a flat or rounded stem tip. Clover, marigold.

Umbel. A cluster of pedicelled flowers arising from one point at the tip of the stem. The pedicels are all of about the same length. Onion.

Compound umbel. A cluster of simple umbles. Queen-Anne's-lace.

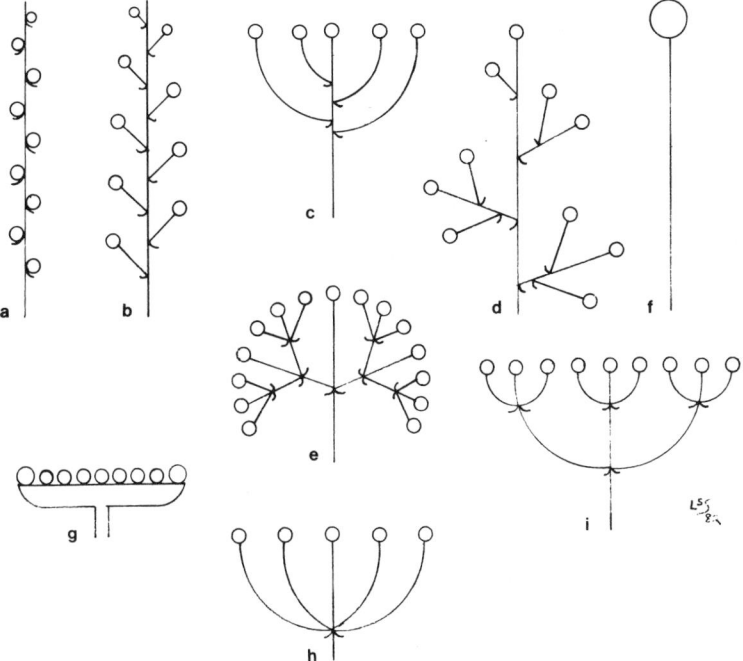

Types of inflorescences: *a*. spike, *b*. raceme, *c*. corymb, *d*. panicle, *e*. cyme, *f*. solitary, *g*. head, *h*. umbel, *i*. coumpound umbel.

Fruit Morphology

Fruits develop from the ovary of flowers that have been pollinated. In some fruits, accessory flower parts may become a part of the fruit. Fruits are classified as either dry or fleshy. The following fruit types are common in herbaceous flowering plants:

DRY FRUITS

Dehiscent dry fruits (those that split open to shed their seeds).

Legume (pod). Composed of one carpel that splits open along two sutures, with seeds attached in a single row. Example: sweet pea.

Follicle. Composed of one carpel that splits open along a single suture. A many-seeded fruit. Examples: delphinium, milkweed.

Capsule. Composed of more than one carpel, opening near the tip by pores or by longitudinal splitting. Many-seeded. Examples: poppy, lily.

Silique. A special type of capsule in the mustard family in which the two valves separate from the thin longitudinal partition called the replum. Example: Lunaria.

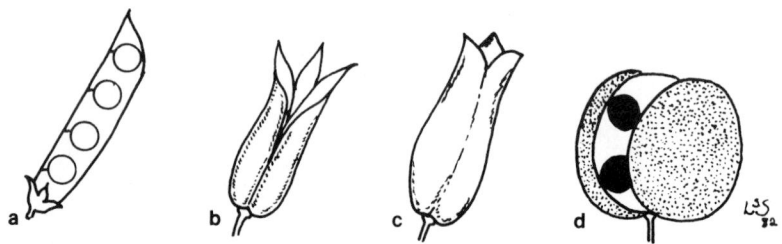

Dry dehiscent fruits: *a*. legume, *b*. follicle, *c*. capsule, *d*. silique.

Indehiscent dry fruits (those that do not open to shed their seeds).

Achene. A one-seeded fruit enclosed by a thin ovary wall. Example: Anemone.

Nutlet. A small, one-seeded fruit in which the seed is enclosed by a thickened ovary wall. Example: Mertensia.

Schizocarp. Fruit formed from a compound ovary in which the carpels separate at maturity, each segment containing a single seed. Example: cow parsnip.

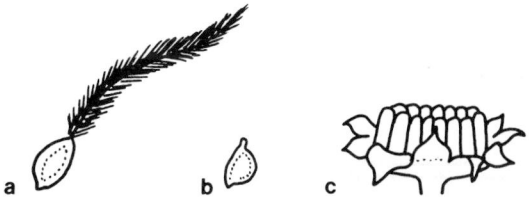

Dry indehiscent fruits: *a*. achene, *b*. nutlet, *c*. schizocarp.

FLESHY FRUITS

Berry. A many-seeded fleshy fruit with a thin pericarp. Example: baneberry.

Accessory. A fruit in which the fleshy portion is not derived from the pistil but where the fleshy edible portion is the enlarged receptacle; the true fruits (achenes) being embedded in the surface.

Fleshy fruits: *a*. berry, *b*. accessory.

PLANT HARDINESS

Plants differ greatly in their hardiness, or ability to grow and thrive in a given area. This hardiness is genetically determined. In general, in species that have a wide natural range, plants grown from seeds collected from northern plants will be hardier than those from southern plants. Fortunately, most garden flowers can be grown north of their natural range because of winter snow cover. Most perennials die to the ground in the fall and only the underground parts of the plants must be protected from the winter cold. Where snow cover cannot be depended on to provide winter protection, a mulch of straw or hay is usually sufficient. With tender plants that produce fleshy storage organs, such as fleshy roots, bulbs, corms, and rhizomes, the storage organs should be dug in the fall and stored over winter. With annual flowers, we are concerned only with frost tolerance. With tender annuals, planting outdoors should be delayed until after danger of frost has passed.

HARDINESS ZONES

Several plant hardiness zone maps are in use. The map used here and by most nurseries was prepared by the United States Department of Agriculture. (See page 19.) A few nurseries may use the zone map developed by the Arnold Arboretum. In Canada, the Canadian Government has prepared their own map for the provinces. It is important to know which map is being used when hardiness zones are mentioned. The Minneapolis and St. Paul area is Zone 4 in the U.S.D.A. map and Zone 3 in the Arnold Arboretum Map. Both maps are based on minimum winter temperatures. Other factors besides minimum winter temperatures can affect hardiness. Some of these factors are soil type, amount of rainfall, and snow cover. The best guide is to look around and see what is growing in your area. You may also want to do some experimenting yourself. Performance in your garden is what really counts. This book is intended to cover United States Department of Agriculture Zones 1 through 4 (see map).

METRIC SYSTEM

In this book all measurements are given in terms of the metric system. Those readers accustomed to measuring in feet and inches should find that the following metric rule will help them visualize the length of a meter, centimeter, and millimeter. A meter equals 100 cm. (centimeters) or 1000 mm. (millimeters) and is equivalent to a little over 39 inches.

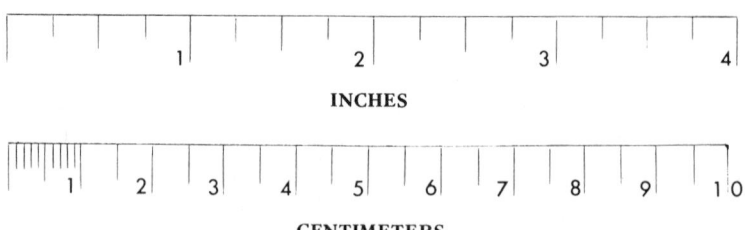

Metric ruler

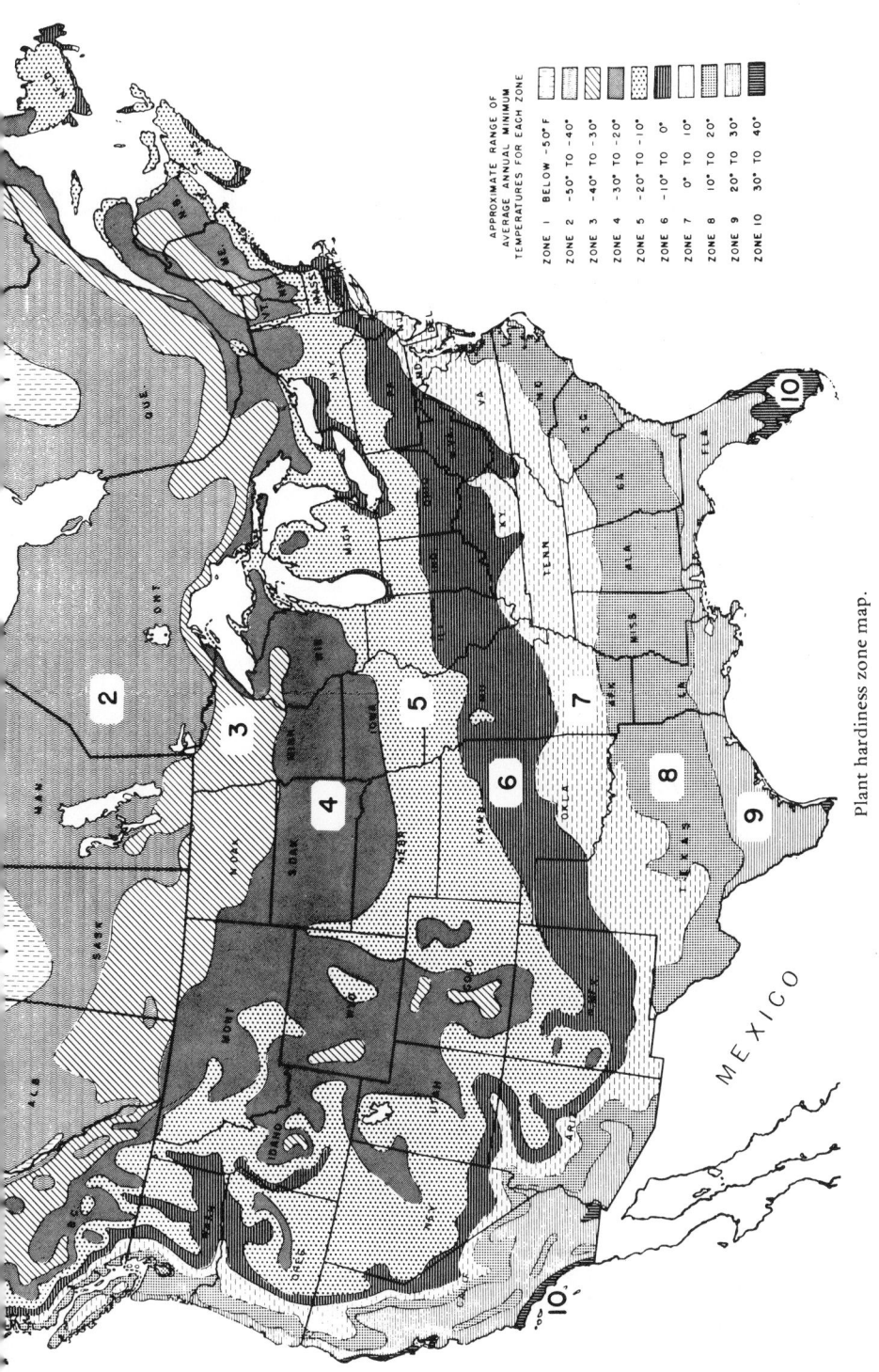

Plant hardiness zone map.

APPROXIMATE RANGE OF
AVERAGE ANNUAL MINIMUM
TEMPERATURES FOR EACH ZONE

ZONE 1 BELOW -50°F
ZONE 2 -50° TO -40°
ZONE 3 -40° TO -30°
ZONE 4 -30° TO -20°
ZONE 5 -20° TO -10°
ZONE 6 -10° TO 0°
ZONE 7 0° TO 10°
ZONE 8 10° TO 20°
ZONE 9 20° TO 30°
ZONE 10 30° TO 40°

PLANT CULTURE

Every gardner wants to grow healthy, attractive plants. To do this requires some basic understanding of how plants grow, their nutrient requirements, and cultural practices that will ensure success. In this chapter we will explore a number of subjects pertaining to plant culture: types of soil, soil as a source of plant nutrients, fertilizing the soil, site selection and soil preparation, starting plants indoors, vegetative propagation, transplanting, weed control, rodent and deer control, insect and disease control, training plants, and winter protection.

TYPES OF SOIL

Knowing the type of soil on your property, is essential for selecting the best plants for your garden. Some plants, such as the butterfly weed, do best on a sandy, well-drained soil. Others do best on a moisture retentive soil. A few plants, such as trailing arbutus and clintonia, require an acid soil.

Soils are classified as mineral or organic, depending on their origin. Mineral soils are made up of rock particles, whereas organic soils are derived from decomposed organic matter. The size of the rock particles in mineral soils varies greatly. Sand is made up of rock particles ranging in size from .05 to 2.0 mm.; silt of particles ranging from .002 to .05 mm.; and clay of particles smaller than .002 mm. Sand particles are visible with the unaided eye, silt particles under an ordinary microscope, and clay particles only with the aid of an electron microscope.

A loam soil is a mixture of various sizes of rock particles plus varying amounts of organic matter. A sandy loam contains a high percentage of sand particles, a silt loam a high percentage of silt, and a clay loam a high percentage of clay. Sandy loams are generally droughty and low in plant nutrients. Clay loams, on the other hand, are moisture retentive and high in plant nutrients. Silt loams are intermediate in fertility and moisture retention. Owing to the small size of clay particles, the particles tend to stick together and form hard clumps if clay loam soils are worked when wet.

Regardless of the type of soil in your garden, it will probably require the addition of organic matter to improve its productivity. Adding organic matter to sandy soil improves its moisture and nutrient retention. On clay soils, the organic matter loosens the soil and improves its physical structure. Since organic matter is constantly being broken down, it is necessary to replenish the organic matter frequently.

SOIL AS A SOURCE OF PLANT NUTRIENTS

The soil is a reservoir of chemical elements, present in both soluble and insoluble forms. Only those elements that are in solution in the soil water can enter the plant through the root hairs that penetrate between soil particles.

At least 16 elements are known to be essential to plant growth. These are carbon (C), hydrogen (H), oxygen (O), nitrogen (N), phosphorus (P), potassium (K), calcium (C), magnesium (Mg), manganese (Mn), iron (Fe), sulfur (S), boron (B), zinc (Zn), copper (Cu), molybdenum (Mo), and vanadium (Va). Some of the elements that enter the plant are not essential to growth. These include aluminum (Al), silicon (Si), and sodium (Na).

Carbon, hydrogen, and oxygen are used in photosynthesis, a process that occurs only in green plants in the presence of light. In this process carbon dioxide (CO_2) combines with water (H_2O) to form simple sugars ($C_6H_{12}O_6$) plus oxygen (O_2). The chemical equation for this process is $6CO_2 + 6H_2O + $ chlorophyll $+$ light $\rightarrow C_6H_{12}O_6 + 6O_2$. The carbon dioxide used in this process makes up over .03 percent of the atmosphere and enters the leaves through tiny openings called stomates. Water enters through the roots from the soil. The oxygen is returned to the air. The carbon dioxide, used in photosynthesis, is replenished by a reverse process, respiration, that occurs in all living cells, and by the burning of fossil fuels.

Nitrogen is a constituent of plant proteins and chlorophyll. It is associated with vegetative growth and a healthy green color in plants. The proteins are synthesized in plants by the addition of nitrogen to the simple sugars formed in photosynthesis.

Phosphorus is needed for flowering and fruiting and is an essential constituent of certain plant proteins. It also hastens maturity of plant cells and aids in carbohydrate movement within the plant.

Potassium plays a catalytic role in the movement of carbohydrates within the plant. It is also associated with strong root development and sturdy stems.

Calcium serves as a cementing substance to hold cells together and aids in cell division. In the soil it neutralizes soil acidity and minimizes the toxic effect of excessive amounts of aluminum and iron.

Magnesium is a constituent of chlorophyll and aides in the movement of phosphorus within the plant.

Iron is essential for chlorophyll synthesis, although it is not a constituent of the chlorophyll molecule. It probably serves a catalytic role.

Sulfur is a constituent of certain plant proteins. Molybdenum acts as a catalyst in the reduction of nitrate nitrogen in the synthesis of amino acids, the building blocks of plant proteins. The exact roles of the other essential elements are not so clearly understood.

Of all the essential elements, only nitrogen, phosphorus, and potassium are apt to be deficient in the soil. These must be replaced to maintain soil fertility. The most likely is a deficiency of nitrogen. Although 80 percent of the air is nitrogen, this gaseous nitrogen cannot be utilized by green plants. Certain soil bacteria and bacteria that live in the root nodules of certain leguminous plants can change the nitrogen in the soil air to the nitrate (NO_3) form by oxidation. By this process a certain amount of nitrogen is made available to green plants. Nitrogen is also returned to the soil by decaying organic matter, the proteins of which are acted on by soil organisms and changed to the nitrate form. Occasionally some gaseous nitrogen is fixed during electric storms and enters the soil in the rainwater. In spite of these natural means for replenishing the soil nitrogen, it is often necessary to add nitrogen in the form of fertilizers. This is especially important in the early spring, when the soil is too cold for the nitrification bacteria to work. In fact, in cold wet soils, denitrification bacteria can reduce the nitrate nitrogen to ammonia, which escapes from the soil as a gas.

Phosphorus is contained in most soils as rock phosphate, which is insoluble and unavailable to plants except as it is released by soil acids. Soils relatively high in organic matter are highest in available phosphorus. On very acid soils and on very alkaline soils, the phosphorus is less available to plants. Phosphorus is sometimes added as rock phosphate or bone meal, forms that are slowly available to plants. These forms are useful for mixing with soil before long-lived perennials such as peonies are planted. Most commercial fertilizers contain the phosphorus in the acid form (HPO_4), which is readily available to plants. The phosphorus that is added should be mixed with the soil so it will be available in the root zone, since it moves very slowly in the soil.

Potassium is present as soluble salts in the soil. When it is needed, it can be added in commercial fertilizers as potassium chloride. Wood ashes also contain some potassium. Potassium, being soluble in water, moves more freely in the soil than phosphorus but not as freely as nitrogen.

Occasionally it may be necessary to add magnesium, manganese, and boron to the soil. Iron, although usually present in adequate amounts, may not be available to certain plants growing on soils that are high in lime ($CaCO_3$); this is particularly true of certain members of the rose family. The leaves of susceptible plants will show a yellowing between the leaf veins. This symptom is called iron chlorosis. Clematis growing near the house foundation often show this symptom because of lime that leaches out from the foundation wall. Adding iron sulfate or iron chelates to the soil usually corrects a chlorosis problem. Foliar sprays containing iron can also be used.

FERTILIZING THE SOIL

To maintain a satisfactory level of soil fertility it is necessary to replenish the elements used by plants or lost from the soil by leaching or erosion, usually by adding organic matter and commercial fertilizers. The organic matter improves the physical properties of the soil and its moisture and nutrient retention. It also adds certain essential elements. Commercial fertilizers contain the essential elements in a readily available form and are relatively cheap to use. Since they are concentrated, it is essential to apply them evenly and at the proper rate. Too heavy an application may do more harm than good. Two good methods may be used to determine when your soil needs fertilizer: the first, a soil test, available for a fee from the Soils Department of your Agricultural Experiment Station and from certain private laboratories, will tell you which elements may be deficient and what kind and how much fertilizer to use. Another method is to study your plants. If they are making satisfactory growth and have a good green color and have abundant bloom, there will be no need to add fertilizer.

Kinds of Fertilizer

For flowering plants, a fertilizer relatively high in phosphorus is best. A 5-10-5 or a 5-10-10 fertilizer is good. If your soil is low in organic matter, a 10-10-10 or a 12-12-12 fertilizer will give good results. The first number in the fertilizer refers to the percentage of nitrogen, the second to the percentage of phosphorus pentoxide (P_2O_5), and the third to that of potassium oxide (K_2O). The form of nitrogen in the fertilizer should be considered. Nitrogen derived from organic sources like cottonseed or soybean meal, tankage, dried blood, or fish is slowly available to green plants, whereas nitrogen from inorganic sources such as ammonium nitrate, ammonium sulfate, and synthetic urea is quickly available. Organic nitrogen produces visible results over a longer period than does inorganic nitrogen, but these results are not noticeable until the soil warms up and soil organisms become active in the spring. The cost of the fertilizer is another factor to consider. Inorganic nitrogen is much cheaper than organic nitrogen. The plant really does not care, since the nitrogen enters the plant in the nitrate (NO_3) form regardless of the source. For acid-loving plants, the fertilizer used should give an acid reaction. Most garden centers will have a brand specifically recommended for acid-loving plants.

When to Fertilize

The best time to apply fertilizer is at the time the soil is being prepared for planting. At that time the fertilizer can be thoroughly worked into the soil. Often, one application in the spring is all that is needed. For some plants that are heavy feeders, a second application just after bloom starts will give an added boost. For fall planted bulbs, a fertilizer high in phosphorus should be worked into the soil beneath the bulbs.

How to Fertilize

It is essential to apply the fertilizer evenly over the entire surface and at the correct rate. A whirlwind spreader can be used. Large areas may require a push-type spreader such as is used on lawns; for small areas, a small plastic spreader turned by hand will do a good job. For best results the fertilizer should be worked into the soil. When sidedressing individual plants, spread the fertilizer by hand, being careful not to get it too close to the plant. The rate of application is very important. If a little is good, it certainly is not true that a lot is better. Fertilizer burn is common, and plants are often killed by too much fertilizer. Since fertilizers vary so much in their analysis, it is difficult to specify an exact rate for application; a safe rule is to never apply at a rate that will exceed 1 pound of actual nitrogen per 1,000 square feet. If your fertilizer contains 10 percent nitrogen, you can safely apply 10 pounds per 1,000 square feet. If the fertilizer contains 5 percent nitrogen, you can apply 20 pounds. It is the nitrogen that "burns."

Many gardeners prefer to use a liquid fertilizer and foliar feed their plants. This method gives good results but is more expensive and requires more frequent applications. When using a liquid fertilizer, apply at the rate recommended on the package.

Site Selection and Soil Preparation

Since most flowering plants do best in full sunlight, the site selected for the flower border should have direct sun for at least 8 hours a day. If you have only shade or partial shade, be careful to select shade tolerant plants. The border should be located where it can be seen and enjoyed from inside the house. A suitable background of shrubs or an attractive fence should be provided. The soil should be free of perennial weeds and annual weed seeds. If quack grass or Canadian thistle are present, they should be eliminated before the soil is prepared. The time to add organic matter is before you plant. Apply three to four bushels of well-rotted manure or compost per 100 square feet of surface and the required amount of fertilizer. If the organic matter is undecomposed, you will need to add additional nitrogen to aid in decomposition. Work this organic matter into the soil, using a spade or power rotovator. The soil should be worked to a depth of at least 6 inches. Deeper is even better. A sandy soil can be worked at almost any time but a clay soil should not be worked when it is wet. Pick up a handful of soil and squeeze it. If it crumbles, it is dry enough to work. Since most flowers are planted in the spring, the time to prepare the soil is just as soon as the soil is dry enough, usually in late April.

STARTING PLANTS INDOORS

Most annual flowers and many perennials are grown from seeds. You have your choice of purchasing plants from garden centers or nurseries or of growing your own plants from seeds. If you have the right conditions, you can grow quality plants. By growing your own plants, you can grow cultivars that are not usually available from garden centers. The growing of plants indoors can be challenging and rewarding.

Purchase your seeds from a reputable seed company. Order the seeds early to be sure of getting the cultivars that you would like to grow. Seeds can be started in a sunny window or under fluorescent lights. I start mine under lights with excellent results. I prepare a separate plastic flower pot about 4 inches in diameter for each kind of seed, and I use a sterile medium. The pots should be clean and rinsed with household disinfectant. Most garden stores sell a starting medium containing vermiculite and peat moss fortified with plant nutrients. This medium is sterile and free of "damping-off" organisms. If you use soil, be sure that the soil has been sterilized by heat to kill harmful organisms.

Fill the pot with the starting medium, then tap the pot on the bench to settle the medium. Scatter the seeds evenly over the surface. Do not put too many seeds in a single pot; too many seedlings will result in tall spindly plants. It may not be necessary to plant all of the seeds in the packet. After scattering the seeds, sift some of the medium through a fine screen to cover the seeds. I use a window screen for this purpose. Next, label each pot, giving the variety and seeding date. You can water the medium well by submersing the base of the pot in a shallow pan of water. When the surface shows moisture, the medium is sufficiently watered. Another method is to apply water in a fine mist until the medium is moist. Set the pots under the lights and cover them with glass or a sheet of clear plastic, providing a moist atmosphere for seed germination. The temperature should be at least 70° F. (21° C.). The time necessary for germination can vary from a few days to several weeks, depending on the kind of seed. Examine the pots each morning. When the green seedlings can be seen, remove the pot from the plastic cover or remove the glass if you cover each pot separately. Put the pot directly under the lights so the tops of the seedlings are about 6 inches (15 cm.) from the lights. I use cool white lights and keep them on for 16 hours each day. It is best to use a time clock. Care must be used to water the seedlings at regular intervals once they are removed from the plastic cover. I find it necessary to water once a day.

When the seedlings develop their first true leaves, it is time to transplant them to individual containers or plant trays. This provides proper spacing to develop short stocky plants. A sharp, pointed stick or "dibble" is used to open the planting holes and to firm the soil around the roots. The seedlings should be carefully lifted from the seed pot to avoid breaking the roots. Water as soon as a flat is transplanted and place the plants back under the lights.

Before planting into the garden, harden off the seedlings in a cold frame to get them accustomed to the outdoor temperatures. If you move them directly from the lights to the garden, the shock may be too great.

When to start seeds is a difficult question for many beginning gardeners. It takes anywhere from 6 to 10 weeks to grow a suitable transplant, depending on the variety and the growing conditions. Since most gardeners plant their flowers about Memorial day, the first seeds should be started about March 15. Some flowers, such as pansies, are frost tolerant and can be set outdoors in early May. Such seeds should be started earlier, often in mid February. Geraniums, grown from seed, require a longer time to develop a flowering size plant. Geranium seeds may be planted in mid January. Experience will soon tell you which seeds to plant early and which ones to plant late. I usually start snapdragons, sweet alyssum, petunias, and impatiens in mid March and wait until mid April to start seeds of zinnias and marigolds.

STARTING SEEDS OF PERENNIALS

Most perennials, except for the named cultivars, can be grown from seed. Some, like delphinium, that bloom the first year, can be started indoors. Others are started outdoors either in a cold frame or in a nursery row. The advantage of starting seeds in a cold frame is that you can protect the plants over the first winter by covering the frame with a protective cover of hay or straw. The exact time to sow the seeds varies. Some seeds must be planted as soon as ripe. Others can be stored over winter for spring planting. Seeds are usually planted in flats or pots. The seedlings are then transplanted in rows with the proper spacing between plants. Some gardeners may prefer to seed directly in rows and thin the seedlings. Spring is the best time to transplant the plants to the flower border.

VEGETATIVE PROPAGATION

Most perennials, especially the named cultivars, are propagated by vegetative means, such as cuttings, layering, and division. Some perennials develop fleshy storage organs and these are used to produce new plants.

Softwood cuttings are taken from healthy plants that are actively growing. These cuttings are usually tip cuttings 3 to 4 inches (7 to 10 cm.) long. Remove the lower leaves and insert the cutting in a sterile rooting medium such as coarse sand or perlite. The medium should be in a shallow flat, enclosed by a glass or clear plastic cover to provide a moist atmosphere for rooting the cuttings. I use window glass, cut to size, for the sides, which are held in place by plastic tape at the corners. I then cover the top with two pieces of glass that can be separated to provide ventilation after roots form. Cuttings that are easy to root will form roots in from 4 to 6 weeks. Cuttings that are difficult to root are dipped in a rooting compound such as Rootone or Hormodin before they are inserted in the rooting medium. These compounds contain hormones that stimulate rooting. Cuttings can also be rooted in sterilized soil. As soon as the cuttings are rooted, they should be potted in soil. Commercially, cuttings are usually propagated under intermittent mist.

Layering is used to propagate certain plants that are difficult to root from cuttings. A branch is bent over and covered with soil, with the tip projecting above the soil. Roots will form along the covered portion of the stem. Some plants can be rooted this way and it is a common method for shrubs. Notching the underside of the covered portion of the stem will often enhance root formation.

Division is probably the most common method of propagating perennial flowers. Plants that have multiple stems are readily propagated using this method. The entire plant can be dug and divided using a spade or knife. If one wants only a few divisions to share with friends, a portion of the plant can be removed with a spade without injury to the parent plant. Fibrous-rooted plants are best divided in the spring. Fleshy-rooted plants, such as the peony, are best divided in the fall.

Many perennials develop fleshy stems called bulbs, corms, or rhizomes. These organs can be used to start new plants. Fall is the time to plant bulbs and corms of hardy perennials. For tender perennials that reproduce from bulbs or corms, spring is the time to plant.

TRANSPLANTING TO THE GARDEN

Plants grown from seeds or divisions are usually planted in the spring. Frost resistant plants such as pansies should be planted early, as soon as the ground can be worked. Frost tender plants should not be planted until danger of frost has passed and the soil has warmed up.

The less that the root system is disturbed in transplanting, the better. Potted plants are better than plants that are grown close together and pulled apart just before planting. Remove the plant from the container. Even when plants are grown in the peat pots, I find it desirable to remove the plant from the pot. Make a hole with a trowel or make a slit in the soil, using a spade, and place the plant in the opening, filling the soil in around the roots. When a slit is opened by a spade, the plant should be place in the slit before removing the spade; then as the spade is lifted, soil will fall in around the roots. With either method, the soil should be firmed around the roots to eliminate air pockets. The depth of planting should be such that the roots will be at the same depth as they were growing in the container. In the case of tall, spindly seedlings, the plants can be set at an angle, so the basal portion of the stem will be covered but the roots will not be too deep. Plants should be thoroughly watered soon after planting. This can be done with a sprinkling can or a garden hose. A transplanting solution can be used instead of plain water. Use a soluble fertilizer, diluted according to the manufacturers' recommendations. If you use a garden fertilizer such as 10-10-10, use one half cup per gallon of water. The transplanting solution will help the plant overcome the shock of transplanting.

TRAINING AND PRUNING

Herbaceous vines must be grown on a trellis or fence. Certain tall plants such as delphinium, dahlia, and gladiolus need to be tied to suitable plant stakes to prevent being blown over by the wind. Very little pruning is done on mature plants. Occasionally young plants are pinched back to encourage them to branch out near the ground. The terminal bud on some plants produces a growth inhibiting hormone that prevents the lateral buds from developing. With the removal of the tip of the stem, this growth inhibiting hormone is removed and the lateral buds develop a compact, bushy plant. This method is especially efficacious for chrysanthemums and leggy annuals. Removal of faded flowers might be considered to be a type of pruning. By preventing fruit and seed formation, gardeners can foster bloom in some plants for a longer time. Pansies and sweet peas are examples.

INSECT AND DISEASE CONTROL

Many garden flowers can be grown with little attention to insect and disease problems. Others are very susceptible and to grow them successfully requires careful attention to symptoms of injury. Learning to recognize the harmful insects and diseases when they first appear and then taking the necessary steps to control them will prevent a great deal of damage. To discuss all of the insects and diseases that can affect garden flowers would take a volume larger than this one. Most libraries will have reference books on insect and disease control, and your County Agricultural Extension Service can help you with such problems. Most land grant universities that teach Horticulture will have a Plant Disease Clinic where affected plants can be taken to have the problem diagnosed. Garden Centers that sell pesticides can also be helpful.

WEED CONTROL

It is important to plant your flowers in weed-free soil. Annual weeds can be easily controlled by cultivation and hand weeding. The weeds must be killed before they become established, which means removing them while they are small seedlings. Large weeds are difficult to remove without injuring the flowering plants. A

preemergence weed killer can be used in the flower border to reduce the necessity for hand weeding. Dacthal is such a chemical.
The soil must be weed free at the time of application and the plants
must be well established. Dachtal kills germinating seeds but does
not injure established plants.

If perennial weeds such as quack grass, Canadian thistles, or
common milkweed get started in the flower border, you are in
trouble. These weeds grow from underground rhizomes, and cutting
the plants off with a hoe does not kill them. When such weeds are
established, the only real solution is to move your plants to a new,
weed free location. Once the flowering plants have been transplanted, the infected area can be sprayed with either Kleen Up or
Round Up to kill the perennial weeds. Avoid getting these chemicals
on desired plants and follow instructions carefully. These chemicals
leave no harmful soil residues and the area can be replanted in a
few weeks after treatment. Since new weed control chemicals are
introduced each year and old ones are removed, it is wise to con-
sult with your County Agricultural Extension Service or the Horticulture Department of your land grant University for up-to-date
recommendations.

WINTER PROTECTION

Winter injury is not a serious threat to most garden flowers. Perennials die to the ground in the fall and snow cover protects the roots
from serious winter injury. In a few of the perennials, a basal rosette
of green leaves could be injured in an open winter. Some of the
biennials have leaves that stay green all winter. These must have
some protection against the winter cold.

A mulch of leaves, straw, or hay is the usual method of providing
winter protection. It should be applied after the plants have hard-
ened but before severe cold weather sets in, usually in early November. Some gardeners use a cold frame to protect certain plants
of borderline hardiness, such as chrysanthemums and Canterbury-
bells. Specific recommendations are given for those plants requiring
winter protection.

PLANT SELECTION

With thousands of species and named cultivars to choose from, it is a challenging task to select appropriate plants to beautify your yard. Most plants prefer full sunlight but some are shade tolerant and others actually prefer shade. Plants also differ in their moisture requirements. A few require acid soil.

The following lists suggest plants that can be used for different purposes and for special growing conditions. The lists are not all inclusive; other species might serve your needs equally well. Before selecting a plant, learn all you can about it. Read the descriptions and look at the photographs in this book.

ACID SOIL PLANTS

Chimaphila umbellata
Clintonia borealis
Cypripedium acuale
Cypripedium reginae
Hepatica americana
Iris kaempferi

Linnaea borealis
Mitchella repens
Pyrola species
Tiarella cordifolia
Trillium undulatum

AQUATIC PLANTS

Alisma plantago-aquatica
Eichhornia crassipes
Nelumbo lutea
Nelumbo nucifera

Nymphaea species and cultivars
Nymphoides indica
Pontederia cordata
Sagittaria latifolia

BOG PLANTS

Acorus calamus
Asclepias incarnata
Calla palustris
Caltha palustris
Chelone species
Cypripedium acaule *
Cypripedium reginae *
Iris pseudoacorus

Iris versicolor
Lobelia cardinalis
Lythrum salicaria
Mimulus species
Pontentilla palustris
Sarracenia purpurea *
Symplocarpus foetidus

---

*Require an acid bog.

EDGING PLANTS

Ageratum houstonianum
Alternanthera ficoidea
Antirrhinum majus —dwarf types

Begonia x *semperflorens-cultorum*
Catharanthus roseus
Centaurea cineraria

Chrysanthemum parthenium
Impatiens wallerana
Lobelia erinus
Lobularia maritima

Nierembergia hippomanica
Senecio cineraria
Tagetes patula
Viola x *wittrockiana*

EVERLASTING PLANTS FOR DRIED ARRANGEMENTS

Ammobium alatum
Anaphalis margaritacea
Celosia cristata
Gomphrena globosa
Gypsophila paniculata
Helichrysum bracteatum

Helipterum roseum
Limonium sinuatum
Lunaria annua
Mollucella laevis
Physalis alkekengi

FRAGRANCE PLANTS

Arabis caucasica
Centaurea moschata
Convallaria majalis
Dianthus plumarius
Heliotropium arborescens
Hesperis matronalis
Hyacinthus orientalis
Iris species and cultivars
Lathyrus odoratus

Lilium species and cultivars
Linnaea borealis
Matthiola species
Narcissus jonquilla
Nicotiana alata
Nymphaea odorata
Paeonia lactiflora
Reseda odorata
Viola odorata

GROUND COVER PLANTS

Aegopodium podograria 'Variegata'*
Ajuga species and cultivars*
*Anemone quinquefolia**
Asarum species*
Cerastium tomentosum
*Convallaria majalis**
Coronilla varia

Dianthus deltoides
Duchesnia indica
Epimedium species*
Lamium maculatum
Lobularia maritima
*Lysimachia nummularia**
Myosotis species*

*Omphalodes cappadocica**
*Pachysandra terminalis**
Phlox borealis
Phlox subulata
Polygonum capitatum
Polygonum cuspidatum var.
    compactum

Potentilla species
Sedum species
Thymus species
Vinca species*

---

*Plants that tolerate shade.

PLANTS WITH SPECIALIZED STEMS AND ROOTS USED IN PROPAGATION

Hardy

Allium species (bulb)
Arisaema triphyllum (corm)
Chionodoxa luciliae (bulb)
Colchicum autumnale (corm)
Convallaria majalis (rhizome)
Crocus species and cultivars
    (corm)
Dicentra species (rhizome, tuber)
Endymion hispanicus (bulb)
Eranthis hyemalis (tuber)
Galanthus nivalis (bulb)
Hyacinthus orientalis (bulb)
Iris species and cultivars (bulb,
    rhizome)
Leucojum vernum (bulb)

Lilium species and cultivars
    (bulb)
Lycoris squamigera (bulb)
Mertensia virginica (fleshy root)
Muscari botryoides (bulb)
Narcissus species and cultivars
    (bulb)
Ornithogalum umbellatum
    (bulb)
Paeonia species and cultivars (fleshy
    root)
Scilla species (bulb)
Tulipa species and cultivars
    (bulb)

Tender

Anemone coronaria (rhizome)
Begonia x *tuberhybrida* (tuber)
Caladium x *hortulanum* (tuber)
Canna x *generalis* (rhizome)
Crocosmia x *crocosmiiflora* (corm)

Dahlia cultivars (fleshy root)
Gladiolus x *hortulanus* (corm)
Hymenocallis narcissiflora (bulb)
Polianthes tuberosa (tuber)
Tigridia pavonia (bulb)

PRAIRIE PLANTS

Anemone species
Asclepias tuberosa
Aster species
Campanula rotundifolia
Cypripedium candidum
Dodecatheon meadia
Echinacea purpurea
Eupatorium species
Gaillardia aristata
Gentiana andrewsii
Geum triflorum
Liatris species

Lilium species
Lithospermum canescens
Monarda species
Petalostemon species
Phlox pilosa
Ratibida pinnata
Rudbeckia hirta
Sisyrinchium angustifolium
Solidago species
Tradescantia virginiana
Viola pedata

ROCK GARDEN PLANTS

Achillea tomentosa
Adonis vernalis
Aethionema saxatile
Androsace species
Anemone species
Anemonella thalictroides
Antennaria species
Arabis species
Arenaria species
Armeria species
Aubrieta deltoidea
Campanula carpatica
Cerastium species
Claytonia virginica
Coryphantha vivipara
Cyclamen hederifolium
Dianthus species
Dicentra species
Dodecatheon meadia
Draba species
Dryas octopetala
Eranthis hyemalis

Euphorbia species
Gentiana acaulis
Geranium species
Gypsophila repens
Hedyotis caerulea
Iberis species
Iris species
Leontopodium alpinum
Lewisia rediviva
Linaria alpina
Narcissus species
Oenothera species
Opuntia species
Pentstemon species
Potentilla species
Primula species
Saxifraga species
Scilla species
Sedum species
Silene species
Sisyrinchium species
Veronica species

SHADE-TOLERANT PLANTS FOR
THE FLOWER BORDER**

Aconitum species
Anemone sylvestris
Antirrhinum majus
Aquilegia species and cultivars
Astilbe x *arendsii*
Begonia species and cultivars*
*Browallia speciosa**
*Catharanthus roseus**
Coleus x *hybridus**
Dicentra
Digitalis species and cultivars
Helleborus niger

Hemerocallis species and cultivars
Hesperis matronalis
Hosta species and cultivars
Impatiens species and cultivars*
*Lobelia erinus**
Mertensia virginica
Narcissus species and cultivars
Physostegia virginiana
Platycodon grandiflorus
Primula species
Viola species and cultivars

---

*Annuals or tender perennials grown as annuals.

**For other shade-tolerant plants see special lists for ground covers and woodland wildflowers.

SILVER FOLIAGE PLANTS

Artemisia ludoviciana
Artemisia schmidtiana 'Nana'
Artemisia stellerana
*Centaurea cineraria**
*Centaurea gymnocarpa**

Cerastium alpinum subsp. *lanatum*
Cerastium tomentosum
*Senecio cineraria**
*Senecio vira-vira**
Stachys byzantina

---

*Annuals or tender perennials grown as annuals.

SUN-LOVING PLANTS FOR THE FLOWER BORDER

Achillea species and cultivars
*Ageratum houstonianum**
Alcea rosea (annual strains)*
Amaranthus species and cultivars

Amsonia tabernaemontana
Anchusa azurea
Anthemis tinctoria
*Antirrhinum majus**

Arctotis stoechadifolia*
Aster species and cultivars
Baptisia tinctoria
Brunnera macrophylla
Calendula officinalis*
Callistephus chinensis*
Campanula species and cultivars
Catharanthus roseus*
Celosia cristata*
Centaurea species and cultivars*
Chrysanthemum species and cultivars
Clematis species and cultivars
Cleome hasslerana*
Coreopsis lanceolata
Coreopsis tinctoria*
Cosmos species and cultivars*
Dahlia cultivars*
Delphinium species and cultivars
Dianthus species and cultivars*
Dictamnus albus
Echinops species
Eremurus stenophyllus
Erigeron species and cultivars
Filipendula rubra
Gaillardia x grandiflora
Helenium autumnale
Heliopsis helianthoides*
Heliotropium arborescens*

Hemerocallis species and cultivars
Heuchera sanguinea
Hibiscus species and cultivars
Hunnemannia fumariifolia*
Iris species and cultivars
Lilium species and cultivars
Lobularia maritima*
Lythrum species and cultivars
Monarda didyma
Nicotiana alata*
Paeonia species and cultivars
Pelargonium species and cultivars*
Petunia x hybrida*
Phlox drummondii*
Phlox paniculata
Physostegia virginiana
Platycodon grandiflorus
Rudbeckia hirta
Salvia species and cultivars*
Scabiosa caucasica
Tagetes species and cultivars*
Thermopsis caroliniana
Tithonia rotundifolia*
Trollius europaeus
Verbena x hybrida*
Veronica species and cultivars
Yucca species and cultivars
Zinnia species and cultivars*

---

*Annuals or tender perennials grown as annuals.

VINES

Adlumia fungosa
Ipomoea species and cultivars
Lathyrus species and cultivars
Phaseolus coccineus

Polygonum aubertii
Thunbergia alata
Tropaeolum peregrinum

WOODLAND WILDFLOWERS

Actaea species and cultivars
Anemone species
Anemonella thalictroides
Aquilegia species
Aralia nudicaulis
Arisaema species
Cassia marilandica
Chimaphila umbellata
Cimicifuga species
Claytonia virginica
Cypripedium species
Dicentra species
Erythronium species
Eupatorium coelestinum
Geranium maculatum

Hepatica species and cultivars
Jeffersonia diphylla
Maianthemum canadense
Mertensia virginica
Monarda fistulosa
Orchis spectabilis
Phlox divaricata
Podophyllum peltatum
Polygonatum species
Sanguinaria canadensis
Smilacina species
Thalictrum species
Trillium species
Uvularia grandiflora
Viola species

PLANT FAMILIES

❧

Brief family descriptions are given to aid the reader in learning to recognize some of the characteristics that place a plant in a certain family. A list of the genera included in this book is given after each family.

ACANTHACEAE Juss. (Acanthus Family)

DESCRIPTION: A family of about 250 genera of dicotyledonous herbs or shrubs, native in the tropics; **leaves** opposite, simple, mostly entire; **flowers** perfect, mostly in spikes, racemes, or clustered, often with prominent, brightly colored bracts; calyx 4- to 5-parted; corolla regular or slightly irregular, tubular, with 5-lobed, or 2-lipped limbs; stamens 2 or 4, in pairs; **fruit** a 2-celled capsule.

GENERA: *Thunbergia*.

AGAVACEAE Endl. (Agave Family)

DESCRIPTION: A small family of about 20 genera of monocotyledonous plants, native in dry regions of the warmer parts of both hemispheres; **plants** are rhizomatous perennial herbs with a basal rosette of leaves, or woody, tree-like plants; **leaves** mostly narrow, sometimes with sharp, marginal teeth; **flowers** showy, in spikes or panicles; perianth segments often united basally to form a tube; stamens 6; **fruit** a capsule or berry.

GENERA: *Polianthes, Yucca*.

ALISMATACEAE Venten. (Water Plantain Family)

DESCRIPTION: A small family of about 10 species of monocotyledonous marsh and aquatic herbs of worldwide distribution; **leaves** below water are bladeless; leaves above water are linear to ovate-sagittate with sheathing petioles; **flowers** usually white, in racemes or panicles; sepals 3; petals 3 or lacking; stamens 6 to many, rarely 3; **fruit** a head of achenes.

GENERA: *Alisma, Sagittaria.*

AMARANTHACEAE Juss. (Amaranth Family)

DESCRIPTION: A large family of 60 or more genera of herbaceous, dicotyledonous plants, native in all parts of the world; **leaves** opposite or alternate; **flowers** small, subtended by dry scales, often showy in mass; perianth 2- to 5-parted; stamens 1 to 5; ovary superior; **fruit** a utricle or achene, or berrylike.

GENERA: *Alternanthera, Amaranthus, Celosia, Gomphrena.*

AMARYLLIDACEAE Jaume St. Hil. (Amaryllis Family)

DESCRIPTION: A large family of 90 or more genera of monocotyledonous plants, native in the warm regions South America, southern Europe, and Africa; **plants** with tunicate bulbs, corms, or rarely rhizomes; **leaves** few, basal, or rarely on the flowering stems; **flowers** solitary to many in a terminal umbel, subtended by 1 or more membranous bracts on a hollow or solid scape, perfect, mostly regular, showy; perianth 6-lobed, sometimes with a corona; stamens 6, opposite the perianth lobes; ovary superior or inferior, 3-celled or rarely 1-celled by abortion; **fruit** a capsule or berry. This family differs from LILIACEAE by the umbellate inflorescence and from the IRIDACEAE by having 6 stamens.

GENERA: *Allium, Galanthus, Hymenocallis, Leucojum, Lycoris, Narcissus.*

APOCYNACEAE Juss. (Dogbane Family)

DESCRIPTION: A large family of about 130 genera of herbs, shrubs, and trees, often with milky juice, of worldwide distribution; **leaves** opposite, simple, without stipules; **flowers** regular, variously colored; stamens borne on the corolla, alternating with the corolla lobes; pistil of 2 united carpels; **fruit** a pair of follicles, drupelets, or capsules.

GENERA: *Amsonia, Catharanthus, Vinca.*

ARACEAE Juss. (Arum Family)

DESCRIPTION: A family of about 13 genera of monocotyledonous herbs of wide distribution, but mostly tropical, including terrestrial, aquatic, and epiphytic plants; **plants** stemless with leaves arising from fleshy corms or rhizomes or with erect or climbing stems with aerial roots; **leaves** in basal rosettes

or alternate along the stems, entire or deeply dissected, usually with long, basally sheathing petioles; **flowers** small, perfect or imperfect, borne on a fleshy spadix, subtended by a usually showy spathe; when flowers are imperfect, the staminate flowers are produced above the pistillate flowers; **fruits** are fleshy berries.
GENERA: *Acorus, Arisaema, Caladium, Calla, Lysichiton, Symplocarpus, Zantedeschia.*

ARALIACEAE (Ginseng Family)
DESCRIPTION: A family of about 80 genera of dicotyledonous herbs, shrubs, trees, or vines, widely distributed in temperate and tropical regions; **stems** frequently prickly; **leaves** alternate, rarely opposite or whorled, simple or palmately or pinnately compound, often stellate-hairy; **flowers** small, in umbels or heads, often massed in compound inflorescences, greenish white or yellow, regular; calyx of 5 minute teeth; petals 5 to 10, sometimes 4; stamens 5 to many; ovary inferior; **fruit** a drupe.
GENERA: *Aralia.*

ARISTOLOCHIACEAE (Birthwort Family)
DESCRIPTION: A small family of 5 genera of dicotyledonous herbs or climbing woody plants, native mostly in tropical and warm climates; **leaves** alternate, petioled, often heart-shaped; **flowers** perfect; calyx corollalike, 3-lobed, of various colors and irregular in form; stamens 3 to 36; ovary usually inferior, 4- to 6-celled; **fruit** a capsule.
GENERA: *Asarum.*

ASCLEPIADACEAE R. Br. (Milkweed Family)
DESCRIPTION: A family of over 100 genera of dicotyledonous herbs, shrubs, and vines, often succulent and with reduced leaves, mostly with milky sap, widely distributed but most common in the tropics and subtropics; **leaves** generally opposite or whorled, simple, usually entire, without stipules; **flowers** in cymes, but often appearing to be in umbels, regular, perfect; calyx deeply 5-lobed; corolla 5-lobed, often with an annulus in the throat; stamens 5, with filaments coherent into a tube basally and united with corolla tube and bearing 1 or 2 whorls of appendages called the corona; anthers winged and united with the stigma; ovaries superior, the 2 carpels free at the base but joined above in a common stigma; **fruit** a pair of follicles; seeds with a tuft of hairs at the apex.
GENERA: *Asclepias.*

BALSAMINACEAE A. Rich. (Balsam or Touch-me-not Family)
DESCRIPTION: A small family of 2 genera of dicotyledonous herbs or subshrubs, widely distributed, especially in the tropics and subtropics of Asia and

Africa; **stems** usually succulent, often swollen at the nodes; **leaves** simple; **flowers** perfect, irregular, solitary or in axillary or terminal clusters; sepals 3, rarely 5, the upper 2 small, the lower one petaloid, asymmetrically funnelform, usually with a nectariferous spur; petals 5, the upper one flat or helmet-shaped, the lower 4 usually united in lateral pairs; stamens 5, alternating with the petals and united toward the top; ovary superior, 5-celled; **fruit** a 5-valved, elastically and explosively dehiscent capsule.

GENERA: *Impatiens*.

BEGONIACEAE Agardh. (Begonia Family)

DESCRIPTION: A small family of only 3 genera of succulent dictoyledonous perennial herbs, native mostly in the tropics or subtropics; **leaves** alternate, usually oblique at the base and asymmetrical, with stipules; **flowers** imperfect, radially or bilaterally symmetrical; tepals separate; stamens many; ovary inferior, usually 3-celled and 3-winged; **fruit** a capsule.

GENERA: *Begonia*.

BERBERIDACEAE Juss. (Barberry Family)

DESCRIPTION: A small family of about 10 genera of dicotyledonous herbs and shrubs, native to the north temperate regions of the world; **leaves** basal or alternate, simple or compound; **flowers** solitary or in racemes or panicles; sepals and petals often similar, usually overlapping in 2 or more series; stamens as many or twice as many as the petals; ovary superior, 1-celled; **fruit** a berry or a dry capsule and irregularly dehiscent.

GENERA: *Caulophyllum, Epimedium, Jeffersonia, Podophyllum*.

BORAGINACEAE Juss. (Borage Family)

DESCRIPTION: A large family of about 100 species of dicotyledonous herbs, shrubs, or trees, or rarely vines, native on all continents; **plants** mostly with stiff hairs, rarely smooth; **leaves** simple, mostly alternate; **flowers** blue, purple, pink, yellow, orange, red, or white, mostly perfect and regular, usually in a coiled inflorescence that unrolls and straightens out as the flowers mature; calyx mostly 5-lobed; corolla 5-lobed; stamens 5; ovary superior, 2- to 4-celled; **fruit** mostly of 4 nutlets.

GENERA: *Anchusa, Brunnera, Cynoglossum, Heliotropium, Lithospermum, Mertensia, Myosotis, Omphalodes, Pulmonaria*.

BUXACEAE Dumort. (Box Family)

DESCRIPTION: A small family of about 7 genera of dicotyledonous herbs, shrubs, or trees, with watery sap and persistant, usually evergreen leaves, widely distributed in temperate and subtropical regions; **leaves** alternate or opposite, simple; **flowers** imperfect, small; calyx lobes usually 4, sometimes as many as 12 in pistillate flowers; petals lacking; stamens usually 4, opposite the sepals; ovary superior, mostly 3-celled; **fruit** a capsule.

GENERA: *Pachysandra*.

CACTACEAE Juss. (Cactus Family)

DESCRIPTION: A large family of over 200 genera of dicotyledonous, mostly spiny, succulent, perennial herbs, shrubs, trees, or vines, native mostly in the drier regions of North and South America; **stems** fleshy, simple or usually branched, cylindrical to flattened or triangular, often jointed, tubercled, or ribbed; **leaves** broad, flat, and more or less persistent or more often cylindrical or rudimentary and soon deciduous; **flowers** sessile or stalked, solitary, or rarely clustered; perianth made up of intergrading sepal-like and petal-like segments that form a tube that connects to the inferior ovary; stamens many, on the inside of the perianth tube; **fruit** a fleshy berry.

GENERA: *Coryphantha, Opuntia*.

CAMPANULACEAE Juss. (Bellflower Family)

DESCRIPTION: A family of about 40 genera of dicotyledonous herbs, rarely shrubs or trees, mostly with a milky sap, native in temperate and tropical regions of the world; **leaves** alternate, simple, and only rarely lobed or divided; **flowers** solitary or in spikes, racemes, or panicles, regular or nearly so, 5-merous; calyx tube usually joined to the ovary; corolla lobed, lilac to blue or purple, sometimes white; stamens 5, sometimes inserted on the corolla, separate or united; ovary usually inferior, 2- to 5-celled with 1 style; **fruit** a dehiscent capsule, rarely berrylike.

GENERA: *Campanula, Platycodon*.

CANNACEAE Juss. (Canna Family)

DESCRIPTION: A single genus of monocotyledonous herbs, native to tropical and subtropical regions; **leaves** alternate, simple, entire, with sheathing petioles; **flowers** in terminal spikes, racemes, or panicles, red or yellow, with a peculiar structure; sepals 3, small, overlapping; petals 3, erect or reflexed, sepal-like, more or less united at base; fertile stamen 1, petal-like, bearing a half anther on one side; staminodes 1 to 4, petal-like, an inner one reflexed and forming a lip; ovary inferior; **fruit** a capsule.

GENERA: *Canna*.

CAPPARACEAE Juss. (Capper Family)

DESCRIPTION: About 40 genera of dicotyledonous herbs, shrubs, and trees, native in tropical, subtropical, and temperate regions; **leaves** alternate, simple or palmately compound; **flowers** perfect, irregular; sepals mostly 4, rarely 8; petals 4, rarely 8 or lacking; stamens 4 to many; ovary superior, 1-celled; **fruit** an elongated capsule or berry.

GENERA: *Cleome.*

CAPRIFOLIACEAE Juss. (Honeysuckle Family)

DESCRIPTION: A small family of about 15 genera of mostly shrubs, rarely herbs, native in the temperate regions of the northern hemisphere; **leaves** opposite, simple or pinnate; **flowers** few and in cymes or many and in flat-topped or rounded clusters; calyx 4- to 5-toothed; corolla 4- to 5-lobed, sometimes irregular; stamens 4 to 5; ovary inferior, usually 1- to 5-celled; **fruit** a berry, drupe, achene, or capsule.

GENERA: *Linnaea.*

CARYOPHYLLACEAE Juss. (Pink Family)

DESCRIPTION: About 70 genera of dictoyledonus herbs and a few subshrubs of wide distribution; stems often swollen at the nodes; **leaves** opposite, simple, entire; **flowers** in terminal cymes or solitary, regular, white or brightly colored; sepals 4 or 5; petals 4 or 5; stamens 8 to 10; ovary superior, 1- to 5-celled, with 2 to 5 styles; **fruit** a many-seeded capsule.

GENERA: *Agrostemma, Arenaria, Cerastium, Dianthus, Gypsophila, Lychnis, Petrorhagia, Saponaria, Silene.*

CHENOPODIACEAE Venteen. (Goosefoot Family)

DESCRIPTION: A family of about 75 genera of dicotyledonous herbs and shrubs of wide distribution; **plants** often troublesome weeds; **leaves** mostly alternate and simple; **flowers** small, often bracted, having no perianth or only a 1- to 5-lobed calyx; stamens 1 to 5, opposite the calyx lobes; ovary usually superior, 1-celled, with 1 ovule; **fruit** a utricle or achene.

GENERA: *Kochia.*

CISTACEAE Juss. (Rock Rose Family)

DESCRIPTION: A small family of only 8 genera of dicotyledonous herbs or shrubs, native to warmer parts of the northern hemisphere, chiefly in the Mediterranean region; **plants** often with star-shaped hairs; **leaves** mostly opposite, simple; **flowers** solitary or in cymes or racemes, regular; sepals 3 to 5, often unequal; petals usually 5, soon deciduous; stamens many; **fruit** a capsule.

GENERA: *Nummularia.*

COMMELINACEAE (Spiderwort Family)

DESCRIPTION: About 40 genera of monocotyledonous herbs, widely distributed, especially in the tropics; **leaves** alternate, simple, parallel-veined, with sheathing leaf bases; **flowers** in axillary or terminal cymes and often subtended by leafy bracts; sepals 3; petals 3, separate or basally united; stamens 1 to 3 or 6; ovary superior, 2- to 3-celled; **fruit** a capsule or berry.

GENERA: *Tradescantia*.

COMPOSITAE Gieske (Sunflower Family)

DESCRIPTION: A very large family of about 1,000 genera of dicotyledonous herbs, or rarely shrubs and trees, of worldwide distribution; **leaves** alternate or opposite, rarely whorled, entire to pinnatifid or compound; **flowers** in heads that are solitary or arranged in spikes, racemes, cymes, corymbs, or panicles; involucral bracts in 1 to several rows, of various shapes, textures, and colors; receptacle flat, convex, conical, or columnar, naked or with various scales or bristles; flowers perfect, imperfect, or sterile, of various colors; corolla either regular, tubular, and 4- to 5-lobed, or irregular and strap-shaped, or 2-lipped; outer flowers are usually strap-shaped and called ray flowers; inner flowers are usually tubular and called disc flowers; stamens usually 5; borne on the corolla tube; anthers usually united into a tube around the style; style usually 2-branched; **fruit** an achene, usually bearing a persistent or deciduous pappus of bristles or scales.

The family is divided into the following tribes:

Anthemis Tribe

DESCRIPTION: About 50 genera of aromatic annual or perennial herbs or rarely subshrubs, native mostly in the Old World, most numerous in the Mediterranean region; **leaves** alternate, usually pinnatifid or pinnately parted or dissected, rarely simple; involucral bracts usually scarious or with scarious margins or tips, overlapping in several rows; **flower** heads discoid or radiate; flowers yellow, white or greenish; disc flowers perfect; ray flowers pistillate or sterile; pappus either absent or present as a scarious cup or crown.

GENERA: *Achillea, Anthemis, Chrysanthemum, Tanacetum*.

Arctotis Tribe

DESCRIPTION: About 20 genera of perennial herbs or rarely shrubs, native mostly in South Africa; **leaves** alternate or in rosettes, usually lobed or divided, sometimes spiny; involucral bracts sometimes scarious, often spine-tipped, overlapping in several rows; receptacle usually naked; **flower** heads usually radiate; disc flowers usually yellow; ray flowers yellow, red, or purple; pappus of scales or a crown or lacking.

GENERA: *Arctotis, Gazania.*

Aster Tribe

DESCRIPTION: Over 100 genera of mostly perennial herbs, rarely shrubs or trees of temperate and mountain regions; **leaves** alternate, entire to toothed or sometimes divided; involucral bracts overlapping in several rows; receptacle naked; **flower** heads usually radiate; disc flowers usually perfect, yellow or white; ray flowers blue, red, or white, rarely yellow; pappus usually of awns or bristles, rarely of scales or lacking.

GENERA: *Aster, Brachycome, Callistephus, Chrysopsis, Erigeron, Machaeranthera, Solidago.*

Calendula Tribe

DESCRIPTION: About 10 genera of herbs or shrubs, native in Africa and in the Mediterranean region; **leaves** alternate or occasionally opposite, entire to toothed or lobed, rarely divided; involucral bracts often with a scarious margin, nearly equal, in 1 to 3 rows; receptacle naked or rarely with a few bristles; **flower** heads radiate; disc flowers perfect, male or sterile, orange or yellow; ray flowers in 1 row, pistillate or sterile, orange or yellow; pappus lacking.

GENERA: *Calendula, Dimorphotheca.*

Carduus Tribe

DESCRIPTION: About 50 genera of thistles or thistle herbs, native chiefly in the northern hemisphere; **leaves** alternate, sinuate to divided, rarely entire, usually spiny or prickly; involucral bracts in many rows, tips often spiny; receptacle bristly or hairy, seldom naked; **flower** heads discoid; flowers tubular, the marginal ones sometimes enlarged, 2-lipped or deeply 5-cleft, commonly pistillate or sterile; disc flowers perfect, deeply 5-lobed; achenes with bristly or plumose pappus.

GENERA: *Centauria, Echinops.*

Cichorium Tribe

DESCRIPTION: About 75 genera of herbs, shrubs, or small trees, with milky sap, mostly native in the North Temperate Zone; **leaves** alternate or basal, entire to pinnatifid or rarely divided; involucral bracts nearly equal, overlapping in one to several rows; **flowers** all strap-shaped, perfect, white, yellow, orange, red, purple, or blue; **achenes** often beaked; pappus of 1 or more rows of simple or plumose bristles.

GENERA: *Catananche.*

Eupatorium Tribe

DESCRIPTION: About 50 genera of herbs or shrubs, native in North and South America, mostly in the tropics; **leaves** mostly opposite, sometimes alternate or whorled, mostly simple, involucral bracts overlapping in several rows; receptacle naked; **flower** heads discoid; disc flowers purple, red, or white; pappus usually of rigid bristles.

GENERA: *Ageratum, Eupatorium, Liatris*.

Helenium Tribe

DESCRIPTION: About 60 genera of herbs or subshrubs, native mostly in North America; **leaves** alternate or opposite, entire or divided, sometimes gland-dotted; involucral bracts in 1 to 3 rows; receptacle usually naked, sometimes with bristles or hairs; **flower** heads usually radiate; disc flowers usually yellow; ray flowers usually pistillate, yellow; pappus of scales, awns, or bristles.

GENERA: *Gaillardia, Helenium*.

Helianthus Tribe

DESCRIPTION: Over 150 genera of coarse herbs or shrubs, native mostly to North and South America; **leaves** often glandular, entire or divided; involucral bracts overlapping in several rows; receptacle scaly; **flower** heads usually radiate; disc flowers and ray flowers usually yellow; pappus of scales or awns or lacking.

GENERA: *Coreopsis, Cosmos, Dahlia, Echinacea, Helianthus, Heliopsis, Ratibida, Rudbeckia, Sanvitalia, Tithonia, Zinnia*.

Inula Tribe

DESCRIPTION: About 300 genera of wide distribution, but mainly in South America and Australia; **leaves** alternate, opposite, or basal, entire or occasionally toothed, often woolly or glandular; involucral bracts usually white or scarious, frequently very hairy, overlapping in several rows; receptacle naked or scaly; **flower** heads discoid; pappus usually of hairs.

GENERA: *Ammobium, Anaphalis, Antennaria, Helichrysum, Inula, Leontopodium*.

Senecio Tribe

DESCRIPTION: About 50 genera of herbs or shrubs or sometimes trees of wide distribution; **leaves** usually alternate or basal, entire or toothed or divided; involucral bracts usually in 1 row; receptacle usually naked; **flower** heads discoid or radiate; disc flowers perfect; ray flowers, when present, pistillate; pappus of many hairlike bristles.

GENERA: *Doronicum, Ligularia, Senecio*.

Vernonia Tribe

DESCRIPTION: About 50 genera of herbs, shrubs, or rarely trees, native to North and South America and Africa; **leaves** usually alternate, entire to toothed; involucral bracts overlapping in several rows; receptacle usually naked, rarely hairy or pitted; **flower** heads discoid; flowers perfect, reddish purple to white; pappus of many bristlelike hairs.

GENERA: *Stokesia*.

CONVOLVULACEAE Juss. (Morning-glory Family)

DESCRIPTION: A family of about 50 dicotyledonous climbing herbs, or rarely shrubs or trees, often with milky juice, native mostly in tropical and subtropical climates; **leaves** alternate, simple or compound; **flowers** often large and showy, regular, perfect; calyx 5-parted; corolla funnelform, pleated or often twisted in bud; stamens 5; ovary superior; **fruit** a capsule or berry.

GENERA: *Convolvulus, Ipomoea*.

CRASSULACEAE DC. (Orpine Family)

DESCRIPTION: About 30 genera of succulent dictoyledonous herbs, rarely shrubs, widely distributed; **leaves** fleshy; simple; **flowers** usually 5-merous, in cymes, spikes, racemes, or panicles; sepals and petals separate or united; stamens as many or twice as many as the petals; ovary superior, made up of several carpels that separate to near the base.

GENERA: *Sedum*.

CRUCIFERAE Juss. (Mustard Family)

DESCRIPTION: A large family of about 350 genera of dicotyledonous pungent or acrid herbs of wide distribution; **leaves** alternate, **flowers** in terminal racemes or corymbs, usually perfect, regular; sepals 4, deciduous; petals 4, their spreading limbs forming a cross; stamens 6, 2 of these shorter and inserted lower than the other 4; pistil of 2 carpels; ovary superior; **fruit** 2-celled, called a silique if elongated and cylindrical, or a silicle if short and flat.

GENERA: *Aethionema, Alyssum, Arabis, Aubrieta, Aurinia, Draba, Erysimum, Hesperis, Iberis, Lobularia, Lunaria, Matthiola*, and *Nasturtium*.

DIPSACACEAE Juss. (Teasel Family)

DESCRIPTION: A small family of 9 dicotyledonous genera of mostly annual, biennial, or perennial herbs, or rarely shrubs, native in Europe, Asia, and Africa; **leaves** opposite, rarely whorled; **flowers** small, irregular, perfect, in dense involucrate heads or interrupted spikes; calyx cup-shaped, tubular, or divided into 5 to 10 segments; corolla 4- to 5-lobed; stamens usually 4, sometimes 2 or 3, arising from the base of the corolla tube; ovary inferior, 1-celled; **fruit** an achene, frequently crowned by the persistant calyx.

GENERA: *Scabiosa*.

EUPHORBIACEAE Juss. (Spurge Family)
DESCRIPTION: A large family of dicotyledonous herbs, shrubs, or trees, and often spiny, cactuslike succulents, often with milky juice, widely distributed; **flowers** monoecious or dioecious, in varying types of inflorescences, sometimes solitary; stamens 1 to several, separate or their filaments united; ovary superior, usually 3-celled; **fruit** a capsule, splitting into 3, 1-seeded sections.

GENERA: *Euphorbia, Ricinus*.

FUMARIACEAE (Fumitory Family)
DESCRIPTION: A small family, sometimes included in the PAPAVARACEAE, of about 20 genera of dicotyledonous herbs, native in the North Temperate Zone and in South Africa; **leaves** basal or alternate to nearly opposite, much dissected and fernlike; **flowers** often irregular, perfect; sepals 2, small, deciduous; petals 4, outer 2 often basally saccate or spurred, inner 2 narrower and crested; stamens 4, separate and opposite the petals, or 6 united in 2 bundles; ovary superior, 1-celled; **fruit** a capsule or nutlet.

GENERA: *Adlumia, Corydalis, Dicentra*.

GENTIANACEAE (Gentian Family)
DESCRIPTION: About 70 genera of dicotyledonous herbs, or rarely shrubs, of worldwide distribution; **leaves** mostly opposite, simple, entire; **flowers** regular, perfect; sepals, petals, and stamens 4 to 12; ovary superior, 1- or 2-celled; **fruit** a capsule.

GENERA: *Gentiana, Gentianopsis, Nymphoides*.

GERANIACEAE Juss. (Geranium Family)
DESCRIPTION: A family of only 11 genera of dicotyledonous herbs or shrubs, widely distributed throughout the world; **leaves** usually opposite, simple or compound, often palmately cleft; **flowers** perfect, mostly regular, usually 5-merous; sepals separate or partly united; petals separate, overlapping, rarely absent; stamens 5, 10, or 15, sometimes lacking anthers; ovary superior, 3- to 5-lobed; **fruit** a capsule.

GENERA: *Geranium, Pelargonium*.

HYDROPHYLLACEAE R. Br. (Waterleaf Family)
DESCRIPTION: A family of about 25 genera of dicotyledonous herbs, rarely

shrubs, native chiefly in western North America; **plants** usually hairy, often glandular or bristly; **leaves** entire, divided, or compound; **flowers** solitary or in cymes, regular, perfect; calyx 5-lobed or 5-parted; corolla 5-lobed; stamens 5; pistil 1, superior and 1-celled; **fruit** a capsule.

GENERA: *Nemophila*.

IRIDACEAE (Iris Family)

DESCRIPTION: A family of about 60 genera of bulbous, cormous, or rhizomatous monocotyledonous perennial herbs with fibrous roots, of wide distribution; **leaves** mostly basal, usually 2-ranked, linear to sword-shaped; **flowers** perfect, regular or irregular, solitary or in clusters with 2 spathelike bracts (spathe valves) or in racemes or panicles; perianth segments 6, separate or basally united into a tube; stamens 3; ovary inferior, usually 3-celled; **fruit** a 3-valved capsule.

GENERA: *Balamcanda, Crocosmia, Crocus, Gladiolus, Iris, Sisyrinchium, Tigridia*.

LABIATAE Jus. (Mint Family)

DESCRIPTION: A family of about 180 genera of dicotyledonous herbs and shrubs of wide distribution, native in the Mediterranean region; stems mostly square in cross section; **leaves** opposite, 4-ranked, simple, mostly with glands secreting pungent, volatile oils; **flowers** irregular, in cymes in the axils of opposite bracts or leaves, forming verticillasters, arranged in a simple or compound inflorescence, sometimes subtended by bractlets; calyx 4- to 5-lobed, 2-lipped, persistent; corolla 4- to 6-lobed, usually 2-lipped; stamens 4, rarely 2, inserted on the corolla; ovary superior, deeply lobed, with a single style and 2-lobed stigma; **fruit** of 4, 1-seeded nutlets.

GENERA: *Agastache, Ajuga, Coleus, Lamium, Mentha, Mollucella, Monarda, Nepeta, Ocimum, Physostegia, Prunella, Salvia, Stachys, Thymus*.

LEGUMINOSAE Juss. (Pea Family)

DESCRIPTION: A large family of about 600 genera of dicotyledonous herbs, shrubs, trees, or vines of wide distribution; **leaves** mostly alternate, usually compound, sometimes reduced to a single leaflet or to a flattened, leaflike petiole (phyllode); stipules present, sometimes modified into thorns; **flowers** mostly irregular, solitary or in racemes, panicles, spikes, or heads; calyx 5-lobed; petals usually 5, rarely 1 or lacking, all separate or the lower 2 united; stamens usually 10, all separate or 9 united into a tube and 1, the uppermost, separate; pistil 1-celled, with 2 to many ovules; **fruit** a legume, sometimes constricted into 1-seeded sections and then called a loment.

GENERA: *Baptisia, Cassia, Coronilla, Lathyrus, Lupinus, Petalostemon, Phaseolus, Thermopsis*.

LILIACEAE Juss. (Lily Family)

DESCRIPTION: A family of about 240 genera of monocotyledonous herbs of wide distribution, most abundant in temperate and subtropical regions; **plants** with fleshy bulbs, corms, rhizomes, or tubers; **leaves** basal or on the stems, usually alternate or sometimes opposite or whorled; **flowers** regular, perfect, mostly showy, in various types of inflorescences; perianth usually of 6 separate segments; stamens 6, rarely 3; ovary usually superior, 3-celled; **fruit** a berry or 3-valved capsule.

GENERA: *Aletris, Camassia, Chamaelirium, Chionodoxa, Clintonia, Colchicum, Convallaria, Endymion, Eremurus, Erythronium, Fritillaria, Hemerocallis, Hosta, Hyacinthus, Lilium, Maianthemum, Muscari, Ornithogalum, Polygonatum, Puschkinia, Scilla, Smilacina, Trillium, Tulipa,* and *Uvularia.*

LINACEAE S. F. Gray (Flax Family)

DESCRIPTION: A family with about 14 genera of dicotyledonous herbs, or rarely shrubs, of wide distribution; **leaves** alternate, rarely opposite or whorled, simple, entire; **flowers** regular, perfect, mostly produced in cymes, sometimes in corymbs, racemes, or panicles; sepals 4 or 5; petals 4 or 5, falling early, often clawed; stamens 5, united at base, alternating with staminodes; **fruit** a capsule or rarely a drupe.

GENERA: *Linum.*

LOBELIACEAE R. Br. (Lobelia Family)

DESCRIPTION: A family of about 25 genera of dicotyledonous herbs, shrubs, or trees, native mostly in tropical regions; sap often acrid, milky; **leaves** alternate, sometimes in rosettes, simple, entire, toothed or pinnately parted; **flowers** solitary or in spikes, racemes, or panicles; calyx 5-lobed or 5-parted; corolla irregular, often 2-lipped, 5-lobed, the tube often split nearly to the base on 1 side; stamens 5, sometimes inserted on petals; anthers united into a tube around the style; ovary mostly inferior; **fruit** a capsule or berry.

GENERA: *Lobelia.*

LYTHRACEAE (Loosestrife Family)

DESCRIPTION: A family of about 22 genera of dicotyledonous herbs, shrubs, or trees, mostly native in tropical America; **leaves** opposite or whorled, rarely alternate, entire; **flowers** perfect; calyx tubular with 4 to 6 lobes, often alternating with triangular appendages; petals 4 to 6, inserted toward the top of the calyx tube, or sometimes absent; stamens few to many; **fruit** a capsule.

GENERA: *Lythrum.*

MALVACEAE Juss. (Mallow Family)

DESCRIPTION: A family of about 95 genera of dicotyledonous herbs, shrubs, or trees, native in tropical and temperate regions; **leaves** alternate, generally with stipules, simple, usually palmately veined or lobed, or palmately compound; **flowers** regular, perfect; calyx 5-lobed, often subtended or enclosed by an involucre of distinct or united bracts; petals 5, obovate, united at base to staminal column; stamens united into a tube enclosing the pistil; ovary superior, with 1 to many carpels; **fruit** a dehiscent capsule or a schizocarp separating at maturity into individual mericarps.

GENERA: *Alcea, Althaea, Hibiscus, Lavatera, Malva.*

MARTYNIACEAE Stapf. (Martynia Family)

DESCRIPTION: A small family of 5 genera of sticky-hairy, dicotyledonous herbs, native in the tropics or subtropics of America; **leaves** opposite or alternate, palmately veined; **flowers** irregular; corolla 5-lobed; stamens 4 or 2; **fruit** a curved, long-beaked capsule.

GENERA: *Proboscidea.*

NYCTAGINACEAE Juss. (Four-O'clock Family)

DESCRIPTION: A family of about 32 genera of dicotyledonous herbs, shrubs, or trees, native in warm and tropical regions; **flowers** often subtended by an involucre, which is sometimes petal-like and showy; calyx often or usually corollalike; petals lacking; ovary superior, 1-celled; **fruit** an achene on which the calyx is persistent.

GENERA: *Mirabilis.*

NYMPHAEACEAE Salisb. (Waterlily Family)

DESCRIPTION: A family of 8 genera of dicotyledonous aquatic herbs of wide distribution; **leaves** usually large with long petioles, sometimes floating, commonly arising from submerged rhizomes; **flowers** solitary, usually showy, regular, perfect; sepals 4 or more; petals, stamens, and carpels few to many; **fruits** various.

GENERA: *Nelumbo, Nymphaea.*

ONAGRACEAE Juss. (Evening Primrose Family)

DESCRIPTION: A family of about 200 genera of dicotyledonous herbs, shrubs, or trees, native largely in North and South America; **flowers** regular, often showy, mostly 4-merous; stamens usually 8; ovary inferior, elongate; **fruit** a thin-walled or woody capsule or berry.

GENERA: *Clarkia, Oenothera.*

ORCHIDACEAE Juss. (Orchid Family)

DESCRIPTION: A large family of over 600 genera of monocotyledonous perennial herbs of worldwide distribution, especially abundant in the tropics; **stems** leafy or scapose, often more or less swollen and forming a pseudobulb; **leaves** usually alternate, simple; **flowers** irregular, solitary or in spikes, racemes, or panicles, perfect or imperfect and either monoecious or dioecious; sepals 3, usually narrow, often colored and petal-like, all alike or the middle one larger and differently colored; petals 3, the lateral ones alike, the middle one (labellum) usually different and much modified in size, shape, and color, usually 3-lobed, sometimes extended at the base into a spur or sac; stamens 3, usually only 1 fertile, united with the style and stigma to form a single structure (column); ovary inferior; **fruit** a capsule.

GENERA: *Cypripedium, Orchis.*

OXALIDACEAE R. Br. (Oxalis Family)

DESCRIPTION: A family of 7 genera of dicotyledonous herbs, shrubs, or rarely trees, native mostly in the tropics, but also in temperate regions; **leaves** pinnately or palmately compound, alternate; leaflets 1 to many; **flowers** regular, perfect, solitary or in racemes, cymes, or umbels; sepals and petals 5; stamens 5 or 10; ovary superior, 5-celled, with 5 styles and stigmas; **fruit** a capsule or berry.

GENERA: *Oxalis.*

PAEONIACEAE F. Rudolphi. (Peony Family)

DESCRIPTION: A single genus of dicotyledonous herbs or rarely shrubs, native in Eurasia and western North America; **leaves** alternate, pinnate or 2-ternate; **flowers** showy, perfect, regular; sepals 5, persistent; petals many; stamens many, spirally arranged, the inner ones maturing before the outer ones; pistils 2 to 8, borne on a fleshy disc; **fruit** of 2 to 8 leathery or woody follicles. This family is often included in the RANUNCULACEAE but differs in having persistent sepals and by having the stamens mature from the center outward.

GENERA: *Paeonia.*

PAPAVERACEAE Juss. (Poppy Family)

DESCRIPTION: A family of about 25 genera of dicotyledonous herbs, rarely shrubs, of worldwide distribution; sap usually milky or colored; **leaves** usually alternate, entire or pinnately or palmately cleft; **flowers** usually solitary, showy, perfect, regular; sepals 2 or 3, early deciduous; stamens many; ovary superior; **fruit** a capsule opening by valves or pores.

GENERA: *Escholtzia, Hunnemannia, Macleaya, Papaver, Sanguinaria.*

PLUMBAGINACEAE Juss. (Plumbago Family)

DESCRIPTION: A family of about 10 genera of dicotyledonous perennial herbs or shrubs, sometimes vines, native along seacoasts in alkaline or saline soils; **leaves** alternate, simple, entire, sometimes auricled or clasping at the base; **flowers** in terminal, spikelike racemes; calyx tubular, glandular, 5-ribbed; corolla tube slender, twice as long as the calyx, with 5 spreading lobes; stamens 5, free from the corolla tube; **fruit** a capsule, splitting into 5 parts.

GENERA: *Armeria, Limonium.*

POLEMONIACEAE Juss. (Phlox Family)

DESCRIPTION: A family of 18 genera of dicotyledonous perennial herbs, rarely shrubs, trees, or vines, native chiefly in North and South America, Europe, and Asia; **leaves** alternate or opposite, simple or compound; **flowers** perfect, mostly regular, terminal or axillary, solitary or in cymes or dense heads; calyx and corolla 5-lobed; stamens 5; **fruit** a capsule.

GENERA: *Ipomopsis, Phlox, Polemoneum.*

POLYGONACEAE Juss. (Buckwheat Family)

DESCRIPTION: A family of about 40 genera of dicotyledonous herbs, shrubs, trees, or vines, of wide distribution; **stems** jointed; **leaves** simple, with stipules usually united into a more or less tubular sheath; **flowers** small; calyx lobes 2 to 6, petal-like, often with wings, spines, or hooks; petals absent; ovary superior, 1-celled; **fruit** an achene, often triangular.

GENERA: *Polygonum.*

PONTEDERIACEAE Kunth. (Pickerel Weed Family)

DESCRIPTION: A family of 6 genera of tropical and temperate herbs, native in swamps or ponds, and floating or rooted in the mud; **leaves** various; **flowers** perfect, somewhat irregular; perianth 6-parted, corollalike, usually showy; stamens 3 or 6; ovary superior; **fruit** a capsule or achene.

GENERA: *Eichhornia, Pontederia.*

PORTULACACEAE Juss. (Purslane Family)

DESCRIPTION: A family of about 16 genera of dicotyledonous herbs or subshrubs of wide distribution; **leaves** alternate or opposite, simple, entire, often fleshy; **flowers** in cymes or racemes, or solitary, often showy, regular, perfect; sepals usually 2, sometimes more; petals usually 4 or 5, falling early; stamens few to many; ovary superior or rarely half-inferior, usually 1-celled; **fruit** a capsule.

GENERA: *Claytonia, Lewisia, Portulaca.*

PRIMULACEAE (Primrose Family)

DESCRIPTION: A family of about 25 genera of dicotyledonous herbs, native mostly in the northern hemisphere; **leaves** usually simple, mostly opposite or whorled, or occasionally all basal or alternate; **flowers** perfect, regular, solitary or in various types of inflorescences; calyx usually 5-lobed; corolla typically 5-lobed; stamens usually 5, opposite the corolla lobes; ovary superior; **fruit** a capsule.

GENERA: *Anagallis, Androsace, Cyclamen, Dodecatheon, Lysimachia, Primula.*

PYROLACEAE Lindl. (Wintergreen Family)

DESCRIPTION: A family of about 10 genera of dicotyledonous herbs, native in cooler regions of the northern hemisphere; **plants** mostly evergreen with scaly, creeping rhizomes, or sometimes saprophytes or root parasites without chlorophyll; **leaves** simple, sometimes scalelike; **flowers** solitary or in scapose umbels or racemes, perfect, regular or nearly so; sepals 4 or 5, separate or sometimes united; stamens 8 or 10, with filaments often expanded at the base and anthers often opening by a pore; **fruit** a capsule.

GENERA: *Chimaphila, Pyrola.*

RANUNCULACEAE Juss. (Buttercup Family)

DESCRIPTION: A family of about 50 genera of dicotyledonous herbs, rarely shrubs, mostly native in the North Temperate Zone; **leaves** alternate or opposite; **flowers** chiefly perfect; sepals and petals 2 to many; petals sometimes lacking; stamens many; **fruit** an achene, follicle, or berry.

GENERA: *Aconitum, Actaea, Adonis, Anemone, Anemonella, Aquilegia, Caltha, Cimicifuga, Clematis, Consolida, Delphinium, Eranthis, Helleborus, Hepatica, Nigella, Ranunculus, Thalictrum,* and *Trollius.*

RESEDACEAE S. F. Gray (Mignonette Family)

DESCRIPTION: A family of 6 genera of dicotyledonous herbs, native in the Mediterranean region of northern Africa; **leaves** alternate, simple or pinnate, with small glandlike stipules; **flowers** mostly perfect, irregular; sepals 4 to 7; petals 4 to 7 or lacking, often laciniate; stamens 3 to 40, with filaments separate or basally united; carpels 2 to 6, separate or united; **fruit** a capsule or berry.

GENERA: *Reseda.*

ROSACEAE Juss. (Rose Family)

DESCRIPTION: A family of about 100 genera of dicotyledonous herbs, shrubs, or trees, of wide distribution; **leaves** mostly alternate, simple or compound; **flowers** perfect, regular; sepals and petals 4 or 5, or petals sometimes lacking; stamens 5 to many, borne on the edge of the calyx tube; pistils 1 to many, with superior or inferior ovaries; **fruit** an achene, follicle, berry, pome, or drupe.

GENERA: *Alchemilla, Dryas, Duchesnea, Filipendula, Geum, Gillenia, Potentilla, Waldsteinia.*

RUBIACEAE Juss. (Madder Family)

DESCRIPTION: A family of nearly 400 genera of dicotyledonous herbs, shrubs, trees, or vines, native chiefly in the tropics or subtropics; **leaves** opposite or whorled, simple, with stipules; **flowers** in cymes, sometimes crowded in globelike heads; usually regular, perfect; calyx and corolla mostly 4- or 5-lobed; stamens 4 or 5 or more, borne on the corolla; ovary inferior, with 2 or more cells; **fruit** a capsule, berry, or drupe.

GENERA: *Hedyotis, Mitchella.*

RUTACEAE Juss. (Rue Family)

DESCRIPTION: A family of about 150 genera of dicotyledonous herbs, trees, and shrubs, native in tropical and temperate regions; **leaves** simple or compound, glandular-dotted; **flowers** sometimes imperfect, usually regular, in various types of inflorescences; sepals 3 to 5; petals 3 to 5, rarely lacking; stamens 3 to 10, rarely 20 to 60, arising from a disc; ovary superior, usually 4- to 5-celled; **fruit** a capsule, berry, drupe, samara, or follicle.

GENERA: *Dictamnus.*

SARRACENIACEAE Dumort. (Pitcher Plant Family)

DESCRIPTION: A family of 3 genera of dicotyledonous, carnivorous, rhizomatous, perennial herbs of North and South America; **leaves** clustered, erect, tubular, or trumpet-shaped, bearing a ridge on the inner side and terminated by an expanded hood or lid; **flowers** usually solitary, on erect, naked scapes, regular, perfect; sepals 4 or 5, subtended by 3 appressed bracts; petals 5 or lacking, early deciduous; stamens many; pistil with a superior ovary and a 3- to 5-lobed style; **fruit** a capsule.

GENERA: *Sarracenia.*

SAXIFRAGACEAE (Saxifrage Family)

DESCRIPTION: A family of about 80 genera of dicotyledonous herbs, shrubs, or small trees, rarely vines, mostly of temperate regions; **leaves** alternate or sometimes opposite; **flowers** in few-flowered cymes or in many-flowered racemes or panicles, usually perfect and regular; sepals and petals 4 or 5, sometimes partly united to form a tube; stamens as many as twice as many as the sepals; carpels 2 to 5, united or partly separate; **fruit** a capsule or berry.

GENERA: *Astilbe, Bergenia, Heuchera, Mitella, Saxifraga, Tiarella.*

SCROPHULARIACEAE Juss. (Figwort Family)

DESCRIPTION: A family of about 200 genera of dicotyledonous herbs, shrubs, or rarely trees, of wide distribution; **leaves** alternate or opposite, rarely whorled or clustered, entire or lobed to pinnatifid; **flowers** perfect, irregular, in various types of inflorescences; calyx 4- to 5-lobed; corolla 4- to 5-lobed, often 2-lipped, rarely nearly regular; stamens usually 4, sometimes 2 or 5; **fruit** a capsule, rarely a berry.

GENERA: *Antirrhinum, Chelone, Digitalis, Erinus, Linaria, Mimulus, Nemesia, Pentstemon, Scutellaria, Torenia, Verbascum,* and *Veronica.*

SOLANACEAE Juss. (Nightshade Family)

DESCRIPTION: A family of about 90 genera of dicotyledonous herbs, shrubs, trees, and vines of tropical and temperate regions, chiefly in Central and South America; **stems** often prickly; **leaves** usually alternate, simple or pinnate; **flowers** perfect; calyx 5-lobed, persistent; corolla usually rotate, funnelform or salverform, 5-lobed, rarely 2-lipped; stamens usually 5, borne on the corolla, 1 or more of these sometimes sterile; **fruit** a berry or capsule.

GENERA: *Browallia, Datura, Nicotiana, Nierembergia, Petunia, Physalis, Salpiglossis.*

TROPAEOLIACEAE A. DC. (Nasturtium Family)

DESCRIPTION: A family of 2 genera of dicotyledonous succulent herbs, native in the mountains of Mexico and South America; **stems** prostrate or climbing by sensitive petioles; **leaves** mostly simple, entire, or palmately lobed or parted, peltate, often long-petioled; **flowers** perfect, irregular, solitary or rarely in umbels; calyx 2-lobed, spurred; petals 5, often clawed, entire or notched or fimbriate; stamens 10; **fruit** separating at maturity into 3, 1-seeded sections.

GENERA: *Tropaeolum.*

UMBELLIFERAE Juss. (Carrot Family)

DESCRIPTION: A family of about 250 genera of dicotyledonous herbs of wide distribution; **leaves** alternate, mostly compound; **flowers** small, in simple or compound umbels, or rarely in heads, perfect or rarely imperfect; calyx 5-lobed; petals and stamens 5; ovary inferior, 2-celled; **fruit** a schizocarp of 2-ribbed or winged carpels that contain oil tubes in the pericarp and separate at maturity.

GENERA: *Aegopodium, Eryngium.*

VALERIANACEAE Batsch. (Valerian Family)

DESCRIPTION: A family of about 10 genera of dicotyledonous perennial herbs or rarely subshrubs of widespread distribution; **leaves** opposite, simple, pinnatifid, or compound; **flowers** small, perfect or imperfect, in cymes or heads; calyx lacking or variously toothed or inrolled in flower and becoming pappuslike in fruit; corolla 5-lobed, often 2-lipped, saccate or spurred at base; stamens 1 to 4, arising from the corolla tube; ovary inferior, usually 3-celled; **fruit** indehiscent, dry, usually with 1 fertile and 2 infertile cells, often crowned with the persistent calyx.

GENERA: *Centranthus, Valeriana.*

VERBENACEAE (Vervain Family)

DESCRIPTION: A family of over 75 genera of dicotyledonous herbs, shrubs, or trees, often with square **stems**, of wide distribution; **leaves** usually opposite or whorled, mostly simple, rarely compound; **flowers** usually perfect, irregular or regular, in spikes, racemes, or cymes; calyx usually 4- to 5-lobed or toothed; corolla usually with as many lobes as the calyx, mostly salverform, sometimes campanulate or 2-lipped; stamens usually 4, sometimes 2 or 5; ovary superior; **fruit** a drupe or dry and separating into nutlets.

GENERA: *Verbena.*

VIOLACEAE Batsch (Violet Family)

DESCRIPTION: A family of about 18 genera of dicotyledonous, perennial herbs, or rarely shrubs widely distributed on all continents; **leaves** alternate, rarely opposite, usually simple, sometimes lobed or divided, with minute or leafy stipules; **flowers** perfect or rarely imperfect, regular or irregular, sometimes cleistogamous; sepals and petals 5, the lower petal often spurred or saccate; stamens 5; **fruit** a capsule or berry.

GENERA: *Viola.*

Plant Descriptions

The entries are alphabetically arranged by genus, followed by the family name. Descriptions are brief and contain only that information that would be useful in recognizing the plant. Culture and use are described under the species description. Only those species that are commonly planted and that are commercially available are described. Important botanical varieties are included. Cultivar descriptions are brief and not all cultivars are included. Family descriptions are given in the hopes that the reader will learn to recognize the family characteristics. Important genera are listed after each family.

The scientific names used are those found in *Hortus Third*. Sometimes nurseries list plants under some other scientific name. These names are alphabetically listed, with reference to the correct name as given in *Hortus Third*. Common names are alphabetically listed in the appendix with reference to their correct scientific name.

Longevity, height, and blooming dates, and common names are given after the species.

PLANT DESCRIPTIONS

Achillea L. (Yarrow)

COMPOSITAE (Sunflower Family)

Anthemis Tribe

DESCRIPTION: A large genus of about 80 species of aromatic herbs native to the north temperate regions of the Old World; **leaves** alternate or in basal rosettes, simple, toothed to pinnately dissected; **flowers** in small radiate heads arranged mostly in corymbs; ray flowers white, pink, or yellow, pistillate; disc flowers tubular, perfect; **fruits** are strongly compressed, smooth achenes.

Achillea filipendula Lam. (Fern-leaf Yarrow). Perennial to 1.5 m. tall. June-August.

DESCRIPTION: **Plants** stiff, erect, with furrowed stems, native in Asia Minor and the Caucasus; **leaves** to 25 cm. long, linear to elliptic, 1- to 2-pinnatifid into linear-lanceolate, toothed segments, hairy, with a strong spicy odor and a fernlike texture; **flowers** yellow, in small heads to 5 mm. across, clustered into compound, convex corymbs to 12 cm. across.

USE: Plant at the back of the flower border. Use for cut flowers or dry for winter arrangements.

CULTURE: Plants grow in any well-drained soil in full sun. Plant in early spring about 60 cm. apart. The species can be propagated by seeds sown in the spring or by division. Cultivars must be vegetatively propagated by cuttings taken in June or by division of the clumps every 3 or 4 years. There are few insect or disease problems.

CULTIVARS

'Coronation Gold'. Plants 90 cm. tall, shorter than the species.

'Gold Plate'. Flower clusters to 15 cm. across.   PLATE 1

'Moonshine'. Plants 60 cm. tall; flowers canary yellow.

Achillea millefolium L. (Common Yarrow). Perennial to 90 cm. tall. June-September.

DESCRIPTION: **Plants** strongly aromatic, rhizomatous, densely hairy, native in Europe and western Asia, naturalized in America; **leaves** 2- to 3-pinnately dissected into linear or lanceolate segments, fernlike; **flowers** white or occasionally pink, in small heads clustered into round or flat corymbs to 7.5 cm. across.

USE: Only the named cultivars should be planted in the flower border. Flowers are excellent for fresh or dried arrangements.

CULTURE: Same as for *A. filipendula* except plants can be spaced 45 cm. apart.

CULTIVARS

'Cerise King'. Flowers cherry red.

'Fire King'. Leaves finely divided; flowers rose red.   PLATE 2

'Red Beauty'. Plants 45 cm. tall; flowers bright red.

'Rose Beauty'. Flowers rose red.

Achillea ptarmica L. (Sneezewort Yarrow). Perennial to 70 cm. tall. June-September.

DESCRIPTION: **Plants** rhizomatous, native in Europe and Asia, naturalized in eastern North America; **leaves** sessile, linear to linear-lanceolate, to 10 cm. long, finely serrate to nearly entire, smooth; **flowers** white, in heads to 2 cm. across, clustered in loose corymbs.

USE: Plant in flower border but be prepared to check its growth as it can spread. Flowers are excellent for cutting.

CULTURE: Same as for *A. filipendula*. Plants should be spaced 30 cm. apart.

CULTIVARS

'Angel's Breath'. Flower heads fully double, white.

'The Pearl'. Flower heads fully double, white.

Achillea--other species

A. ageratifolia (Sibth, and Sm.) Benth. (Greek Yarrow). A low, tufted perennial from northern Greece, to 20 cm. tall; **leaves** linear-lanceolate, in basal rosettes, silvery-pubescent, to 4 cm. long; **flowers** white, in solitary heads to 3 cm. across.

A. tomentosa L. (Woolly Yarrow). **Plants** mat-forming, woolly, to 30 cm. tall, native in Europe and western Asia; **flowers** bright yellow in small clustered heads from June to August. 'Aurea', with dark yellow flowers, 'Moonlight', with cream-colored flowers, and 'King Edward', with primrose yellow flowers are cultivars.

Aconitum L. (Aconite, Monkshood)

RANUNCULACEAE (Buttercup Family)

DESCRIPTION: A genus of 100 or more species of perennial herbs, native in the north temperate regions of the world; **plants** usually with stiff, erect, branched stems and tuberous roots; **leaves** palmately veined and usually lobed or cleft; **flowers** irregular, blue, white, or sometimes yellow, in racemes or panicles; sepals 5, petal-like, with upper sepal large and hood or helmet-shaped; petals 2 to 5, small, the upper 2 spurlike and included in the hood or helmet, the others minute or lacking; stamens many; pistils 3 to 5; **fruit** a follicle.

Aconitum carmichaelii Debeaux. (Azure Monkshood). Perennial to 1.5 m. tall. August, September. PLATE 3

DESCRIPTION: **Plants** native in eastern Asia; **leaves** leathery, dark green, 3-cleft; **flowers** deep purple-blue, in dense wandlike panicles.

USE: Plant toward the back of the flower border. The blue flowers are welcome in late summer when there are few blue flowers in the garden. Cut flowers make striking arrangements.

CULTURE: Monkshood thrive in rich, deeply prepared soil in either sun or partial shade. Plants may need to be staked in windy sites. Propagation is by seeds or division. It takes several years for plants to bloom from seeds. Plant seeds as soon as ripe. Once established, plants should not be disturbed until they become overcrowded. Powdery mildew is sometimes a problem. The roots are poisonous and should never be eaten.

Aconitum fischeri Rehb. Material sold under this name is usually *A. carmichaelii*.

Aconitum napellus L. (Garden Monkshood, Helmet Flower). Perennial to 1 m. tall. July, August.

DESCRIPTION: **Plants** with slender stems, native in northern Europe; **leaves** to 10 cm. wide, 3-parted to base, with lanceolate segments; **flowers** violet, to 4 cm. high, with hemispheric helmet, borne in dense racemes to 20 cm. long.

USE: Same as for *A. carmichaelii.*

CULTURE: Same as for *A. carmichaelii.* Plants may be a little more shade tolerant.

CULTIVARS
'Bicolor'. Flowers white with a blue border.
'Bressingham Spire'. Flowers dark blue.
'Newry Blue'. Flowers a true blue.
'Sparks Variety'. Flowers a deep purple.

Aconitum wilsonii — see *Aconitum carmichaelii*

Acorus L. (Sweet Flag)

ARACEAE (Arum Family)

DESCRIPTION: A small genus of only two species of perennial herbs, native in North America and Eurasia; **plants** aromatic, with fleshy rhizomes buried in wet soil; **leaves** irislike or grasslike; **flowers** small, perfect, borne on a spadix, partially enclosed by a leaflike spathe.

Acorus calamus L. (Sweet Flag). Perennial to 2 m. tall. July, August

DESCRIPTION: **Plants** grow from stout, pink rhizomes; **leaves** irislike, to 2 cm. wide, with a prominent midrib; **flowers** yellow, on a stout spadix.

USE: These are handsome plants for planting in shallow water or in wet soil at the edge of a stream or pond.

CULTURE: Plant the rhizomes in early spring in water no deeper than 20 cm. They multiply quickly and the size of the clumps may need to be restricted.

CULTIVAR
'Variegatus'. Leaves with yellow stripes.

Acorus gramineus Ait. (Grassy-leaved Sweet Flag). Perennial to 45 cm. tall. July, August.

DESCRIPTION: **Plants** with slender rhizomes, native in southeastern Asia and Japan; **leaves** grasslike, rarely more than 6 mm. wide; **flowers** borne on a slender spadix.

USE: Same as for *A. calamus.*

CULTURE: Same as for *A. calamus.*

CULTIVARS
'Pusillus'. Plants dwarf.
'Variegatus'. Leaves with white stripes.

Acroclinum roseum —see *Helipterum roseum*

Actaea L. (Baneberry)

RANUNCULACEAE (Buttercup Family)

DESCRIPTION: A genus of about 8 species of erect, perennial herbs, native in rich woods in north temperate regions of the world; leaves large, compound; flowers small, white, in terminal racemes; sepals 4 or 5, petaloid, falling early; petals 4 to 10, small, spatulate, clawed; stamens many; pistil 1; fruit a glossy berry.

Actaea alba —see *Actaea pachypoda*

Actaea pachypoda Elliott (White Baneberry, Doll's-eyes). Perennial to 60 cm. tall. May.

DESCRIPTION: **Plants** form upright clumps, native from Minnesota to Nova Scotia, and south to Missouri and Georgia; leaves ternately compound; leaflets mostly ovate with pointed teeth; **flowers** in oblong racemes; petals square at the apex; **fruit** a white berry with a black "eye" on top, borne on a stout pedicel.

USE: Plant in a woodland wildflower garden.

CULTURE: Plants grow best in a rich fertile loam soil high in organic matter and in partial shade. Propagation is by seeds or division. Plant seeds in early summer. Seedlings are transplanted to a shaded nursery bed and grown until large enough to plant in their permanent location. Division is best done in early spring.

CULTIVAR
'Rubrocarpa'. Fruits pinkish purple with a lighter pink blotch.

Actaea rubra (Ait.) Willd. (Red Baneberry). Perennial to 60 cm. tall. May.   PLATE 4

DESCRIPTION: **Plants** form upright clumps, native from South Dakota to Nova Scotia, south to Nebraska and Pennsylvania; leaves ternately compound; leaflets ovate, toothed to deeply cleft; **flowers** in ovoid racemes; fruits red, on slender pedicels.

USE: Same as for *A. pachypoda.*

CULTURE: Same as for *A. pachypoda.*

CULTIVARS AND VARIETIES

'Alba'. Fruits white.

subsp. *arguta* (Nutt.) Hult. Native in western North America; leaves smaller and more deeply incised than in species.

Adlumia Raf.

FUMARIACEAE (Fumitory Family)

DESCRIPTION: A small genus of but a single species of herbaceous, biennial vines, native in eastern North America; **leaves** alternate, 3- to 4-pinnate; **flowers** narrow, heart-shaped, perfect, in axillary panicles; petals 4, united and persistent, enclosing the stamens and pistil; stamens 6, united at base into a tube; **fruit** a few-seeded capsule.

Adlumia fungosa (Ait.) Greene (Alleghany Vine, Mountain-fringe, Climbing Fumitory). Biennial vine to 4 m. long. June, July.

DESCRIPTION: **Plants** climbing by the petioles twisting around the supports, native from Ontario to North Carolina; **leaves** fernlike, to 25 cm. long; **flowers** white to purple, to 1.5 cm. long; corolla persistent and enclosing the capsule.

USE: A climbing plant useful for covering stumps in a woodland wildflower garden. Grown for its fernlike foliage as well as its flowers.

CULTURE: Plant in soil that is well-drained and high in organic matter. A shady location is preferred. Propagation is by seeds planted in early spring. Since it is a biennial, the plant dies after flowering. To maintain a planting, start seeds every spring. A support, such as a stump or trellis, is needed.

Adonis L. (Pheasant's-eye)

RANUNCULACEAE (Buttercup Family)

DESCRIPTION: A genus of about 40 species of Eurasian herbs; **leaves** alternate, divided into narrow segments; **flowers** solitary, terminal, mostly red or yellow; sepals 5; petals 5 to many; pistils numerous; **fruit** an achene.

Adonis aestivalis (Summer Adonis). Annual to 40 cm. tall. July.

DESCRIPTION: **Plants** well-branched, native in Europe; **leaves** 3-pinnate with ultimate segments linear, acute; **flowers** crimson; sepals appressed to the spreading petals; fruit an achene with sharp teeth at the base of the inner side.

USE: Plant toward the front of the flower border or in the rock garden.

CULTURE: Plants like a sandy loam soil enriched with organic matter. They thrive in either full sun or partial shade. Propagation is by seeds started indoors in late March.

VARIETY

f. *citrina* (Hoffm.) Voss. Flowers citron yellow.

Adonis vernalis L. (Spring Adonis). Perennial to 50 cm. tall. April, May.   PLATE 5

DESCRIPTION: **Plants** native in central and southern Europe; lower **leaves** reduced to scales; **flowers** yellow, to 8 cm. across; petals 10 to 15, narrow; **achenes** with long beaks.

USE: An excellent rock garden plant.

CULTURE: Soil and shade requirements same as for *A. aestivalis*. Propagation is by seeds or division. Seeds are sown in a cold frame in sandy soil in late summer. Plants are divided in early spring.

Adonis — other species

A. amurensis Regel & Radde. (Amur Adonis), native in southeastern Asia, is a perennial with yellow, white, or rose flowers in June and July.

A. annua L. (Autumn Adonis, Pheasant's-eye), native in southern Europe and southwestern Asia, is an annual with scarlet flowers in July and August.

Aegopodium L. (Goutweed)

UMBELLIFERAE (Carrot Family)

DESCRIPTION: A small genus of about 5 species of coarse herbs with creeping rhizomes, native in Europe and Asia; **leaves** biternate; **flowers** small, yellow or white, in compound umbels.

Aegopodium podagraria L. (Goutweed). Perennial to 35 cm. tall. May, June.

DESCRIPTION: **Plants** native in Europe, naturalized in North America; **leaflets** oblong to ovate, to 8 cm. long, sharply serrate; **flowers** white, in dense umbels to 12 cm. across.

USE: An excellent ground cover for shady places.

CULTURE: Plants grow in any soil and compete well with tree roots. They spread by rhizomes and may invade the lawn area unless confined by a soil barrier. Do not plant in the flower border. Old plants can be mowed to the ground in early spring with a rotary mower.

CULTIVARS: The species is seldom planted but the following cultivar is widely used.

'Variegata'. Leaves with white margins. Commonly called Silver Edge Goutweed.   PLATE 6

Aethionema R. Br. (Stone Cress)

CRUCIFERAE (Mustard Family)

DESCRIPTION: A genus of about 40 species of low growing, smooth, annual or perennial herbs, native in the Mediterranean region; **leaves** simple, sessile, often glaucous; **flowers** pink, lilac, or white, in showy, terminal racemes; sepals and petals 4; **fruit** a flattened, usually winged silicle.

Aethionema grandiflorum Boiss. & Hohen. (Persion Stone Cress). Perennial to 30 cm. tall. May, June.

DESCRIPTION: **Plants** with many erect stems, native in Turkey, Iraq, and Iran; **leaves** linear-oblong, to 4 cm. long, evenly distributed along the stem; **flowers** pink, to 3 cm. across, in terminal racemes; **silicles** flat, ovate, or rounded, to 1.5 cm. long.

USE: An excellent rock garden plant or use in masses toward the front of the flower border. The flowers are excellent for cutting.

CULTURE: Plants prefer a sandy or rocky soil in full sun. A winter mulch is needed. Once established, the plants are long lived. Propagation is by cutting. Trim the plants after flowering and take the cuttings from the new growth. Rooted cuttings are potted and carried over winter in a cold frame. Plants can also be grown from seed planted in a cold frame in sandy soil in late summer.

CULTIVAR

'Warley Rose'. Flowers bright pink with lighter veins.

Aethionema saxatile (L.) R. Br. (Persian Candytuft, Cliff Stone Cress). Tender perennial grown as an annual to 30 cm. tall. June, July.

DESCRIPTION: **Plants** with several stems, native in southern Europe and Asia Minor; **leaves** usually ovate or oblong, obtuse; **flowers** white or pink, to 1.5 cm. across, in loose or dense racemes; **silicles** to 1 cm. across.

USE: Same as for *A. grandiflorum.*

CULTURE: Same site requirements as *A. grandiflorum*. Propagation is by seeds started indoors in late March. Space the plants about 20 cm. apart.

Aethionema — other species

A. coridifolium DC. (Lebanon Stone Cress), native in Turkey and Lebanon, is a perennial to 30 cm. tall, with pink or rosy lilac flowers in May and June.

A. iberidium (Boiss.) Boiss. (Persian Candytuft, Spanish Stone Cress), native in Turkey and Greece, is a perennial to 20 cm. tall. with white flowers in May and June.

A. x *warleyense* Bergmans. (Warley Stone Cress) is a perennial of hybrid origin (*A. armenum* x *A. grandiflorum*). It produces rose pink to carmine flowers in May.

Agastache Clayt. (Giant Hyssop)

LABIATAE (Mint Family)

DESCRIPTION: A genus of about 30 species of coarse herbs, native in North America and Asia; **stems** mostly square in cross section; **leaves** opposite, serrate, petioled; **flowers** small, blue or purple, in many-flowered verticillasters arranged in interrupted terminal spikes; calyx tubular, oblique, 15-veined, 5-toothed; corolla 2-lipped, with upper lip erect, 2-lobed, and lower lip 3-lobed; stamens 4, exserted; **fruit** of 4 nutlets.

Agastache foeniculum (Pursh.) O. Kuntze (Anise Giant Hyssop, Fennel Giant Hyssop). Perennial to 1 m. tall. July.   PLATE 7

DESCRIPTION: **Plants** upright, coarse, branched, native in north central North America; **leaves** ovate, acute, serrate, to 7 cm. long, white beneath; **flowers** blue, in cylindrical spikes to 10 cm. long; calyx teeth acute, corolla to 1 cm. long.

USE: Plant toward the back of the flower border in a woodland wildflower garden.

CULTURE: Plants prefer a rich, moist soil high in organic matter in full sun or partial shade. Propagation is by seeds or division in early spring.

Agastache — other species

A. nepatoides (L.) O. Kuntze (Yellow Giant Hyssop), native from Ontario to Quebec, south to Kansas and Georgia, is 1.5 m. tall, with small blue flowers to 8 mm. long in August and September.

A. rugosa (Fisch. & C. A. Mey.) O. Kuntze (Wrinkled Giant Hyssop), native in eastern Asia, is 1.2 m. tall, with purple flowers in August and September.

A. urticifolia (Benth.) O. Kuntze (Nettleleaf Giant Hyssop), native from British Columbia to Montana, south to California, is 1 m. tall with rose to violet flowers larger than those in *A. nepatoides.*

Ageratum L. (Flossflower)

COMPOSITAE (Sunflower Family)

Anthemis Tribe

DESCRIPTION: A small genus of about 30 species of annual herbs or shrubs, native to the southeastern United States, Central America, and South America; **leaves** mostly opposite, ovate or lanceolate, usually serrate or crenate; **flowers** blue, purple, rose, or white, in compact heads, arranged in irregular panicles or corymbs, all funnelform or tubular, perfect; involucres bell-shaped; hemispherical, or top-shaped; involucral bracts overlapping in 2 to 3 rows; **fruit** an achene with a pappus of 5 or 6 scales.

Ageratum houstonianum Mill. (Flossflower). Annual to 90 cm. tall. June-September.

DESCRIPTION: **Plants** are native in central and southern Mexico and adjacent Guatemala and British Honduras; **leaves** ovate to triangular, to 12 cm. long, cordate or square at base, crenate or rarely dentate, hairy; **flowers** blue, lilac, or lavender, in heads to 1 cm. across; involucral bracts linear-lanceolate, glandular.

USE: Plants are used for mass effects in the flower border or for edging.

CULTURE: Plants prefer a rich, moisture retentive soil in either full sun or partial shade. Propagation is by seed started indoors in early April, Plants are spaced about 20 cm. apart in the garden.

CULTIVARS: Numerous cultivars have been named. Most of these are compact and suitable for edging purposes.

'Blue Blazer'. Dwarf plants with bluish mauve flowers.   PLATE 8
'Blue Chip'. Uniform plants with bluish mauve flowers.
'Blue Mink'. Tetraploid. Plants vigorous with lavender blue flowers.
'Blue Moon'. Plants low, with soft, powder blue flowers.
'Fairy Pink'. Flowers salmon pink.
'Midget Blue'. All-America Winner. Flowers bluish mauve on uniform dwarf plants.
'Snow Carpet'. Plants dwarf; flowers pure white.
'Spindrift'. Flowers uniform, white, or medium-sized plants.

Agrostemma L. (Corn Cockle)

CARYOPHYLLACEAE (Pink Family)

DESCRIPTION: A small genus of only 3 species of annual herbs, native in the Mediterranean region; **leaves** opposite, entire; **flowers** solitary or in a loose few-flowered cyme; calyx 10-ribbed, with 5 lobes; petals 5, clawed; stamens 10; **fruit** a 1-celled capsule.

Agrostemma githago L. (Common Corn Cockle). Annual to 1 m. tall. July-September.

DESCRIPTION: A much-branched annual, native in the Mediterranean region, naturalized and often a weed in North America; **leaves** linear, to 10 cm. long; **flowers** magenta purple, rarely white, to 3 cm. across; calyx teeth longer than the calyx tube; petals shorter than the sepals; **capsule** with 5 teeth.

USE: Named cultivars are sometimes planted in the flower border.

CULTURE: Plants grow in most any soil with very little care. Seeds are planted directly where the plants are to grow in early spring. Remove faded flowers to prevent self seeding.

CULTIVAR
'Milas'. Flowers are rosy purple, to 7.5 cm. across.

Ajuga L. (Bugleweed)

LABIATAE (Mint Family)

DESCRIPTION: A genus of about 40 species of annual or perennial herbs, native in the temperate regions of the Old World; **stems** mostly square in cross section; **leaves** opposite, simple, often crenate or entire; **flowers** blue, white, or rose, in axillary verticillasters arranged in terminal spikes; calyx cup-shaped, 5-toothed; corolla with tube exserted with a ring of hairs inside; limbs 2-lipped, with upper lip very short and lower lip 3-lobed; stamens 4, in 2 pairs, usually exserted; **fruit** of 4 obovoid, net-veined nutlets.

Ajuga reptans L. (Carpet Bugleweed). Perennial to 25 cm. tall. May, June.

DESCRIPTION: **Plants** hairy, native in Europe; basal **leaves** to 6 cm. long, ovate, nearly sessile; **flowers** blue, rarely pink or white, in whorls of 6.

USE: Ajugas are suitable for planting toward the front of the flower border, in rock gardens, or as ground cover.

CULTURE: Plants grow in most any well-drained soil in either full sun or partial shade. Cultivars with colored leaves have brighter colors in full sun. Some winter protection is needed in exposed sites where the snow is apt to blow off in winter. Propagation is mainly by division in early spring.

CULTIVARS

'Alba'. Flowers creamy white.

'Albovariegata'. Leaves variegated with white.

'Atropurpurea'. Leaves bronzy purple; flowers dark purple.

'Bronze Beauty'. Leaves dark purple; flowers purple.

'Burgundy Glow'. Leaves tricolor, first burgundy, later aging to creamy white and dark pink.   PLATE 9

'Burgundy Lace'. Leaves variegated with green and white, spotted red.

'Pink Beauty'. Flowers delicate pink.

'Silver Beauty'. Leaves variegated with light cream and dark green.

Ajuga —other species

A. genevensis L. (Geneva Bugleweed), native in Eurasia, is a perennial to 40 cm. tall, with blue or violet flowers in June and July. 'Alba' with creamy white flowers, 'Bronze Beauty' with bronze leaves and deep blue flowers, 'Rosea' with rose pink flowers, and 'Variegata' with green leaves mottled with creamy white, are named cultivars.

A. pyramidalis L., native in Europe, is a perennial to 30 cm. tall, with pale violet blue, rarely pink or white, flowers in June and July. 'Metalica Crispa' is a cultivar with purplish brown leaves with crisped margins.

Alcea L. (Hollyhock)

MALVACEAE (Mallow Family)

DESCRIPTION: A genus of about 60 species of mostly biennial or short-lived perennial herbs, native in the eastern Mediterranean region and in central Asia; **stems** usually erect, unbranched; leaves simple, unlobed or palmately parted; **flowers** yellow, white, or pink to purple, in elongated racemes; stamens usually 10, united in a tubular column; **fruit** a schizocarp of about 40 mericarps in a single whorl.

Alcea rosea L. (Hollyhock). Typically a biennial to 3m. tall. June-September.

DESCRIPTION: **Plants** with spirelike flowering stems, native in Asia Minor; **leaves** large, sub or bicular, palmately 3- to 7-lobed; **flowers** yellow, white, pink, and purple, to 10 cm. across, in erect racemes; **mericarps** with a narrow dorsal furrow, bordered by parallel wings.

USE: Plant toward the back of the flower border or plant in front of a fence.

CULTURE: Hollyhocks require a well-drained soil, in full sun. Although a short-lived perennial, it is best to treat them as biennials. In recent years, annual strains have been developed that flower the first-year when seeds are started indoors. Propagation is by seeds. For biennial types, seeds should be planted in a nursery row in late June or July. Thin the plants to about 15 cm. apart. Transplant to where the plants are to bloom the following spring.

CULTIVARS

Chaters Double (strain). Plants to 2 m. tall; flowers double, to 10 cm. across, in a wide color range.

Fordhook Giants (strain). Flowers large, in shades of scarlet, crimson, pink, rose, and deep yellow.

'Marjorette'. All-America Winner. Plants annual, to 75 cm. tall; flowers semi-double, fluffy, in a wide color range.

'Powder Puffs'. Plants annual, to 2 m. tall; flowers double, in a wide color range.

'Silver Puffs'. Plants annual, dwarf; flowers double, with a rose pink or silvery pink "eye."   PLATE 10

'Summer Carnival'. All-America Winner. Plants annual, to 1.5 m. tall; flowers fully double, in shades of white, primrose, pink, deep rose, or crimson.

Alchemilla L. (Lady's-mantle)

ROSACEAE (Rose Family)

DESCRIPTION: A large genus of about 200 species of annual or perennial herbs, native mostly in north temperate zones of the world; **leaves** palmately lobed or divided; **flowers** small, green or yellow, in mostly compound cymes; stamens 1 to 4; pistils 1 to 10; **fruits** are achenelike and embedded in the dry, persistent calyx.

Alchemilla pubescens — see *Alchemilla glaucescens*

Alchemilla vulgaris L. (Common Lady's-mantle). Perennial to 50 cm. tall. May-August.   PLATE 11

DESCRIPTION: Mound-shaped **plants**, native in Europe, naturalized in eastern North America; **leaves** mostly basal, palmately lobed with 7 to 11 shallow toothed lobes, green on both surfaces; **flowers** small, to 3 mm. across.

USE: Plant in rock gardens or toward the front of the flower border. Grown for its attractive leaves and mound-shaped form.

CULTURE: Plants prefer light shade and a soil that is high in organic matter. Propagation is by seeds or by spring division. Seeds should be sown in a sandy soil in a cold frame in May. The seedlings should be thinned to 10 cm. apart.

Alchemilla —other species

A. alpina L. (Alpine Lady's-mantle), native in the mountains of Europe, is a low, mound-shaped plant to 20 cm. tall, suitable for rock gardens.

A. glaucescens Wallr., native in Europe, is a mound-shaped plant to 20 cm. tall, with hairy leaves.

Aletris L. (Star Grass)

LILIACEAE (Lily Family)

DESCRIPTION: A small genus of about 10 species of perennial, fibrous rooted herbs, native in North America and eastern Asia; **leaves** basal, grasslike, from a short, thick rhizome; **flowers** white or yellow, in erect, spikelike racemes; perianth segments 6; stamens 6; **fruit** a capsule.

Aletris farinosa L. (Unicorn Root, White-tube Star Grass). Perennial to 1 m. tall. June, July.

DESCRIPTION: **Plants** spreading by rhizomes, native from Minnesota to Maine, south to Texas and Florida; leaves pale yellowish green, to 15 cm. long; **flowers** white, in spikelike racemes; perianth tubular with 6 spreading lobes.

USE: A useful plant in a sunny prairie wildflower garden.

CULTURE: Plants require a moist, acid soil and full sun. Propagation is by spring division or by seeds planted in an acid, peaty soil in a cold frame in September.

Aletris —other species

A. aurea Walt. (Yellow Colicroot), native from Maryland to Florida, is similar but has yellow flowers.

Alisma L. (Water Plantain)

ALISMATACEAE (Water Plantain Family)

DESCRIPTION: A small genus of 6 or 7 species of aquatic, perennial herbs of wide distribution; **leaves** basal, linear to heart-shaped, with sheathing petioles;

flowers white, small, perfect, in whorls on a scapose panicle; sepals and petals 3; stamens 6; **fruit** a head of achenes.

Alisma plantago-aquatica L. (Water Plantain, Mad-dog Weed). Perennial to 1 m. tall. June, July.

DESCRIPTION: An aquatic **plant** with fleshy corms, native in the temperate regions of North America and Asia; **leaves** usually above the water, lanceolate or elliptic to broadly ovate, to 15 cm. long, rounded or subcordate at base; **flowers** white, sometimes purple-tipped, to 1.3 cm. across; **achenes** clustered in heads to 7 mm. across.

USE: Sometimes planted in shallow pools or wet soils along a stream.

CULTURE: Fleshy corms are planted in spring in wet soil either directly or in containers submerged in water. Seeds can also be planted in containers and submerged in water in the spring.

Allium L. (Onion)

AMARYLLIDACEAE (Amaryllis Family)

DESCRIPTION: A large genus of 400 or more species of strongly odorous, perennial, bulbous or rhizomatous herbs, native mostly in the northern hemisphere; **bulbs** tunicate, with fleshy, concentric leaf bases, outer coats usually membranous with parallel fibers or fibers forming a netted pattern; **leaves** mostly basal, narrow, tubular or flat, sheathing the stem at the base; **flowers** usually showy, in umbels subtended by a spathe of 1 or 2, sometimes more, united valves; perianth segments 6, separate or united at base; stamens 6; ovary superior, 3-celled, with 1 to 10 ovules; **fruit** a capsule.

Allium albopilosum —see *Allium christophii*

Allium azureum —see *Allium caeruleum*

Allium giganteum Regel (Giant Garlic, Giant Onion). Perennial to 1 m. tall. June, July.   PLATE 12

DESCRIPTION: **Plants** native in central Asia; **bulbs** large, ovoid, with membranous outer scales; **leaves** strap-shaped, to 5 cm. wide, glaucous; **flowers** bright lilac, in dense umbels to 10 cm. across.

USE: Plant toward the back of the flower border in small clumps. Flowers are good for cutting.

CULTURE: Plants need a well-drained soil that is high in organic matter. Propagation is largely by bulbs planted in the fall of the year in September. Space the bulbs about 20 cm. apart and 15 cm. deep. Mulch the first winter.

Allium moly L. (Lily Leek). Perennial to 50 cm. tall. May, June.

DESCRIPTION: **Plants** native in southern Europe; **bulbs** small, ovoid, with a leathery outer coat; **flowers** yellow, to 3 cm. across, in several- to many-flowered umbels.

USE: This is an excellent rock garden plant.

CULTURE: Plant the bulbs 10 cm. deep and 10 cm. apart. Soil requirements same as for *A. giganteum*.

Allium oreophyllum var. *ostrowskianum*—see *Allium ostrowskianum*

Allium tuberosum Rottl. (Garlic Chives). Perennial to 60 cm. tall. July, August.

DESCRIPTION: **Plants** native in southeastern Asia; **bulbs** elongate on stout rhizomes, with fibrous-netted outer coat; **leaves** 4 to 9, not hollow, keeled on the back, to 5 mm. wide; **flowers** white, fragrant, in many-flowered umbels.

USE: Grown for its edible leaves and white flowers.

CULTURE: Thrives in any well-drained soil. Remove all faded flowers before they go to seed or seedlings will volunteer all over.

Allium—other species

A. caeruleum Pall. (Blueglobe Onion), native in Asia, is a perennial to 60 cm. tall, with blue flowers in July.

A. cernuum Roth. (Nodding Onion, Wild Onion), native from British Columbia to New York, south to California and South Carolina, is a perennial to 70 cm. tall, with rose or white flowers in nodding umbels in July and August.

A. christophii Trautv. (Stars-of-Persia), native in Iran, is a perennial to 85 cm. tall, with silvery blue flowers in June.

A. cyaneum Regel., native in China, is a perennial to 30 cm. tall, with violet or purplish blue flowers in June.

A. karataviense Regel (Turkestan Onion), native in Turkestan, is a perennial to 25 cm. tall, with red flowers in June.   PLATE 13

A. neapolitanum Cyr. (Daffodil Garlic, Flowering Onion), native in southern Europe, Asia Minor, and northern Africa, is a perennial to 50 cm. tall, with white flowers in May and June.

A. ostrowskianum Regel (Ostrowsky Onion), native in Turkestan, is a perennial to 30 cm. tall, with rose colored flowers in May and June.

A. roseum L. (Rosy Onion), native in southern Europe, northern Africa, and Asia Minor, is a perennial to 45 cm. tall, with rose or white flowers in June. 'Grandiflorum' has larger flowers than the species.

A. schoenoprasum L. (Chives), native in Europe and Asia, is a clump-forming perennial to 70 cm. tall, with rose violet flowers in dense umbels in July and August. Used for food flavoring.

A. senescens L., native in Europe and Siberia, is a popular rock garden plant to 30 cm. tall, with rose pink to white flowers in July and August. Cultivars are 'Glaucum' with rose pink flowers and blue green leaves and 'Rose Beauty' with flowers a deeper rose color than species.   PLATE 14

A. sphaerocephalum L. (Ballhead Onion, Round-headed Garlic), native in northern Africa, Europe, and western Asia, is a perennial to 70 cm. tall, with purplish red flowers in rounded umbels in June and July.

A. stellatum Ker. (Prairie Onion), native in the north central United States, is a perennial to 50 cm. tall, with lavender pink flowers in July and August. Sometimes planted in prairie gardens.

A. tanguticum Regel (Lavender Globe Lily, Tangute Onion), native in western China, is a perennial to 45 cm. tall, with purple flowers in July.

A. tricoccum Ait. (Wild Leek), native from Minnesota to New Brunswick, south to Iowa and North Carolina, is a perennial to 30 cm. tall, with greenish white flowers in June and July. This is a shade tolerant onion that often imparts an onion flavor to milk from cows pasturing in the woods in early spring.

Alternanthera Forssk, (Joseph's-coat, Copperleaf)

AMARANTHACEAE (Amaranth Family)

DESCRIPTION: A genus of more than 100 species of herbs or shrubs, native in tropical or subtropical countries; **leaves** opposite, entire, green, or variously colored or variegated; **flowers** small, perfect, produced in small axillary heads.

Alternanthera ficoidea (L.) R. B. (Joseph's-coat, Copperleaf). Tender perennial grown as an annual, to 15 cm. tall. July-September.

DESCRIPTION: **Plants** dwarf, native from Mexico to Argentina; **leaves** elliptic to broadly ovate or obovate, tipped with a short spine, green or variously colored; **flowers** white or straw-colored, in dense axillary heads.

USE: Used for carpet bedding and for edging. For formal effects, the plants must be sheared.

CULTURE: Plants grow well in most soils in full sun. Since only the cultivars with colored foliage are used, propagation is vegetative. Stock plants are dug in the fall, potted, and wintered in a cool greenhouse or as a house plant. Cuttings are taken in February or March from the tips of new shoots. When rooted, they are potted and planted outdoors after danger of frost.

CULTIVARS

'Aurea Nana'. Plants dwarf; leaves yellow.
'Bettzkyana'. Leaves blotched with shades of red and yellow.
'Brilliantissima'. Leaves bright red.
'Versicolor'. Leaves copper or blood red.

Althaea rosea — see *Alcea rosea*

Alyssum L. (Madwort)

CRUCIFERAE (Mustard Family)

DESCRIPTION: A genus of about 160 species of annual, biennial, or perennial herbs, native in Europe and Asia; **plants** mostly gray-pubescent, with star-shaped, often scalelike hairs; **leaves** alternate, simple, entire; **flowers** usually yellow; sepals and petals 4; stamens 4, of two lengths.

Alyssum argenteum — see *Alyssum murale*

Alyssum maritima — see *Lobularia maritima*

Alyssum montanum L. (Mountain Alyssum). Perennial to 25 cm. tall. April-August.

DESCRIPTION: A low, compact, mound-forming **plant**, native in the mountains of Europe; **leaves** obovate-oblong to linear, gray-pubescent; **flowers** golden yellow, fragrant, in axillary clusters; **fruits** elongated, gray-pubescent silicles.

USE: A charming rock garden or dry wall plant.

CULTURE: Plants require a well-drained soil and full sun. Propagation is by seeds, cuttings, or root division in early spring. Seeds are planted in a sandy soil in May. Cuttings are taken in June.

Alyssum murale Waldst. & Kit. (Yellow-tuft). Perennial to 70 cm. tall. April, May.

DESCRIPTION: **Plants** upright, gray green, native in eastern Europe; basal **leaves** obovate-spatulate, usually disappearing before flowering; stem leaves lanceolate or oblanceolate, to 2 cm. long; **flowers** yellow, small, in terminal corymbs; **silicles** orbicular.

USE: Rock gardens and dry walls.

CULTURE: Same as for *A. montanum*.

Alyssum saxatile —see *Aurinia saxatilis*

Amaranthus L. (Amaranth)

AMARANTHACEAE (Amaranth Family)

DESCRIPTION: A genus of about 50 species of coarse annual herbs, native in mild and tropical climates of the world, often escaping from cultivation and becoming troublesome weeds; **leaves** alternate; **flowers** imperfect, small and inconspicuous, in chaffy, often colored heads or spikes; perianth segments mostly 5; stamens mostly 5, with 4-celled anthers; **fruit** a 1-seeded utricle.

Amaranthus tricolor L. (Joseph's-coat, Tampala). Annual to 1.3 m. tall. August, September.

DESCRIPTION: **Plants** erect, branched, native in the tropics; **leaves** elliptic to ovate, to 10 cm. long, typically green but often blotched with red; **flowers** small, in axillary clusters or panicles.

USE: Planted in the flower border for their colored foliage. Leaves are sometimes eaten as greens.

CULTURE: Easy to grow in any good garden soil in full sun. Seeds should be started indoors in late March at 70° F, or they can be planted outdoors as soon as the soil warms up in mid-May. Space plants about 30 cm. apart.

CULTIVARS AND VARIETIES

var. *salicifolius* Hort. Aellen (Fountain Plant). Leaves narrow, to 18 cm. long.

'Early Splendor'. Leaves pendant, flaming rosy crimson.

'Illumination'. Upper leaves bright rosy red, tipped with gold.

'Molten Fire'. Leaves scarlet and green.   PLATE 15

'Sunrise'. Upper leaves scarlet crimson.

Amaranthus — other species

A. caudatus L. (Love-lies-bleeding, Tassel Flower), native in the tropics, has small red flowers in slender drooping spikes in August and September.

A. hybridus var. *erythrostachys* Moq. (Princess Feather), native in tropical America, has red leaves and flowering spikes in August and September.

Ammobium R. Br.

COMPOSITAE (Sunflower Family)

Inula Tribe

DESCRIPTION: A small genus of only 2 or 3 species of herbs native in Austrailia; **leaves** alternate; **flowers** yellow, all tubular, in solitary, discoid heads; involucral bracts numerous, scarious, white; receptacles with chaffy scales between the flowers; **fruit** a 4-angled achene.

Ammobium alatum R. Br. (Winged Everlasting). Tender perennial grown as an annual, to 60 cm. tall. July, August.

DESCRIPTION: **Plants** with winged stems, white tomentose, native in Austrailia; **leaves** ovate to lanceolate, tapering to base, to 25 cm. long; **flowers** in heads to 2.5 cm. across.

USE: Planted for dried flower arrangements. Cut before the flowers are fully open and dry in a dry, airy place by hanging the stems upside down.

CULTURE: Plants are of easy culture in any well-drained soil in full sun. Although a perennial, the plants are not hardy and are grown as annuals. Start seeds indoors in late March. Transplant the seedlings to the garden about Memorial Day. Space the plants 30 cm. apart.

Amsonia Walt. (Bluestar)

APOCYNACEAE (Dogbane Family)

DESCRIPTION: A small genus of about 20 species of perennial herbs with milky sap, native in North America and eastern Asia; **leaves** alternate or more or less whorled, entire; **flowers** in terminal cymes, regular, perfect, 5-merous; corolla salverform, hairy inside; stamens attached above the middle of the corolla tube, included; **fruit** a pair of cylindrical follicles.

Amsonia tabernaemontana Walt. (Bluestar, Willow Amsonia). Perennial to 1 m. tall. June, July.   PLATE 16

DESCRIPTION: **Plants** with numerous stems, native in the eastern and southern United States; **leaves** alternate, elliptic or lanceolate, to 15 cm. long; **flowers** light blue, in short cymes; corolla tubular, with spreading, starlike lobes, to 1 cm. across; **fruit** a slender follicle.

USE: An attractive plant toward the back of the flower border or in the woodland wildflower garden.

CULTURE: Plants thrive in most well-drained soils in full sun or partial shade. Propagation is by seeds, cuttings, or spring division. Seeds should be planted as soon as ripe in a cold frame or a nursery row.

Anagallis L. (Pimpernel)

PRIMULACEAE (Primrose Family)

DESCRIPTION: A genus of about 30 species of glabrous annual or perennial herbs, native to all continents but most abundant in tropical Africa; **stems** are erect to creeping, often rooting at the nodes; **leaves** simple, alternate, opposite or whorled; **flowers** red, blue, pink, or white, solitary and axillary, or in terminal racemes; calyx mostly 5-lobed; corolla campanulate to rotate, mostly 5-lobed; stamens 5; **fruit** a capsule.

Anagallis arvenis L. (Scarlet Pimpernel, Poor Man's Weatherglass). Annual to 30 cm. tall. July-September.

DESCRIPTION: **Plants** spreading with 4-angled stems, native in Europe but naturalized in the eastern United States; **leaves** opposite, ovate, to 2 cm. long; **flowers** scarlet or white, solitary in leaf axils, to .6 cm. across; corolla rotate.

USE: Sometimes planted toward the front of the flower border or in rock gardens.

CULTURE: Plants grow best in a well-drained sandy loam soil in full sun. Seeds should be started indoors in late March or outdoors as soon as the soil can be worked. Plants should be spaced about 20 cm. apart in the garden.

VARIETY

f. *caerulea* (Schreb.) Baumg. Flowers blue.

Anagallis monelli L. (Pimpernel). Tender perennial grown as an annual, to 50 cm. tall. July-September.

DESCRIPTION: **Plants** upright, native in the Mediterranean region; **leaves** opposite, ovate or oblong, to 2.5 cm. across; **flowers** blue, reddish beneath, to 2 cm. across, solitary and axillary, rotate to nearly campanulate.

USE: Same as for *A. arvensis*.

CULTURE: Same as for *A. arvensis*.

CULTIVARS AND VARIETIES

subsp. *linifolia* (L.) Marie. Leaves linear-lanceolate.
'Breweri'. Flowers red.
'Phillipsii'. Flowers gentian blue.

Anaphalis DC. (Everlasting)

COMPOSITAE (Sunflower Family)

Inula Tribe

DESCRIPTION: A genus of about 35 species of dioecious or polygamodioecious, gray or white-woolly perennial herbs, native in Europe, Asia, and North America; **stems** leafy; **flower** heads small, discoid, produced in corymbs; involucral bracts stiff, dry, white or gray; flowers all tubular, yellow; **achenes** oblong-obovate.

Anaphalis margaritacea (L.) Benth. & Hook. (Pearly Everlasting). Perennial to 1 m. tall. July, August.   PLATE 17

DESCRIPTION: **Plants** erect, white-woolly, rhizomatous, native in northern North America and eastern Asia; **leaves** alternate, sessile, linear-lanceolate to lanceolate to 10 cm. long, white-woolly; **flower** heads small, clustered, each 6 mm. across; involucres white-hairy.

USE: Sometimes planted in wildflower gardens. Flowering stems are cut and dried to use in winter flower arrangements. Tie the stems in bundles and hang upside down in a dry, well-ventilated room.

CULTURE: Plants grow well in poor, well-drained soils in full sun. Propagation is by seeds or by division in early spring. Seeds sown in July will produce plants that bloom the next year. Space the plants about 30 cm. apart.

Anchusa L. (Bugloss, Alkanet)

BORAGINACEAE (Borage Family)

DESCRIPTION: A genus of between 30 and 40 species of coarse, hairy, erect, annual or perennial herbs of Europe, Asia Minor, and Africa; **leaves** simple, alternate and basal; **flowers** blue, violet, white, or seldom yellow, tubular or funnelform, many, in leafy-bracted cymes; calyx 5-lobed or 5-parted; corolla 5-lobed, with scales in the throat; stamens 5, included; **fruit** 4 rough nutlets, each surrounded at the base by an annular rim.

Anchusa azurea Mill. (Alkanet, Italian Bugloss). Perennial to 1.5 m. tall. June-September.

DESCRIPTION: **Plants** branched, hispid, native in Europe; **leaves** oblong to lanceolate to 20 cm. long; **flowers** bright blue, to 2 cm. across, in leafy-bracted cymes.

USE: Plant in small groups toward the back of the flower border. The blue flowers provide color to the summer border.

CULTURE: Plants do best in a moist but well-drained soil. They prefer full sun but will bloom in partial shade. Propagation is by seeds or root cuttings. Plants are short-lived, so a fresh supply of plants should be available. Seeds can be planted in early spring where plants are to bloom. A winter protection with evergreen boughs is advised. Space the plants 50 cm. apart.

CULTIVARS
'Blue Angel'. Plants dwarf; flowers brilliant blue.
'Dropmore'. Flowers deep blue.
'Little John'. Plants compact; flowers brilliant blue.
'London Royalist'. Flowers large, true blue.
'Pride of Dover'. Flowers sky blue.
'Royal Blue'. Plants pyramidal; flowers royal blue.

Anchusa capensis Thunb. (Alkanet). Biennial, grown as an annual, to 70 cm. tall. July-September.

DESCRIPTION: **Plants** erect, native in southern Africa; **leaves** linear-lanceolate with bulbous-based hairs; **flowers** blue, margined with red, with a white throat, to 7 mm. across.

USE: Plant in groups in the center of the flower border.

CULTURE: Same as for *A. azurea*. Start seeds early indoors for earlier bloom.

CULTIVARS

'Blue Angel'. Flowers starlike, ultramarine blue.

'Blue Bird'. Flowers blue.

'Pink Bird'. Flowers pink.

Anchusa myosotiflora —see *Brunnera macrophylla*

Androsace L. (Rock Jasmine)

PRIMULACEAE (Primrose Family)

DESCRIPTION: A genus of about 125 species of tufted annual, biennal, or perennial herbs of Europe, Asia, and North America; **leaves** simple, mostly basal; **flowers** red or white, in scapose umbels, or solitary; calyx 5-cleft; corolla funnelform or salverform, 5-lobed; **fruit** a 5-valved capsule.

Androsace primuloides Duby (Primula Rock Jasmine). Perennial to 10 cm. tall. May.

DESCRIPTION: **Plants** stoloniferous, native in the Himalayas; **leaves** in basal rosettes, oblanceolate, to 5 cm. long, covered with silky hairs; **flowers** pink, to 1.25 cm. across; bracts subtenting the umbels broadly lanceolate.

USE: An excellent plant for the rock garden.

CULTURE: A partially shaded site with a sandy or gritty, well-drained soil is required. Water during dry periods. Propagation is by seeds, cuttings, or division. Seeds are sown as soon as ripe in a sandy soil in a cold frame. Cuttings are taken in June or July and rooted in sand. Division is done immediately after flowering.

CULTIVAR

'Chumbyi'. Plants compact with silky hairs.

Androsace sarmentosa var. *primuloides* —see *Androsace primuloides*

Androsace —other species

A. carnea L. (Rock Jasmine), native in the Alps and Pyrenees mountains, is a perennial to 8 cm. tall, with rose to white flowers with a yellow eye in May.

A sarmentosa Wallich, native in the Himalayas, is a perennial to 15 cm. tall, with rose-colored flowers in May.

A. septentrionalis L., native in Asia, Europe, and northern North America, is an annual to 20 cm. tall, with white or pink flowers in May and June.

Anemone L. (Windflower, Pasqueflower)

RANUNCULACEAE (Buttercup Family)

DESCRIPTION: A genus of about 120 species of perennial herbs, native in the north temperate regions of the world; **leaves** mostly divided, dissected, or compound; **flowers** white or variously colored, solitary, subtended by a leaflike involucre; sepals petal-like; petals lacking; stamens many; pistils numerous, forming **achenes** with long, plumose styles.

Anemone sylvestris L. (Snowdrop Anemone). Perennial to 50 cm. tall. May, June.

DESCRIPTION: **Plants** stoloniferous, native in Europe and Siberia; **leaves** 5-parted, hairy, unequally dentate, on long petioles; involucral leaves 3-parted; **flowers** white, solitary, fragrant, often nodding, to 7 cm. across.

USE: Plant in flower border or in woodland wildflower garden. Flowers are nice in arrangements.

CULTURE: Plants like a rich, moist soil high in organic matter. They like partial shade but will grow in full sun. Propagation is by seeds or division in early spring. Seeds should be sown in early fall in a cold frame. Space the plants about 30 cm. apart.

CULTIVARS
'Flore Pleno'. Flowers double.
'Grandiflora'. Flowers larger than in species.   PLATE 21

Anemone — other species

Anemone blanda Schott. & Kotschy (Greek Anemone, Grecian Windflower), native in southern Europe and Asia Minor, has sky blue flowers in May on short plants. Winter protection is needed. 'Blue Star' with intense blue flowers, 'Bridesmaid' with white flowers, and 'Pink Star' with pink flowers with yellow centers are named cultivars.   PLATE 18

A. canadensis L. (Meadow Anemone), native in North America, has white flowers in June. It likes moist soil and spreads by rhizomes.

A. coronaria L. (Poppy Anemone), native in the Mediterranean region, is a popular florist's plant. It produces fleshy, tuberous rhizomes. These rhizomes can be potted in March and planted outdoors in May for June bloom. The flowers are large and brightly colored. The rhizomes must be dug in the fall and stored in a cool moist place.

A. halleri All. (Haller's Pasqueflower), native in the European Alps, has beautiful lilac purple flowers in April and May. It requires a well-drained soil and is suitable for planting in a rock garden.   PLATE 19

Anemone nemerosa L. (European Wood Anemone), native in Eurasia, is shade-loving and suitable for planting in a woodland garden. The flowers are white or rose-colored from April to June.

Anemone patens L. (American Pasqueflower), native in sandy or rocky soils in the northern United States, has hairy, light blue flowers in April. It is an excellent rock garden plant. It is difficult to transplant so start with small seedlings.   PLATE 20

A. pulsatilla L. (European Pasqueflower), native in Europe, is similar to *A. patens*. The flowers range from blue to red purple. It is easier to divide and transplant than the American species.

A. quinquefolia L. (Wood Anemone), native in the northern United States and Canada, is a low, shade-loving groundcover that spreads by rhizomes. The flowers are white in June.

Anemonella Spach. (Rue Anemone)

RANUNCULACEAE (Buttercup Family)

DESCRIPTION: A genus with a single species native in eastern North America; **plants** with tuberous roots and basal leaves; **flowers** are white to pale pink in few-flowered umbels; sepals petal-like; petals lacking; stamens numerous.

Anemonella thalictroides (L.) Spach. (Rue Anemone). Perennial to 20 cm. tall. May, June.

DESCRIPTION: **Plants** glabrous, native from Minnesota to New Hampshire, south to Kansas and Florida; **leaves** 2- to 3-ternate, with ovate segments to 2.5 cm. long; **flowers** white to pale pink, in few-flowered umbels, subtended by sessile involucral leaves.

USE: A delightful plant in the rock garden or in the woodland wildflower garden.

CULTURE: Plants grow well in a well-drained soil high in organic matter in full sun or partial shade. Propagation is largely by division of the tuberous roots in September. Plant the tubers about 4 cm. deep and about 15 cm. apart.

CULTIVARS
'Rosea'. Flowers rosy red.
'Shoaf's Double Pink'. Flowers fully double on compact plants. An excellent
rock garden plant.   PLATE 22

Antennaria Gaertn. (Pussy-toes)

COMPOSITAE (Sunflower Family)

Inula Tribe

DESCRIPTION: A genus of about 50 species of dioecious white- or gray-
woolly perennial herbs, native in North and South America, and northern
Europe and Asia; **stems** simple, erect; **leaves** in basal rosettes and also alternate
on stems; **flower** heads discoid, small, in racemes or dense corymbs; involucral
bracts overlapping, with white or scarious tips; flowers white, the pistillate
tubular, the staminate funnelform.

Antennaria dioica (L.) Gaertn. (Common Pussy-toes). Perennial to 25 cm. tall. July, August.

DESCRIPTION: **Plants** stoloniferous, native in North America, Europe, and
northern Asia; **leaves** green and smooth above, white-woolly beneath, basal
leaves spatulate, to 2.5 cm. long, stem leaves linear; heads 2 to 12; involucral
bracts with white or rose tips.

USE: Planted as ground covers in dry sites, in rock gardens, and between
stepping stones.

CULTURE: Pussy-toes are of easy culture, thriving on poor soils in full sun.
Propagation is largely by division in early spring. Seeds can also be planted in
sandy soil in early spring. Space plants about 15 cm. apart.

CULTIVARS
'Rosea'. Involucral bracts with rose colored tips.
'Tomentosa'. Leaves densely white-woolly.

Antennaria microphylla — see *Antennaria rosea*

Antennaria — other species

A neglecta Greene (Field Pussy-toes), native from southern Canada south to
California and Virginia, has involucral bracts that are green or purple with
white tips.

A. rosea Greene (Rose Pussy-toes), native from Alaska south to California and New Mexico, has involucral bracts that are usually rose colored at the tips.

Anthemis L. (Dog Fennel, Chamomile)

COMPOSITAE (Sunflower Family)

Anthemis Tribe

DESCRIPTION: A genus of about 100 species of aromatic herbs, native to Europe, western Asia, and northern Africa; **stems** leafy; **leaves** alternate, incised to pinnately dissected; **flower** heads solitary, terminal; involucre saucer-shaped; involucral bracts overlapping in several rows, usually with dry margins; receptacle flat to conical, with more or less chaffy scales; disc flowers tubular, perfect, yellow; ray flowers pistillate or sterile, white or yellow; **achenes** cylindrical or sometimes flattened.

Anthemis aizoon — see *Achillea ageratifolia* var. *aizoon*

Anthemis biebersteiniana — see *Anthemis marschalliana*

Anthemis tinctoria L. (Golden Marguerite, Golden Chamomile). Biennial or short-lived perennial to 1 m. tall. July-September.

DESCRIPTION: **Plants** with ascending stems, native in central and southern Europe, and western Asia; **leaves** pinnately dissected, to 8 cm. long, smooth above, white-woolly beneath; **flower** heads to 4 cm. across; ray flowers golden yellow; **achenes** cylindrical or angled.

USE: Named cultivars are excellent for the flower border. The species should be used in a naturalized area. The flowers are used in flower arrangements.

CULTURE: The Golden Marguerite thrives in any well-drained soil and in full sun. It prefers a sandy loam. It is apt to winter kill in a wet soil. Propagation is by seeds or by division in the spring. The species can be propagated by seeds planted in early spring. Space the plants about 40 cm. apart.

CULTIVARS

'E. C. Buxton'. Flowers creamy yellow, fading to nearly white.
'Grallagh Gold'. Flowers golden orange.
'Kelwayi'. Flowers bright yellow.
'Moonlight'. Flowers creamy yellow.   PLATE 23
'St. Johannis'. Flowers brilliant orange.

Anthemis —other species

A carpatica Waldst. & Kit., native in the mountains of Europe, has white flowers in May. It is mat-forming and a good rock garden plant.

A. marschalliana Willd, native in the Caucasus, is a low plant to 30 cm. tall, with showy yellow flowers. It is an excellent rock garden plant.

Antirrhinum (Snapdragon)

SCROPHULARIACEAE (Figwort Family)

DESCRIPTION: A genus of about 40 species of tender perennial herbs, native in temperate regions; **leaves** opposite, simple; **flowers** variously colored; corolla broadly tubular with 2 lips and a throat partially closed by a palate and a swollen projection on the underside.

Antirrhinum majus L. (Snapdragon). Tender perennnial grown as an annual, to 1 m. tall. June-October.   PLATE 24

DESCRIPTION: **Plants** erect, branched, native in the Mediterranean region; **leaves** lanceolate, to 7 cm. long; **flowers** in shades of orange, pink, red, and yellow, produced in terminal racemes; corolla 4 to 5 cm. long.

USE: A common bedding plant for the flower border. An excellent cut flower for flower arrangements.

CULTURE: Plants thrive in any good garden soil in full sun or partial shade. Start seeds indoors in late March. Space the plants about 30 cm. apart in the garden. The flowering season is lengthened by the removal of old flowering stems. Snapdragons are quite resistant to insects and disease.

CULTIVARS
'Floral Carpet'. Plants dwarf, free-flowering; flowers in a wide color range.
'Little Darling'. All-America Winner. Plants base-branching, compact; flowers in a wide color range.
'Madame Butterfly'. All-America Winner. Flowers double, in a wide color range.
'Magic Carpet'. Plants base-branching, compact, flowers yellow, white, rose, pink, orchid, crimson, cherry, and bronze.
'Pixie'. Plants dwarf; flowers in a wide color range.
'Wedding Bells'. Plants tall, base-branching; flowers bell-shaped, in shades of white, yellow, pink, rose, orange, and crimson.

Aquilegia L. (Columbine)

RANUNCULACEAE (Buttercup Family)

DESCRIPTION: A large genus of about 70 species of perennial herbs, native in north temperate regions; **leaves** 2- to 3-ternate; **flowers** white, yellow, blue, lavender, or red, solitary, showy, pendent or upright; sepals 5, petal-like; petals 5, with a short, broad lip and usually a long, hollow, backward projecting spur; stamens many; **fruit** a many-seeded follicle.

Aquilegia x *hybrida* Sims. (Garden Columbine). Perennial to 1 m. tall. May-July.

DESCRIPTION: **Plants** of hybrid origin involving several species including *A. caerulea, A. canadensis, A. chrysantha*, and *A. vulgaris*; **leaves** 2- to 3-ternate with rounded lobes; **flowers** various, with short or long spurs.

USE: This is one of the most widely grown of our garden perennials. They are planted in masses in the flower border or in the wildflower garden. The flowers are commonly used in flower arrangements.

CULTURE: Columbines prefer a moist, well-drained soil of high fertility. They prefer a light shade. Plants are not long-lived so it is necessary to have young plants coming along to replace the older plants. Propagation is by spring division and by seeds. Seeds can be started indoors in late March or sown directly as soon as the soil can be worked. Space the plants about 40 cm. apart in the border. They are sometimes susceptible to leaf miners and stem borers.

CULTIVARS AND STRAINS

Bierdermeier (strain). Dwarf plants to 20 cm. tall with upfacing flowers in a good color range.

'Crimson Star'. Plants to 75 cm. tall; flowers with long spurs, crimson with a white center.

Dreer's Long-spurred (strain). Flowers in many shades of red, pink, yellow, blue, and purple.

Langdon's Rainbow (strain). Developed in England, flowers in many bright colors.

McKana's Giants (strain). All-America Winner. Flowers very large, long-spurred, in shades of blue, pink, maroon, purple, red, deep yellow, primrose, white, and show combinations of color.   PLATE 25

'Rose Queen'. Flowers in shades of rose and pink.

Aquilegia—other species.

A. alpina L. (Alpine Columbine), native in the European Alps, is low growing with bright blue flowers in June. A good rock garden species.

A. caerulea James (Rocky Mountain Columbine), native in the Rocky Mountain states, has light blue flowers to 7 cm. across in June and July. 'Alba' with white flowers, 'Citrina' with citron yellow flowers, 'Cuprea' with copper red flowers, and 'Rosea' with pink or red flowers are named cultivars.

A. canadensis L. (Wild Columbine), native in the eastern United States and Canada, has red flowers in June and July, and is often planted in woodland wildflower gardens.

A. chrysantha A. Gray (Golden Columbine), native in New Mexico and Arizona, has golden yellow flowers with long spurs in June and July. 'Alba' with white flowers, 'Alba Plena' with double, white flowers, 'Flore Pleno' with double yellow flowers, and 'Silver Queen' with pure white flowers are named cultivars.

A. discolor Levier & Leresche, native in Spain, has attractive foliage and blue and white flowers with incurved spurs in June and July.

A. flabellata Siebold & Zucc., native in Japan, has nodding bluish purple flowers on low plants in June and July.

A. vulgaris L. (European Garden Columbine), native in Europe, has nodding violet-colored flowers with spurs that are strongly hooked, in June and July. Named cultivars are 'Alba Plena' with double, white flowers, 'Atrorosea' with red flowers, 'Caryophylloides' with white flowers flushed with red, 'Flore Pleno' with double, violet-colored flowers, and 'Stellata' with flowers lacking spurs.

Arabis L. (Rock Cress)

CRUCIFERAE (Mustard Family)

DESCRIPTION: A genus of about 100 species of low, annual, biennial, or perennial herbs, native in North America or Eurasia; **leaves** entire, lobed, or pinnatifid; **flowers** white, pink, purple, in terminal spikes or racemes; sepals and petals 4; **fruits** long, narrow siliques.

Arabis albida — see *Arabis caucasica*

Arabis caucasica Schlechtend. (Wall Rock Cress). Perennial to 30 cm. tall. May.

DESCRIPTION: A procumbent **plant** with soft white pubescence, native in southern Europe and Iran; basal **leaves** usually obovate, tapering to the base, stem leaves auriculate to sagittate; **flowers** white, fragrant, in loose racemes; petals to 1.5 cm. long; **siliques** to 6 cm. long.

USE: An excellent plant for rock and wall gardens and for edging the flower border. The cut flowers are effective in miniature bouquets.

CULTURE: Rock Cresses need a well-drained soil that is neutral, or slightly alkaline, and full sun. Best results are obtained on a sandy loam soil. Plants should be pruned back after flowering. Propagation is by seeds, cuttings, and spring division. Seeds should be planted in a nursery row or in a cold frame in May. Cuttings are taken soon after flowering and rooted in sand. Plants are spaced about 30 cm. apart.

CULTIVARS

'Coccinea'. Flowers are red.

'Flore-Pleno'. Flowers are double, white.

'Snowcap'. Plants very dwarf; flowers snow white.

'Variegata'. Leaves with white margins.

Arabis — other species

A. alpina L. (Mountain Rock Cress, Alpine Rock Cress), native in the mountains of Europe, is similar to *A. caucasica* except the flowers and fruits are smaller.   PLATE 26

A. blepharophylla Hook. & Arn., native in California, has rose purple flowers in May. A very good rock garden plant.

A. procurrens Waldstein, & Kit., native in mountains of Europe, has small, white flowers from April to early June.

Aralia L.

ARALIACEAE (Ginseng Family)

DESCRIPTION: A genus of about 30 species of herbs, shrubs, or trees, native in North America, Asia, and the Malay Peninsula; **leaves** alternate, 1- to 3-pinnate; **flowers** small, white or green, in umbels that are often arranged in panicles; petals 5, more or less overlapping; stamens 5; **fruit** a drupe.

Aralia nudicaulis L. (Wild Sarsaparilla). Perennial to 30 cm. tall. May, June.

DESCRIPTION: **Plants** stemless, native from British Columbia to Newfoundland, south to Colorado and Georgia; **leaves** 2- to 3-pinnate with leaflets that are elliptic to lanceolate and 15 cm. long; **flowers** in terminal umbels; **fruits** black.

USE: Plant in a shaded wildflower garden. Grown mainly for the attractive foliage.

CULTURE: Plants require a moist soil high in organic matter and some shade. Propagation is by seeds or by spring division. Plant the seeds in May in a nursery row, and keep the seedlings shaded.

Aralia racemosa L. (American Spikenard). Perennial to 2 m. tall. June, July.

DESCRIPTION: **Plants** stemless, native from Utah to New Brunswick, south to Arizona and South Carolina; **leaves** few, 2- to 3-pinnate, to 85 cm. long, arising from a fleshy rhizome; **flowers** small in many umbels arranged in a dense raceme or panicle; **fruits** brown or purple.

USE: Same as for *A. nudicaulis*.

CULTURE: Same as for *A. nudicaulis*.

Arctotis L. (African Daisy)

COMPOSITAE (Sunflower Family)

Arctotis Tribe

DESCRIPTION: A genus of about 30 species of annual and perennial herbs and subshrubs, native in South Africa; **leaves** in basal rosettes or alternate on the stems; **flower** heads solitary on long, rather stout peduncles; disc flowers tubular, perfect; ray flowers strap-shaped, pistillate; **achenes** usually with 3 to 5 wings.

Arctotis stoechadifolia Berguis (Blue-eyed African Daisy). Tender perennial grown as an annual, to 85 cm. tall. June-September.

DESCRIPTION: **Leaves** oblong to obovate, to 10 cm. long, pinnately lobed or lyrate, entire to irregularly toothed, white-woolly; **flower** heads to 7.5 cm. across; ray flowers creamy white above, reddish underneath; disc flowers violet.

USE: Planted in the flower border and for cutting. Flowers close at night.

CULTURE: Plants grow in most soils and withstand drought. They like full sun but do not bloom well in extremely hot weather. Propagation is by seeds started indoors in early April. Space the plants about 30 cm. apart.

CULTIVARS AND VARIETIES: Hybrid strains are sold with flowers in shades of red, pink, yellow, and orange.

var. *grandis* (Thunb.) Less. Leaves and flowering stems are longer than in species.

Arenaria L. (Sandwort)

CARYOPHYLLACEAE (Pink Family)

DESCRIPTION: A large genus of about 150 species of low, often mat-forming annual or perennial herbs of the temperate and arctic regions of the northern hemisphere; **leaves** opposite, mostly linear; **flowers** usually white, in terminal or axillary cymes; sepals 4 or 5; petals 5; stamens 10; **fruit** an ovoid capsule.

Arenaria caespitosa — see *Arenaria verna*

Arenaria montana L. (Mountain Sandwort). Perennial to 30 cm. tall. May, June. PLATE 27

DESCRIPTION: **Plants** gray green, hairy, native in Portugal and Spain; **leaves** oblong to linear, to 2.5 cm. long; **flowers** white, in few-flowered cymes.

USE: An interesting plant for rock and wall gardens.

CULTURE: Plants require a well-drained soil. A sandy loam high in organic matter is preferred. Plant at the base of rocks on the shaded side. Some winter protection is needed. Propagation is by seeds or spring division. Seeds should be started in a cold frame in early spring.

Arenaria — other species

A. hookeri Nutt. (Hooker Sandwort), native in the Rocky Mountains, is similar to *A. montana* but has stiffer, more pointed leaves.

A. verna L. (Irish Moss, Tufted Sandwort), native from Spain to northern Russia, is low and mosslike. 'Aurea' has yellowish green leaves.

Arisaema Mart.

ARACEAE (Arum Family)

DESCRIPTION: A large genus of 190 or more species of stemless, tuberous-rooted herbs, native mostly in the Old World; **leaves** 1 to 3, 3-lobed or 3-parted, to palmately dissected with 5 to 15 segments, on long petioles; spathe convolute below, expanded above into narrow or often very broad blade colored or marked with purple; **flowers** small, imperfect, monoecious or dioecious, borne on a spadix that is terminated by an elongated, sterile appendage; perianth lacking; **fruit** a berry.

Arisaema triphyllum (L.) Torr. (Jack-in-the-pulpit, Indian Turnip).
Perennial to 75 cm. tall. May.   PLATE 28

DESCRIPTION: **Plants** native from Minnesota to Nova Scotia, south to Texas
and Florida; **leaves** mostly 2, 3-lobed, to 22 cm. long, on petioles up to 70 cm.
long; **flowers** borne on an erect spadix; spathe green with purple stripes, with
a hood that arches over the spadix; **fruits** bright red, in dense clusters.

USE: Plant in a woodland wildflower garden. It is grown for the curious bloom
and handsome foliage. Indians used the tuberous root for food. The tuberous
roots must be cooked to remove the acrid taste of the fresh roots.

CULTURE: Plants are easy to grow in any moist soil high in organic matter in
shade. Propagation is by seeds sown as soon as ripe or by offsets that occur at
the base of the tuberous roots.

CULTIVAR
'Zebrinum'. Spathe purple to bronze with white longitudinal stripes on the
inside.

Arisaema — other species

A. draconitum (L.) Schott. (Green-dragon, Dragonroot), native from Kansas
to Maine, south to Mexico and Florida, has leaves that are palmately dissected
into 7 to 19 segments, and a spadix with an appendage 15 cm. long. The hood
is erect.

Armeria Willd. (Thrift, Sea Pink)

PLUMBAGINACEAE (Leadwort Family)

DESCRIPTION: A genus of about 35 species of perennial, evergreen, low
growing, tufted herbs or subshrubs, native in alpine meadows of the northern
hemisphere; **stems** much-branched; **leaves** in rosettes at the ends of short
branches, linear or lanceolate; **flowers** perfect, 5-merous, in terminal, globose
heads on cylindrical scapes and subtended by involucral bracts; calyx funnelform, 5-lobed, 10-ribbed, scarious, with colored base sometimes prolonged to
form a spur; petals united at the base; styles 5 with capitate stigmas; **fruits**
1-seeded.

Armeria caespitosa — see *Armeria juniperifolia*

Armeria cephalotes — see *Armeria pseudarmeria*

Armeria formosa — see *Armeria pseudarmeria*

Armeria latifolia — see *Armeria pseudarmeria*

Armeria maritima (Mill.) Willd. (Common Thrift, Common Sea Pink. Perennial to 35 cm. tall. May, June.   PLATE 29

DESCRIPTION: **Plants** tufted, native along the coast in eastern and western North America and in Europe; **leaves** linear, to 10 cm. long; **flowers** pink or white, in terminal heads to 2.5 cm. across.

USE: Used in rock gardens and for edging. It also makes an attractive cut flower.

CULTURE: Plants require a well-drained sandy loam soil and full sun. Propagation is by seeds and division. Seeds should be soaked in warm water before seeding in a cold frame in May. Division is best done in the spring.

CULTIVARS
'Alba'. Flowers white.
'Brilliant'. Flowers cherry red.
'Laucheana'. Flowers deep pink.
'Royal Rose'. Flowers rose-colored.
'Vindictive'. Flowers dark pink.

Armeria — other species

A. juniperifolia (Vahl.) Willd. (Pyrenees Thrift), native in Spain, has sharp-pointed linear leaves and pink or white flowers in May and June. This is an excellent rock garden plant. 'Alba' with white flowers, and 'Rosea' with rose colored flowers are named cultivars.

A. plantaginea Willd., native in Europe, is similar to *A. maritima* except the leaves are lanceolate with scarious margins. 'Bee's Ruby' has rose carmine flowers.

A. pseudarmeria (J. Murr.) Mansf. (Sea Lavender), native in Portugal, is taller than *A. maritima* with lanceolate leaves up to 25 cm. long. The flowers are white to dark rose pink from May to July. 'Rubra' has striking red flowers.

Armeria — garden hybrids. The Armerias cross readily and several named hybrids are on the market.
CULTIVARS
'Glory of Holland'. Flowers deep pink in May and June.
'Royal Rose'. Flowers bright pink on stiff stems.

Artemisia L. (Sagebrush, Wormwood)

COMPOSITAE (Sunflower Family)

Anthemis Tribe

DESCRIPTION: A large genus of over 200 species of aromatic, annual, biennial, and perennial herbs and shrubs, native in dry areas of the northern hemisphere; **leaves** alternate, entire to lobed or dissected; **flower** heads small, in spikes, racemes, or panicles; involucre cylindrical to globose, with overlapping bracts in several rows; receptacle flat or hemispherical, naked or with long hairs; disc flowers white, yellow, brown, or purple; ray flowers pistillate or absent.

Artemisia ludoviciana (Woot.) Keck. (Western Mugwort, White Sagebrush, Louisiana Sagebrush). Perennial to 1 m. tall. July, August.

DESCRIPTION: **Plants** rhizomatous, aromatic, native from Washington to Michigan, south to California to Arkansas; **leaves** lanceolate to elliptic-lanceolate, to 11 cm. long, entire or lobed, white-tomentose beneath, nearly smooth above; **flowers** in small heads in dense panicles.

USE: Grown mostly for its silvery and aromatic foliage. Plant as an accent plant in the flower border.

CULTURE: Plants thrive in full sun in well-drained soils of low fertility. Propagation is chiefly by spring division or stem cutting. Cuttings are easily rooted in sand in July.

CULTIVARS AND VARIETIES
var. *albula* (Woot.) Shinn. Leaves shorter than in species and white-tomentose on both surfaces.
'Silver King'. Same as the var. *albula*.
'Silver Queen'. Leaves glistening and silvery.

Artemisia purshiana — see *Artemisia ludoviciana*

Artemisia — other species

A. frigida Willd. (Fringed Wormwood), native from Alaska to Wisconsin south to Arizona and Kansas, has silvery foliage and is sometimes planted in prairie gardens.

A. schmidtiana Maxim., native in Japan, is a perennial to 70 cm. tall with finely cut, silvery foliage. The cultivar 'Nana', also called 'Silver Mound', is a compact, mound-shaped plant that is commonly planted for color accent in the border.   PLATE 30

A. stellerana Bess. (Beach Wormwood, Dusty-miller), native in northeastern Asia, has felty-white foliage and is sometimes planted in rock gardens.

Asarum L. (Wild Ginger)

ARISTOLOCHIACEAE (Birthwort Family)

DESCRIPTION: A genus of about 75 species of perennial, rhizomatous herbs, native in the north temperate regions of the world; **leaves** mostly heart-shaped on long petioles; **flowers** purple or brown, produced singly near the ground and covered over by the leaves; calyx corollalike, campanulate, regular, 3-parted; corolla vestigial or lacking; stamens 12; **fruit** a fleshy, globose capsule.

Asarum canadense L. (Canada Wild Ginger). Perennial to 30 cm. tall. April, May.   PLATE 31

DESCRIPTION: **Plants** dying to the ground in the fall, native from Minnesota to New Brunswick, south to Arkansas and North Carolina; **leaves** few, heart-shaped, to 15 cm. across; **flowers** purple-brown, to 3 cm. across.

USE: This is the most commonly planted species in the north. It makes an excellent ground cover in shaded areas.

CULTURE: Plants require a rich, moist soil high in organic matter. Propagation is mainly by division of established clumps in early spring.

Asarum — other species.

A. caudatum Lindl. (British Columbia Wild Ginger), native from British Columbia to California, has leaves similar to *A. canadense* except they are evergreen.

A. europaeum L. (European Wild Ginger), native in Europe, has small, evergreen leaves. It forms dense clumps and makes an excellent ground cover in shade.

A. shuttleworthii Britten & Bak., native in the southeastern states, has large evergreen leaves that are mottled.

The above evergreen species have been less vigorous in our arboretum trials than the deciduous *A. canadense*, and they require winter snow cover or protection from the winter sun.

Asclepias L. (Milkweed)

ASCLEPIADACEAE (Milkweed Family)

DESCRIPTION: A large genus of about 200 species of mostly perennial herbs, widely distributed but native mainly in North America and Africa; **plants** with milky sap; **leaves** simple, opposite or sometimes whorled or alternate; **flowers** in axillary or terminal, umbellate cymes; corolla white, yellow, red, or purple, rotate, 5-lobed and reflexed thus hiding the sepals; corona present, with 5 hoodlike lobes, each with or without a horn; follicles usually paired and erect on deflexed or erect pedicels; **seeds** usually with a tuft of hairs.

Asclepias incarnata L. (Swamp Milkweed). Perennial to 1 m. tall. July, August.

DESCRIPTION: Moisture-loving **plants**, native from Utah to Nova Scotia, south to New Mexico and Florida; **leaves** opposite, linear to ovate-elliptic, to 15 cm. long; **flowers** rose-purple, rarely white; follicles about 9 cm. long, slender.

USE: Plant toward the back of the flower border in moist soil or plant along a stream or pond. The flowers are excellent for cutting.

CULTURE: Plants thrive in any good soil that is not too dry. Propagation is by seeds or by spring division. Seeds can be planted in a cold frame or in a sheltered area in early summer. Transplant to their permanent location in early spring.

Asclepias tuberosa L. (Butterfly Weed). Perennial to 1 m. tall. July, August.   PLATE 32

DESCRIPTION: **Plants** from woody rootstocks, native from North Dakota to New England, south to California and Florida; **leaves** spirally arranged, narrow lanceolate to oblanceolate, to 10 cm. long; **flowers** orange or occasionally red or yellow, in upper leaf axils; corolla lobes to 8 mm. long; follicles narrowly fusiform, to 15 cm. long.

USE: A beautiful border plant, often planted in prairie gardens.

CULTURE: Plants must have a well-drained soil, preferably a sandy loam, and full sunlight. Once established, the plants should not be moved. The usual method of propagation is by seeds sown in early summer in a sandy soil. Seedlings can be transplanted the following spring.

Asclepias — other species

A. curassavica L. (Bloodflower), native in South America, is a tender perennial that can be grown as an annual by starting the seeds early indoors. The flowers are bright crimson in July and August.

A. verticillata L. (Horsetail Milkweed), native in eastern and central North America, has narrow, whorled leaves and small, white flowers in July and August. It is sometimes planted in prairie restoration plantings.

Aster L.

COMPOSITAE (Sunflower Family)

Aster Tribe

DESCRIPTION: A large genus of up to 500 species of mostly perennial herbs, native in North and South America, Europe, Asia, and Africa; **plants** frequently rhizomatous or fibrous-rooted; **leaves** alternate, simple, entire to toothed; **flower** heads usually radiate, rarely solitary, in racemes, corymbs, or panicles; involucre campanulate, hemispherical, or turbinate; involucral bracts in several rows, herbaceous or scarious; receptacle flat, pitted; disc flowers perfect, usually yellow, sometimes orange, white, or purple; ray flowers in a single outer row, pistillate or sterile, purple, blue, violet, pink, or white.

Aster novae-angliae L. (New England Aster). Perennial to 2 m. tall. September, October.

DESCRIPTION: **Plants** rhizomatous, native from North Dakota to Vermont, south to New Mexico and Alabama; **leaves** sessile, auriculate-clasping, lanceolate, to 12 cm. long, entire, rough; **flower** heads to 5 cm. across, in corymbs; ray flowers deep violet purple, occasionally in other colors.

USE: Plant toward the back of the flower border or use in a wildflower garden.

CULTURE: Asters like a well-drained soil and preferably full sun. They will grow in partial shade but will not bloom as well. Propagation is by seeds or spring division. Seeds can be sown in a nursery row in spring. Named cultivars must be vegetatively propagated.

CULTIVARS

'Albus'. Flowers white.
'Elmer Potschke'. Flowers a warm pink with a trace of violet.
'Harrington's Pink'. Flowers salmon pink.
'Rosea'. Flowers rose pink.
'September Ruby'. Flowers deep crimson.
'Treasurer'. Flowers deep lilac.

Aster novi-belgii L. (New York Aster, Michaelmas Daisy). Perennial to 1.5 m. tall. September, October.

DESCRIPTION: **Plants** rhizomatous, native from Newfoundland to Georgia; **leaves** sessile and more or less auriculate-clasping to winged-petioled, linear-lanceolate to lanceolate or elliptic, to 18 cm. long, entire to sharply serrate; **flower** heads to 2.5 cm. across, in cymose panicles; ray flowers blue violet.

USE: Same as for *A. novae-angliae*.

CULTURE: Same as for *A. novae-angliae*.

CULTIVARS

'Ada Ballard'. Flower heads semi-double; ray flowers lavender blue.
'Autumn Glory'. Flower heads semi-double; ray flowers rich red.
'Chorister'. Flower heads single; ray flowers white.
'Eventide'. Flower heads semi-double; ray flowers violet blue.
'Lassie'. Flower heads fully double; ray flowers pink.
'Marie Ballard'. Flower heads double; ray flowers powder blue.

Aster—other species

A. alpinus L. (Alpine Aster), native in the mountains of Europe and Asia, is a low-growing species with blue to violet flowers in September and October. This is a good rock garden plant. Named cultivars are 'Albus' with white ray flowers, 'Coeruleus' with blue ray flowers, 'Roseus' with pale rose ray flowers, 'Rubra' with rosy purple ray flowers, and 'Happy End' with pink ray flowers.   PLATE 33

A. amellus L. (Italian Aster), native in central and southeastern Europe and western Asia, has large flower heads to 5 cm. across from August to October. The ray flowers are bluish lilac. It is less hardy than *A. novae-angliae*. 'Brilliant' has pink ray flowers.

A. ericoides L. (Heath Aster), native in the eastern United States, has small, white flower heads in September and October. It is sometimes planted in prairie restoration projects.

A. x *frikarti* Frikart (Wonder-of-Staffa), developed from a cross between *A. amellus* x *A. thomsonii*, has large violet blue flower heads to 6 cm. across from June to October. It is one of our most beautiful asters. It requires winter protection.

Aster—garden hybrids. Numerous species have been used to develop garden hybrids. The aim has been to produce a shorter plant with earlier bloom. The following are only a few of the recent introductions:
'Blue Horizon'. Ray flowers blue.
'Melba Pink'. Ray flowers rose.
'Red Star'. Ray flowers rose red.

'Snow Cushion'. Ray flowers pure white.   PLATE 34
'Violet Carpet'. Ray flowers deep violet blue.

Astilbe Buch.-Ham. (Perennial Spirea)

SAXIFRAGACEAE (Saxifrage Family)

DESCRIPTION: A genus of about 14 species of perennial herbs, native in North America and eastern Asia; **leaves** 2- to 3-ternately compound, with leaflets toothed; **flowers** small, white or pink, in dense panicles; calyx small, usually 4- to 5-parted; petals 4 to 5 or more, or absent; stamens as many or twice as many as the petals; **fruit** a follicle.

Astilbe x *arendsii* Arends. (Garden Astilbe). Perennial to 1 m. tall. June-August.   PLATE 35

DESCRIPTION: A variable hybrid species resulting from crossing *A. chinensis* var. *davidii* with other species.

USE: Astilbes are often planted in the flower border or along streams or pools.

CULTURE: The astilbes require a rich, moisture retentive soil. They will tolerate some shade but bloom best in full sun. They are moisture-loving plants and frequent watering is required during dry weather. Propagation is by spring division of established clumps. Some winter protection is advisable.

CULTIVARS: Hundreds of cultivars have been named.

'Amethyst'. Flowers deep violet.
'Avalanche'. Flowers pure white.
'Bridal Veil'. Flowers white in feathery panicles.
'Fanal'. Foliage reddish green; flowers carmine red.
'Ostrich Plume'. Flowers salmon pink.
'Peach Blossom'. Flowers light rose.

Astilbe sinensis — see *Astilbe chinensis*

Astilbe — other species

A. chinensis (Maxim.) Franch. (Chinese Astilbe), native in China and Japan, and its var. *davidii* Franch. are parents of many garden hybrids. 'Finale' with soft pink flowers, 'Pumila' with deep pink flowers and a compact form, and 'Intermezzo' with deep salmon pink flowers are named cultivars.

A. japonica (C. Morr. & Dechny.) A. Gray (Silver-feathers) has loose panicles of white flowers in June. This is the florist's spirea.

Aubrieta Adans. (Purple Rock Cress)

CRUCIFERAE (Mustard Family)

DESCRIPTION: A small genus of mat-forming herbs from southern Europe and Iran; **leaves** simple, usually hairy; **flowers** many, lilac magneta to bright purple; sepals 4, petals 4, long-clawed; **fruit** an oblong to globose silique.

Aubrieta deltoidea (L.) DC. (Purple Rock Cress). Short-lived perennial to 30 cm. tall. April-June.   PLATE 36

DESCRIPTION: Low, mat-forming **plants**, native in Sicily, Greece, and Asia Minor; **leaves** rhombic to ovate-cuneate, covered with simple and stellate hairs; **flowers** rose lilac to purple, to 2 cm. across; **siliques** elliptic, to 2 cm. long.

USE: Plants are usually planted in rock and wall gardens for their spring bloom.

CULTURE: The Purple Rock Cress prefers partial shade and a soil that is light, porous, and well-drained. A cool, moist climate such as the Pacific Northwest is ideal. Plants are apt to be short-lived where summers are hot. A winter mulch is required. Propagation is by seeds, by division, and by cuttings. Seeds are planted in early spring. Division is done in the spring. Cuttings are taken soon after plants finish flowering in early July. Space plants about 25 cm. apart.

CULTIVARS
'Bengale'. Flowers semi-double, in shades of lilac, purple, and red.
'Borsch's White'. Flowers pure white.
'Dr. Mules'. Flowers dark royal blue.
'Purple Cascade'. Flowers purple.
'Red Cascade'. Flowers red, on spreading plants.

Aubrieta eyrei — see *Aubrieta deltoidea*

Aurinia Desv.

CRUCIFERAE (Mustard Family)

DESCRIPTION: A small genus of about 7 species of biennial or perennial herbs, native in central and southern Europe; basal **leaves** in tufted rosettes, with sinuate or dentate margins, on long, deeply grooved petioles, and stem leaves much reduced; **flowers** yellow or white, in racemes or panicles; sepals and petals 4; **fruit** a flattened or somewhat inflated silicle.

Aurinia saxatilis (L.) Desv. (Basket-of-gold). Short-lived perennial to 30 cm. tall. April, May. PLATE 37

DESCRIPTION: **Plants** low, mat-forming, native in southern and central Europe and Turkey; basal **leaves** spatulate, sinuate, and dentate and stem leaves linear-lanceolate; **flowers** yellow, in large panicles; **siliques** orbicular.

USE: A useful plant for rock gardens and dry walls.

CULTURE: To flower well, the plant requires a sunny location and a well-drained soil. Prune the plants back after flowering to reduce seed formation and to shape the plants. Propagation is by seeds and by division. Seeds planted in August should produce plants that will flower the next spring. Division of old plants should be done in early spring. Named cultivars can be reproduced by softwood cuttings taken in June.

CULTIVARS

'Argentea'. Flowers lemon yellow.
'Citrina'. Flowers pale yellow.
'Compacta'. Plants more dwarf than in species.
'Flore Pleno'. Flowers double, bright yellow.
'Silver Queen'. Flowers soft yellow.

Baptisia Venten. (False Indigo, Wild Indigo)

LEGUMINOSAE (Pea Family)

DESCRIPTION: A genus of about 35 species, native in North America; **leaves** alternate, mostly with 3 leaflets; **flowers** pealike, in racemes; stamens 10, separate; **fruit** a short inflated legume.

Baptisia australis (L.) R. Br. (Blue False Indigo). Perennial to 2 m. tall. June, July. PLATE 38

DESCRIPTION: **Plants** forming large clumps, native from Pennsylvania south to Tennessee and North Carolina; **leaflets** oblanceolate to ovate, to 6 cm. long; **flowers** indigo blue, in long terminal racemes.

USE: Plant as specimen plants toward the back of the border or plant in prairie garden.

CULTURE: Plants thrive in most any garden soil. Once established, they are long-lived. Owing to their deep taproot they are difficult to divide. Propagation is largely by seeds but it will take several years to produce flowering-sized plants. Space plants about 1 m. apart.

Baptisia tinctoria (L.) Venten. (Yellow False Indigo). Perennial to 1 m. tall. June, July.

DESCRIPTION: **Plants** native from Minnesota to Massachusetts, south to Florida; **leaflets** are 2.5 cm. long; **flowers** are bright yellow.

USE: Same as for *B. australis*.

CULTURE: Same as for *B. australis*.

Begonia L.

BEGONIACEAE (Begonia Family)

DESCRIPTION: A very large genus of over 1,000 species of mostly tropical and subtropical monoecious perennial herbs or subshrubs; **plants** fibrous-rooted, rhizomatous, tuberous-rooted, or bulbous, with erect or procumbent, sometimes climbing stems; **leaves** alternate, variable in size and shape, usually oblique and asymmetrical, petioled, with 2 stipules; **flowers** monoecious, white, pink, red, orange, or yellow, usually in axillary cymes, sometimes with showy bracts; staminate flowers with 2 to 4 sepals and 0 to 2 petals, the sepals and petals of different sizes and shapes but usually of the same color; stamens many, forming a yellow, globose mass or column; pistillate flowers with 2 to 5 equal tepals and an inferior ovary that is 3-winged; **fruit** a capsule or rarely berrylike.

Begonia x *semperflorens—cultorum* Hort. (Wax or Bedding Begonia). Tender perennial grown as an annual, to about 20 cm. tall. June-October. PLATE 39

DESCRIPTION: Low, compact plants developed by crossing *B. cucullata* with *B. schmidtiana* and other species; **plants** fibrous rooted with fleshy, brittle stems; **leaves** ovate to broad-ovate, usually smooth, green to bronzy red or mahogany red or green variegated with white; **flowers** single or double, white, pink, or red, in small axillary clusters.

USE: Begonias are planted outdoors in window boxes, and in planters on the terrace, and are used for edging and for mass plantings.

CULTURE: Plants prefer partial shade although some of the newer cultivars will grow in full sun. They like a moist but well-drained soil that is high in organic matter. Propagation is by seeds or cuttings. Plants can be wintered as house plants and cuttings can be taken in late winter. The usual method is by seed started in mid March. Space the plants about 20 cm. apart in the garden.

CULTIVARS AND STRAINS

'Calico'. Leaves a blend of bronze and green; flowers a sparkling blend of red, rose, pink, and white.

Foremost (strain). Plants sun-tolerant with large flowers in a wide color range, and green leaves.

'Gin'. Leaves bronze; flowers deep pink.

Glamour (strain). Leaves green; flowers very large, to 5 cm. across, in pink, red, rose, and white colors.

'Linda'. Leaves green; flowers large, deep rose.

'Ruffles'. Flowers large, ruffled, in red, white, and pink colors.

'South Pacific'. Flowers double, reddish orange.

Begonia x *tuberhybrida* Voss. (Tuberous Begonia). Tender perennial to 50 cm tall. June-October.   PLATE 40

DESCRIPTION: A complex hybrid developed by crossing several species, including *B. boliviensis*, *B. clarkei*, *B. davisii*, *B. pearcei*, *B. rosiflora*, *B. veitchii*, and others; **plants** develop a tuberous corm at the base of the stem; **leaves** are variable owing to the hybrid origin; **flowers** are large, single or double, in many colors.

USE: Tuberous begonias are sometimes planted in the foundation planting on the north side of the house. More often they are planted in hanging baskets or containers.

CULTURE: Plant in a soil that is high in organic matter. Start corms in late March or early April in a mixture containing acid peat, pressing the corms into the soil with the tops showing. After the corms develop roots, the buds develop into leafy shoots. The rooted corms are then transplanted into flower pots about 6 inches in diameter. After the danger of frost has passed, the plants can be planted outdoors. In the fall, the plants are dug and the fleshy corms are stored in a cool, moist place over winter. Powdery mildew can be difficult to control in late summer, but good air circulation helps to keep the mildew in check. It may be necessary to spray with a good fungicide.

CLASSIFICATION: In Europe a number of named cultivars are sold but in America most of the corms sold are grown from seed. The American Begonia Society classifies the tuberous begonias into the following classes:

Single Group. Flowers large, with 4 tepals.

Crispa or Frilled Group. Flowers large, single, with margins of tepals frilled and ruffled.

Cristata or Crested Group. Flowers large, single, with a frilled tuft or crest near the center of each tepal.

Narcissiflora or Daffodil-flowered Group. Flowers large, more or less double with central tepals forming a trumpet.

Camellia Group. Flowers large, double, resembling camellias, of various solid colors, unruffled.

Ruffled Camellia Group. Same as Camellia Group except the tepals are ruffled.

Rosebud or Rosiflora Group. Flowers large, double, with raised rosebudlike centers.

Fimbriata Plena or Carnation Group. Flowers large, double, carnationlike, with fringed tepals.

Picotee Group. Flowers large, usually double and camellialike, with tepals margined with a different shade or color blending with the dominant color.

Marginata Group. Flowers as in the Picotee Group, but tepals edged by a precise line of color different from the dominant color.

Marmorata Group. Flowers as in the Camellia Group, but rose-colored, blotched or spotted with white.

Pendula or Hanging-basket Group. Stems trailing or pendant; flowers small to large, single or double.

Multiflora Group. Plants compact; flowers many, small, single or double.

Belamcanda Adans.

IRIDACEAE (Iris Family)

DESCRIPTION: A small genus of 2 species of perennial herbs, native in China and Japan; **leaves** growing from fleshy, irislike rhizomes, long and narrow; **flowers** twisting spirally as they fade; perianth segments 6, separate, about equal; **fruit** a capsule that opens to expose the black seeds.

Belamcanda chinensis (L.) DC. (Blackberry Lily, Leopard Flower). Perennial to 1 m. tall. June, July.   PLATE 41

DESCRIPTION: **Plants** rhizomatous with upright flowering stems, native in China and Japan; basal **leaves** to 25 cm. long, stem leaves smaller; **flowers** orange with red dots, to 5 cm. across, starlike; perianth segments 6, acute; filaments of stamens purple; capsules opening to show a column of black **seeds** resembling a blackberry fruit.

USE: Plant in perennial flower border. Seed pods are dried for winter flower arrangements.

CULTURE: Plants require full sun and a well-drained sandy loam soil for best results. Propagation is by seeds or division in the spring of the year. A winter covering of straw or marsh hay is recommended.

CULTIVARS
'Freckle Face'. Flowers light orange with darker freckles.
'Hello Yellow'. Flowers pure yellow.

Bergenia Moench.

SAXIFRAGACEAE (Saxifrage Family)

DESCRIPTION: A small genus of about 12 species of perennial herbs, native in temperate Asia; **plants** with thick fleshy rhizomes, forming clumps or colonies; **leaves** large, thick, wavy, entire or toothed, with glandular pits; petioles sheathed at the base; **flowers** pink or white, showy, in clusters on long scapes; sepals and petals 5; stamens 10; ovary superior with 2 styles; **fruit** a capsule.

Bergenia cordifolia (Haw.) Sternb. (Heartleaf Bergenia). Perennial to 40 cm. tall. May.

DESCRIPTION: **Plants** native in Siberia and Mongolia; **leaves** orbicular, to 25 cm. long, rounded or cordate at base. crenulate-serrate, glabrous, often bullate; **flowers** pink or white, to 2 cm. across; sepals and petals 5.

USE: Plants used in flower borders, woodland gardens, and along streams and pools.

CULTURE: Plants like a moist site in either full sun or partial shade. The soil should be high in organic matter. A winter cover of snow or a mulch material is needed. Propagation is mainly by spring division. The species can be propagated by seeds started in a sandy soil in May.

CULTIVARS
'Evening Glow'. Leaves purplish brown; flowers dark red.
'Morning Red'. Leaves bronzy green; flowers purplish red.
'Perfecta'. Flowers rosy red.
'Silver Light'. Flowers white.

Bergenia—other species

B. crassifolia (Haw.) Sternb. (Siberian Tea, Leather Bergenia), native in Siberia and Mongolia, has leathery leaves and rose purple flowers.

B. x *schmidtii* (Regel) Silva-Tar. is a hybrid resulting from a cross between *B. ciliata* x *B. crassifolia*. This hybrid is planted more often than the above species.   PLATE 42

Bocconia cordata—see *Macleaya cordata*

Brachycome Cass.

COMPOSITAE (Sunflower Family)

Aster Tribe

DESCRIPTION: A genus of about 70 species of annual or perennial herbs or rarely subshrubs, native in Australia and New Zealand; **leaves** basal or alternate, entire or variously dissected; **flower** heads radiate, solitary or loosely clustered; involucre hemispherical; involucral bracts scarious, in 2 or 3 rows; receptacle flat to convex, naked; disc flowers perfect, yellow; ray flowers in 1 row, pistillate, white, blue, lilac, pink, or yellow; **achenes** compressed or 4-angled.

Brachycome iberidifolia Benth. (Swan River Daisy). Annual to 50 cm. tall. July, August.

DESCRIPTION: **Plants** with daisylike flowers, native in Australia; **leaves** pinnately dissected into linear segments, to 7 cm. long; **flower** heads solitary on slender peduncles; ray flowers blue, rose, or white; **achenes** 4-angled.

USE: Plants used in rock gardens and window boxes and for edging.

CULTURE: Plants grow best in a light, well-drained soil in full sun. They bloom best before hot weather. Propagation is by seeds started indoors in early April. Space the plants about 25 cm. apart.

Browallia L. (Bush Violet)

SOLANACEAE (Potato Family)

DESCRIPTION: A small genus of about 8 species of annual or perennial herbs, native in tropical America; **leaves** mostly simple, alternate; **flowers** blue, violet, or white, solitary in leaf axils or in racemes; calyx usually 5-toothed; corolla salverform, 5-lobed, with 15 veins in tube; stamens 4, borne on the corolla; **fruit** a capsule enclosed in the calyx.

Browallia speciosa Hook. (Lovely Browallia). Tender perennial grown as an annual to 60 cm. tall. July-September.   PLATE 43

DESCRIPTION: Low, spreading **plant**, native in the lowlands of tropical America; **leaves** narrowly ovate, to 6 cm. long, obtuse to acute; **flowers** blue, violet, or white, to 5 cm. across, solitary in upper leaf axils; corolla tube about 2.5 cm. long.

USE: Sometimes planted for summer bloom in shaded areas and also used in window boxes, hanging baskets, and patio containers.

CULTURE: Plants grow either in full sun or partial shade. Bloom is best where the plants receive the afternoon shade. Propagation is by seeds or cuttings. Plants may be wintered as houseplants and cuttings can be taken in March. Seeds are sown in late March. The seeds need light and a temperature of 70° F. Plants are set outdoors in late May with a 25 cm. spacing.

CULTIVARS

'Blue Bells'. Plants compact; flowers violet blue.

'Jingle Bells'. Plants compact; flowers in shades of white, blue, and lavender.

'Powder Blue'. Plants compact; flowers powder blue.

'Silver Bells'. Plants compact; flowers snow white.

'Velvet Bells'. Plants compact; flowers deep blue.

Browallia — other species

B. americana L. (Amethyst Browallia), native in tropical America, has smaller, bluish purple flowers with a yellow center.

B. viscosa HBK. (Sticky Browallia), native in Peru, is similar to *B. americana* except the leaves are clammy-viscid. 'Sapphire' has dark blue flowers.

Brunnera Stev.

BORAGINACEAE (Borage Family)

DESCRIPTION: A small genus of only 3 species of perennial herbs, native in western Siberia and the eastern Mediterranean region; **stems** hairy; **leaves** simple, alternate, ovate, conspicuously veined; **flowers** blue, numerous, in bractless, paniculate cymes; calyx and corolla 5-lobed; stamens 5; **fruit** of 4 nutlets.

Brunnera macrophylla (Adams) I. M. Johnst. (Siberian Bugloss, Forget-me-not Anchusa, Heartleaf Anchusa). Perennial to 50 cm. tall. May.

DESCRIPTION: **Plants** with large basal leaves and slender stems, native in the Caucasus and western Siberia; basal **leaves** ovate, cordate, or reniform, with long petioles; stem leaves ovate, sessile, or with short petioles; **flowers** blue, small, to 7 mm. across, in bractless, paniculate cymes.

USE: Sometimes planted toward the front of the flower border or in naturalistic plantings as a ground cover.

CULTURE: It thrives in moist, rich soil high in organic matter in either sun or partial shade. Propagation is by seeds planted in late summer in a nursery row or by spring division. It can also be grown from root cuttings. Space the plants about 30 cm. apart.

Caladium Venten.

ARACEAE (Arum Family)

DESCRIPTION: A small genus of about 15 species of tuberous, stemless herbs, native in tropical America; **leaves** often beautifully marked with red, white, and other colors; **flowers** imperfect, small, borne on a spadix; spadix enclosed by a partly expanded spathe.

Caladium x *hortulanum* Birdsey. (Fancy-leaved Caladium). Tender perennial to 60 cm. tall, grown for its ornamental leaves. Flowers insignificant.   PLATE 44

DESCRIPTION: A garden hybrid of mixed origin; **plants** stemless; **leaf** blades often peltate, ovate to lanceolate, basally bifid, cordate, or truncate, variously variegated with red, rose, salmon, white, and green, on long petioles.

USE: Grown as specimen plants in sheltered, shady areas or as container plants.

CULTURE: Caladiums require a moist soil high in organic matter and a sheltered location. The humidity must be kept high around the plants. Propagation is by seeds or in the case of named cultivars by division of the fleshy tubers. In March, the tubers can be cut with a sharp knife into sections with each section containing 2 or more buds. Each division is planted in a pot in a soil mixture consisting of 2 parts garden loam and one part each of peat and leaf mold. Plants can be left in pots over summer or planted directly in a shady garden after danger of frost. In the fall, the pots are placed in the basement in a dry moderately warm place and water is withheld. The tops dry down and the tubers rest until divided and repotted the following March. Plants that are growing in the garden soil are dug in the fall and placed in flats with the tubers covered with soil and treated as above.

CULTIVARS
'Ace of Hearts'. Leaves rose colored with scarlet veins.
'Blaze'. Leaves red with scarlet veins.
'Candidum'. Leaves white with dark green veins.
'Pink Beauty'. Leaves pink with darker edges.
'Pink Cloud'. Leaves crinkled, pink with green mottling.
'White Christmas'. Leaves pure white blotched with green.

Calendula L.

COMPOSITAE (Sunflower Family)

Calendula Tribe

DESCRIPTION: A genus of about 15 species of annual or perennial herbs or shrubs, native from the Canary Islands through southern Europe and northern Africa; **leaves** alternate, simple; **flower** heads solitary; radiate; involucral bracts overlapping in 1 or 2 rows; receptacle naked or bristly; disc flowers sterile; ray flowers pistillate; **achenes** incured, smooth.

Calendula officinalis L. (Pot Marigold), Annual to 60 cm. tall. June-October.   PLATE 45

DESCRIPTION: **Plants** coarse, much branched, native in southern Europe; **leaves** oblong-lanceolate, entire or remotely toothed, more or less clasping; **flowers** yellow to deep orange, in solitary heads to 10 cm. across.

USE: Calendulas are often planted in the flower border for their showy flowers. The flowers are excellent for cutting.

CULTURE: Plants like full sun and a well-drained soil. They bloom best in cool weather. Seeds can be planted early for early bloom or direct-seeded in late May for fall bloom. Aster yellows disease can affect them, causing a yellowing of the foliage and deformed flower heads.

CULTIVARS

'Apricot Beauty'. Ray flowers apricot colored.

'Art Shades'. Flower heads fully double; ray flowers in shades of apricot, orange, cream, lemon, and white.

'Geisha Girl'. Flower heads fully double; ray flowers incurved, burnt orange.

'Golden Gem'. Ray flowers a golden yellow.

'Lemon Beauty'. Ray flowers lemon yellow.

Calla L.

ARACEAE (Arum Family)

DESCRIPTION: A genus with but a single species of perennial herbs, growing in bogs, often in shallow water, in the north temperate regions of the world; **stems** creeping; **leaves** simple; spathe white, open on one side; spadix short, covered by the small, imperfect **flowers**; perianth lacking.

Calla palustris L. (Water Arum, Wild Calla, Water-dragon). Perennial to 25 cm. tall. June, July.

DESCRIPTION: **Plants** native in north temperate regions of the world; **leaves** ovate-cordate, to 15 cm. long, on long petioles; spathe green outside, white inside, about 5 cm. long; **fruit** a red berry, produced in clusters.

USE: Plant in wet soils or in shallow water at the edge of streams or pools.

CULTURE: A sunny site and a soil high in organic matter and permanently wet are needed for the proper culture of this plant. Propagation is largely by division of established clumps in early spring or by seed sown in boggy soil as soon as ripe.

Calliopsis tinctoria — see *Coreopsis tinctoria*

Callistephus Cass.

COMPOSITAE (Sunflower Family)

Aster Tribe

DESCRIPTION: A genus of a single species of annual herbs, native in China; **stems** erect, rather stiff; **leaves** alternate; **flower** heads radiate, showy, solitary on terminal peduncles; involucral bracts in several rows, the outer ones herbaceous, the inner ones membranous; receptacle pitted, naked; disc flowers perfect, fertile; ray flowers violet to rose or white, pistillate; **achenes** compressed with a pappus consisting of 2 rows of bristles.

Callistephus chinensis (L.) Nees (China Aster). Annual to 90 cm. tall. July-September.   PLATE 46

DESCRIPTION: **Plants** native in China; **leaves** simple, broadly ovate to triangular-ovate, to 8 cm. long, deeply and irregularly toothed; ray **flowers** in shades of violet, rose, and white.

USE: Plant in flower border. Flowers excellent for cutting.

CULTURE: This is a popular annual in regions where "aster yellows" disease is not a difficulty. The plants grow well in most soils in either full sun or partial shade. Propagation is by seeds started indoors in early April. Space the plants about 25 cm. apart in the border. The disease "aster yellows," transmitted by the 6-spotted leaf hopper, usually appears in August; affected plants are stunted, with yellow foliage and flower heads that fail to open fully. Control the leaf hoppers by frequent spraying with a good insecticide. The area immediately surrounding your garden should also be sprayed to kill the leaf hoppers before they infect the asters. Florists often grow the plants under a structure enclosed with aster cloth to exclude the pest.

CULTIVARS AND STRAINS

Extra Early (strain). Plants to 50 cm. tall; flower heads fully double, to 7.5 cm. across, with incurved ray flowers in shades of blue, rose, scarlet, and white.

Perfection (strain). Plants to 60 cm. tall; flower heads double, well-formed, to 8 cm. across, in shades of blue, white, crimson, and pink.

Pompom (strain). Plants to 40 cm. tall; flower heads fully double, to 5 cm. across, with quilled center flowers and broarder outer flowers, in shades of white, pink, crimson, lavender, blue, and violet.

Powder Puffs (strain). Plants base-branching, to 60 cm. tall; flower heads fully double, to 8 cm. across, in shades of various colors.

Totem Pole (strain). Plants to 60 cm. tall; flower heads large, to 18 cm. across. The following are named cultivars of this strain:
'Azure Blue'. Ray flowers azure blue.
'Dark Blue'. Ray flowers dark blue.
'Rose Pink'. Ray flowers rose pink.
'Scarlet Cerise'. Ray flowers scarlet cerise.

Calonyction aculeatum — see *Ipomoea alba*

Caltha L. (Marsh Marigold)

RANUNCULACEAE (Buttercup Family)

DESCRIPTION: A genus of about 20 species of low, succulent, perennial herbs of cold marshes of the temperate zones of the world; **leaves** alternate, petioled, entire or serrate; **flowers** yellow, white, or pink, axillary or terminal, on short peduncles; sepals usually 5 to 9, petal-like; petals lacking; stamens many; pistils 4 or more; **fruit** a follicle.

Caltha palustris L. (Marsh Marigold, Common Cowslip). Perennial to 60 cm. tall. May, June.   PLATE 47

DESCRIPTION: **Plants** native in moist, boggy soils from Alaska to Newfoundland, south to Tennessee and North Carolina, and in Eurasia; **stems** fleshy, hollow, branched; **leaves** rounded, heart-shaped, to 18 cm. across; **flowers** bright yellow, to 5 cm. across.

USE: Marsh marigolds are often planted in moist soil at the edge of a stream or pond or even in a moist portion of the flower border.

CULTURE: Plants require a moist site and will grow in shallow water in early spring. They bloom best in full sun but they will tolerate some shade. Propagation is by seeds or by division in early spring.

CULTIVARS

'Alba'. Flowers creamy white.

'Monstrosa-Pleno'. Flowers fully double.

Camassia Lindl. (Camas)

LILIACEAE (Lily Family)

DESCRIPTION: A genus of 5 species of bulbous perennials, native in North America; **bulbs** tunicate with brown or black outerscales; **leaves** basal, linear; **flowers** regular to slightly irregular, white, blue, or violet blue, in terminal racemes; perianth segments 6, similar; **fruit** a 3-valved capsule.

Camassia esculenta — see *Camassia quamash*

Camassia quamash (Pursh) Greene (Common Camas). Perennial to 90 cm. tall. May, June.

DESCRIPTION: **Plants** native from British Columbia to Alberta, south to Oregon and Montana; **leaves** to 50 cm. long, glaucous; **flowers** ranging in color light to dark blue; capsules ovate to oblong.

USE: Bulbs are often planted in the rock garden, flower border, or a woodland wildflower garden.

CULTURE: Plants thrive in most soils and will even tolerate semi-boggy situations. Propagation is by seeds sown as soon as ripe in sandy soil in a cold frame or by division of the bulbs. Bulbs are planted in early September about 12 cm. apart and 10 cm. deep.

Camassia — other species

C. cusickii S. Wats., native in Oregon, has pale blue to blue violet flowers in May. Some winter protection is needed.

C. scilloides (Raf.) V. L. Cory (Wild Hyacinth), native from Minnesota to Pennsylvania and south to Texas and Georgia, has small, white, blue, or blue violet flowers in May.

Campanula L. (Bellflower)

CAMPANULACEAE (Bellflower Family)

DESCRIPTION: A large and important genus of about 300 species of annual, biennial, and perennial herbs, distributed throughout the northern hemisphere; **plants** ranging from low, mat-forming to coarse, erect; **leaves** alternate, without stipules; the basal leaves larger and with longer petioles than the stem leaves; **flowers** bell-shaped, violet-blue, purple, white, or pink, usually borne in racemes, spikes, heads, or narrow panicles; calyx tube regular, united to the ovary, with needle-shaped to triangular lobes; corolla campanulate to rotate, 5-lobed; stamens 5, with filaments flattened at the base; **fruit** a capsule, dehiscing by lateral pores or slits.

Campanula carpatica Jacq. (Carpathian Bellflower). Perennial to 40 cm. tall. June-August.   PLATE 48

DESCRIPTION: **Plants** forming clumps with slender stems, native in the Carpathian Mountains of Austria; **leaves** ovate-triangular to broadly lanceolate, to 5 cm. long, deeply serrate, on long petioles; **flowers** blue lilac, erect, on long, slender pedicels; corolla broadly cup-shaped, to 5 cm. across.

USE: Plant in rock garden or toward the front of the flower border.

CULTURE: Plants thrive in most any well-drained soil in full sun. Best results are obtained by using a fertilizer high in phosporus. Propagation of the species is by seeds started in the spring. Named cultivars are propagated by division in the spring or by cuttings rooted in late spring.

CULTIVARS
'Alba'. Flowers white.
'Blue Carpet'. Plants compact; flowers blue.
'China Doll'. Flowers soft blue.
'White Star'. Flowers are star-shaped, white.

Campanula garganica —see *Campanula elatines*

Campanula glomerata L. (Clustered Bellflower). Perennial to 50 cm. June, July.

DESCRIPTION: **Plants** erect, with simple or branched stems, native in Eurasia; **leaves** oblong-ovate to lanceolate, to 12 cm. long, minutely serrate, the lowest with long petioles; **flowers** blue or white, to 2.5 cm. long, in dense terminal and axillary clusters.

USE: An excellent plant for the border or woodland garden.

CULTURE: Plants grow in full sun or partial shade and spread rapidly by underground rhizomes. They like a rich, fertile loam soil. Propagation is mainly by divison in spring.

CULTIVARS AND VARIETIES

var. *acaulis* Rehn. Flower stems only 15 cm. tall.

'Alba'. Flowers white.

var. *dahurica* Fisch. (Dahurian Bellflower). Flower clusters larger than in species.   PLATE 49

'Joan Elliott'. Flowers deep, royal blue in dense terminal clusters.

'Superba'. Flowers royal purple, very showy.

Campanula medium L. (Canterbury-bells). Biennial to 1 m. tall. June, July.

DESCRIPTION: **Plants** native in southern Europe; basal **leaves** ovate to obovate, to 25 cm. long, crenate-undulate, with winged petioles; stem **leaves** sessile, smaller; **flowers** white to blue, in open racemes, calyx bristly-ciliate, with large, ovate appendages; corolla to 5 cm. long, campanulate, somewhat inflated at the base.

USE: A popular border flower where winters are not too severe.

CULTURE: Plants do best in a well-drained soil of good fertility. Propagation is by seeds sown in July or August. Seeds should be started in a cold frame and except in regions with dependable snow cover, the seedlings should be wintered in the cold frame and in early spring transplanted to the border where they will bloom.

CULTIVAR

'Calycanthema'. Sepals also petal-like, and up to 7.5 cm. across. This cultivar is sometimes called Cup-and-saucer flower.

Campanula persicifolia L. (Peach-leaved Bellflower, Peach-bells, Willow Bellflower). Perennial to 1 m. tall. June-August.

DESCRIPTION: **Plants** erect, mostly unbranched, native in Europe and northeastern Asia; basal **leaves** oblong-lanceolate, to 15 cm. long, entire or serrulate, smooth; stem leaves linear; **flowers** white to deep blue, axillary, solitary, or in a few-flowered racemes; calyx without appendages; corolla campanulate, to 3 cm. long.

USE: Plant toward the back of the flower border or in the wildflower garden. A good cut flower.

CULTURE: It grows well in most garden soils of average fertility or above. It likes sun but tolerates some shade. Propagation is by seeds sown in the spring or by spring division of old clumps.

CULTIVARS
'Alba'. Flowers pure white.
'Grandiflora'. Flowers very large, sky blue.
'Telham Beauty'. Plants tall; flowers blue.
'Wedgewood'. Plants compact; flowers violet blue.

Campanula poscharskyana — see *Campanula elatines*

Campanula — other species

C. arvatica Lag., native in Spain, is similar but smaller than *C. carpatica*. It is a good rock garden plant.

C. elatines L. (Adriatic Bellflower), native near the Adriatic Sea, has a trailing habit of growth and blue, star-shaped flowers in June and July. It is sometimes planted in dry walls and in rock gardens.

C. isophylla Moretti (Italian Bellflower), native in Italy, is not hardy but it is sometimes planted in hanging baskets. It blooms all summer with blue or white, bell-shaped flowers.

C. rotundifolia L. (Bluebell, Harebell), native in North America, has deep lavender blue flowers in loose terminal racemes from June to September. It is sometimes planted in flower borders and rock gardens.   PLATE 50

Canna L.

CANNACEAE (Canna Family)

DESCRIPTION: A genus of about 60 species of tall, perennial herbs, native in the tropics and subtropics; **plants** with thick, branched rhizomes and mostly unbranched, erect stems; **leaves** large, simple, entire, with sheathing petioles; **flowers** irregular, large, showy, in various colors, produced in terminal spikes, racemes, or panicles; sepals and petals 3, small, and usually green; fertile stamen 1, petal-like, bearing a half anther on one side; staminodes 1 to 4, petal-like; ovary inferior; **fruit** a 3-valved capsule.

Canna x *generalis* L. H. Bailey (Common Garden Canna). Tender perennial to 1.5 m. tall. August, September.   PLATE 51

DESCRIPTION: **Plants** of garden origin; **leaves** variously colored, often reddish; **flowers** large, to 10 cm. across, in terminal panicles, in many colors including shades of yellow, pink, and red.

USE: Cannas are often planted in beds in parks and other public gardens. They can be planted toward the back of the flower border where space permits.

CULTURE: This tender perennial is grown from fleshy rhizomes that must be dug in the fall and stored in a fairly warm, dry place at a temperature of about 60° F. The rhizomes are divided in the spring and started indoors in late April. The plants can be set outdoors about Memorial Day. Space the plants about 40 cm. apart. Cannas like full sun and a rich, well-drained soil.

CULTIVARS: Numerous cultivars have been named. The following are only a few of those available.

'Chinese Coral'. Plants to 75 cm. tall; flowers soft pink coral.

'Eureka'. Plants to 1.2 m. tall; flowers creamy white.

'Primrose Yellow'. Plants to 75 cm. tall; flowers primrose yellow.

'Salmon Pink'. Plants to 75 cm. tall; flowers salmon pink.

'Scarlet Beauty'. Plants to 80 cm. tall; flowers scarlet.

Cassia L. (Senna)

LEGUMINOSAE (Pea Family)

DESCRIPTION: A large genus of over 500 species of trees, shrubs, and herbs, mostly native in tropical and subtropical regions; **leaves** alternate, even-pinnate; **flowers** in racemes that are sometimes corymbose, panicled, clustered or solitary; mostly yellow, showy, nearly regular, 5-merous; stamens 10, with 7 fertile and 3 sterile anthers; **fruit** a flat or cylindrical legume.

Cassia marilandica L. (Wild Senna). Perennial to 120 cm. tall. July, August.

DESCRIPTION: **Plants** glabrous or nearly so; native from Iowa to Pennsylvania, south to Texas and Florida; **leaflets** oblong or oblong-lanceolate, nearly acute; stipules linear-lanceolate; **flowers** in axillary racemes, showy, yellow, regular; **fruits** flat, to 8 cm. long.

USE: Plant toward the back of the flower border or in a woodland wildflower garden.

CULTURE: Plants require a well-drained soil in full sun or partial shade. Protect in winter with a light mulch. Propagation is by seeds or spring division. Seeds are planted in early spring in a nursery row and transplanted to their permanent location as soon as they are large enough. Plants should be spaced about 50 cm. apart.

Catananche L. (Cupid's-dart)

COMPOSITAE (Sunflower Family)

Cichorium Tribe

DESCRIPTION: A small genus of 5 species of biennial or perennial herbs native in the Mediterranean region; **plants** with milky sap; **leaves** alternate, linear, lanceolate, or oblanceolate; **flower** heads solitary on long peduncles; involucral bracts in several rows, with scarious tips; receptacle bristly; flowers all strap-shaped, perfect, blue, white, or yellow; **achenes** oblong, bristly.

Catananche caerulea L. (Cupid's-dart). Tender perennial grown as an annual, to 60 cm. tall. June-September.

DESCRIPTION: **Leaves** lanceolate to oblanceolate, to 30 cm. long, entire to few-toothed; **flowers** blue.

USE: Planted for cut flowers and dried flower arrangements, and for mass effect in the flower border.

CULTURE: Plants require a well-drained soil and full sun. Propagation is by seeds started indoors in late March. Space the plants about 25 cm. apart.

CULTIVARS
'Alba'. Flowers white.
'Bicolor'. Flowers blue, edged with white.
'Blue Giant'. Flowers large, blue.
'Major'. Flowers deep violet blue.

Catharanthus G. Don (Periwinkle)

APOCYNACAE (Dogbane Family)

DESCRIPTION: About 5 species of annual or perennial herbs, native in the Old World tropics; **leaves** opposite, entire; **flowers** solitary or few in axillary cymes, 5-merous, perfect; corolla salverform with throat closed by bristlelike hairs; stamens borne on tube of corolla; **fruit** a pair of slender follicles.

Catharanthus roseus (L.) G. Don (Rose Periwinkle). Tender perennial grown as an annual, to 60 cm. tall. June-October.

DESCRIPTION: **Leaves** simple, oblong-lanceolate, to 5 cm. long, glossy; **flowers** typically rose pink, occasionally white.

USE: Use for mass effect in the flower border, for edging, for window boxes and patio containers, and as an annual ground cover.

CULTURE: Plant in any well-drained soil in full sun or in partial shade. Propagation is by seeds started indoors in late March. Space the plants about 25 cm. apart in the garden. Plants carried over winter as house plants can be propagated by cuttings.

CULTIVARS

'Little Blanche'. Plants to 25 cm. tall; flowers pure white.

'Little Bright Eyes'. Plants to 25 cm. tall; flowers white with red eye.   PLATE 52

'Little Delicata'. Plants to 25 cm. tall; flowers pink with red eye.

'Pink Carousel'. Plants to 15 cm. tall; flowers rose pink.

'Polka Dot'. Plants to 10 cm. tall; flowers white with cherry red centers.

Celosia L. (Woolflower)

AMARANTHACEAE (Amaranth Family)

DESCRIPTION: About 60 species of annual and perennial herbs, native in warm regions of America and Africa; **leaves** alternate, entire or lobed; **flower** small, in dense chaffy spikes; sepals 5, white or colored; petals lacking; stamens 5, with 4-celled anthers and filaments united into a tube.

Celosia cristata L. (Cockscomb, Feathered Amaranth). Annuals to 1 m. tall. July-October.   PLATE 54

DESCRIPTION: **Plants** are tetraploids of unknown origin; **leaves** linear to ovate-lanceolate, to 5 cm. long; **flowers** in crested spikes or feathery panicles, small, white, yellow, purple, or red.

USE: Plant in the flower border for summer and fall color. Flowers can be dried for winter bouquets.

CULTURE: Celosias thrive in any good garden soil in full sun. Propagation is by seeds started indoors in early/late March. The seedlings are very susceptible to damping-off diseases, so use sterilized containers and a sterile growing medium. Space the plants about 25 cm. apart in the border.

CULTIVARS: Many cultivars have been named in both the cockscomb and plumosa groups.

Cockscomb group. Flowers crested in vibrant shades of golds and reds. Excellent for drying for winter bouquets.

'Fireglow'. All-America Winner. Plants to 45 cm. tall; flowers bright scarlet.

'Floradale Rose-pink'. Plants to 40 cm. tall; flowers in delicate rose pink combs.

'Toreador'. All-America Winner. Plants to 45 cm. tall; flowers bright crimson red.

Plumosa Group. Plants well-branched, crowned with silky, feathery plumes; flowers in a variety of colors.

'Apricot Brandy'. All-America Winner. Plants to 40 cm. tall; flowers apricot orange.

'Crusader'. Plants to 40 cm. tall; flowers deep crimson.

'Forest Fire'. Plants to 75 cm. tall; flowers scarlet.

'Golden Triumph'. All-America Winner. Plants to 60 cm. tall; flowers golden yellow. PLATE 53

'Red Fox'. All-America Winner. Plants to 60 cm. tall; flowers rich bronzy red.

'Tango'. Plants to 90 cm. tall; flowers golden tangerine in giant plumes.

Centaurea L. (Knapweed, Centaurea)

COMPOSITAE (Sunflower Family)

Carduus Tribe

DESCRIPTION: A large genus of over 400 species of annual, biennial, and perennial herbs, rarely subshrubs, native in the Mediterranean region and Near East, with 2 species in North America and 1 in Austrailia; **leaves** basal or alternate, entire or pinnately dissected; **flower** heads solitary or sometimes in small clusters; involucre campanulate, ovoid, globose, or cylindrical; involucral bracts overlapping in several rows; receptacle flat, densely bristly; flowers blue to shades of purple, yellow, or white, all tubular and perfect, or the outer enlarged, raylike, and sterile; **achenes** often compressed.

Centaurea candidissima—see *Centaurea cineraria*

Centaurea cyanus L. (Bachelor's-button). Annual to 50 cm. tall. July-September. PLATE 55

DESCRIPTION: **Plants** with slender stems, often decumbent, native in Europe and Near East; basal **leaves** lyrate-pinnatifid or narrowly lanceolate, entire or with a few remote teeth; stem leaves linear-lanceolate, entire, sessile, with gray, cottony hairs; **flowers** blue, sometimes purple or pink, outer ones enlarged and raylike.

USE: Planted in the flower border for summer bloom and for cut flowers.

CULTURE: Plants thrive in most soils and prefer full sun. Propagation is by seed started indoors in early April or direct seeding in early spring. Space the plants about 25 cm. apart.

CULTIVARS
'Blue Boy'. Flowers cornflower blue.
'Jubilee Gem'. All-America Winner. Plants, dwarf; flowers double, cornflower blue.
'Pinkie'. Flowers pink.
'Polka Dot'. Plants dwarf; flowers in a full color range.
'Snow Man'. Flowers white.

Centaurea imperialis—see *Centaurea moschata*

Centaurea moschata L. (Sweet Sultan). Annual to 60 cm. tall. July-September.

DESCRIPTION: **Plants** erect, branched, native in the orient; **leaves** lyrate to pinnatifid, sparsely pubescent; **flower** heads to 5 cm. across; flowers yellow, white, pink, or purple, fragrant, the outer ones much enlarged, raylike.
USE: Same as for *C. cyanus*.
CULTURE: Same as for *C. cyanus*.
CULTIVARS
'Alba'. Flowers white.
'Imperialis'. Flowers in wide color range.
'Purpurea'. Flowers purple.
'Rosea'. Flowers rose pink to purple pink.

Centaurea—other species

C. americana Nutt. (Basket Flower), native from Missouri south to Arizona and Louisiana, is a tall-growing annual with large purple flower heads in late summer. Plant toward the back of the flower border.

C. cineraria L. (Dusty-miller), native in southern Europe, is a tender perennial grown as an annual for its attractive silvery foliage.

C. dealbata Willd. (Persian Centaurea), native in the Caucasus, is a perennial with rose purple to pink flower heads in August and September.

C. gymnocarpa Moris & DeNot. (Dusty-miller), native in Capri, is a tender perennial grown as an annual for its silvery foliage.

C. macrocephala Pushk. (Globe Centaurea), native in the Caucasus, is a coarse perennial with large golden yellow flower heads in August, suitable for naturalizing.   PLATE 56

C. *montana* L. (Mountain Bluets), native in Europe, is a perennial about 50 cm. tall, with blue violet flowers in heads to 2.5 cm. across in July and August.

Centranthus DC. (Centranth)

VALERIANACEAE (Valerian Family)

DESCRIPTION: A small genus of about 12 species of annual or perennial herbs native in Europe and the Mediterranean region; **leaves** opposite, simple; **flowers** small, red or white, in dense terminal clusters; calyx pappuslike with 5 to 15 narrow divisions; corolla tubular, 5-parted, spurred at base; stamen 1; ovary inferior; **fruit** a 1-seeded nut.

Centranthus ruber (L.) DC (Red Valerian). Short-lived perennial to 1 m. tall. June-August.

DESCRIPTION: **Plants** glaucous and glabrous, native in Europe, North Africa, and Asia Minor; **leaves** lanceolate to ovate, to 10 cm. long, sessile, slightly toothed to entire; **flowers** numerous, in dense terminal clusters, crimson to pale red, about 1 cm. long, fragrant.

USE: Plant toward the back of the flower border for summer bloom and for cut flowers.

CULTURE: Plants grow in any well-drained soil either in full sun or in partial shade. Propagation is largely by seeds planted in spring in a nursery row. This is a short-lived perennial but it usually reseeds itself and seedlings can be transplanted to a desired location.

CULTIVARS
'Coccinea'. Flowers carmine red.
'Roseus'. Flowers deep rose.

Cerastium L. (Mouse-ear Chickweed)

CARYOPHYLLACEAE (Pink Family)

DESCRIPTION: A genus of about 60 species of annual or perennial herbs of wide distribution; **plants** mostly mat-forming or tufted, usually hairy; **leaves** opposite, usually gray to gray-green; **flowers** white, solitary or in cymes; sepals 5, rarely 4, separate; petals 5, rarely 4, often bifid or emarginate; stamens 5 to 10; **fruit** a cylindrical capsule, dehiscing with 10 teeth.

Cerastium tomentosum L. (Snow-in-summer). Perennial to 20 cm. tall. May, June.

DESCRIPTION: **Plants** creeping, native in the mountains of Italy and Sicily; **leaves** lanceolate to 2.5 cm. long, white-woolly; **flowers** white, to 2.5 cm. across; petals notched.

USE: Plant in rock garden or use as a ground cover. It also makes an attractive plant in a dry rock wall.

CULTURE: Plants like full sun and a well-drained soil of low fertility. Propagation is by spring division or by seeds sown in early spring. Divide when plants become crowded.

CULTIVAR

'Yoyo'. Leaves silvery; flowers white.

Cerastium — other species

C. alpinum L., native in the Arctic, North America, and Europe, is similar to *C. tomentosum*. The subsp. *lanatum* (Lam.) Asch. & Groebn. is more woolly than the species.

C. bierbersteinii DC. (Taurus Mouse-ear Chickweed), native in the Crimea, is also similar to *C. tomentosum*, but the flowers are larger, to 5 cm. across. This is also a good rock garden plant.

Chamaelirium Willd. (Devil's-bit)

LILIACEAE (Lily Family)

DESCRIPTION: A small genus with but a single perennial species native in eastern North America; **plants** dioecious, with tuberous roots; **flowers** white, aging to yellow, in terminal, spikelike racemes; perianth segments 6; stamens 6; **fruit** a 3-valved capsule.

Chamaelirium luteum (L.) A. Gray (Blazing-star, Fairy-wand, Rattlesnake Root). Perennial to 50 cm. tall. May, June.

DESCRIPTION: **Plants** native from Michigan to Massachusetts, south to Arkansas and Florida; basal **leaves** spatulate to obovate, to 15 cm. long; stem leaves reduced upward. **Flowers** dioecious, white, turning yellow with age, produced in terminal racemes.

USE: A good plant for the rock garden or woodland garden.

CULTURE: Plants like soil high in organic matter and a site that is partially shaded; propagation is by fall division or by seeds sown as soon as ripe in a cold frame.

Cheiranthus allionii — see *Erysimum hieraciifolium*

Chelone L. (Turtlehead)

SCROPHULARIACEAE (Figwort Family)

DESCRIPTION: A small genus of about 6 species of summer-flowering, pernnial herbs of North America; **leaves** opposite, serrate, mostly glabrous; **flowers** white or purple, in spikelike racemes; sepals 5; corolla irregular, 2-lipped, lower lip bearded inside; fertile stamens 4, woolly; staminode 1, shorter than fertile stamens; **fruit** a capsule containing many winged seeds.

Chelone glabra L. (White Turtlehead). Perennial to 2 m. tall. July, August.

DESCRIPTION: **Plants** upright, native from Minnesota to Newfoundland, south to Missouri and Georgia; **leaves** lanceolate to ovate, to 15 cm. long, subsessile or with short, winged petiole; **flowers** white or partly greenish yellow or tinged with pink or purple, to 3.5 cm. long; lower lip white-bearded; staminode white or green.

USE: The turtlehead is best planted along a stream or at the edge of a pool. It also can be planted in moist soil in a woodland garden.

CULTURE: Plant in moist soil in a partially shaded location. Propagation is by division in early spring, by seed sown in early spring, or by cuttings taken in July. Space the plants about 50 cm. apart.

Chelone obliqua L. (Shellflower, Rose Turtlehead). Perennial to 70 cm. tall. July, August.   PLATE 57

DESCRIPTION: **Plants** native from Minnesota to Indiana, south to Alabama and Maryland; **leaves** lanceolate to lanceolate-elliptic, short-petioled; **flowers** purple, to 2.5 cm. long; lower lip with pale yellow beard; staminode white.

USE: Same as for *C. glabra*.

CULTURE: Same as for *C. glabra*.

Chelone — other species

C. lyonii Pursh. (Pink Turtlehead), native in the mountains of the Carolinas and Tennessee, has rose purple flowers with a yellow beard on the lower lip. Culture and use are the same as for *C. glabra*.

Chimaphila Pursh. (Pipsissewa, Prince's Pine)

PYROLACEAE (Wintergreen Family)

DESCRIPTION: A small genus of about 8 species of glabrous, evergreen herbs or subshrubs with creeping stems, native in the North Temperate Zone; **leaves** in irregular whorls, simple, toothed; **flowers** white to rose pink, in few-flowered terminal corymbs; sepals and petals 5; stamens 10, with filaments expanded at base; **fruit** a 5-celled capsule.

Chimaphila maculata (L.) Pursh. (Spotted Wintergreen, Striped Pipsissewa). Perennial to 25 cm. tall. June, July.

DESCRIPTION: **Plants** native from Minnesota to Nova Scotia, south to Indiana and Virginia; **leaves** lanceolate to ovate-lanceolate, to 5 cm. long, variegated with white along the veins; **flowers** white, fading to pink, fragrant.

USE: Use in rock gardens or in woodland wildflower gardens.

CULTURE: The pipsissewa requires a moist, acid soil and partial shade. Propagation is by seeds started in a mixture of acid peat and sand in July in a cold frame or by division in early spring.

Chimaphila umbellata (L.) W. Barton (Common Pipsissewa, Prince's Pine). Perennial to 25 cm. tall. June, July.

DESCRIPTION: **Plants** native in Eurasia and northern North America; **leaves** oblong-obovate, to 5 cm. long, broadest above the center, not varigated; **flowers** pink; calyx lobes longer than broad.

USE: Same as for *C. maculata*.

CULTURE: Same as for *C. maculata*.

VARIETIES

var. *cisatlantica* S. F. Blake. Native in eastern North America. Differs from the species in the calyx lobes that are broader than long.

var. *occidentalis* (Rydb). S. F. Blake. Native to western North America. Leaves larger than in species; calyx lobes similar.

Chionodoxa Boiss. (Glory-of-the-snow)

LILIACEAE (Lily Family)

DESCRIPTION: A genus of about 5 species of alpine, bulbous, perennial herbs, native in Crete, Cypress, and Asia Minor; **bulbs** tunicate; **leaves** basal; **flowers** blue, white, or pink, in terminal racemes; perianth segments 6, united into a tube at base; stamens 6; **fruit** a 3-valved capsule.

Chionodoxa luciliae Boiss. (Glory-of-the-snow). Bulbous perennial to 15 cm. tall. April, May. PLATE 58

DESCRIPTION: **Plants** native in Asia Minor; **leaves** basal, linear to oblanceolate; **flowers** bright blue with white centers to 2.5 cm. across, in few-flowered terminal racemes.

USE: Plant in a rock garden or use for naturalizing in sunny locations.

CULTURE: Chionodoxas need a moist, well-drained soil and full sun. Propagation is by bulbs planted in September or early October. Space the bulbs about 10 cm. apart and plant them 8 cm. deep. The plants are not long-lived and replanting every third year may be required.

CULTIVARS

'Alba'. Flowers white.

'Gigantea'. Flowers larger than in species, star-shaped, clear blue.

Chrysanthemum L.

COMPOSITAE (Sunflower Family)

Anthemis Tribe

DESCRIPTION: A large genus of over 100 species of often aromatic annual or perennial herbs or rarely subshrubs, native mainly in Europe and Asia; **leaves** alternate, sometimes in a basal rosette, entire, toothed, or sometimes pinnatifid; **flower** heads usually radiate, solitary, or in corymbs; involucral bracts overlapping in 2 to 5 rows; receptacle flat or convex, naked; flowers white, yellow, orange, pink, red, or purple; disc flowers all perfect; ray flowers pistillate, sometimes lacking; **achenes** nearly cylindrical or ribbed.

Chrysanthemum coccineum Willd. (Pyrethrum, Painted Daisy). Perennial to 60 cm. tall. June, July. PLATE 59

DESCRIPTION: **Plants** with unbranched stems, native in southwestern Asia; **leaves** pinnatifid, fernlike; **flower** heads solitary on long peduncles, to 7.5 cm. across; disc flowers yellow; ray flowers white, pink, or red.

USE: The painted daisy is an attractive plant for the sunny flower border. The flowers are attractive in flower arrangements.

CULTURE: Plants grow best in full sun although they will tolerate shade for part of the day. A well-drained loam soil high in organic matter is required. Too much moisture, especially in the spring, can be fatal. Propagation is by seed sown in early spring or by spring division. Space the plants about 25 cm. apart.

CULTIVARS

'Buckeye'. Heads semi-double; ray flowers rose scarlet.

'Helen'. Heads double; ray flowers light pink with a pink crest.

'James Kelway'. Ray flowers velvety blood red.

'Snowball'. Heads double; ray flowers white.

Chrysanthemum maximum — see *Chrysanthemum* x *superbum*

Chrysanthemum x *morifolium* Ram. (Florist Chrysanthemum, Garden Chrysanthemum). Perennial to 1 m. tall. August-October.   PLATE 60

DESCRIPTION: A garden hybrid involving several species including *C. indicum*, *C. japonense*, *C. makinoi*, *C. ornatum*, and *C. zawadskii*; **leaves** thick, lanceolate to ovate, lobed, strongly aromatic; **flower** heads of various sizes and shapes, usually clustered on branches peduncles; ray flowers white, yellow, bronze, pink, red, and purple; disc flowers, when present, yellow.

USE: The garden chrysanthemum is one of the most widely planted of all perennials. They can be used in the mixed flower border or they can be planted in the foundation planting to add fall color. The flowers are excellent for cutting and flower arranging.

CULTURE: Breeding work on this hybrid began in China about 500 B.C. The Japanese soon started breeding work to improve the size and form of the flowering heads. In the 1930s, breeding work began in the North Central states and adjoining Canadian provinces to obtain earlier blooms and plants that were adapted to outdoor culture. Up until that time, the florist's chrysanthemum bloomed only during short days and usually few, if any, flowers would be produced out-of-doors before frost. By introducing an early-flowering species from Korea into the breeding program, outdoor cultivars have been produced that now bloom as early as August. Literally hundreds of named cultivars are now available to add color to the fall garden. These range in size of plants from low, mound-shaped plants to tall plants that may require staking. The size of the flower heads range from a few cm. across to 15 or more cm. The form of the flower heads vary from single, daisylike heads to fully double with all of the flowers being raylike.

Although chrysanthemums are a perennial, the plants do not always live over winter. Most growers treat them as annuals, starting with new plants each spring that are readily available from most nurseries and garden centers. Even when plants do live over winter it is advisable to dig them up in the spring and divide them into single-stemmed divisions. Propagation is by cuttings. Commercial growers dig up stock plants in the fall after they finish flowering, cut the tops off, place the plants in flats, and set the plants in cold frames. In February or March, the flats are brought into a greenhouse and cuttings are taken from new growth that starts at the base of the plant. These cuttings are rooted and potted. Young plants are ready for sale in mid May. This method of wintering and propagation can also be used by the home owner.

Chrysanthemums require a well-drained soil and bloom best in full sun. As soon as the plants grow to a height of about 6 inches, the tops are pinched back to force lateral branching. A second pinch may also be needed to obtain a well-branched plant. Do not pinch the plants back after July 1 or you will delay bloom.

Chrysanthemums are susceptible to several leaf problems including foliar nematodes. These problems are usually worse in a wet year or where the plants are crowded. Tarnished plant bugs can also affect the opening flowers, causing distorted flower heads. A spray program using a good fungicide and an insecticide will assure healthy plants and better bloom.

CULTIVARS: It is impossible to list more than a few of the thousands of named cultivars on the market. The following are some of the most popular of the cultivars introduced by the University of Minnesota:

'Autumn Fire'. Plants tall; flower heads midseason, to 8 cm. across; ray flowers burnt orange.

'Golden Fantasy'. Plants of medium height; flower heads midseason, to 5 cm. across; ray flowers golden yellow.

'Gold Strike'. Plants of medium height; flower heads early, pompom, to 5 cm. across; ray flowers golden yellow.

'Lindy'. Plants tall; flower heads midseason, to 10 cm. across; ray flowers quilled, incurved, lavender pink.

'Minn-Autumn'. Plants low, mound-shaped; flower heads midseason, to 6 cm. across; ray flowers reddish bronze.

'Minnrose'. Plants low, mound-shaped; flower heads midseason, to 4 cm. across; ray flowers deep rose pink.

'Minnyellow'. Plants low, mound-shaped; flower heads late, to 5 cm. across; ray flowers lemon yellow.

'Royal Pomp'. Plants of medium height; flower heads midseason, pompom, to 5 cm. across; ray flowers bright purple.

'Vulcan'. Plants of medium height; flower heads early, flat, to 6 cm. across; ray flowers dark red.

'Zonta'. Plants of medium height; flower heads midseason, to 6 cm. across; ray flowers apricot bronze.

Chrysanthemum x *superbum* Bergmans (Shasta Daisy). Short-lived perennial to 1 m. tall. June-September.   PLATE 62

DESCRIPTION: This hybrid species was developed by crossing *C. lacustre* x *C. maximum*; **leaves** coarsely toothed; lower leaves oblanceolate to 30 cm. long including petioles; upper leaves lanceolate, sessile; **flower** heads to 10 cm. across, solitary on long peduncles; disc flowers yellow; ray flowers pure white.

USE: Grow in cutting garden or plant in flower border. Flowers are excellent for cutting.

CULTURE: The culture of the Shasta daisy is similar to that of the garden chrysanthemum. The plants are not very hardy and it is best to start them in a cold frame where they can be protected over winter. The plants can be transplanted in early spring to where they will bloom.

CULTIVARS: Numerous cultivars are on the market.

'Alaska'. Flower heads single, to 12 cm. across.

'Esther Read'. Flower heads fully double with high centers.

'Little Miss Muffet'. Flower heads single on short stems.

'Marconii'. Flower heads double, frilled.

'Mount Shasta'. Flower heads fully double with a high crested center.

'Polaris'. Flower heads single.

'Silver Princess'. Plants compact, to 30 cm. tall; flower heads single.

Chrysanthemum tricolor — see *Chrysanthemum carinatum*

Chrysanthemum — other species

C. carinatum Schousb. (Tricolor Chrysanthemum), native in Morocco, is an annual with daisylike flowers in which the ray flowers are white, yellow, red, or purple, with a band of a different color near the base. Seeds should be started early indoors for summer bloom.

C. leucanthemum L. (Oxeye Daisy), native in Europe and Asia, and naturalized all over, is a common roadside weed with white, daisylike flowers from June to October. 'Selma Star' is a named cultivar with large flower heads to 10 cm. across. Plants can reseed and become a weed.

C. parthenium (L.) Bernh. (Feverfew), native in southeastern Europe, produces clusters of small, rayless flower heads in August and September. 'Golden

Ball' with golden yellow flowers and 'Snowball' with white flowers are popular cultivars. Although a tender perennial, this species blooms from seed started indoors in early April, so it is treated as an annual. Seedlings also volunteer in the garden where the plants grew the previous year.   PLATE 61

C. zawadskii Herbich, native in Japan and Korea, is important as one of the parents in our modern garden chrysanthemums. 'Clara Curtis' is a cultivar of this species with pink ray flowers in August and September.

Chrysopsis (Nutt.) Elliott (Golden Aster)

COMPOSITAE (Sunflower Family)

Aster Tribe

DESCRIPTION: About 30 species of annual, biennial, and perennial herbs, native in North America; **stems** leafy, erect to decumbent; **leaves** alternate, simple, usually entire; **flower** heads few to many in corymbs; involucre campanulate to hemispherical; involucral bracts overlapping in several rows; receptacle naked; disc and ray flower yellow; **achenes** obovoid, compressed with double pappus.

Chrysopsis villosa (Pursh.) Nutt. (Golden Aster). Perennial to 1 m. tall. July, August.

DESCRIPTION: **Plants** with taproots, native from British Columbia to Wisconsin, south to California and Texas; **leaves** oblong-elliptic to linear-oblanceolate; **flower** heads to 4 cm. across; disc and ray flowers yellow.

USE: Plant in the sunny border or in prairie restoration plantings.

CULTURE: Plants will grow and bloom on poor soils providing they have full sun. Propagation is by division in the early spring or by seeds sown in July in a nursery row.

CULTIVARS
'Golden Sunshine'. Ray flowers bright yellow.
'Goldflake'. Ray flowers deep golden yellow.

Cimicifuga L. (Bugbane)

RANUNCULACEAE (Buttercup Family)

DESCRIPTION: A genus of about 15 species of tall perennial herbs, native in the North Temperate Zone; **leaves** large, ternately compound; **flowers** small, white, numerous, in long racemes or panicles; sepals 2 to 5, petal-like, falling early; petals 1 to 8 or lacking, small, clawed, mostly 2-lobed; stamens many; pistils 1 to 8; **fruit** a follicle.

Cimicifuga americana Michx. (American Bugbane). Perennial to 1.5 m. tall. June-August. PLATE 63

DESCRIPTION: **Plants** native in eastern United States; **stems** slender; **leaves** 2- to 3-ternate, then pinnate with 3 to 5 leaflets; leaflets ovate, oblong, incised, acuminate, to 7.5 cm. long; **flowers** in loose, elongated panicles; petals 2-horned with basal concave nectary.

USE: Often planted in the woodland wildflower garden. They can also be used as a background plant in the flower border.

CULTURE: Plants like a rich, well-drained soil high in organic matter. They will grow in full sun but do best in partial shade. Propagation is by seeds or division in early spring. Once established, the plants should be left undisturbed.

Cimicifuga racemosa (L.) Nutt. (Black Cohosh, Black Snakeroot, Cohosh Bugbane). Perennial to 2 m. tall. June-August.

DESCRIPTION: **Plants** native from Ontario to Massachusetts, south to Missouri and Georgia; **leaves** 2- to 3-ternate, then often pinnate; leaflets wedge-shaped to cordate at base, to 10 cm. long; **flowers** in a few, erect, wandlike racemes; petals with 1 or 2 horns; follicle 1.

USE: Same as for *C. americana*.

CULTURE: Same as for *C. americana*.

CULTIVARS
'Armleuchter'. Racemes larger than in species.
'White Pearl'. Flowers white, in large trusses.

Cimicifuga — other species

C. foetida L. (Skunk Bugbane), native in Siberia, is a tall species suitable for the wildflower garden.

C. simplex (DC.) Turcz. (Kamchatka Bugbane), native from Siberia to Japan, is another tall species with leaves to 30 cm. across.

Clarkia Pursh (Godetia)

ONAGRACEAE (Evening Primrose Family)

DESCRIPTION: A genus of about 30 species of annual herbs native in western North America and South America; **leaves** simple, linear to ovate; **flowers** showy, in leafy spikes or racemes; calyx tube short with 4-sepal lobes; petals 4, sessile or clawed at base; stamens 8 or 4; ovary inferior; **fruit** a capsule.

Clarkia elegans — see *Clarkia unguiculata*

Clarkia unguiculata Lindl. (Rose Clarkia). Annual to 90 cm. tall. June-August.

DESCRIPTION: An erect glabrous annual, native in California; **leaves** lanceolate to ovate, to 5 cm. long; **flowers** lavender pink to salmon or purple, often double in cultivated strains, produced in erect, leafy racemes; petals triangular to rhombic, to 2 cm. long, with slender basal claws.

USE: An attractive annual for the flower border.

CULTURE: Clarkias require a moist, well-drained soil and full sun. Seedlings do not transplant well, so it is best to sow the seeds directly where the plants are to bloom as early in the spring as the soil can be worked. The plants dislike hot muggy weather and bloom best in cool weather. Thin the plants to about 30 cm. apart.

Clarkia — other species

C. amoena (Lehm.) A. Nels. & Macbr. (Satin Flower) is another native of California, with pink to lavender flowers with red centers from June to August.

C. pulchella Pursh., native from the Rocky Mountains to the Pacific coast, has large pink to lavender flowers from June to August.

Claytonia L. (Spring Beauty)

PORTULACAEAE (Purslane Family)

DESCRIPTION: A small genus of about 20 species of smooth, fleshy, perennial herbs, with fleshy taproots, corms, or stolons, native mostly in western North America; basal **leaves** 1 or more; stem leaves opposite, usually 1 pair; **flowers** white or rose, in terminal racemes; **fruit** a capsule.

Claytonia virginica L. (Spring Beauty). Perennial to 20 cm. tall. April, May.   PLATE 64

DESCRIPTION: **Plants** with fleshy corms, native from Minnesota to Nova Scotia, south to Texas and Georgia; **leaves** linear to linear-lanceolate, to 12 cm. long; **flowers** white with pink veins, to 2 cm. across.

CULTURE: Spring beauties like a moist soil high in organic matter and grow best in light shade. Plants die down after flowering and maturing their seeds. Propagation is by seeds or by division of their fleshy corms in the fall, preferably in September.

Clematis L. (Virgin's Bower)

RANUNCULACEAE (Buttercup Family)

DESCRIPTION: A large genus of over 200 species of perennial herbs or woody climbing vines, native in the North Temperate Zone; **leaves** opposite, compound or simple; **flowers** showy, solitary or in panicles; urn-shaped, bell-shaped, or opening flat; sepals petal-like; petals lacking; stamens many; **fruit** an achene with a long feathery style. Only the herbaceous, nonclimbing species are considered in this book.

Clematis heracleifolia DC. (Tube Clematis). Perennial to 1 m. tall. July, August.

DESCRIPTION: A spreading **plant**, native in eastern China; **leaflets** 3, coarsely toothed, to 12 cm. long; **flowers** tubular, to 2.5 cm. long; sepals blue, recurved.

USE: Plant toward the back of the flower border.

CULTURE: The Tube Clematis likes a well-drained soil of average fertility. It flowers best in full sun. The species spreads by rhizomes and can become invasive. Propagation is by division in early spring. The tops should be cut down either in the fall or early in the spring.

CULTIVAR AND VARIETY

var. *davidiana* (Decne.) Hemsl. Not as tall as the species, with light, violet blue, fragrant flowers.

'Davidiana Wyvale'. Flowers deep blue.

Clematis integrifolia L. (Solitary Clematis). Perennial to 1 m. tall. June-August.

DESCRIPTION: **Plants** erect, native in Europe and Asia; **leaves** simple, entire, to 10 cm. long; **flowers** nodding, blue, open urn-shaped, to 3.5 cm. long; **achenes** with styles to 5 cm. long.

USE: Same as for *C. heracleifolia*.

CULTURE: Plants prefer full sun and a well-drained soil. Staking is required in windy sites. Propagation is by seeds or by spring division.

Clematis mandshurica — see *Clematis recta* var. *mandshurica*

Clematis recta L. (Ground Clematis). Perennial to 1.5 m. tall. June-August.

DESCRIPTION: Tall perennial with weak **stems** that require support, native in southern Europe; **leaflets** 5 to 9, ovate-lanceolate, to 6 cm. long, pointed, entire; **flowers** white, fragrant to 2 cm. across, in panicles.

USE: An excellent background plant for the perennial border.

CULTURE: Plants require a well-drained soil and full sun. Plants should be staked to keep the flowering stems from falling over. Propagation is by spring division.

CULTIVARS AND VARIETY

var. *mandshurica* (Rupr.) Maxim. Stems to 2 m. tall; flowers larger than in species.   PLATE 65

'Grandiflora'. Flowers pure white, larger than in species.

'Purpurea'. Plants with purple foliage.

Cleome L. (Spider Plant)

CAPPARACEAE (Capper Family)

DESCRIPTION: A large genus of about 200 species of herbs, subshrubs, and shrubs, native mostly in the tropics and subtropics; **plants** mostly with a fetid odor; **leaves** simple or palmately compound; **flowers** white, green, yellow, or purple, in bracted racemes; petals 4, usually clawed; stamens usually 6, with long filaments; **fruit** a narrow capsule.

Cleome hasslerana Chodat. (Spider Flower). Annual to 1.5 m. tall. July-September.

DESCRIPTION: **Plants** erect, strongly scented, native in southern Brazil and Argentina; **leaves** palmately compound with pairs of short spines at base; leaflets 5 to 7, acuminate; **flowers** dark pink, fading to white, in bracted racemes; **capsules** to 5 cm. long.

USE: Plant toward the back of a sunny flower border.

CULTURE: Plants thrive in any well-drained soil in full sun. Propagation is by seeds started indoors in early April or by direct seeding. Space plants about 60 cm. apart.

CULTIVARS

'Alba'. Flowers white.

'Cherry Queen'. Flowers cherry-colored.

'Pink Queen'. Flowers pink.
'Rose Queen'. Flowers salmon pink.   PLATE 66

Clintonia Raf.

LILIACEAE (Lily Family)

DESCRIPTION: A small genus of only 6 species of perennial, rhizomatous herbs, native in North America and eastern Asia; **leaves** mostly basal; **flowers** white to greenish yellow or rose purple, in terminal umbels, rarely solitary; perianth segments 6; stamens 6; **fruit** a blue or black berry.

Clintonia borealis (Ait.) Raf. (Bluebead Lily). Perennial to 50 cm. tall. May, June.   PLATE 67

DESCRIPTION: **Plants** with erect flowering stems, native in eastern North America; **leaves** 2 to 5, oblong to elliptic or obovate, to 30 cm. long, glossy green; **flowers** greenish yellow, nodding, in 3- to 8-flowered umbels; **fruit** a blue berry.

USE: A good plant for the woodland wildflower garden.

CULTURE: Plants require an acid soil. They like partial shade and a soil that is high in organic matter. Propagation is largely by plant division in early spring. They can also be grown from seed started in a mixture of acid sand and peat in spring.

Clintonia — other species

C. *andrewsiana* Torr., native in northern California, has rose purple flowers. A winter protection is needed.

C. *umbellata* (Michx.) Morong. (Speckled Wood Lily), a native of eastern North America, has spotted leaves and white flowers spotted with green and purple.

Colchicum L.

LILIACEAE (Lily Family)

DESCRIPTION: A genus of about 70 species of cormous, perennial herbs, native in Europe, North America, and western and central Asia; **stem** and scape develops underground; **leaves** linear, lanceolate, oblong, or strap-shaped, appearing either with flowers or in the autumn flowering species in the early spring; **flowers** white to purple, rarely yellow; perianth segments 6, joined basally into a long tube extending underground, expanding above into a crocuslike flower; stamens 6, **fruit** a capsule.

Colchicum autumnale (Autumn Crocus, Meadow Saffron). Perennial to 20 cm. tall. September, October. PLATE 68

DESCRIPTION: **Plants** of unknown origin but cultivated for centuries for the medicinal drug colchicum, and for colchicine, used in plant breeding to induce spores; **leaves** 3 to 8, in spring, linear to lanceolate, to 25 cm. long; **flowers** pale violet to deep magenta red; anthers golden yellow.

USE: The autumn crocus is suitable for planting in rock gardens or intermixed with a low ground cover. They are also massed under trees.

CULTURE: Colchicums like a well-drained soil and prefer partial shade. The leaves come out early in the spring and then die down during summer. Propagation is by lifting and dividing the fleshy corms in August or September. Space the corms about 25 cm. apart and plant about 5 cm. deep.

Colchicum speciosum Steven. (Meadow Saffron). Perennial to 40 cm. tall. September, October.

DESCRIPTION: **Plants** native in the Caucasus, Asia Minor, and the eastern Mediterranean region; **leaves** 4 to 6, in the spring, widely oblong, to 40 cm. long; **flowers** rose to purple, with a white throat, to 10 cm. across, tapering to a tube that may be 30 cm. long; anthers yellow or brown.

USE: Same as for *C. autumnale*.

CULTURE: Same as for *C. autumnale*.

Colchicum —garden hybrids.

Beautiful garden hybrids have been developed by crossing *C. autumnale* x *C. speciosum*.

CULTIVARS
'Autumn Queen'. Flowers deep violet.
'Lilac Wonder'. Flowers violet mauve.
'The Giant'. Flowers very large, rosy lilac.
'Violet Queen'. Flowers deep purple violet.
'Waterlily'. Flowers double pink.

Coleus Lour. (Flame Nettle)

LABIATAE (Mint Family)

DESCRIPTION: A genus of about 150 species of annual or perennial herbs, native in the tropics of the Old World; **stems** square in cross section; **leaves** opposite crenate-serrate or doubly crenate-serrate, often variously colored; **flowers** in 6- to many-flowered verticillasters, crowded toward the tip of the stem but more distant toward the base, arranged in terminal panicles; calyx campanulate, 5- to 10-veined, 2-lipped; corolla blue or lilac to violet, with tube longer than calyx, limb 2-lipped, upper lip short, 2- to 4-lobed, lower lip entire, boat-shaped; stamens 4; **fruit** of 4 smooth nutlets.

Coleus x *hybridus* Voss. (Garden Coleus). Tender perennial grown as an annual to 1 m. tall. July-September.   PLATE 69

DESCRIPTION: An assemblage of hybrids derived from crossing *C. blumei* and other species; **leaves** usually variegated and multicolored; **flowers** blue or lilac to purple.

USE: Coleus are grown as house plants and also to add foliage color to out-door flower borders.

CULTURE: They require a rich soil high in organic matter and full sun for best foliage color. They can be propagated by seeds sown in mid-March or from cuttings. To obtain well-branched plants, the tips of the seedlings should be pinched out. Space the plants about 30 cm. apart. Removal of flowering stems as they appear will improve the appearance of the foliage.

CULTIVARS AND STRAINS

Brilliant (strain). Plants vigorous, bushy; leaves in many bright colors.

Carefree (strain). Plants short, leaves oaklike, in a wide color range.

'Chartreuse'. Leaves light green.

Fiji (strain). Plants short; leaves broad with fringed or ruffled edges, in bright colors.

Rainbow (strain). Leaves in a rainbow of colors.

'Red Velvet'. Leaves deep crimson red.

'Volcano'. Leaves scarlet red.

Consolida (DC.) S. F. Gray (Larkspur)

RANUNCULACEAE (Buttercup Family)

DESCRIPTION: A genus of about 40 species of annual herbs, native from the Mediterranean region to Central Asia; **leaves** palmately laciniate; **flowers** in bracted racemes or panicles, irregular; sepals 5, petal-like, the upper most spurred; petals seemingly 1, nearly entire or 3- to 5-lobed, spurred, the spur nectariferous and extending into the sepal spur; stamens 5; **fruit** a follicle.

Consolida ambigua (L.) P. W. Ball & Heyw. (Rocket Larkspur). Annual to 60 cm. tall. July-September.

DESCRIPTION: **Plants** pubescent, seldom branched, native in the Mediterranean region; **leaves** palmately laciniate; **flowers** in few-flowered racemes, bright blue, rarely white or pink; sepals to 1.5 cm. long with a slender spur; follicles to 2.5 cm. long, gradually tapering to a point.

USE: Commonly planted in the flower border and excellent for cut flowers.

CULTURE: The larkspur is easy to grow in most soils. The plants require full sun to bloom well. Since the seedlings are difficult to transplant, it is best to sow the seeds directly where the plants are to bloom as soon as the soil can be worked. Thin the plants to about 20 cm. apart. Bloom is best in cool weather.

CULTIVARS
'Blue Bell'. Flowers double, azure blue.
'Dark Blue Spire'. Flowers dark blue.
'Pink Perfection'. Flowers pink.
'White King'. Flowers white.

Convallaria L. (Lily-of-the valley)

LILIACEAE (Lily Family)

DESCRIPTION: A small genus of only 3 species of rhizomatous perennial herbs, native in the temperate regions of the northern hemisphere; **leaves** basal; **flowers** white to pink, in terminal, bracted, 1-sided racemes; perianth segments united, bell-shaped, with recurved lobes; stamens 6; **fruit** a berry.

Convallaria majalis L. (Lily-of-the valley). Perennial to 20 cm. tall. May, June.

DESCRIPTION: Low, spreading plants, native in Europe; **leaves** 2 or 3, lanceolate-ovate to elliptic, to 20 cm. long; **flowers** white, rarely pink, nodding, fragrant; **fruit** a berry.

USE: Plant as a ground cover under trees or on the north side of a building. Also good for cut flowers.

CULTURE: Plants like a fertile, well-drained soil that is high in organic matter. Plants do spread so it is best not to plant in the flower border. Plants tend to die down in late summer and present an untidy appearance. Propagation is by division in the fall or spring.

CULTIVARS

'Aureo-variegata'. Leaves variegated with yellow.

'Flora Plena'. Flowers double.

'Giant Bells'. Flowers larger than in species.

'Rosea'. Flowers pink.

Convolvulus L. (Bindweed)

CONVOLVULACEAE (Morning-glory Family)

DESCRIPTION: A genus of about 225 species of mostly climbing or twining herbs, native mostly in temperate regions; **leaves** simple, often lobed, with cordate, sagittate, or hastate base; corolla campanulate or funnelform, with 5-angled, pleated limb; **fruit** a capsule.

Convolvulus tricolor L. (Dwarf Morning-glory). Annual to 30 cm. tall. July-September.

DESCRIPTION: **Plants** with erect or ascending stems, much branched, native in southern Europe; **leaves** simple, linear-oblong; **flowers** produced in clusters of 3, blue with yellow throat, to 4 cm. across; **fruit** a capsule.

USE: Plant toward the front of the flower border in full sun.

CULTURE: Many of the perennial species are noxious weeds and should never be planted. *C. tricolor* is an annual that presents no such difficulties. It thrives in any good garden soil. Propagation is by seeds that can be planted directly in the border as soon as the soil can be worked, or seeds can be started indoors in late March.

CULTIVAR

'Royal Ensign'. Flowers petunia-shaped.

Coreopsis (Tickseed)

COMPOSITAE (Sunflower Family)

Helianthus Tribe

DESCRIPTION: A genus of over 100 species of annual or perennial herbs, seldom shrubs, native in North and South America and Africa; **leaves** entire or pinnately lobed or cut; **flower** heads radiate, solitary or long-peduncled panicles; involucral bracts in 2 rows; disc flowers yellow or purple; ray flowers brown, rose, or bicolored; **achenes** compressed, usually winged; pappus usually of smooth or barbed awns or short scales.

Coreopsis grandiflora Hogg. (Bigflower Coreopsis). Perennial to 60 cm. tall. May, June.

DESCRIPTION: **Plants** leafy to the top, native from Kansas to Missouri, south to New Mexico and Florida; **leaves** opposite, linear to lanceolate, simple to pinnately compound; **flower** heads mostly solitary, to 6 cm. across; disc flowers orange yellow; ray flowers sterile, yellow.

USE: An excellent plant for the sunny flower border and for cutting.

CULTURE: Coreopsis likes a rich soil and full sun. Plants should be spaced about 30 cm. apart for a mass effect. Propagation is by seed sown in early spring or by division of established plants in early spring.

CULTIVARS
'Double New Gold'. Flower heads double; ray flowers golden yellow.
'Gold fink'. Plants dwarf; ray flowers deep yellow.
'Sunburst'. Flower heads semi-double; ray flowers sparkling yellow.

Coreopsis tinctoria Nutt. (Calliopsis). Annual to 1 m. tall. July-September.

DESCRIPTION: **Plants** much branched, native from Washington to Minnesota, south to California and Louisiana; **leaves** opposite, 1- to 2-pinnate; leaflets linear or linear-lanceolate; **flower** heads to 3 cm. across, in loose corymbose panicles; outer involucral bracts only one-fourth as long as the inner; disc flowers dark red or purple; ray flowers sterile, bicolored, yellow with brown base or entirely yellow, brown, or purple; **achenes** slender, wingless, without a pappus.

USE: A popular plant for the sunny flower border.

CULTURE: Same as for *C. grandiflora* except it is propagated only from seeds. Seeds should be started indoors for earlier bloom.

CULTIVARS
'Crimson King'. Ray flowers crimson.
'Golden Crown'. Disc flowers golden.
'Golden Sovereign'. Ray flowers golden.

Coreopsis—other species

C. auriculata L. (Eared Coreopsis), native in the southeastern United States, is a showy perennial with basal lobes on the leaves, suggesting "ears." Flowers are yellow in summer. 'Nana' is a good rock garden plant.

C. lanceolata L. (Lance Coreopsis), native over most of the United States, is similar to *C. grandiflora* and used in much the same way. 'Grandiflora' has larger flower heads than the species.

C. verticillata L. (Threadleaf Coreopsis), native in the eastern United States, has showy yellow ray flowers from June to August.   PLATE 70

Coronilla L. (Crown Vetch)

LEGUMINOSAE (Pea Family)

DESCRIPTION: A small genus of about 20 species of herbs or shrubs, native in the Old World; **leaves** odd-pinnate; **flowers** pealike, in axillary umbels, yellow, or sometimes purple or white; standard orbicular, reflexed; stamens 10, 9 united and 1 free; **fruit** a slender legume, constricted between the seeds.

Coronilla varia L. (Crown Vetch). Perennial to 60 cm. tall. July, August.   PLATE 71

DESCRIPTION: A sprawling **plant**, native in Europe but naturalized in the eastern United States; **leaflets** oblong, in 5 to 10 pairs; **flowers** pink or white, to 1.25 cm. long; petals with claws about as long as the calyx.

USE: A coarse ground cover for steep banks.

CULTURE: This coarse ground cover should be planted only for erosion control on steep banks. It should not be planted in the flower border since it will crowd out more desirable plants. It thrives on any good garden soil in full sun or partial shade. Propagation is by direct seeding or by the use of transplants.

CULTIVARS
'Goldleaf'. Leaves golden yellow.
'Penngift'. Very vigorous plants.

Corydalis Venten

FUMARIACEAE (Fumitory Family)

DESCRIPTION: A genus with about 300 species of annual and perennial herbs, native to the North Temperate Zone and South Africa; perennial species with rhizomes or tubers; **leaves** pinnately compound; **flowers** irregular, perfect, in racemes; sepals 2 or lacking; petals 4, one of the outer pair with a basal spur; stamens 6, in 2 bundles; **fruit** a slender capsule.

Corydalis lutea (L.) DC. (Yellow Corydalis). Perennial to 40 cm. tall. May, June.   PLATE 72

DESCRIPTION: A many-stemmed, tuber-forming perennial, native in Europe; **leaves** green above, glaucous below; **flowers** golden yellow, to 2 cm. long, in axillary racemes.

USE: A good plant for rock or wall gardens and sometimes planted in the woodland garden.

CULTURE: Plants require a well-drained soil in full sun or partial shade. Propagation is by seeds sown as soon as they are ripe. If seeds are saved for spring seeding, they must be stored in a cool dry place. Seeds should be sown directly where plants are to grow as the seedlings are difficult to transplant.

Corydalis sempervirens (L.) Pers. (Rock Harlequin). Annual to 1 m. tall. July, August.

DESCRIPTION: **Plants** much-branched, native from Alaska to Newfoundland, south to Minnesota and Georgia; **flowers** pale pink to nearly purple, with yellow tips, to 2 cm. long, in few-flowered racemes.

USE: Same as for *C. lutea*.

CULTURE: Same as for *C. lutea*.

Corydalis — other species

C. bulbosa (L.) DC. (Fumewort, Bulb Corydalis), native in Europe, is a corm-producing perennial with rose to purple flowers in May.

C. mobilis (L.) Pers., native in central Asia, spreads by rhizomes and has yellow flowers in May and June.

Coryphantha (Engelm.) Lem.

CACTACEAE (Cactus Family)

DESCRIPTION: A genus of low, tubercled cacti, native in Mexico, Cuba, and the United States; **stems** fleshy, cespitose, usually globose or oblong, with watery juice; **tubercles** fleshy, succulent, cylindrical or angled, with terminal spines; **leaves** lacking; **flowers** showy, usually red or yellow; **fruits** are globose or oblong, many-seeded.

Coryphantha vivipara (Nutt.) Brit. & Rose (Nipple Cactus). Perennial to 15 cm. tall. May, June.   PLATE 73

DESCRIPTION: **Plants** with tufted stems covered with tubercles; native from Alberta to Minnesota, south to Texas; **tubercles** with 3 to 4 terminal spines and a cluster of spreading ones; **flowers** bright purple, to 4 cm. across; sepals and petals united at base; stamens numerous; **fruit** a fleshy berry.

USE: Sometimes planted in rock gardens.

CULTURE: Plants require well-drained soil and full sun. Propagation is by seeds started in a sandy soil mix in July. Seedlings should be wintered in a cold frame.

Cosmos Cav. (Mexican Aster)

COMPOSITAE (Sunflower Family)

Helianthus Tribe

DESCRIPTION: A genus of about 25 species of annual or perennial herbs, native from the southwestern United States to tropical America; **leaves** opposite, pinnately divided; **flower** heads radiate, solitary or in panicles; ray flowers white, rose, purple, or yellow; **achenes** narrowed upward into a beak; pappus of barbed awns.

Cosmos bipinnatus Cav. (Common Cosmos). Annual to 1.5 m. tall. July-September.

DESCRIPTION: **Plants** native in Mexico; **leaves** 2-pinnated into linear segments; **flower** heads to 10 cm. across; disc flowers yellow; ray flowers white, pink, or crimson.

USE: Commonly planted in the flower border for summer bloom and for cut flowers.

CULTURE: Plants require a well-drained soil and a sunny location. Propagation is by seeds started indoors in early April. Space the plants about 30 cm. apart.

CULTIVARS
'Candy Stripe'. Plants dwarf, early flowering; ray flowers bicolor.
'Dazzler'. Ray flowers crimson.
'Pinkie'. Ray flowers pink.
'Purity'. Ray flowers white.

Cosmos sulphureus Cav. (Yellow Cosmos). Plants to 1.5 m. tall. July-September.

DESCRIPTION: **Plants** native in Mexico; **leaves** 2- to 3-pinnate, with lanceolate leaflets; **flower** heads to 7.5 cm. across; disc flowers yellow; ray flowers pale or golden-yellow or orange; **achenes** with long beaks.

USE: Same as for *C. bipinnatus*.

CULTURE: Same as for *C. bipinnatus*.

CULTIVARS

'Bright Lights'. Ray flowers lemon yellow, gold, golden orange, or vermillion red.

'Diablo'. All-America Winner. Ray flowers a brilliant fiery red.   PLATE 74

'Goldcrest'. Flowers semi-double, orange.

'Lemon Twist'. Ray flowers bright yellow.

'Sunset'. All-America Winner. Flowers semi-double, vermillion.

Crocosmia Planch. (Montebretia)

IRIDACEAE (Iris Family)

DESCRIPTION: A small genus of 5 species of corm-producing herbs of South Africa; **leaves** linear; **flowers** orange to crimson, in a simple raceme, enclosed at base by 2 brown spathes; perianth tube tapering at base but dilated toward the tip into broad throat, usually shorter than the perianth lobes; **fruit** a globose, 3-lobed capsule.

Crocosmia x *crocosmiiflora* (V. Lemoine) N.E. Br. (Montebretia). Tender perennial to 1 m. tall. July-September.

DESCRIPTION: A garden hybrid developed by crossing *C. aurea* x *C. pottsii*; flowering **stems** upright, branched; **leaves** irislike, to 2 cm. wide; **flowers** orange-crimson, to 5 cm. across, in short racemes.

USE: Plant in clumps in the flower border. The flowers are excellent for cutting.

CULTURE: The montebretias have about the same cultural requirements as gladiolus, which see. Propagation is by offsets at the base of the corms. Corms must be dug in the fall and stored in a cool dry place over winter. Plant in mid-May, spacing the corms about 20 cm. apart. Cover with about 10 cm. of soil.

CULTIVARS

'Aurantiaca'. Flowers orange.

'Brightest and Best'. Flowers orange, shaded red.

'His Majesty'. Flowers rich yellow, shading to scarlet.

'Lady Oxford'. Flowers pale yellow, shading to peach-pink.

'Rheingold'. Flowers golden yellow.

Crocus L.

IRIDACEAE (Iris Family)

DESCRIPTION: A genus of about 80 species of corm-producing herbs, native from Spain to North Africa and Afghanistan; corms tunicate; **leaves** linear, keeled; flower peduncle and ovary develop below ground, sometimes sub-tended by a tubular spathe; **flowers** white, yellow, lilac, or purple, made up of 6 perianth segments and 3 stamens that arise from the perianth tube; **fruit** a 3-valved capsule that matures at or below the soil line.

Crocus chrysanthus (Herb.) Herb. Perennial to 15 cm. tall. April.

DESCRIPTION: **Plants** native to Caucasus and Crimea; tunic or covering of the corms smooth with short stiff fibers; **leaves** 4 to 6; **flowers** typically yel-low and globose to 3 cm. across; named cultivars come in various colors.

USE: Plant in rock gardens or under shrubs or trees, or naturalize in a lawn.

CULTURE: The corms should be planted in the fall as soon as they can be purchased, preferably in September. Space the corms about 10 cm. apart and cover with about 8 cm. of soil. If rodents are a threat to the corms; cover the planting with quarter-inch hardware cloth or window screen. The plants may become crowded because of division of the corms. If crowding occurs, dig the corms after the leaves die down and replant in the fall.

CULTIVARS
'Blue Pearl'. Flowers lobelia blue.
'Cream Beauty'. Flowers cream-colored.
'Lady Killer'. Flowers sulphur yellow.
'Princess Beatrix'. Flowers lobelia blue with yellow base.
'Zwanenburg Bronze'. Flowers golden yellow.

Crocus vernus (L.) J. Hill (Dutch Crocus). Perennial to 15 cm. tall. April, May.   PLATE 75

DESCRIPTION: **Plants** native in central and southern Europe; tunic of corm re-ticulate; **leaves** several, widest at the middle; **flowers** white to lilac, purple, often striped with darker purple, with white throat; stamen filaments white, anthers lemon yellow; style branches not divided or only fringed at apex, orange scarlet.

USE: Same as for *Crocus chrysantha*.

CULTURE: Same as for *Crocus chrysantha*.

CULTIVARS
'Albiflorus'. Flowers white.
'Harlem Gem'. Flowers lilac blue.

Crocus —other species

C. medius Balb., native in the mountains of France and Italy, is autumn-flowering with bright lilac colored flowers with purple stripes.

C. pulchellus Herb., native in Greece and Turkey, is also autumn-flowering with pale lavender to bright lilac flowers with an orange yellow throat.

C. sativus L. (Saffron Crocus) is not known in the wilds. It flowers in September with purplish violet flowers with orange stigmas. It is a commercial source of a yellow food colorant.

C. sieberi J. Gay (Sieber Crocus), native in Greece and Crete, blooms in April with star-shaped flowers that are dark purple to white with an orange throat. 'Firefly', with lilac blue flowers, and 'Violet Queen', with violet blue flowers, are named cultivars.

C. tomasinianus Herb., native in Yugoslavia, blooms in April with lavender flowers with white-bearded throats.

Crocus — garden hybrids.

Numerous cultivars have been named from crosses between several species. These are larger flowered and of better substance than the species.

CULTIVARS

'Ancyrensis'. Flowers brilliant orange.
'Little Dorrit'. Flowers amethyst blue.
'Peter Pan'. Flowers large, white.
'Remembrance'. Flowers blue.
'Yellow Mammoth'. Flowers yellow.

Cyclamen L.

PRIMULACEAE (Primrose Family)

DESCRIPTION: A small genus of about 15 species of tuber-forming herbs, native from central Europe and the Mediterranean region to Iran; **leaves** basal, long-petioled, ovate, orbicular, or reniform, usually cordate, sometimes lobed, usually blotched or marbled above, often dentate; **flowers** pink, carmine, magenta, or white, nodding, solitary on scapes that usually coil downward, bringing the mature fruits to the ground; calyx 5-lobed; corolla with a short tube, 5-lobed, blotched at base, usually reflexed and twisted; stamens 5; **fruit** a 5-valved capsule.

Cyclamen hederifolium Ait. (Baby Cyclamen, Neapolitan Cyclamen). Perennial to 10 cm. tall. August, September.   PLATE 76

DESCRIPTION: **Plants** native in southern Europe and western Asia Minor; corms to 15 cm. across, depressed-globose, with corky surface, rooting from the upper surface; **leaf** blades cordate, often angled or lobed, to 14 cm. long, marbled above, green or beet-red beneath, margins dentate; **flowers** rose pink to white, with basal crimson blotch, to 2.5 cm. across; corolla lobes acute, eared at base.

USE: This is the hardiest species and is sometimes planted in rock gardens or in woodland gardens under trees.

CULTURE: The tuberous corms are planted in early fall in well-drained soil that has been enriched with leaf mold. Plant the corms about 5 cm. deep and mulch with straw or marsh hay in early November. The plant may not be long-lived.

CULTIVAR
'Album'. Flowers white.

Cyclamen neapolitanum — see *Cyclamen hederifolium*

Cyclamen — other species

C. cilicium Boiss. & Heldr., native in Asia Minor, has rose pink flowers in September. It requires winter protection.

C. coum Mill., native in southeastern Europe and Asia Minor, blooms in May with white to pink or carmine flowers. It requires winter protection.

Cynoglossum L. (Hound's-tongue)

BORAGINACEAE (Borage Family)

DESCRIPTION: A genus of about 80 species of herbs native to temperate regions; **stems** usually hairy; **leaves** simple, alternate; **flowers** blue, purple, pink, or white, in terminal cymes; calyx 5-cleft or 5-lobed; corolla funnelform to salverform, 5-lobed, with 5 scales in the throat; stamens 5, included in the tube; **fruit** of 4 nutlets, each with short barbed prickles, forming a burr of "stick-tight."

Cynoglossum amabile Stapf. & J. R. Drumm. (Chinese Forget-me-not). Biennial to 60 cm. tall. June-August. PLATE 77

DESCRIPTION: **Plants** native in eastern Asia; basal **leaves** lanceolate to oblong-lanceolate, to 20 cm. long, petioled; stem leaves smaller, sessile; **flowers** blue, white, or pink to 7 mm. long.

USE: Plant in the flower border for summer bloom.

CULTURE: Although a biennial, this species is usually grown as an annual, with the seeds started indoors. It thrives in full sun and in most soils. It has a tendency to reseed itself and volunteer plants are not uncommon.

CULTIVARS

'Blanche'. Flowers in shades of white and blue.

'Firmament'. Flowers deep brilliant blue.

'Snowbird'. Flowers white.

Cypripedium L. (Lady's-slipper)

ORCHIDACEAE (Orchid Family)

DESCRIPTION: A genus of about 50 species of herbs, native to Eurasia and North America; **leaves** broad, pleated; **flowers** solitary or in few-flowered terminal racemes; lip inflated, saclike; column with 2 fertile anthers flanking a glandlike staminode; **fruit** a many-seeded capsule. See ORCHIDACEAE for flower structure.

Cypripedium acaule Ait. (Moccasin Flower, Pink Lady's-slipper). Perennial to 25 cm. tall. June.   PLATE 78

DESCRIPTION: **Plants** native in acid bogs or in Jack Pine woods from Minnesota to Newfoundland, south to North Carolina; **leaves** 2, basal, to 20 cm. long and 7.5 cm. wide; **flowers** solitary on a scape, to 12 cm. across; sepals and petals greenish brown; lip rose pink with darker crimson veins.

USE: Sometimes planted in wild flower gardens.

CULTURE: The moccasin flower is difficult to establish. It requires either an acid, sandy soil or a specially constructed acid bog. Unless you have the right soil conditions it is best not to plant this species. Native plants are on the protected list, so plants must be purchased from a nursery.

Cypripedium calceolus L. (Yellow Lady's-slipper). Perennial to 60 cm. tall. June.   PLATE 80

DESCRIPTION: **Plants** native from British Columbia to Newfoundland, south to Texas and Georgia; **leaves** ovate to elliptic-lanceolate, to 20 cm. long; **flowers** 1 or 2 on erect, leafy stems; sepals and petals greenish yellow to purplish brown; upper sepal lanceolate to lanceolate-ovate, lateral sepals usually united behind the lip; petals lanceolate-linear, flat to spirally twisted; lip light to deep yellow, usually veined or spotted with purple.

USE: Commonly planted in woodland wildflower gardens.

CULTURE: This is the easiest of the lady's-slippers to grow. It likes a soil high in organic matter and light shade. Propagation is by division in the fall.

VARIETIES: A variable species.

var. *parviflorum* (Salisb.) Fern. (Small Yellow Lady's-slipper). Flowers smaller and stems more slender than in typical species.

var. *pubescens* (Willd.) Correll (Large Yellow Lady's-slipper). Flowers larger and stems more robust than in species.

Cypripedium candidum Muhlenb. (Small White Lady's-slipper). Perennial to 30 cm. tall. June.

DESCRIPTION: **Plants** native in meadows near lime outcrops from Minnesota to New York, south to Missouri and Kentucky; **leaves** 3 to 4, to 13 cm. long and 3.5 cm. wide; **flowers** solitary; sepals and petals green, veined with brown purple; lip white, with purple spots around the mouth and inside.

USE: Plant in wildflower garden in either full sun or partial shade.

CULTURE: This lady's-slipper is easy to grow. It is the only species that likes a soil high in lime. It grows in river bottoms near lime outcrops. It can be increased by division.

Cypripedium pubescens — see *Cypripedium calceolus* var. *pubescens*

Cypripedium reginae Watt. (Showy Lady's-slipper). Perennial to 80 cm. tall. June, July.   PLATE 81

DESCRIPTION: **Plants** native in eastern North America west to Minnesota and Missouri; stems leafy; **leaves** to 20 cm. long and 12 cm. wide; **flowers** to 7.5 cm. across; sepals and petals white; lip white, striped with rose or purple.

USE: Plant in wildflower garden.

CULTURE: This is Minnesota's state flower and rather demanding in its requirements. The soil must be high in organic matter and quite acid. Acid peat moss or decomposed pine needles should be mixed with existing soil unless the soil is naturally acid. The plants like light shade and no competiton from nearby plants. The soil should be kept moist.

Cypripedium spectabile — see *Cypripedium reginae*

Cypripedium — other species

C. arietinum R. Br. (Ram's-head Lady's-slipper), native in northeastern North America, is a rare species with an odd-shaped flower. It is sometimes planted in collections but is not as showy as other species.   PLATE 79

Dahlia Cav.

COMPOSITAE (Sunflower Family)

Helianthus Tribe

DESCRIPTION: A small genus of about 27 species of fleshy-rooted perennials, native in Mexico, Central America, and Columbia; **stems** to 6 m. tall, usually unbranched, often woody at the base; **leaves** opposite or whorled, 1- to 3-odd-pinnate; **flower** heads radiate, long peduncled; involucral bracts in 2 rows, the inner membranous, the outer somewhat fleshy; receptacle flat or curved, scaly; disc flowers perfect; replaced in many cultivars by star-shaped flowers; ray flowers pistillate or sterile, white, yellow, orange, scarlet, or purple; **achenes** oblong or obovate, compressed; pappus of 2 obscure teeth or absent.

Dahlia—garden hybrids.

None of the wild species are in cultivation. The garden dahlias are the result of hybridizing the wild species such as *D. pinnata* and *D. coccinea*. The American Dahlia Society classifies dahlias according to size as follows:

AA or Giant, over 25 cm. in diameter.

A or Large, 20 to 25 cm. in diameter.

B or Medium, 15 to 20 cm. in diameter.

BB or Small, 10 to 15 cm. in diameter.

M or Miniature, under 10 cm. in diameter.

They also classify dahlias as to form into 15 groups as follows:

Formal Decorative. Flower heads fully double with the majority of the ray flowers broad, pointed or rounded at the tips, flat or slightly revolute, regularly arranged, and tending to recurve; the central rays cupped and spirally displayed.

Informal Decorative. Flower heads fully double with the majority of the ray flowers broad, pointed or rounded at the tips, and tending to recurve; the ray flowers may be more or less lanciniated, slightly revolute, twisted or curled, giving an irregular appearance to their arrangement; the central rays cupped and more or less spirally displayed.

Semi-cactus. Flower heads fully doube with the majority of the ray flowers broad at the base, straight, incurved or slightly recurved; ray flowers somewhat revolute but fully revolute for less than half their length.

Straight Cactus. Flower heads fully double with the majority of the ray flowers fully revolute for at least half their length, pointed, and straight or slightly incurved or recurved.

Incurved Cactus. Flower heads fully double with the majority of the ray flowers fully revolute for at least half their length, pointed, with a pronounced curvature toward the center front of the head.

Ball. Flower heads fully double, ball-shaped or slightly flattened; ray flowers blunt, rounded or indented, involute for most of their length and normally spirally displayed.

Miniature Ball. Same as ball except for their small size.

Pompon. Flower heads fully double, similar to Ball dahlias but more globe-shaped and smaller in size; ray flowers involute for most of their length and fully involute for more than half their length.

Waterlily. Flower heads fully double, characterized by large, broad, and generally sparse ray flowers that are straight or slightly incurved, giving the flower a flat appearance with the depth normally not more than half the diameter of the head.

Peony-flowered. Flower heads open-centered with two or more rows of ray flowers surrounding the disc flowers. Some or all of the ray flowers in the row adjacent to the disc may be irregularly formed, curled, or twisted.

Anemone-flowered. Flower heads with one or more rows of ray flowers surrounding a dense group of colored elongated disc flowers.

Single. Flower heads open-centered with only one row of ray flowers.

Mignon Single. Same as single except flower heads are less than 5 cm. across and plants are less than 45 cm. tall.

Orchid-flowered. Flower heads open-centered with one row of ray flowers. The ray flowers are involute for two-thirds or more of their length with margins meeting or overlapping for some portion of their length.

USE: Dahlias are grown chiefly for cut flowers. Some of the smaller flowered and seed propagated dahlias are planted in the flower border to provide late summer and fall color.

CULTURE: The garden dahlias are tender plants that require a long growing season to get maximum bloom. They like a fertile soil high in organic matter and ample moisture. Propagation is both by seeds and by root divisions. Many seed companies have strains that bloom freely the first year from seed. Most of the named cultivars are vegetatively propagated. Stem cuttings are often used to increase the number of plants. Dahlias produce a cluster of fleshy roots. These are dug in the fall of the year soon after the tops are killed by frost. The roots are stored over winter in a frost-free room at a temperature of $35°$ to $40°$ F. The roots are usually covered with sand, vermiculite, sawdust, or some other material to minimize dessication.

The roots can be planted directly in the garden in mid-May, or roots can be potted and new plants started indoors. Before planting, the roots should be carefully separated. The vegetative buds are not on the roots but rather at the base of the old stem; it is important to separate the roots carefully so some of the old stem will be attached to the neck portion of the root. When planting outdoors, cover the fleshy root with about 4 inches of soil. Dahlias should be spaced from 45 cm. to 1 m. apart depending on the cultivar. The tall, exhibition dahlias must be staked with sturdy stakes about 2 m. tall driven into the ground soon after planting. A single stem should be allowed to grow for each plant and this should be tied to the stake. The tip of the stem should be cut or pinched out just above the third pair of leaves to force lateral branching. Further pinching back of lateral branches may be required on vigorous plants. Growth should be continuous after the plants start to grow. Use ample quantities of fertilizer and water and mulch. For best results remove early flower buds until the plants reach 2/3 of their mature size. For large exhibition blooms, lateral buds should also be removed. Spraying may be required to control.

CULTIVARS AND STRAINS: There are thousands of named cultivars to choose from. Visit a public or private garden featuring dahlias to make your selections, or visit a flower show featuring dahlias. Most seed companies sell strains of dahlias that can be grown from seed. A few of these strains are:

Early Bird. Plants dwarf, to 35 cm. tall; flower heads double or semi-double, in a mixture of bright colors.

Redskin. All-America Winner. Plants dwarf, to 35 cm. tall; leaves dark, bronzy green; flower heads double or semi-double, to 8 cm. across, in shades of white, yellow, pink, rose, orange, and red.

Rigoletto. Plants dwarf, to 30 cm. tall; flower heads double or semi-double, to 6 or more cm. across, in shades of white, yellow, pink, orange, red, and purple.

Sunburst. Plants to 60 cm. tall; flowering heads double or semi-double, to 10 cm. across, in a wide color range, suitable for cutting.

The following named cultivars were recommended by a member of the Minnesota Dahlia Society:

'Alfred C.'. Flower heads giant, semi-cactus, orange.

'Billy'. Flower heads miniature, mignon single, yellow.

'Commando'. Flower heads large, formal decorative, purple.

'Dr. Les'. Flower heads giant, incurved cactus, dark red.

'Duet'. Flower heads medium, formal decorative, bicolor, dark red on white.

'Edna C.'. Flower heads medium, formal decorative, yellow.

'Emory Paul'. Flower heads giant, formal decorative, purple.

'Envy'. Flower heads giant, informal decorative, dark red.

'Gerry Hoeck'. Flower heads small, water lily, pink.   PLATE 82

'Golden Heart'. Flower heads medium, semi-cactus, flame blend.

'Hallmark'. Flower heads pompom, dark pink.

'Hamari Girl'. Flower heads giant, formal decorative, dark pink.

'Holland Festival'. Flower heads giant, informal decorative, bicolor, orange on white.

'Joe K.'. Flower heads miniature, formal decorative, red.

'Juanita'. Flower heads medium, straight cactus, dark red.

'Kelvin Floodlight'. Flower heads giant, formal decorative, yellow.

'Kiss'. Flower heads miniature, formal decorative, lavender.

'Klankstad Kerkrade'. Flower heads small, straight cactus, variegated, yellow on red.

'Light Music'. Flower heads medium, incurved cactus, lavender.

'Match'. Flower heads small, semi-cactus, bicolor, white on purple.

'Moorplace'. Flower heads pompom, dark red.

'Paulie Pal'. Flower heads miniature, formal decorative, white.

'Purple Royalty'. Flower heads miniature, formal decorative, purple.

'Sassy'. Flower heads miniature, formal decorative, pink.

'Small World'. Flower heads pompom, white.

'The Queen'. Flower heads small, semi-cactus, lavender.

'Walter Hardisty'. Flower heads giant, informal decorative, white.

'White Kerkrade'. Flower heads small, straight cactus, white.

'Wiggles'. Flower heads miniature, straight cactus, orange.

'Windlassie'. Flower heads medium, informal decorative, white.

Datura L. (Thorn Apple)

SOLANACEAE (Potato Family)

DESCRIPTION: A small genus of 8 species of annual or perennial herbs, native in tropical and subtropical regions, mostly in America; **leaves** alternate, entire to sinuately dentate, strong-smelling; **flowers** solitary in the axils of branches, erect, to 25 cm. long, often fragrant, generally nocturnal and lasting for 1 day; calyx tubular, spathelike, or with 2 to 5 acute or acuminate teeth, falling with the corolla after flowering, the persistent base then expanding to form a cup, reflexed frill, or membranous disc; corolla funnelform, pleated in bud, sometimes double, white or white with purple markings, yellow, or purple to violet; stamens 5, equal, borne on the corolla, with long-linear anthers; stigmas often capitate; **fruit** a dehiscent capsule, usually prickly or spiny.

Datura inoxia Mill. (Angel's-trumpet). Tender perennial grown as an annual to 1 m. tall. July, August.

DESCRIPTION: **Plants** spreading, hairy, native in Mexico and the southwestern United States; **leaves** ovate, to 25 cm. long; flowers pink or lavender, to 20 cm. long; calyx 5-toothed.

USE: Plant in sunny flower border.

CULTURE: Plants are of easy culture in most any garden soil in full sun. Propagation is by seeds started indoors in early April.

Datura metel L. (Downy Thorn Apple). Annual to 1.5 m. tall. July, August.

DESCRIPTION: **Plants** glabrous, native in southwestern China; **leaves** ovate, to 20 cm. long; **flowers** typically white, occasionally yellow or purple, to 18 cm. long, single or double.

USE: Same as for *Datura inoxia*.

CULTURE: Same as for *Datura inoxia*.

Daucus L. (Carrot)

UMBELLIFERAE (Carrot Family)

DESCRIPTION: A genus of about 25 species of herbs of wide distribution; **leaves** pinnately compound; **flowers** small, white or yellow, in compound umbels; involucre and involucels of many-toothed or entire bracts; **fruit** ovate or oblong, flattened prickly-winged.

Daucus carota var. *carota* L. (Queen-Anne's-lace). Biennial to 90 cm. tall. June to September.

DESCRIPTION: **Plants** native to Eurasia, escaped from cultivation and naturalized in many areas; **leaves** ovate in outline, finely cut into many narrow segments; **flowers** small, white, in compound umbels.

USE: Plant in flower borders. The flowers are used in flower arrangements.

CULTURE: The Queen-Anne's-lace is of easy culture. It thrives in most soils in full sun. Propagation is by seeds. The garden carrot also belongs to this species.

Delphinium L. (Larkspur)

RANUNCULACEAE (Buttercup Family)

DESCRIPTION: A large genus of more than 300 species of annual, biennial, or perennial herbs, native in the North Temperate Zone; **leaves** palmate, variously cut or divided; **flowers** in racemes, usually blue, but in garden hybrids pink, white, scarlet, red, and yellow colors occur; calyx showy, of 5 sepals, one of which is spurred; petals 2 or 4, smaller than the sepals, often crowded in the throat and called the "bee," the upper pair with spurs that project into the calyx spur; stamens many; pistils 2 to 5; **fruit** a follicle.

Delphinium ajacis — see *Consolida ambigua*

Delphinium x *belladonna* Hort. (Garland Larkspur). Perennial to 1 m. tall. June-August.

DESCRIPTION: **Plants** of hybrid origin resulting from a cross between *D. elatum* x *D. grandiflorum*; **flowers** rich blue with long spurs over 2.5 cm. long, in short racemes; petals yellow.

USE: Plant in perennial flower border in full sun.

CULTURE: The plants are mostly grown from seeds. Seeds are planted in a nursery row and transplanted to their permanent location.

CULTIVARS
'Bellamosa'. Flowers deep blue.
'Casa Blanca'. Flowers pure white.
'Connecticut Yankee'. Flowers in shades of blue, lavender, white, and violet.

Delphinium chinensis — see *Delphinium grandiflorum*

Delphinium x *cultorum* Voss. (Garden Delphinium). Perennial to 2.5 cm. tall. June-August.   PLATE 83

DESCRIPTION: **Plants** of hybrid origin involving several species; **flowers** very large in tall indeterminate racemes, in a wide color range.

USE: This beautiful garden delphinium is commonly planted toward the back of the flower border for accent.

CULTURE: Although the garden delphinium will tolerate some shade, it is best to plant it where it will receive full sun. Because of their tall height, the plants should be tied to stakes, especially in windy locations. After flowering, the flowering stem should be cut back to prevent seed formation. When this is done, a second crop of bloom may be expected. In Europe, selected cultivars are often vegetatively propagated by division and cuttings. In America, most plants are grown from seed. By starting seeds early indoors, plants will often bloom the first year. Space the plants about a meter apart in the garden. Powdery mildew is the most common disease, most often in shady locations. It can be controlled by spraying. Aphids and cyclamen mites are common pests, often requiring control measures.

CULTIVARS AND STRAINS: Many named cultivars have been developed in England and in Europe. In America, special seed strains are more commonly planted.
Blackmore and Langdon strain. An imported strain from England with large flowers in blue or mauve colors with "bees" of contrasting colors.
Pacific Coast strains. Numerous strains of large-flowered hybrids have been developed on the West Coast and are often in a wide variety of colors.

Delphinium grandiflorum L. (Chinese Larkspur). Perennial to 1 m. tall. June-August.

DESCRIPTION: **Plants** with slender hairy stems, native in Siberia and China; lower **leaves** with long petioles and upper leaves sessile, with narrow segments; **flowers** blue or violet, to 3.5 cm. across, with yellow or blue "bees."

USE: Plant in flower border for colorful bloom.

CULTURE: Similar to *D.* x *cultorum* except the plants do not require staking.

CULTIVARS

'Album'. Flowers blue.

'Blue Butterfly'. Flowers marine blue.

'Blue Mirror'. Flowers navy blue.

Dianthus L. (Pink)

CARYOPHYLLACEAE (Pink Family)

DESCRIPTION: A genus of about 300 species of annual, biennial, and perennial herbs, native in Eurasia and South Africa; **leaves** opposite, the bases often uniting to form a sheath around the stem; nodes swollen; **flowers** solitary, in panicles, or in heads surrounded by bracts; calyx tubular, 5-toothed, many-veined; petals usually 5, limb often abruptly narrowed into an elongated claw; blade entire, many-toothed, or fimbriate; stamens 10; **fruit** a 4-valved capsule.

Dianthus barbatus L. (Sweet William). Biennial to 60 cm. tall. June, July.

DESCRIPTION: **Plants** native in the Pyrenees and Carpathian Mountains, and on the Balkan Peninsula; **leaves** often short-petioled, lanceolate, with a prominent midrib; **flowers** in many-flowered, flat-topped cymes, white, pink, rose, red, purple, violet, and bicolored; petals bearded inside.

USE: A popular border flower, used for massing.

CULTURE: This biennial is grown from seed started in July in a cold frame. Protect the plants over winter and transplant to the border in early spring. The plants like full sun and a soil that is nearly neutral.

CULTIVARS

'Albus'. Flowers white.

'Midget'. Plants 15 cm. tall; flowers in a wide color range.

'Red Monarch'. All-America Winner. Flowers rich red.

'Scarlet Beauty'. Flowers scarlet.

'Summer Beauty'. Flowers in many colors, some star-shaped and mottled, others with white centers.

'Wee Willie'. Plants only 8 cm. tall; flowers in a wide color range.

Dianthus caryophyllus L. (Carnation, Clove Pink). Short-lived perennials, often grown as annuals to 1 m. tall. July-September. PLATE 84

DESCRIPTION: **Plants** tufted, glaucous, with stiff stems, probably native in the Mediterranean region; **leaves** narrow, to 15 cm. long, acuminate, blue-glaucous; **flowers** to 10 cm. across, often double, white, pink, red, purple, yellow, or apricot orange, often very fragrant, 2 to 5-flowered on erect stems.

USE: Plant in flower border or cutting garden.

CULTURE: Small-flowered forms of this popular florist's flower are sometimes planted in the garden. They like a rich soil and full sun. If seeds are started indoors, plants will bloom the first year. Plants also root easily from cuttings. Some cultivars will live over winter if heavily mulched in the fall.

CULTIVARS: Besides the many named cultivars grown by florists, a number of cultivars are bred for outdoor culture.

'Dwarf Baby'. Plants to 30 cm. tall; flowers fully double, in many colors.

'Grenadin'. Plants to 35 cm. tall; flowers double, in shades of copper red, salmon, rose, scarlet, white, and pink.

'Juliet'. All America Winner. Plants to 25 cm. tall; flowers rich scarlet red, fragrant, to 6 cm. across.

'King of Blacks'. Flowers dark red.

'Pixie Delight'. Plants to 25 cm. tall; flowers double, in shades of bluish white, pink rose, scarlet, and purple.

Dianthus chinensis L. (Rainbow Pinks). Tender perennial grown as an annual to 75 cm. tall. July-September.

DESCRIPTION: **Plants** native of central and eastern China; basal **leaves** soon withering, stem leaves to 7.5 cm. long, ciliate; **flowers** in loose clusters, rosy lilac with a purple eye, to 2.5 cm. across; petals obovate.

USE: Plant in flower border and for cut flowers.

CULTURE: This popular plant likes a rich soil and full sun. Propagation is by seeds started indoors in late March.

CULTIVARS

'Baby Doll'. Plants 20 cm. tall; flowers in many colors.

'China Doll'. All-America Winner; flowers double, salmon, red, or white.

'Magic Charms'. All-America Winner; plants 18 cm. tall; flowers in many brilliant colors.

'Queen of Hearts'. All-America Winner. Plants to 30 cm. tall; flowers deep scarlet red.

'Snowfire'. All-America Winner. Plants to 20 cm. tall; flowers white, fringed, with red centers.   PLATE 85

Dianthus — other species

D. x *allwoodii* Hort. (Allwood Pink), a hybrid species resulting from a cross between *D. caryophyllus* and *D. plumarius*, is a tufted perennial with showy flowers in many colors from May to August.

D. alpinus L. (Alpine Pink), native in the European Alps, is a popular rock garden plant with red purple flowers speckled pink in May and June.

D. deltoides L. (Maiden Pink), native in Europe, is a low, spreading plant with deep pink flowers in May and June. It is planted in rock gardens and also as a ground cover.

D. gratianopolitanus Vill. (Cheddar Pink), native in Europe, is a low, tufted perennial with fragrant, rosy pink flowers in May and June.

D. plumarius L. (Cottage Pink), native in Europe, forms a dense mat with fragrant flowers in shades of rose, purple, or white in May and June.

Dicentra Bernh. (Bleeding-heart)

FUMARIACEAE (Fumitory Family)

DESCRIPTION: A small genus of about 20 species of perennial herbs, native in North America and Asia; **plants** usually with fleshy rhizomes or tubers, often stemless; **leaves** alternate or basal, mostly ternately compound or dissected; **flowers** in racemes, usually nodding, irregular, white or red; corolla laterally flattened, cordate or 2-spurred at base, closed at top, composed of an outer and inner pair of petals; stamens 6, united, in 2 bundles; **fruit** an oblong or linear capsule.

Dicentra cucullaria (L.) Bernh. (Dutchman's-breeches). Perennial to 25 cm. tall. April, May.

DESCRIPTION: Tuber-forming **plants** native from Minnesota to Nova Scotia, south to Kansas and North Carolina; **leaves** all basal, dividing into linear segments, dying down in June; **flowers** nodding in simple racemes, white, tipped with cream yellow; spurs of petals prolonged, widely spreading.

USE: Plant in woodland wildflower garden.

CULTURE: This little woodland wildflower likes a moist soil high in organic matter and moderate shade. Propagation is by the fleshy tubers and by seed. After flowering and fruiting in early spring, the foliage dies down to the ground.

Dicentra eximia (Ker.-Gawl.) Torr. (Wild Bleeding-heart, Fringed Bleeding-heart). Short-lived perennial to 60 cm. tall. May-September.   PLATE 86

DESCRIPTION: **Plants** with short fleshy rhizomes, native in the mountains from New York to Georgia; **leaves** all basal and ternately dissected, staying green all summer; **flowers** nodding, in panicles, everblooming, pink to purple; corolla cordate at base, narrowed above into a long neck.

USE: Plant in rock garden or in flower border.

CULTURE: This bleeding-heart stays green all summer and has repeat bloom. It thrives in full sun or partial shade. Propagation is by seeds or division. It also self sows, and volunteer seedlings can be transplanted.

CULTIVARS
'Alba'. Flowers white.
'Bountiful'. Plants vigorous, 45 cm. tall; flowers pink.
'Luxuriant'. Plants to 50 cm. tall; flowers red.
'Zestful'. Plants to 30 cm. tall; flowers rose red.

Dicentra spectabilis (L.) Lem. (Common Bleeding-heart). Perennial to 60 cm. tall. May, June.   PLATE 87

DESCRIPTION: **Plants** with fleshy roots and leafy stems, native in Japan; **leaf** segments broad, obovate to cuneate, turning yellow and dying in late summer; **flowers** pendent, in simple racemes basally heart-shaped; outer petals rosy red with tips reflexed, inner ones white.

USE: Plant in flower border.

CULTURE: This popular old-fashioned garden flower is of easy culture. It grows in full sun or partial shade in any good garden soil. After flowering, the plants die down in midsummer. Propagation is by division of the fleshy roots in August or September.

CULTIVAR
'Alba'. Flowers white.

Dicentra —other species

D. canadensis (J. Goldie) Walp. (Squirrel Corn), native in eastern North America, is similar to *D. cucullaria* except that the outer petals are not spreading at the base. They flower at the same time and require the same culture.

D. formosa (Andr.) Walp. (Western Bleeding-heart), native on the west coast of North America, has rose purple to white flowers in compound racemes in April.

Dictamnus L. (Gas Plant)

RUTACEAE (Rue Family)

DESCRIPTION: A genus with a single herbaceous species, native from southern Europe to northern China; **leaves** alternate, pinnate, glandular-dotted; **flowers** white to rose, in terminal racemes, irregular; sepals and petals 5; stamens 10; **fruit** a 5-lobed capsule.

Dictamnus albus L. (Gas Plant, Burning Bush). Perennial to 1 m. tall. June, July.

DESCRIPTION: A strong-smelling perennial, native from southern Europe to northern China; **leaflets** 9 to 11, ovate, serrulate, to 7.5 cm. long; **flowers** white to rose, about 2.5 cm. long.

USE: Plant in sunny flower border.

CULTURE: The gas plant gets its name from the fact that the leaves give off a volatile, inflammable oil that will sometimes ignite, without harming the plant, if a flame is placed near it. It thrives in most well-drained garden soils when planted in full sun. Propagation is by seeds planted in spring or by root cuttings, started in sandy soil in early spring.

CULTIVARS

'Albus'. Flowers dazzling white.

'Rubra'. Flowers rosy purple.   PLATE 88

Dictamnus fraxinella —see *Dictamnus albus*

Didiscus coeruleus —see *Trachymene coerulea*

Digitalis L. (Foxglove)

SCROPHULARIACEAE (Figwort Family)

DESCRIPTION: A genus of about 20 species of biennial or perennial herbs, native from southern Europe and northern Africa to central Asia; **leaves** alternate, simple, in basal rosettes in young plants, stem leaves shorter than basal ones; **flowers** showy, in terminal, often one-sided racemes; calyx 5-parted; corolla purple, yellow, brown, or white, often spotted or streaked inside, somewhat 2-lipped, with tube inflated or campanulate; stamens 4; **fruit** a capsule.

Digitalis ambigua — see *Digitalis grandiflora*

Digitalis grandiflora Mill. (Yellow Foxglove). Perennial to 1 m. tall. June, July.

DESCRIPTION: **Plants** hairy, native of Europe and western Asia; basal **leaves** ovate-lanceolate, to 20 cm. long, serrate, becoming smaller and sessile or clasping up the stem; **flowers** yellow, marked with brown, to 5 cm. long; calyx lobes linear.

USE: Plant in woodland wildflower garden.

CULTURE: This species is of easy culture. The soil should be high in organic matter and the area should be in light shade. Propagation is by seed or division in early spring.

Digitalis purpurea L. (Common Foxglove). Biennial of borderline hardiness to 1.5 m. tall. June, July.

DESCRIPTION: **Plants** native in the Mediterranean region, escaped and naturalized in milder regions of the United States; basal **leaves** lanceolate to ovate or broadly ovate, long-petioled, stem leaves sessile or short-petioled; **flowers** drooping, purple or sometimes pink or white, spotted with purple, to 7.5 cm. long; calyx lobes ovate.

USE: Plant in flower border.

CULTURE: The species is seldom planted except in mild climates. It can be grown by planting the seeds in a cold frame and transplanting the seedlings to the border in the spring. Since the cultivar Foxy was introduced a few years ago, this cultivar has largely replaced the species for northern gardens. Seeds of Foxy can be started indoors in March and the plants will bloom in September and October.

CULTIVARS: Numerous cultivars have been named but most of them are not hardy enough for northern gardens.

'Foxy'. All-America Winner. This is the first and only cultivar that will bloom the first year from seed started indoors in March. Similar to the species in flower color. PLATE 89

Digitalis — other species

D. ferruginea L. (Rusty Foxglove), native in southern Europe, is a tall biennial or short-lived perennial to 2 m. tall, with yellow flower, spotted with rusty red markings in June and July.

D. lutea L., native in Europe, has flowers that are yellow or white in racemes to 1 m. tall in June and July.

D. x *mertonensis* Buxt. & Darl., a hybrid species resulting from a cross between *D. grandiflora* and *D. purpurea*, is a vigorous perennial to 2 m. tall, with flowers to 5 cm. long with a crushed strawberry color in June and July.

Dodecatheon L. (Shooting-star)

PRIMULACEAE (Primrose Family)

DESCRIPTION: A genus of about 14 species of scapose, perennial herbs, native mostly in North America; **leaves** simple, in a basal rosette; **flowers** white, magenta, lavender, or purple, nodding, in umbels; calyx and corolla 4- to 5-parted; corolla tube usually maroon with a yellow band at the throat, lobes reflexed; stamens 4 or 5; filaments free or united into a tube; anthers slender; **fruit** a capsule.

Dodecatheon meadia L. (Common Shooting-star). Perennial to 50 cm. tall. May-July.   PLATE 90

DESCRIPTION: **Plants** glabrous, native from Minnesota to Pennsylvania to Wisconsin, south to Texas and Alabama; **leaves** ovate to spatulate, to 30 cm. long; **flowers** magenta or lavender to white, in umbels on scapes.

USE: A delightful plant to grow in a rock garden or in a woodland wildflower garden.

CULTURE: The shooting-star likes a lime-free soil high in organic matter, partial shade, and adequate moisture. Plants can be divided in early spring or new plants can be started from seeds planted as soon as ripe. Individual plants are inclined to be short-lived.

CULTIVAR
'Alba'. Flowers white.

Dodecatheon radicatum — see *Dodecatheon pulchellum*

Dodecatheon — other species

D. pulchellum (Raf.) Merrill, native from Alaska to Mexico and scattered eastward, has flowers that are magenta to lavender in May and June. 'Alba' is a white-flowered cultivar.

Doronicum L. (Leopard's-bane)

COMPOSITAE (Sunflower Family)

Senecio Tribe

DESCRIPTION: A genus of about 30 species of perennial herbs of Europe and temperate Asia; **stems** simple or somewhat branched; basal **leaves** long-petioled;

stem leaves alternate, often clasping; **flower** heads radiate, long-peduncled; involucral bracts in 2 to 3 rows, nearly equal; disc and ray flowers yellow; **achenes** 10-ribbed, with pappus of simple hairs.

Doronicum caucasicum —see *Doronicum cordatum*

Doronicum cordatum (Wulfen) Schultz-Bip. (Heartleaf Leopard's-bane). Perennial to 75 cm. tall. May, June.   PLATE 91

DESCRIPTION: Rhizomatous **plants**, native in southeastern Europe and western Asia; **leaves** cordate-ovate to ovate-lanceolate, toothed or lobed, often clasping at base; **flower** heads solitary, to 5 cm. across; ray flowers yellow.

USE: A colorful perennial wtih daisylike flowers that add color to the perennial flower border.

CULTURE: Plants are of easy culture in either full sun or partial shade. They thrive in any good garden soil. Propagation is by division right after flowering in early June. The species can also be propagated from seeds. Plants may be short-lived unless they are protected over winter.

CULTIVARS
'Finesse'. Ray flowers bright yellow.
'Madame Mason'. Flower heads large; ray flowers bright yellow.
'Magnificum'. Flower heads very large.

Doronicum —other species.

D. plantigineum L. (Plantain Leopard's-bane), native in Europe, is similar to *D. cordatum* except the leaves are narrow and taper toward the base.

Draba L. (Whitlow Grass)

CRUCIFERAE (Mustard Family)

DESCRIPTION: A large genus of about 250 species of annual and perennial herbs, native in north temperate and boreal regions and in mountains, growing in open, rocky, or gravelly soils; **leaves** simple, entire or dentate, mostly basal and forming a rosette; **flowers** small, white, yellow, rose, or purple, in terminal racemes; sepals and petals 4; **fruit** a globular or orbicular silicle.

Draba aizoides L. Perennial to 10 cm. tall. April, May.

DESCRIPTION: **Plants** native in the mountains of southern Europe; **leaves** linear, in basal rosettes; **flowers** yellow, in many-flowered racemes on glabrous scapes.

USE: A good rock garden plant.

CULTURE: Drabas like a well-drained soil and full sun. They do best in a sandy or gravelly soil. Propagation is by division or by seeds started in a cold frame in early spring in a sandy soil mixture.

Draba repens — see *Draba sibirica* 'Repens'

Draba sibirica (Pell.) Thall. (Siberian Draba). Perennial to 30 cm. tall. April, May.

DESCRIPTION: **Plants** with creeping stems, native in Siberia, the Caucasus, and eastern Greenland; **leaves** oblong-lanceolate, acute, somewhat hairy; **flowers** yellow.

USE: Same as for *Draba aizoides*.

CULTURE: Same as for *Draba aizoides*.

CULTIVAR

'Repens'. Plants form a dense mat only 7 cm. tall.

Draba — other species

D. alpina L. (Rockcress Draba), a circumpolar species, has yellow flowers in April and May. A good rock garden plant.

D. altaica (C. A. Mey.) Bunge., native in Asia, has white flowers in April and May.

D. borealis DC. (Northern Draba), native in arctic regions of Canada and Siberia, also has white flowers in April and May and is a good rock garden plant.

D. dedeana Boiss. & Reut. (Dede Draba), native in Spain, has white to sulphur yellow flowers in April and May.   PLATE 92

Dryas L. (Dryad)

ROSACEAE (Rose Family)

DESCRIPTION: A small genus of evergreen, creeping plants, native in alpine regions of the Northern Hemisphere; **leaves** alternate; **flowers** white or yellow, solitary; sepals and petals 7 to 10 with sepals shorter than the petals; **fruit** an achene with a feathery style.

Dryas octopetala L. (Mountain Avens). Perennial to 20 cm. tall. June.   PLATE 93

DESCRIPTION: Creeping evergreen, native from Alaska to Greenland, south to mountains of Colorado; **leaves** ovate-elliptic to oblong, toothed, smooth above, white-tomentose below; **flowers** white, to 2.5 cm. across.

USE: An excellent rock garden plant.

CULTURE: Plants prefer light shade. The soil should be specially prepared by mixing equal parts of garden soil with either peat or leaf mold and a small amount of crushed limestone. Plants can be propagated by cuttings taken in early summer or by seed started in spring. April is the best time to plant.

Dryas —other species

D. drummondii Richardson (Drummond Dryas) has the same natural range as *D. octopetala*. It differs in having yellow flowers.

D. x *suendermannii* Kellerer is a hybrid between *D. drummondii* and *D. octopetala*. The flowers are yellow in bud but open white.

Duchesnea Sm. (Mock Strawberry)

ROSACEAE (Rose Family)

DESCRIPTION: A small genus of 2 Asiatic herbs with runners; **flowers** yellow; calyx bractlets leafy and toothed; achenes borne on a dry receptacle.

Duchesnea indica Sm. (Mock Strawberry). Perennial to 10 cm. tall. May, June.

DESCRIPTION: Strawberrylike **plants**, native in India; **leaves** trifoliate with long petioles, with ovate leaflets that are toothed and silky hairy underneath; **flowers** yellow, to 2.5. cm. across; **fruits** red like a strawberry but white and pithy inside.

USE: The mock strawberry is attractive as a ground cover and is also planted in rock gardens.

CULTURE: Plants are of easy culture in almost any good garden soil and in full sun. Propagation is usually by division in early spring. It can also be grown from seed.

Echinacea Moench (Purple Coneflower)

COMPOSITAE (Sunflower Family)

Helianthus Tribe

DESCRIPTION: A small genus of 3 species of rough, perennial herbs, native in North America; **leaves** alternate, simple, large; **flower** heads **radiate**, solitary or few on a long peduncle; receptacle conical; disc flowers purple-brown; ray flowers purple to white; **achenes** 4-angled; pappus a short crown.

Echinacea purpurea (L.) Moench (Purple Coneflower). Perennial to 1 m. tall. July, August.

PLATE 94

DESCRIPTION: **Plants** native from Iowa to Ohio, south to Louisiana and Georgia; lower **leaves** ovate to broadly lanceolate, coarsely toothed, long-petioled, rough; upper stem leaves narrower, nearly entire, sessile; **flower** heads to 15 cm. across; ray flowers rose purple.

USE: Plant in sunny flower border or in a prairie garden.

CULTURE: The purple coneflower likes full sun and grows well in any well-drained soil. Propagation is by seeds or division in early spring. Seeds should be sown in a cold frame or a nursery row in April for planting the following spring.

CULTIVARS

'Bright Star'. Flower heads to 20 cm. across; ray flowers lavender pink.
'Crimson Star'. Ray flowers crimson.
'The King'. Ray flowers old rose; disc flowers copper.
'White Luster'. Ray flowers white.

Echinops L. (Globe Thistle)

COMPOSITAE (Sunflower Family)

Carduus Tribe

DESCRIPTION: A large genus of about 100 species of biennial or perennial herbs, native from the Mediterranean region to central Asia; **leaves** in basal rosettes or alternate on the flowering stems, mostly pinnatifid or 2- to 3-pinnately dissected, with prickly margins; **flower** heads with 1 flower within its own involucre, but individual heads aggregated to form a dense, globe-shaped, compound head subtended by a common, reflexed involucre; flowers all tubular, blue or white; **achenes** 4-angled to nearly cylindrical, usually hairy.

Echinops ritro L. (Small Globe Thistle). Perennial to 1 m. tall. July, August.

DESCRIPTION: **Plants** with white-woolly stems, native in eastern Europe and Western Asia; **leaves** oblong in outline; to 20 cm. long, pinnately dissected into lanceolate, spiny-toothed segments, green and glossy above, white-woolly beneath; **flowers** bright blue, in heads to 4 cm. across.

USE: A bold accent plant to use toward the back of the flower border.

CULTURE: Plants are of easy culture in a sunny location. The plants are about as wide as tall so allow room for them to develop. Propagation is either by seeds or division in early spring.

Echinops — other species

E. exaltatus Schrad. (Russian Globe Thistle), native in Russia, is similar to *E. rito* but a little coarser. It grows to a height of 1.5 m.　　PLATE 95

E. humilis Bieb. (Siberian Globe Thistle), native in western Asia, grows to a height of 30 cm. and has small, blue flower heads. 'Taplow Blue', with metallic blue flowers, and 'Taplow Purple', with purple flowers, are usually assigned to this species.

Eichhornia Kunth.

PONTEDERIACEAE (Pickerel Weed Family)

DESCRIPTION: A small genus of about 7 species of aquatic herbs, native in tropical America; **leaves** floating or submerged; **flowers** showy, in terminal spikes; **fruit** a capsule.

Eichhornia crassipes (Mart.) Solms-Laub. (Water Hyacinth). Tender perennial to 20 cm. tall. July, August.　　PLATE 96

DESCRIPTION: Floating aquatic **plants**, native in tropical America; **leaf** blades ovate to orbicular; petioles much inflated, serving as floats; **flowers** violet, large and showy, in terminal spikes; upper lobe of perianth segments with a yellow-centered bluish patch.

USE: Sometimes planted in shallow water in pools or streams.

CULTURE: This tender perennnial must be wintered indoors in a tank of water or new plants must be purchased each spring. The plants grow well in shallow water where the roots can grow down into the mud. The floating leaves and the showy flowers add interest to this aquatic plant. In the South this plant multiplies rapidly and often impedes navigation on streams and lakes.

Endymion Dumort. (Wood Hyacinth)

LILIACEAE (Lily Family)

DESCRIPTION: A small genus of 3 or 4 species of bulbous, herbaceous **plants**, native in western Europe and northwestern Africa; **bulbs tunicate, renewed** yearly; **leaves** 6 to 9, all basal; **flowers** campanulate to rotate, blue, pink, or white, subtended by 2 bracts, produced in a raceme; perianth segments 6, united at the base; stamens 6; **fruit** a 3-valved capsule.

Endymion hispanicus (Mill.) Chouard (Spanish Bluebell). Perennial to 50 cm. tall. May.

DESCRIPTION: **Plants** native in Spain, Portugal, and northwestern Africa; **leaves** strap-shaped, to 60 cm. long; **flowers** campanulate, blue to rose-purple, to 2 cm. across, in erect racemes; anthers blue.

USE: Plant in woodland wildflower garden.

CULTURE: The leaves of the Spanish bluebell die down after the seeds mature, leaving a bare spot during the summer and fall. For this reason it is recommended that the bulbs be planted among ferns. The plants come up and bloom before the ferns are fully developed. Plant the bulbs about 10 cm. apart and 15 cm. deep in the fall as soon as the bulbs can be purchased.

CULTIVARS
'Alba Maxima'. Flowers white.
'Blue Queen'. Flowers porcelain blue.
'Rose Queen'. Flowers clear rose.

Endymion — other species

E. non-scriptus (L.) Garcke (English Bluebell), native in western Europe, is quite similar to *E. hispanicus* but the flowers are smaller.   PLATE 97

Epimedium L. (Barrenwort)

BERBERIDACEAE (Barberry Family)

DESCRIPTION: A genus of about 21 species of low, rhizomatous, perennial herbs, native in Europe and Asia; **leaves** small, pinnately or ternately divided; **flowers** small, in simple or compound inflorescences; sepals 8, the outer 4 unequal, in 2 pairs, soon falling, the inner 4 petaloid, spreading or reflexed; petals 4, flat and either petal-like or extended into pouches or spurs; stamens 4.

Epimedium grandiflorum C. Morr. (Longspur Epimedium). Perennial to 30 cm. tall. May, June.

DESCRIPTION: **Plants** native in Japan, Korea, and Manchuria; **leaves** biternate or triternate; **flowers** red to violet, to 5 cm. across; spurs to 2.5 cm. long.
USE: An excellent ground cover for shady areas.

CULTURE: Plants are of easy culture in a cool, moist soil high in organic matter, in partial shade. Propagation is by division of the plants in early spring.

CULTIVARS
'Macranthum'. Flowers rose pink.
'Niveum'. Flowers white.
'Rose Queen'. Flowers rose colored.

Epimedium macranthum —see *Epimedium grandiflorum* 'Macranthum'

Epimedium x *youngianum* Fisch. & C. A. Mey. Perennial to 60 cm. tall. May, June.

DESCRIPTION: **Plants** of hybrid origin developed by crossing *E. diphyllum* x *E. grandiflorum*; **flowers** white or rose, to 2 cm. across, pendulous.

USE: Same as for *E. grandiflorum*.

CULTURE: Same as for *E. grandiflorum*.

CULTIVARS
'Niveum'. Flowers white.
'Roseum'. Flowers rose lilac.
'Sulphureum'. Flowers light yellow.

Epimedium —other species

E. alpinum L. (Alpine Epimedium), native in southern Europe, has red sepals in May and June. A good rock garden plant.

E. pinnatum Fisch. (Persian Epimedium), native in northern Iran and the Caucasus, has yellow sepals and red petals in May and June.

E. x *rubrum* C. Morr. (Red Epimedium) is a hybrid resulting from a cross between *E. alpinum* and *E. grandiflorum*. It has red sepals and yellow petals tinged with red.

E. x *versicolor* C. Morr. Resulted from a cross between *E. grandiflorum* and *E. pinnatum*. It has rose sepals and yellow petals tinged with red. 'Sulphureum' is a named cultivar with pale yellow flowers.

Eranthis Salisb. (Winter Aconite)

RANUNCULACEAE (Buttercup Family)

DESCRIPTION: A small genus of about 7 species of low perennial herbs with short, fleshy tubers, native in Europe and Asia; **leaves** basal, palmately dissected;

involucral leaves sessile; **flowers** solitary, yellow or white, sessile above the involucre or pedicelled; sepals 5 to 8; petal-like; petals modified into small nectaries; stamens many; pistils few to many; **fruit** of many-seeded follicles.

Eranthis hyemalis Salisb. (Winter Aconite). Perennial to 15 cm. tall. April, May.

DESCRIPTION: **Plants** glabrous, native in southern Europe; basal **leaves** mostly solitary with 3 to 5 lobes, then cut into narrow segments; involucre spreads horizontally; **flowers** sessile on involucre, yellow, to 2.5 cm. across; **follicles** brown, to 1.6 cm. long, stipitate.

USE: Plant in a rock garden or under trees and shrubs near the edge of the lawn.

CULTURE: The winter aconite likes a well-drained soil and partial shade. Plant the tubers in the fall in late September or early October. Mulch the planting area in November to provide winter protection.

Eranthis — other species

E. cilicica Schott. & Kotschy., native in Greece and Asia Minor, is similar to *E. hyemalis* but smaller. A good rock garden plant.

Eremurus Bieb. (Desert-candle)

LILIACEAE (Lily Family)

DESCRIPTION: A genus of about 40 species of perennial herbs, native to western and central Asia; **leaves** basal, narrow, forming rosettes; **flowers** white, pink, yellow, orange, or brown, in racemes terminating long scapes; perianth segments 6, almost completely separate; stamens 6; **fruit** a 3-celled capsule with many seeds.

Eremurus bungei — see *Eremurus stenophyllus*

Eremurus stenophyllus (Boiss. & Buhse.) Bak. (Foxtail Lily). Perennial to 1.5 m. tall. June.   PLATE 98

DESCRIPTION: **Plants** native in Persia; **leaves** linear, to 30 cm. long, glabrous, ciliate on margins; **flowers** yellow, about 2.5 cm. across, opening from the bottom of the raceme upwards.

USE: An interesting accent plant for the sunny border.

CULTURE: The foxtail lily likes a well-drained soil and full sun. Mixing in liberal quantities of well-rotted manure or leaf compost will produce the most attractive plants. Propagation is by seeds sown as soon as ripe or by fall division of the crowns. The fleshy, yellow roots are quite brittle, so the plants must be carefully divided. A winter mulch should be used.

Erigeron L. (Fleabane)

COMPOSITAE (Sunflower Family)

Aster Tribe

DESCRIPTION: A large genus of about 200 species of annual, biennial, or perennial herbs, mostly native in North America; **leaves** alternate or basal; **flower** heads mostly radiate, solitary or in corymbs or panicles; involucre campanulate to hemispherical; involucral bracts in 1 or 2 rows, narrow, from nearly equal and herbaceous to overlapping and scarcely herbaceous; receptacle flat, naked; disc flowers perfect, yellow; ray flowers in 2 rows, pistillate, narrow, white to pink, blue, or purple, rarely orange or yellow; **achenes** compressed, with a pappus of capillary bristles.

Erigeron speciosus (Lindl.) DC. (Oregon Fleabane). Perennial to 75 cm. tall. June, July.

DESCRIPTION: **Plants** native from British Columbia to Alberta, south to Arizona and South Dakota; basal **leaves** oblanceolate to spatulate, narrowed to a winged petiole, entire; stem leaves mostly lanceolate, sessile; **flower** heads to 4 cm. across with hairy involucral bracts; ray flowers blue or white, up to 150.

USE: An attractive border plant for its spring and summer bloom.

CULTURE: Plant in a well-drained soil in full sun. Propagation is by division of mature plants in early spring.

CULTIVARS

'Azure Fairy'. Flowering heads semi-double; ray flowers lavender.

'Foerster's Liebling'. Flowering heads semi-double; ray flowers pink.

'Pink Jewel'. Ray flowers baby pink.

Erigeron — other species

E. aurantiacus Regel. (Double Orange Daisy), native in Turkestan, has orange ray flowers in semi-double heads. It is only about 20 cm. tall and makes a good rock garden plant.

E. compositus Pursh. (Fernleaf Fleabane), native in western Idaho and eastern Oregon, is a low, tufted plant with white, pink, or blue ray flowers. Suitable for rock gardens.

Erigeron —garden hybrids

A number of garden hybrids are on the market. These are mostly hybrids of *E. speciosus* crossed with other species.

CULTIVARS

'Azure Beauty'. Flowering heads double; ray flowers blue.
'Blue Beauty'. Flowering heads single; ray flowers blue.
'Pink Jewel'. Flowering heads large; ray flowers pink.
'Prosperity'. Flowering heads semi-double; ray flowers sky blue.
'Red Beauty'. Flowering heads single; ray flowers red.

Erinus L.

SCROPHULARIACEAE (Figwort Family)

DESCRIPTION: A small genus of only 2 species of perennial herbs, native in western and central Europe and North Africa; **leaves** alternate; **flowers** in simple racemes; calyx 5-parted; corolla 5-lobed; stamens 4; **fruit** a capsule.

Erinus alpinus L. (Liver Balsam). Perennial to 15 cm. tall. May, June.

DESCRIPTION: **Plants** tufted, native in the mountains of western and central Europe; **leaves** spatulate, to 4 cm. long, coarsely toothed; **flowers** purple, to 1.25 cm. across, in racemes to 6 cm. long.

USE: A good rock garden plant.

CULTURE: Plants require a well-drained soil and prefer partial shade. Propagation is by seeds sown in a sandy soil in a cold frame in May, or seeds can be mixed with sand and sown in rock crevices. Plants are usually short-lived so it is necessary to have young plants grown from seed to replace plants that die.

CULTIVAR

'Albus'. Flowers white.

Eryngium L. (Eryngo, Sea Holly)

UMBELLIFERAE (Carrot Family)

DESCRIPTION: A genus of about 200 species of perennial herbs, native in many parts of the world; **leaves** simple, spiny-toothed and variously lobed, or divided; **flowers** small, white or blue, sessile, in dense, bracted heads; **fruit** ovoid, usually scaly.

Eryngium amethystinum L. (Amethyst Sea Holly, Amethyst Eryngo). Perennial to 60 cm. tall. July, August.

DESCRIPTION: **Plants** native in Europe; **leaves** obovate, 2-pinnate; **flowers** blue, in bracted heads; bracts long, lancoeolate.

USE: Plant in sunny flower border for its hollylike leaves and blue flowers.

CULTURE: Plants grow best in a rich fertile loam soil that is well drained. Propagation is by seeds started in a sandy soil as soon as ripe. Transplant the seedlings to their permanent location as soon as they are large enough. Once established, the plants should not be disturbed.

Eryngium yuccifolium Michx. (Rattlesnake-master, Button Snake-root). Perennial to 1 m. tall. July, August.   PLATE 99

DESCRIPTION: **Plants** native from Minnesota to Connecticut, south to Texas and Florida; **leaves** linear, rigid, bristly; **flowers** white, in bracted heads.

USE: Same as for *E. amethystinum*.

CULTURE: Same as for *E. amethystinum*.

Eryngium — other species

E. alpinum L. (Bluetop Eryngo), native in Europe, has blue or white flowers in July and August on plants that are about 80 cm. tall.

E. giganteum Bieb. (Stout Eryngo), native in the Caucasus, grows to a height of 2 m. The leaves are silvery gray and the flower heads with blue or pale green flowers are surrounded by large silvery bracts. This species should be planted toward the back of the flower border.

E. planum L., native in Europe and Asia, has steel blue flowers in bracted heads with narrow, rigid bracts. Plants are about 90 cm. tall.

Erysimum L. (Wallflower)

CRUCIFERAE (Mustard Family)

DESCRIPTION: A genus of about 80 species of annual, biennial, and perennial herbs, native in the northern hemisphere; **stems** with branched hairs; **leaves** entire to sinuate-dentate; **flowers** showy, lemon-yellow to golden or orange, or reddish to purple, in crowded racemes; sepals and petals 4; **fruit** an elongate, linear silique.

Erysimum asperum (Nutt.) DC (Western Wallflower). Perennial to
1 m. tall. May, June.   PLATE 100

DESCRIPTION: **Plants** native in western America and as far east as Ohio;
leaves lanceolate, to 10 cm. long, entire or lower leaves remotely toothed;
flowers orange to yellow.

USE: A colorful plant for mass planting in a sunny flower border.

CULTURE: Plants like a well-drained soil and full sun. Propagation is by
seeds. Seeds should be planted about June 1 in a cold frame, and the seedlings
transplanted to the flower border in early spring. Plants may be short-lived.

Erysimum hieraciifolium L. (Siberian Wallflower). Biennial or perennial to 1 m. tall. May, June.

DESCRIPTION: **Plants** native in north central and eastern Europe; **leaves**
linear or oblong, sinuate-dentate, gray or green; **flowers** golden-yellow, in spikelike racemes; **siliques** to 5 cm. long.

USE: Same as for *E. asperum.*

CULTURE: Same as for *E. asperum.*

CULTIVAR
'Golden Bedder'. Flowers golden yellow.

Erythronium L. (Dogtooth Violet, Trout Lily)

LILIACEAE (Lily Family)

DESCRIPTION: A small genus of about 25 species of spring-flowering perennial herbs with membranous-coated corms, native mostly in temperate
America, Europe, and Asia; **leaves** 2, mostly basal, often mottled; **flowers** white,
yellow, pink, rose, or purple, nodding, solitary or several in a raceme; perianth
segments 6, separate, usually recurved; stamens 6; **fruit** a 3-valved capsule.

Erythronium albidum Nutt. (White Dogtooth Violet). Perennial to
30 cm. tall. May.

DESCRIPTION: **Plants** native from Minnesota to Ontario, south to Texas and
Kentucky; **leaves** elliptic, to 15 cm. long, green or rarely mottled; **flowers**
white with a yellow spot at the base of perianth segments, solitary; anthers
creamy white; stigma deeply lobed with spreading lobes.

USE: Plant in woodland wildflower garden or in a shaded portion of the rock
garden.

CULTURE: Plants are of easy culture in a well-drained soil in light shade. Plant the corms in the fall in late September or early October, spacing them about 10 cm. apart and cover with about 6 cm. of soil. The leaves die down soon after flowering. Except for weeding, the soil should not be disturbed during the dormant season. Plants can also be grown from seed but it will take several years for the corms to reach a flowering size.

Erythronium americanum Ker. Gawl. (Yellow Adder's tongue). Perennial to 30 cm. tall. May.

DESCRIPTION: **Plants** native from Minnesota to Nova Scotia, south to Alabama and Florida; **leaves** elliptic to 15 cm. long, mottled with brown; **flowers** yellow, solitary to 5 cm. long; anthers brown or yellow; stigma with short lobes.

USE: Same as for *E. albidum*.

CULTURE: Same as for *E. albidum*.

Erythronium — other species

E. californicum Purdy (California Fawn Lily), native in the coastal mountains of California, has large, white to cream-colored flowers to 3.5 cm. long in May. A winter mulch is recommended.

E. grandiflorum Pursh. (Avalanche Lily), native in the northwestern United States and British Columbia, has large, golden yellow flowers with red or maroon anthers. A winter mulch is recommended. 'Album', with white flowers, and 'Robustum', with very large, yellow flowers, are named cultivars.

E. revolutum Sm. (Mahogany Fawn Lily), native from British Columbia to northern California, has large, rose pink flowers to 4 cm. long. 'Pagoda', with canary gold flowers, 'Rose Beauty', with deep rose-colored flowers with orange centers, and 'White Beauty', with pure white flowers with red centers, are named cultivars.   PLATE 101

Escholtzia Cham. (California Poppy)

PAPAVARACEAE (Poppy Family)

DESCRIPTION: A small genus of about 10 species of annual or perennial herbs with a watery sap, native in western North America; **leaves** alternate, mostly glabrous, much-dissected; **flowers** yellow to orange red; sepals 2, forming a hoodlike cap that is pushed off by the opening 4 petals; stamens 16 or more; **fruit** a slender capsule.

Escholtzia californica Cham. (California Poppy). Tender perennial grown as an annual to 60 cm. tall. June, July.

DESCRIPTION: **Plants** glaucous and glabrous, native in California and Arizona; **leaves** much-dissected; **flowers** deep orange to pale yellow, to 5 cm. across; **capsule** to 10 cm. long.

USE: Plant in the flower border for spring bloom.

CULTURE: Plants prefer a well-drained soil and full sun. Although a perennial in the Southwest, it is grown as an annual in northern gardens. Seed should be sown early in the spring where plants are to bloom.

CULTIVARS

'Aurantiaca Orange'. Flowers rich orange.

'Ballerina Yellow'. Flowers semi-double, delicately fluted.

'Mission Bells'. Flowers double or semi-double in a wide color range. PLATE 102

Eupatorium L. (Boneset)

COMPOSITAE (Sunflower Family)

Eupatorium Tribe

DESCRIPTION: A large genus of about 500 species of mostly perennial herbs and shrubs, native chiefly in tropical America; **leaves** mostly opposite, sometimes whorled or alternate, usually petioled, linear to orbicular, entire or dissected; flowering heads numerous, in corymbs on panicles, discoid; involucral bracts overlapping in 2 or more rows; receptacle flat to convex or conical, naked; **flowers** all tubular, perfect, purple to rose-colored or white, never yellow; **achenes** usually 5-angled, with a pappus of a single row of capillary bristles.

Eupatorium coelestinum L. (Mist Flower, Hardy Ageratum, Blue Boneset). Perennial to 1 m. tall. July-October.   PLATE 103

DESCRIPTION: **Plants** rhizomatous, native from Kansas to New Jersey, south to Texas and Florida; **leaves** triangular-ovate, to 7.5 cm. long, coarsely toothed, sparsely hairy; **flower** heads in dense corymbs; receptacle conical; flowers blue to violet.

USE: Plant in perennial flower border or in a woodland wildflower garden.

CULTURE: Plants prefer a moist soil and partial shade. Propagation is largely by division or by cuttings taken in the spring soon after growth starts.

CULTIVAR

'Alba'. Flowers white.

Eupatorium — other species

E. maculatum L. (Spotted Joe-pye Weed), native in eastern North America, has purple flowers in August and September, and is sometimes planted in wet sites along a stream.

E. perfoliatum L. (Common Boneset), native in eastern North America, has white flowers in July and August. It is sometimes planted in woodland wildflower gardens.

E. purpureum L. (Green-stemmed Joe-pye Weed), native in eastern North America, has pink to purple flowers in August and September. It is sometimes planted in wet soils.

Euphorbia L. (Spurge)

EUPHORBIACEAE (Spurge Family)

DESCRIPTION: A very large genus with over 1,600 species of monoecious or dioecious herbs, shrubs, or trees, of wide distribution; **stems** often spiny and cactuslike; **leaves** opposite or whorled, simple, entire or toothed, petioled or sessile, sometimes rudimentary or absent; **flowers** imperfect, in a compound inflorescence called a cyathium that resembles a flower; cyathia solitary and terminal, or axillary, or clustered in cymes; involucre or cythium cup-shaped, with 5 inner lobes alternating with glands, sometimes with petaloid appendages; **fruit** a 3-valved capsule.

Euphorbia cyathophora J. Murr. (Mexican Fire Plant). Annual to 1 m. tall. August, September.

DESCRIPTION: **Plants** native in Mexico; **leaves** ovate to linear, sometimes fiddle-shaped, entire or toothed, glossy green; upper leaves and floral bracts becoming red or red at the base; **cyathia** in terminal clusters with 1 or 2 glands.

USE: Plant in sunny flower border for the colored bracts.

CULTURE: Easy to grow in any well-drained soil. Sow seeds early in the spring where plants are to grow. Thin the seedlings so plants are spaced about 30 cm. apart.

Euphorbia epithymoides L. (Cushion Spurge). Perennial to 30 cm. tall. April, May.   PLATE 104

DESCRIPTION: **Plants** mound-shaped, native in eastern Europe; **leaves** oblong, dark green; **cyathea** in umbel-like cymes; involucral bracts yellow with 2 to 4 glands.

USE: This is a colorful plant in a rock garden.

CULTURE: Plants thrive in any well-drained soil in full sun. Propagation is by division in the spring of the year or by seeds started in a nursery row in May.

Euphorbia heterophylla —see *Euphorbia cyathophora*

Euphorbia marginata Pursh. (Snow-on-the-mountain). Annual to 60 cm. tall. July, August.

DESCRIPTION: **Plants** native from Montana to Minnesota, south to New Mexico and Missouri; **leaves** ovate to oblong, to 8 cm. long; upper leaves with white margins; **cyathia** white, with petal-like appendages.

USE: Sometimes planted for its variegated leaves.

CULTURE: This annual likes a well-drained soil and full sun. Seeds are sown in early spring directly where plants are to grow. Thin the seedlings to 30 cm. apart. The snow-on-the-mountain has a milky sap and handling the plants can cause a skin irritation on some people. Seedlings may volunteer.

CULTIVAR

'Summer Icicle'. Leaves with broad white margins.

Euphorbia polychroma —see *Euphorbia epithymoides*

Euphorbia variegata —see *Euphorbia marginata*

Euphorbia —other species

E. *corollata* L. (Flowering Spurge), native from Ontario south to Texas and Florida, has white bracts in May and June.

E. *cyparissias* L. (Cypress Spurge), native in Europe and often escaped from cultivation, has yellow bracts in May and June, and finely divided leaves.

E. *myrsinites* L. (Myrtle Spurge), native in Europe, has yellow cyathia and bracts in May and June.

Filipendula Mill. (Meadowsweet)

ROSACEAE (Rose Family)

DESCRIPTION: A small genus of hardy perennial herbs, native in the North Temperate Zone; **leaves** alternate, usually pinnate; **flowers** many, small, in terminal corymbose panicles on leafy stems; sepals and petals usually 5; stamens many; pistils 5 to 15; **fruit** an achene.

Filipendula hexapetala — see *Filipendula vulgaris*

Filipendula rubra (J. Hill.) B. L. Robinson (Queen-of-the-prairie, Prairie Meadowsweet). Perennial to 2 m. tall. June-August.   PLATE 105

DESCRIPTION: **Plants** native from Iowa to Pennsylvania, south to Illinois and Georgia; **leaves** interruptedly pinnate, green and scarcely paler beneath; terminal leaflets 10 to 20 cm. across, 7- to 9-parted, the lobes lanceolate-oblong, incised; **flowers** deep peach blossom pink.

USE: Plant toward the back of the flower border, in a prairie garden, or along a stream.

CULTURE: A sun-loving perennial that thrives in most garden soils. It tolerates light shade. Plants have a tendency to spread so do not plant if space is limited. The fluffy pink flowers are very showy. Propagation is by seeds or division of old clumps in early spring.

CULTIVARS
'Venusta'. Flowers deep rose or purplish red.
'Venusta Magnificum Album'. Flowers white.

Filipendula ulmaria (L.) Maxim. (Queen-of-the-meadow, European Meadowsweet). Perennial to 2 m. tall. June-August.

DESCRIPTION: **Plants** native in Europe and Asia, naturalized in eastern North America; **leaves** to 20 cm. long, with 2 to 5 pairs of lateral leaflets and a terminal leaflet; leaflets doubly serrate and white-tomentose underneath; **flowers** creamy white.

USE: Same as for *F. rubra*.

CULTURE: Same as for *F. rubra*.

CULTIVARS
'Aureo-variegata'. Leaves variegated with yellow.
'Flore Plena'. Flowers double.

Filipendula venusta — see *Filipendula rubra* 'Venusta'

Filipendula vulgaris Moench (Dropwort). Perennial to 1 m. tall. June-August.

DESCRIPTION: **Plants** with tuberous rootstock, native in Europe and Asia; **leaves** glabrous, to 25 cm. long, fernlike; leaflets many, pinnatifid, to about 2.5 cm. long; stipules broad; **flowers** white, often tinged red on outside, to 2 cm. across.

USE: Same as for *F. rubra*.

CULTURE: Same as for *F. rubra*.

CULTIVARS

'Flore Plena'. Flowers double.

'Grandiflora'. Flowers creamy yellow, larger than in species.

Flipendula —other species

F. purpurea Maxim., native in Japan, has flowers that are carmine to pink in June and July. 'Alba', with white flowers, and 'Nana', which is a dwarf, are named cultivars.

Fritillaria L. (Fritillary)

LILIACEAE (Lily Family)

DESCRIPTION: A genus of about 100 species of spring-flowering, bulbous, perennial herbs, native in western North America, Europe, Asia, and northern Africa; **bulbs** tunicate or with 1 or more fleshy scales, sometimes with ricelike bulblets; **leaves** alternate, opposite, or whorled; **flowers** of various colors, sometimes checkered, nodding, funnelform to campanulate, solitary or in terminal racemes or umbels; perianth segments 6, separate; stamens 6; style 1, entire to 3-parted; **fruit** a 3-valved capsule, sometimes 6-winged or 6-angled, with many, flat seeds.

Fritillaria imperialis L. (Crown-imperial Fritillary). Short-lived perennial to 1 m. tall. April, May.

DESCRIPTION: **Plants** with a skunklike odor, native in northern India and Afghanistan; bulbs to 15 cm. across, with several scales; **leaves** alternate, lanceolate, to 15 cm. long; **flowers** red orange, to 5 cm. long, pendent on curved pedicels, produced in a whorl below a tuft of leaves at the top of a naked peduncle.

USE: Plant in the flower border.

CULTURE: Plants require a deep, fertile soil high in organic matter. Bulbs should be planted 15 cm. deep in late September or early October. The plants are of borderline hardiness so a winter mulch is required. Plants may be short-lived.

CULTIVARS

'Aurora'. Flowers red with a coppery overlay.

'Lutea'. Flowers yellow.

'Maxima'. Flowers larger than in species.

A good combination of lawn, flowers, and Minnesota's white birc

Photographs on the next five pages courtesy of the Minneso
State Horticultural Society, exceptions note

Flower border fea
sweet alyssum, lo
and dahlias.

Border of annuals and perennials edged with sweet alyssum.

Entrance steps
flanked by flowers.

Curved border featuring spring bulbs.

Mixed flower border by a gardener trained in England. Photograph by the author.

A curved flower border in midsummer.

An interesting border featuring sculpture and flowers.

A mixed flower border.

Annual flowers with a rose trellis background in the
Minnesota Landscape Arboretum. Photograph by the author.

1. *Achillea filipendula* 'Gold Plate' (Fern-leaf Yarrow) – shape and flowers.

2. *Achillea millefolium* 'Fire King' (Common Yarrow) – shape and flowers.

Aconitum carmichaelii (Azure
nkshood) — shape and flowers

4. *Actaea rubra* (Red Baneberry) — fruits

5. *Adonis vernalis* (Spring Adonis) —
shape and flowers

1egopodium podagraria 'Variegata'
veredge Goutweed) — shape and leaves

7. *Agastache foeniculum* (Anise Giant
Hyssop) — shape and flowers

1geratum houstonianum 'Blue Blazer'
ossflower) — shape and flowers

9. *Ajuga reptans* 'Burgundy Glow' (Carpet
Bugleweed) — shape and leaves

10. *Alcea rosea* 'Silver Puffs' (Hollyhock) —
shape and flowers

11. *Alchemilla vulgaris* (Common Lady's-
mantle) — shape and flowers

12. *Allium giganteum* (Giant Garlic) — flowers

13. *Allium karataviense* (Turkestan Onion) —
shape and flowers

14. *Allium senescens* — shape and flowers

15. *Amaranthus tricolor* 'Molten Fire'
(Joseph's-coat) — shape and flowers

16. *Amsonia tabernaemontana* (Bluestar) —
shape and flowers

17. *Anaphalis margaritacea* (Pearly
Everlasting) — shape and flowers

19. *Anemone halleri* (Haller's Pasqueflower) — shape and flowers

Anemone blanda (Greek Anemone) —)e and flowers

20. *Anemone patens* (American Pasqueflower) — shape and flower

Anemone sylvestris 'Grandiflora' owdrop Anemone) — shape and flowers

22. *Anemonella thallictroides* 'Shoaf's Double Pink' (Double Rue Anemone) — shape and flowers

Anthemis tinctoria 'Moonlight' (Golden rguerite) — shape and flowers

24. *Antirrhinum majus* 'Cream Puff' (Snapdragon) — shape and flowers

25. *Aquilegia* x *hybrida* (McKana strain of Garden Columbine) — shape and flowers

26. *Arabis alpina* (Mountain Rock Cress) — shape and flowers

27. *Arenaria montana* (Mountain Sandwort) — shape and flowers

28. *Arisaema triphyllum* (Jack-in-the-pulpit) shape and flowers

29. *Armeria maritima* (Common Thrift) — shape and flowers

30. *Artemisia schmidtiana* 'Nana' (Silver Mound Sage) — shape

31. *Asarum canadense* (Canada Wild Ginger) shape and leaves

Asclepias tuberosa (Butterfly Weed) — ~~e and flowers~~

33. *Aster alpinus* 'Happy End' (Alpine Aster) — flowers

Aster x 'Snow Cushion' (Garden Hybrid ~~r~~) — shape and flowers

35. *Astilbe* x *arendsii* (Garden Astilbe) — shape and flowers

Aubrieta deltoidea (Purple Rock ~~ss~~) — shape and flowers

38. *Baptisia australis* (Blue False Indigo) — shape and flowers

Aurinia saxatilis (Basket of Gold) — ~~e and flowers~~

39. *Begonia* x *semperflorens – cultorum*
(Wax Begonia) – shape and flowers

40. *Begonia* x *tuberhybrida* (Tuberous
Begonia) – shape and flowers

41. *Belamcanda chinensis* (Blackberry
Lily) – flowers

42. *Bergenia* x *schmidtii* – shape and flowers

43. *Browallia speciosa* (Lovely Browallia) –
shape and flowers

44. *Caladium* x *hortulanum* (Fancy-leaved
Caladium) – shape and leaves

45. *Calendula officinalis* (Pot Marigold) –
shape and flowers

46. *Callistephus chinensis* (Rainbow strain
of China Aster) – shape and leaves

altha palustris (Marsh Marigold) —
and flowers

48. *Campanula carpatica* (Carpathian
Bellflower) — shape and flowers

Campanula glomerata var. *dahurica*
urian Bellflower) — shape and flowers

50. *Campanula rotundifolia* (Bluebell) — flowers

52. *Catharanthus roseus* 'Little Bright Eyes'
(Rose Periwinkle) — shape and flowers

Canna x *generalis* (Common Garden
a) — shape and flowers

53. *Celosia cristata* 'Golden Triumph' (Woolflower — Plumosa Group) — shape and flowers

54. *Celosia cristata* (Woolflower—Cockscomb Group)—shape and flowers

55. *Centaurea cyanus* 'Blue Diadem' (Bachelor's-button)—shape and flowers

56. *Centaurea macrocephala* (Globe Centaurea)—shape and flowers

57. *Chelone obliqua* (Rose Turtlehead)—shape and flowers

58. *Chionodoxa luciliae* (Glory-of-the-snow)—shape and flowers

59. *Chrysanthemum coccineum* (Painted Daisy)—shape and flowers

60. *Chrysanthemum* x *morifolium* (Garden Chrysanthemum)—Arboretum collection

Chrysanthemum parthenium 'Gold Boy'
rfew) — shape and flowers

62. *Chrysanthemum* x *superbum* 'Riestern'
(Shasta Daisy) — shape and flowers

imicifuga americana (American
ane) — shape and flowers

64. *Claytonia virginica* (Spring Beauty) —
shape and flowers

lematis recta var. *mandschurica* (Man-
ian Ground Clematis) — shape and flowers

66. *Cleome hasslerana* 'Rose Queen' (Spider
Flower) — shape and flowers

Clintonia borealis (Bluebead Lily) —
e and flowers

68. *Colchicum autumnale* (Autumn
Crocus) — flowers

69. *Coleus* x *hybridus* (Garden Coleus) —leaves

70. *Coreopsis verticillata* 'Sunray' (Threadle Coreopsis) —shape and flowers

71. *Coronilla varia* (Crown Vetch) —mass planting in bloom

72. *Corydalis lutea* (Yellow Corydalis) — shape and flowers

73. *Coryphantha vivipara* (Nipple Cactus) — shape and flowers

75. *Crocus vernus* (Dutch Crocus) — shape and flowers

74. *Cosmos sulphureus* 'Diablo' (Yellow Cosmos) —flowers

yclamen hederifolium (Baby
men) — shape and flowers

77. *Cynoglossum amabile* (Chinese Forget-
me-not) — shape and flowers

Cypripedium acaule (Pink Lady's-slipper) —
: and flowers

79. *Cypripedium arietinum* (Ram's-head
Lady's-slipper) — shape and flowers

80. *Cypripedium calceolus* (Yellow Lady's-slipper) — shape and flowers

81. *Cypripedium reginae* (Showy Lady's-slipper) – shape and flowers

82. *Dahlia* x 'Gerry Hoeck' (Garden Dahlia) – shape and flowers

83. *Delphinium* x *cultorum* (Garden Delphinium) – shape and flowers

84. *Dianthus caryophyllus* (Carnation) – shape and flowers

Dianthus chinensis 'Snowfire' (Rainbow Pinks) – shape and flowers

Dicentra eximia (Wild Bleeding-heart) –
ɔe and flowers

87. *Dicentra spectabilis* (Common Bleeding-
heart) – flowers

88. *Dictamnus albus* 'Rubra' (Gas Plant) —
shape and flowers

89. *Digitalis purpurea* 'Foxy' (Common
Foxglove) — shape and flowers

90. *Dodecatheon meadia* (Common
Shooting-Star) — shape and flowers

91. *Doronicum cordatum* (Heartleaf
Leopard's-bane) — shape and flowers

92. *Draba dedeana* (Dede Draba) —
shape and flowers

93. *Dryas octopetala* (Mountain Avens) —
shape and flowers

Echinacea purpurea (Purple Coneflower) —
e and flowers

95. *Echinops exaltatus* (Russian Globe
Thistle) — flowers

Eichhornia crassipes (Water Hyacinth) —
e and flowers

97. *Endymion non-scriptus* (English Bluebell) —
shape and flowers

Eremurus stenophyllus (Foxtail Lily) —
e and flowers

99. *Eryngium yuccifolium* (Rattlesnake-
master) — shape and flowers

100. *Erysimum asperum* (Western
Wallflower) — shape and flowers

101. *Erythronium revolutum* (Mahogany Fawn Lily) — shape and flowers

102. *Escholtzia californica* 'Mission Bells' (California Poppy) — shape and flowers

103. *Eupatorium coelestinum* (Mist Flower) — flowers

104. *Euphorbia epithymoides* (Cushion Spruge) — shape and flowers

105. *Filipendula rubra* (Queen-of-the-prairie) — shape and flowers

106. *Gaillardia* x *grandiflora* 'Baby Cole' (Blanket Flower) — flowers

107. *Galanthus nivalis* (Common Snowdrop) — shape and flowers

108. *Gazania ringens* 'Golden Marguerite' (Treasure Flower) — flowers

Gentiana andrewsii (Bottle
an) —flowers

110. *Geranium sanguincum* (Bloodred
Geranium) —shape and flowers

Gillenia trifoliata (Indian-physic) —
: and flowers

112. *Gomphrena globosa* 'Rubra' (Common
Globe Amaranth) —shape and flowers

Gyposophila paniculata 'Compacta'
umon Baby's-breath) —shape and flowers

114. *Helenium autumnale* 'Butterpat
(Common Sneezeweed) —flowers

Helianthus annuus 'Teddy Bear' (Common
lower) —shape and flowers

116. *Heliopsis helianthoides* subsp. *scabra* (False
Sunflower) —shape and flowers

117. *Heliotropium arborescens* (Heliotrope) —
shape and flowers

118. *Helleborus niger* (Christmas Rose) —
shape and flowers

119. *Hemerocallis* x 'Pink Orchid' (Daylily) — shape and flowers

120. *Hepatica acutiloba* (Sharplobe Liverleaf) —
shape and flowers

121. *Hesperis matronalis* (Sweet Rocket) —
shape and flowers

Heuchera sanguinea (Coralbells) —
: and flowers

123. *Hibiscus* x 'Southern Belle' (Garden
Hybrid Hibiscus) — flowers

124. *Hosta crispula* (Plantain Lily) —
shape and leaves

Hosta **'Honeybells'** (Fragrant Plantain
—shape and flowers

Hosta sieboldiana (Seersucker Plantain
) —shape and leaves

127. *Hosta* x 'Betsy King' (Hybrid Plantain
Lily) —shape and flowers

128. *Hosta* x 'Royal Standard' (Hybrid Plantain Lily) — shape and flowers

129. *Hunnemannia fumariifolia* (Mexican Tulip Poppy) — shape and flowers

130. *Hyacinthus orientalis* (Dutch Hyacinth) — shape and flowers

131. *Hymenocallis narcissiflora* (Peruvian Daffodil) — shape and flowers

132. *Iberis sempervirens* (Evergreen Candytuft) — shape and flowers

133. *Impatiens platyphylla* 'Tangerine' (Java Snapweed) — shape and flowers

134. *Impatiens wallerana* (Patience Plant) — shape and flowers

135. *Incarvillea delavayi* (Hardy Gloxinia) — flowers

nula ensifolia (Swordleaf Sunray) –
and flowers

137. *Ipomoea tricolor* 'Heavenly Blue'
(Morning Glory) – flowers

Ipomopsis rubra (Scarlet Gilia) –
and flowers

139. *Iris Kaempferi* (Japanese Iris) –
shape and flowers

Iris sibirica 'Silver Tip' (Siberian Iris) –
and flowers

141. *Iris spuria* (Butterfly Iris) –
shape and flowers

Iris versicolor (Blue Flag) – flowers

143. *Iris* 'Sunworshiper' (Hybrid Bearded
Iris) – flowers

144. *Jeffersonia diphylla* (American Twinleaf) —shape and flowers

145. *Kochia scoparia* f. *trichophylla* (Summ Cypress) —shape

146. *Lathyrus odoratus* (Sweet Pea) —shape and flowers

147. *Lavatera trimestris* (Herb Tree Mallow) —flowers

148. *Liatris spicata* (Spike Gay-feather) — shape and flowers

149. *Lilium canadense* (Canada Lily) —shape and flowers showing turk's-cap type

150. *Lilium philadelphicum* (Wood Lily) —sh and flowers showing upfacing type

Lilium regale (Regal Lily) — shape and
ers showing trumpet type

152. *Lilium* x 'Connecticut King' (Hybrid
Lily) — shape and flowers showing upfacing type

Lilium x 'Orange Light' (Hybrid Lily) —
e and flowers showing upfacing type

154. *Linaria alpina* 'Fairy Delight' (Alpine
Toadflax) — shape and flowers

Linnaea borealis (Twinflower) —
e and flowers

. *Lithospermum canescens* (Hoary
coon) — shape and flowers

157. *Lobelia cardinalis* (Cardinal
Flower) — flowers

158. *Lobelia erinus* (Edging Lobelia) –
shape and flowers

160. *Lobularia maritima* 'Carpet of Snow'
(Sweet Alyssum) – shape and flowers

159. *Lobelia siphilitica* (Blue Lobelia) –
flowers

161. *Lunaria annua* 'Variegata' (Variegated
Money Plant) – shape and flowers

162. *Lupinus perennis* (Wild Lupine) –
shape and flowers

163. *Lupinus* (Russell strain of hybrid lupine) –
shape and flowers

164. *Lychnis chalcedonica* (Maltese Cross) –
flowers

Lychnis viscaria (German Catchfly) – : and flowers

Lysichiton americanum (Yellow Skunk age) – shape and flowers

166. *Lycoris squamigera* (Magic Lily) – flowers

Lysimachia nummularia (Moneywort) – : and flowers

169. *Lysimachia vulgaris* (Garden Loosestrife) – shape and flowers

Lythrum x 'Columbia Pink' (Hybrid rum) – shape and flowers

171. *Maianthemum canadense* (False Lily-of-the-valley) – shape and flowers

172. *Matthiola incana* 'Dwarf Ten-week'
(Common Stock) – shape and flowers

173. *Mertensia virginica* (Virginia Bluebells)
flowers

174. *Mimulus moschatus* (Musk Plant) –
shape and flowers

175. *Mirabilis jalapa* (Four-o'clock) –
shape and flowers

177. *Monarda didyma* 'Cambridge Scarlet'
(Bee Balm) – shape and flowers

176. *Mitella diphylla* (Bishop's-cap) – flowers

Muscari botryoides 'Album' (White Grape inth) — shape and flowers

179. *Myosotis scorpioides* (True Forget-me-not) — shape and flowers

Narcissus x 'Kingscourt' (Hybrid odil) — flowers

180. *Narcissus bulbocodium* (Hoop-petticoat Daffodil) — shape and flowers

182. *Narcissus* x 'St. Louis' (Hybrid Daffodil) — flowers

Nelumbo lutea (American Lotus) — s and flowers

184. *Nelumbo nucifera* (Sacred Lotus) — leaves and flowers

185. *Nemophila menziesii* (Baby-blue-eyes) – shape and flowers

186. *Nicotiana alata* 'Nicki Red' (Flowering Tobacco) – shape and flowers

187. *Nierembergia hippomanica* 'Purple Robe' (Cupflower) – shape and flowers

188. *Nymphaea tuberosa* (Magnolia Water Lily) – leaves and flowers

189. *Nymphaea* (Tropical Hybrid Water Lily) – leaves and flowers

Nymphoides indica (Water Snowflake) —
s and flowers

Oenothera missouriensis (Ozark Gumbo
) —shape and flowers

Omphalodes cappadocica (Navelwort) —
e and flowers

191. *Ocimum basilicum* 'Dark Opal' (Common
Basil) —shape and leaves

194. *Opuntia humifusa* (Common Prickly Pear
Cactus) —shape and flowers

195. *Orchis spectabilis* (Showy Orchid) –
shape and flowers

196. *Oxalis violacea* (Violet Wood Sorrel) –
shape and flowers

197. *Pachysandra terminalis* (Japanese
Spurge) – shape and flowers

198. *Paeonia* x 'Sea Shell' (Hybrid Garden
Peony) – flowers

199. *Papaver nudicaule* (Iceland Poppy) –
shape and flowers

200. *Papaver orientale* 'Helen Elizabeth'
(Oriental Poppy) – shape and flowers

201. *Pelargonium* x *hortorum* 'Show Girl'
(Bedding Geranium) – flowers

2. *Pentstemon* (Hybrid Beard Tongue) – shape and flowers

204. *Petunia* x *hybrida* 'Blushing Maid'
(Grandiflora Type) – flowers

203. *Petalostemon purpureum* (Purple Prairie
Clover) – flowers

205. *Petunia* x *hybrida* 'Sugar Plum' (Multiflora Type) — shape and flowers

206. *Phaseolus coccineus* (Scarlet Runner Bean) — flowers

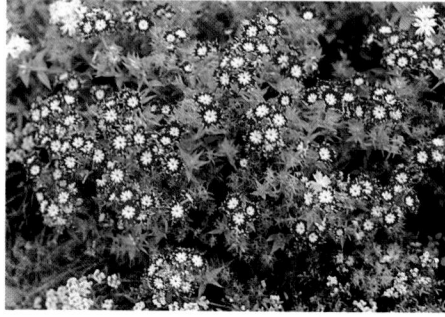

208. *Phlox drummondii* 'Twinkle' (Annual Phlox) — shape and flowers

207. *Phlox divaricata* (Blue Phlox) — shape and flowers

Phlox paniculata 'Leo Schlageter' (Garden x) — flowers

210. *Physostegia virginiana* (False Dragonhead) — shape and flowers

Platycodon grandiflorus (Balloon er) — shape and flowers

212. *Podophyllum peltatum* (Mayapple) — shape and leaves

Polemonium reptans (Creeping Jacob's-er) — shape and flowers

214. *Polygonatum commutatum* (Great Solomon's-seal) — shape and flowers

Polygonum cuspidatum var. *compactum* anese Fleece Flower) — shape and flowers

216. *Portulaca grandiflora* 'Sunglo' (Moss Rose) — shape and flowers

217. *Potentilla nepalensis* 'Miss Willmott' (Nepal Cinquefoil) — shape and flowers

219. *Primula denticulata* (Himalayan Primrose) — shape and flowers

221. *Pulmonaria saccharata* 'Mrs. Moon' (Bethlehem Sage) — leaves and flowers

218. *Primula cortusoides* (Orange-eye Primrose) — shape and flowers

220. *Primula* species (Japanese Primrose) — shape and flowers

222. *Puschkinia scillioides* (Squill Puschkinia) shape and flowers

Ranunculus acris 'Flore Pleno' (Double tercup) – shape and flowers

Ricinus communis (Castor Bean) – pe and leaves

224. *Ratibida columnifera* (Prairie Coneflower) – shape and flowers

226. *Rudbeckia hirta* (Gloriosa Daisy) – shape and flowers

228. *Salpiglossis sinuata* 'Bolero' (Painted Tongue) – shape and flowers

227. *Sagittaria latifolia* (Arrowhead) – leaves and flowers

229. *Salvia farinacea* 'Victoria' (Mealy-cup Sage) — shape and flowers

230. *Salvia splendens* 'Blaze of Fire' (Scarlet Sage) — shape and flowers

231. *Salvia* x *superba* (Garden Sage) — flowers

.232. *Sanguinaria canadensis* (Bloodroot) — shape and flowers

233. *Sanguinaria canadensis* 'Multiplex' (Double Bloodroot) — shape and flowers

234. *Sanvitalia procumbens* 'Gold Braid' (Trailing Sanvitalia) — shape and flowers

235. *Saponaria ocymoides* 'Splendens' (Rock Soapwort) — shape and flowers

Sarracenia purpurea (Common Pitcher t) — shape and flowers

Sedum spectabile 'Brilliant' (Showy ecrop) — shape and flowers

Senecio cineraria 'Silver Lace' (Dusty-r) — shape and leaves

237. *Scabiosa caucasica* (Perennial Scabious) — flowers

238. *Scilla sibirica* (Siberian Squill) — shape and flowers

240. *Sedum spurium* 'Dragon's Blood' (Tworow Stonecrop) — shape and flowers

242. *Silene keiskei* (Catchfly) — shape and flowers

243. *Sisyrinchium angustifolium* (Common Blue-eyed Grass) — shape and flowers

244. *Smilacina racemosa* (False Solomon's-seal) — shape and flowers

245. *Solidago* x 'Golden Mosa' (Hybrid Goldenrod) — shape and flowers

246. *Stachys byzantina* 'Silver Carpet' (Lamb's ears) — shape and flowers

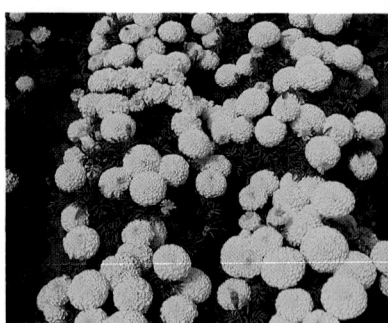

248. *Tagetes erecta* 'First Lady' (American Marigold) — shape and flowers

247. *Symplocarpus foetidus* (Skunk Cabbage) — shape and flowers

249. *Tagetes patula* 'Naughty Marietta' (French Marigold) — shape and flowers

Tagetes tenuifolia 'Lemon Gem' (Signet gold) — shape and flowers

251. *Thermopsis caroliniana* (Carolina False Lupine) — shape and flowers

Thunbergia alata (Black-eyed Susan) — shape and flowers

253. *Thymus* x *citriodorus* (Lemon Thyme) — shape and flowers

Thymus vulgaris 'Aureus' (Garden ne) — shape and leaf color

255. *Tiarella cordifolia* (Foamflower) — shape and flowers

Tithonia rotundifolia 'Torch' (Mexican ower) — flowers

257. *Tradescantia* x *andersoniana* 'Red Cloud' (Garden Spiderwort) — leaves and flowers

258. *Trillium erectum* (Purple Trillium) — flowers

259. *Trillium grandiflorum* (Showy Trillium) — shape and flowers

260. *Trillium grandiflorum* (Double Showy Trillium) — shape and flowers

261. *Trillium nivale* (Snow Trillium) — shape and flowers

262. *Trillium viride* var. *luteum* (Yellow Wood Trillium) — shape and flowers

263. *Trollius europaeus* (Common Globeflower) — shape and flowers

264. *Tropaeolum majus* (Garden Nasturtium) — shape and flowers

265. *Tropaeolum peregrinum* (Canary-bird Vine) — shape and flowers

Tulipa (Garden Hybrid Tulips) — mass
ing showing shape and flowers

267. *Uvularia grandiflora* (Big Merrybells) —
shape and flowers

Verbena x *hybrida* 'Sparkle' —
e and flowers

269. *Veronica* x 'Minuet' (Garden Hybrid
Veronica) — shape and flowers

Viola pedata (Bird's-foot Violet) —
e and flowers

271. *Viola pubescens* (Downy Yellow Violet) —
shape and flowers

Viola x *wittrockiana* 'Imperial Blue'
den Pansy) — shape and flowers

273. *Waldsteinia fragarioides* (Barren
Strawberry) — shape and flowers

274. *Yucca filamentosa* (Adam's-needle) — shape and flowers

275. *Zinnia elegans* (Common Zinnia) — shape and flowers

276. *Zinnia haageana* 'Chippendale' (Mexican Zinna) — shape and flowers

277. Terraced hillside — author's yard

'Rubra'. Flowers red.
'Sulphurea'. Flowers sulphur yellow.

Fritillaria — other species

F. camschatcensis (L.) Ker.-Gawl. (Kamchatka Fritillary), native in Japan and along our west coast from Alaska to Washington, has purple black flowers and whorled leaves in early spring.

F. meleagris L. (Checkered Fritillary), native in northern Europe and the Caucasus, has checkered flowers in shades of red and purple in early spring. 'Aphrodite' is a white flowered cultivar.

Funkia — see *Hosta*

Gaillardia Foug. (Blanket Flower)

COMPOSITAE (Sunflower Family)

Helenium Tribe

DESCRIPTION: A genus of about 14 species of annual, biennial, and perennial herbs, native in North and South America; **leaves** mostly basal, entire, toothed, or pinnatifid, pubescent; **flower** heads radiate, or rarely discoid, solitary, showy; receptacle hemispherical; disc flowers hairy, red-purple or sometimes yellow; ray flowers yellow or red, with ligule 3-toothed; **achene** obpyramidal, hairy, with pappus of awned scales.

Gaillardia x *grandiflora* Van Houtte (Blanket Flower). Perennial to 60 cm. tall. June to October.

DESCRIPTION: A garden hybrid developed by crossing *G. aristita* x *G. pulchella*; **leaves** oblanceolate to linear-lanceolate; **flower** heads to 10 cm. across.

USE: Plant in sunny flower border. Compact forms can also be planted in rock gardens. The flower heads are excellent for flower arranging.

CULTURE: A light well-drained sandy loam soil is best. Plants are usually short-lived in heavy clay soils. Propagation is by seeds sown in May in a nursery row or in a cold frame. Named cultivars can be propagated by division in early spring.

CULTIVARS: Numerous cultivars of this tetraploid hybrid have been named.
'Baby Cole'. Plants compact; ray flowers yellow with red bands.   PLATE 106
'Burgundy'. Ray flowers narrow, red.
'Dazzler'. Ray flowers yellow, with red bands.

'Goblin'. Ray flowers deep red, edged with yellow.
'Tangerine'. Ray flowers orange.
'Torch Light'. Ray flowers deep red, edged with yellow.

Gaillardia pulchella Foug. (Annual Gaillardia). Annual to 60 cm. tall. July to October.

DESCRIPTION: **Plants** native from Colorado to Virginia, south to New Mexico and Florida; **leaves** oblanceolate to spatulate, to 15 cm. long, toothed or pinnately lobed; **flower** heads to 5 cm. across, on long peduncles; involucral bracts green, with papery bases; disc flowers yellow, with red tips; ray flowers red, tipped with yellow or entirely red or yellow.

USE: Annual gaillardias are planted for mass effects in the flower border.

CULTURE: Plants like a light well-drained soil. Propagation is by seeds started indoors in early April. Space the plants about 30 cm. apart in the garden.

CULTIVARS AND VARIETY

var. *picta* (Sweet) A. Gray. Plants more succulent than the species. Most of the named cultivars are from this variety.

'Gaiety'. Flowering heads fully double; ray flowers claret, rose, yellow, sulphur, orange, maroon, with several bicolors.

'Lollipops'. Ray flowers bicolor in shades of butterscotch, lemon, and raspberry.

'Tetra Fiesta'. Ray flowers quilled, in smoky red shades tipped with yellow.

Gaillardia — other species

G. aristata Pursh., one of the parents of *G.* x *grandiflora*, is native from British Columbia to North Dakota, south to Oregon and Colorado. At one time this species was widely planted but it has been largely replaced by hybrids.

Galanthus L. (Snowdrop)

AMARYLLIDACEAE (Amaryllis Family)

DESCRIPTION: A small genus of about 12 species of early spring-blooming bulbous herbs, native in Europe and Asia; **bulbs** membranous-coated; **leaves** 2 or 3, basal; **flowers** solitary, pendent, white, subtended by a papery spathe split on one side; perianth segments 6, separate, the inner 3 shorter, overlapping and appearing tubular; ovary inferior; **fruit** a berry.

Galanthus elwesii Hook. (Giant Snowdrop). Perennial to 24 cm. tall. April, May.

DESCRIPTION: **Plants** native in Asia Minor; **leaves** 2, appearing with the flowers, to 10 cm. long, erect; **flowers** white, to 5 cm. across.

USE: Plant under shrubs, in the lawn, or in a rock garden.

CULTURE: Plants are of easy culture in any well-drained soil. They thrive in full sun or partial shade. Plant the bulbs in late September in clumps of 12 or more. Space the bulbs about 10 cm. apart and cover with 10 cm. of soil. Bulbs should be divided when plants become crowded.

Galanthus nivalis L. (Common Snowdrop). Perennial to 15 cm. tall. April, May.   PLATE 107

DESCRIPTION: **Plants** native in Europe; **leaves** 2, narrow, to 10 cm. long; **flowers** white, about 2.5 cm. across.

USE: Same as for *G. elwessi*.

CULTURE: Same as for *G. elwessi*.

CULTIVARS
'Flore Pleno'. Flowers double.
'Simplex'. Flowers single.

Gazania Gaertn.

COMPOSITAE (Sunflower Family)

Arctotis Tribe

DESCRIPTION: A genus of about 16 species of rhizomatous, perennial, rarely annual, herbs or subshrubs; with milky juice, native mostly in South Africa; **leaves** mostly in basal rosettes, rarely on the stems, entire or lobed or pinnatifid; **flower** heads solitary on long peduncles, radiate, closing at night; involucral bracts in 2 to several rows, united at base to form a cup; receptacle pitted; disc flowers tubular, perfect; ray flowers strap-shaped, sterile, white, yellow, orange, or scarlet, sometimes with basal spots; **achenes** hairy, with pappus of 2 rows of delicate, scarious, toothed scales.

Gazania ringens (L.) Gaertn. (Treasure Flower). Tender perennial grown as an annual, to 40 cm. tall. July, August.

DESCRIPTION: **Plants** rhizomatous with decumbent stems, native in South Africa; **leaves** lanceolate, or obovate-lanceolate, to 8 cm. long, green above, white-tomentose beneath; **flower** heads to 7.5 cm. across, on long peduncles; ray flowers yellow or orange, with a brown black, white-eyed basal spot.

USE: A useful plant for edging a flower border or for an annual ground cover.

CULTURE: Plants like a light, well-drained soil high in organic matter, and full sun. Propagation is by seeds started indoors in late March. Set plants outdoors after danger of frost.

CULTIVARS

'Colorama'. Ray flowers in a color range including white, cream, yellow, and orange.

'Golden Marguerite'. Ray flowers a lively golden yellow.   PLATE 108

'Sunshine'. Ray flowers in bright shades of cream, yellow, orange, pink, bronze, and red, with a contrasting zone of color at the base.

Gazania splendens — see *Gazania ringens*

Gentiana L. (Gentian)

GENTIANACEAE (Gentian Family)

DESCRIPTION: A large genus of over 300 species of annual, biennial, and perennial herbs, native in temperate and arctic regions; **leaves** opposite, sessile or petioled, sometimes clasping; **flowers** white, yellow, blue, purple, or red, often spotted, solitary or many in elongated or capitate clusters; 4- to 5-merous; calyx tubular to campanulate, variously lobed or cleft; corolla funnelform, campanulate, or salverform, sometimes tubular or club-shaped, variously lobed with teeth, pleats, or appendages between the lobes; stamens united with the corolla tube; **fruit** a capsule, with many flat-winged seeds.

Gentiana acaulis L. (Stemless Gentian). Perennial to 10 cm. tall. May, June.

DESCRIPTION: Tufted **plants**, native in the Alps and Pyrenees mountains; **leaves** in basal rosettes, elliptic or lanceolate; **flowers** dark blue, solitary; calyx funnelform, to 1.25 cm. long, with ovate lobes; corolla campanulate, spotted inside, with appendages between the lobes; stigma lobes rounded; fimbriate.

USE: A good rock garden plant.

CULTURE: The stemless gentian likes a moist but well-drained soil and full sun. Propagation is by seeds or by division in early spring. The seeds should be sown in late fall in a shallow container and left in a cold frame over winter. Low temperatures are needed for seed germination. Gentians grow best where summers are cool.

Gentiana andrewsii Griseb. (Bottle Gentian). Perennial to 60 cm. tall. August, September. PLATE 109

DESCRIPTION: **Leaves** ovate to lanceolate; **flowers** clustered at the tips of the stems or borne in the upper leaf axils, blue, becoming purple in age; corolla remaining completely closed with but a porelike opening at the tip, to 4 cm. long.

USE: Plant in a prairie garden or along a stream.

CULTURE: The bottle gentian likes a moist soil high in organic matter. It prefers full sun but will grow in partial shade. Propagation is mainly by division of established plants in early spring.

CULTIVAR
'Alba'. Flowers white.

Gentiana crinata — see *Gentianopsis crinata*

Gentiana — other species

G. cruciata L. (Cross Gentian), native in Europe and northern Africa, has dark blue flowers. It requires a peaty soil.

G. lagodechiana (Kuzn.) Grossh., native in western Asia, has deep blue, tubular-funnelform flowers to 4 cm. long in August and September.

G. verna L. (Spring Gentian), native in Europe and Asia, has deep blue, salverform flowers to 2.5 cm. long in June.

Gentianopsis Ma. (Fringed Gentian)

GENTIANACEAE (Gentian Family)

DESCRIPTION: A genus of about 15 species of annual or biennial herbs of the northern hemisphere; **leaves** opposite; **flowers** showy, blue or purple, rarely white, solitary, on slender bractless pedicels, 4-merous; calyx tubular, 4-angled; corolla funnelform to campanulate, with fringed lobes; stamens borne on upper 1/3 of the corolla tube; ovary on a stalk.

Gentianopsis crinata (Froel.) Ma. (Fringed Gentian). Annual, or sometimes biennal, to 1 m. tall. August-October

DESCRIPTION: **Plants** native in eastern North America; **leaves** ovate to lanceolate; **flowers** bright blue, with corolla lobes delicately fringed.

USE: Plant in woodland wildflower garden.

CULTURE: This beautiful native is difficult to grow. It requires a cool, moist site in partial shade. Propagation is by seeds started early indoors. The seeds should be stored in a refrigerator.

Geranium L. (Cranesbill)

GERANIACEAE (Geranium Family)

DESCRIPTION: A genus of over 300 species of annual or perennial herbs, rarely shrubs, native in temperate regions or in the mountains of the tropics; **leaves** usually palmately parted or divided into usually toothed lobes; **flowers** solitary and axillary, or clustered and terminal, white, pink, or purple; sepals and petals 5; stamens 10; ovary 5-celled with 2 ovules in each cell; **fruit** a long-beaked capsule.

Geranium grandiflorum — see *Gernaium himalayense*

Geranium maculatum L. (Wild Geranium, Wild Cranesbill). Perennial to 60 cm. tall. May, June.

DESCRIPTION: **Plants** native to North America; **stems** with appressed pubescent; **leaves** deeply 3- to 5-parted; **flowers** rose purple, to 2.5 cm. across.

USE: Plant in woodland wildflower garden.

CULTURE: The wild geranium likes a well-drained soil, high in organic matter, and partial shade. Propagation is by seeds started in May in a cold frame or a nursery row. Plants are then transplanted to their permanent location the following spring. Once established, the plants should not be disturbed. Named cultivars must be propagated by division.

CULTIVAR
'Album'. Flowers white.

Geranium sanguineum L. (Bloodred Geranium). Perennial to 45 cm. tall. May-August.   PLATE 110

DESCRIPTION: **Plants** are mound-shaped, with spreading white hairs, native in Eurasia; **leaves** deeply 5- to 7-lobed with long, lanceolate teeth; **flowers** red to purple on axillary pedicels.

USE: Excellent for planting in the flower border or in a rock garden.

CULTURE: This geranium likes a well-drained soil high in organic matter. Plants do well in full sun. Propagation is mainly by division of old plants.

CULTIVARS
'Album'. Flowers white.

'Alpenglow'. Flowers carmine red.
'Lancastriense'. Flowers salmon pink.

Geranium — other species

G. cinereum Cav., native in the Pyrenees mountains, has pink petals with darker stripes. It is a good rock garden species, growing only about 15 cm. tall.

G. dalmaticum (G. Beck) Rech. (Dalmatian Cranesbill), native in Dalmatia, has rose-colored flowers. 'Album' is a named cultivar with white flowers tinged with pink.

G. endresii J. Gay, also native in the Pyrenees mountains, has silvery pink flowers. 'Wargrave Pink', with clear pink flowers, and 'Johnson's Blue', with blue flowers, are named cultivars.

G. himalayense Klotzch (Lilac Geranium), native from Turkestan to northern India, has lilac-colored flowers with purple veins. 'Alpinum' has peacock blue flowers.

G. ibericum Cav. (Caucasus Geranium), native in southwestern Asia, has bright blue to purple flowers.

G. macrorrhizum L., native in Europe, has a thick taproot and magenta-colored flowers. 'Album' has white flowers.

Geum L. (Avens)

ROSACEAE (Rose Family)

DESCRIPTION: A genus of over 50 species of perennial herbs, native of temperate and cold regions; **leaves** pinnate or lyrate, usually with large terminal lobes, mostly basal; **flowers** solitary or in corymbs, perfect, white, yellow, or red; sepals 5, usually with 5 bractlets in between; petals 5, often broad and showy; stamens and pistils many; **fruits** are achenes with persistent styles that are often plumose.

Geum chiloense — see *Geum quellyon*

Geum triflorum Pursh (Old-man's-whiskers, Prairie Smoke). Perennial to 45 cm. tall. May, June.

DESCRIPTION: **Plants** native on well-drained prairie soils from British Columbia to Ontario, south to California and Illinois; **leaves** with many wedge-shaped, shallowly cut leaflets; **flowers** purplish pink, nodding, in terminal clusters of 3; **fruit** with long feathery styles.

USE: Plant in prairie garden.

CULTURE: This interesting native plant grows best in well-drained soil and in full sunlight. It can be propagated by seeds or division in early spring. The seeds should be started in May in a nursery row.

Geum — other species

G. quellyon Sweet (Chile Avens), native in Chile, has showy scarlet flowers to 2.5. cm. across in June. It is one of the parents of our garden hybrids. 'Plenum' has double flowers.

G. reptans L., native in Europe, has yellow petals and purple styles. It is a good rock garden plant, growing about 20 cm. tall.

Geum — garden hybrids

Most of the garden hybrids are the result of crossing *G. coccineum* with *G. quellyon*. These hybrids are short-lived perennials that are often grown as annuals by starting seeds indoors. They bloom from June until frost.
'Ballerina'. Plants dwarf; flowers pink.
'Golden Sunset'. Flowers yellow.
'Lady Stratheden'. Flowers golden yellow.
'Mrs. Bradshaw'. Flowers double, scarlet red.
'Red Wings'. Flower red.

Gilia coronopifolia — see *Ipomopsis rubra*

Gilia rubra — see *Ipomopsis rubra*

Gillenia Moench. (Indian-physic)

ROSACEAE (Rose Family)

DESCRIPTION: A small genus of 2 species of erect, branched perennial herbs, native in North America; **leaves** with 3 leaflets; **flowers** white or pink, or long pedicels in terminal panicles; calyx 5-toothed; petals 5; stamens 10 to 20; **fruit** of 5 follicles.

Gillenia trifoliata (L.) Moench. (Indian-physic, Bowman's-root). Perennial to 1 m. tall. June.   PLATE 111

DESCRIPTION: **Plants** native from Ontario and New York, south to Alabama and Georgia; **leaflets** oblong-ovate, serrate; **flowers** pink.

USE: Plant in woodland wildflower garden.

CULTURE: A moist, shaded site is required for the successful culture of this plant. Propagation is by division in early spring or by seed sown about May 1.

Gladiolus L. (Corn Flag, Sword Lily)

IRIDACEAE (Iris Family)

DESCRIPTION: A large genus of nearly 300 species of perennial herbs with tunicate corms, native in Europe, the Mediterranean region, the Near East, and South Africa; **stems** usually unbranched, leafy; **leaves** sword-shaped; **flowers** showy, in one-sided spikes, irregular, borne in 2 spathe valves; perianth segments 6, united basally into a curved, funnelform tube, the upper 3 segments larger than the lower 3; stamens 3, borne below the perianth throat; style branches 3; **fruit** a 3-valved capsule.

Gladiolus x *hortulanus* L. H. Bailey (Garden Gladiolus). Tender perennial to 1.5 m. tall. August, September.

DESCRIPTION: **Plants** of hybrid origin involving several species, including *G. natalensis*; **leaves** sword-shaped; **flowers** very showy, in a wide color range.

USE: Plants are grown primarily for cut flowers. The usual method is to grow the plants in rows with clean cultivation. If planted in the flower border, it is best to plant several corms of a single cultivar in a group.

CULTURE: Plants grow best in a sandy loam soil and in full sun. Propagation is by division of corms and by cormlets. Corms can be planted in early May or about the time that the leaves appear on trees. Plantings made at 10-day intervals will provide a long season of bloom. The depth of planting depends on the soil and the size of the corms, being planted deeper in a sandy soil. Space the corms from 10 to 15 cm. apart and cover with 8 to 10 cm. of soil. The soil should be a sandy loam. Heavy clay soils can be improved by adding organic matter. Weeds must be controlled by shallow cultivation and hand weeding. Dacthal® is sometimes used to control annual weeds. The gladiolus requires a fertile soil; for specimen blooms, some growers use a liquid fertilizer every 10 days until the flowers begin to open. Thrips are the main insect pest and this insect must be controlled. The flowering stems are usually cut as soon as the first florets open. Use a sharp knife to cut the stems, leaving as many of the leaves on the plants as possible. The gladiolus is susceptible to several diseases, largely soil borne, that affect the corms. Affected plants usually show yellow or brown leaves. Diseased plants should be rogued out and destroyed.

Corms should be dug soon after the first frost in the fall. After lifting the plants, cut the stem about 2 cm. above the corms, then place the corms in shallow flats or paper bags. Keep each variety separate if you wish to retain the identity of the cultivars. Store in a well-ventilated room with the temperature above freezing. As soon as the corms have cured for a few weeks, they can be cleaned by snapping off the old shriveled corm at the base of the new corm. Cleaned corms should be dusted with a good insecticide if thrips attacked the plants during the growing season. Before planting in the spring, it is a good plan to sort the corms by size. Plant the large corms for flower production. The small corms and cormlets can be planted closer together in a separate area to increase your stock for next year.

CULTIVARS: Garden gladiolus cultivars are classified into two major groups, Formal and Informal. The Formal cultivars have their flowers arranged in a regular fashion on the stems, close together and approximately in opposite pairs; the Informal cultivars have their flowers arranged in looser spikes and spaced alternately along the stems. A further classification is based on flower size: Giants, with flowers over 14 cm. in diameter; Large, with flowers 10.5 to 14 cm. in diameter; Small, with flowers 8 to 10.5 cm.; and Miniature, with flowers under 6.25 cm. in diameter. Color classifications within the above size categories are: White and Cream; Yellow and Buff, Orange; Salmon and Scarlet; Pink; Red; Rose and Lavender; Purple and Violet; Smoky; and A.O.C. (any other color). There are literally thousands of named cultivars and new ones are introduced each year. In selecting cultivars it is best to visit a grower who specializes in glads and make your selection when the plants are in bloom. Flower shows are also an excellent place to see some of the newer cultivars. Most states have a chapter of the American Galdiolus Society and members are usually willing to share their knowledge with you.

The following are good cultivars that are reasonably priced and readily available:

'Born Free'. A vigorous plant with tall purple spikes.

'Day Dream'. Vigorous plants with tall, clear pink spikes.

'Debbit T'. Plants with rugged green foliage and deep yellow spikes.

'Galilee'. Plants with tall pastel blue spikes.

'Green Spire'. Plants rugged with tall spikes of green florets.

'Happy Birthday'. Winner of British Gladiolus Society's Trial Garden Award. Tall spikes with ruffled, buff-colored florets.

'Inca Chief'. Florets ruffled, deep bittersweet orange.

'Lilac & Chartreuse'. Florets ruffled, lilac lavender with a green throat.

'Parade'. Florets salmon pink with a cream throat.

'Priscilla'. Florets rose-colored with picoteed edges.

'Red Ginger'. Florets a radiant red.
'Smoky Lady'. Florets a smoky rose violet color.
'Winter Olympics'. Florets white with creamy throat.

Godetia —see *Clarkia*

Godetia amoena —see *Clarkia amoena*

Gomphrena L. (Globe Amaranth)

AMARANTHACEAE (Amaranth Family)

DESCRIPTION: A genus of over 100 species of erect or prostrate annual or perennial herbs, native in tropical America, Australia, and southeastern Asia; **flowers** in dense chaffy heads, perfect; perianth 5-lobed or 5-parted; stamens 5, with filaments united into a tube and anthers 2-celled; **fruit** a utricle.

Gomphrena globosa L. (Common Globe Amaranth). Annual to 45 cm. tall. July-September.

DESCRIPTION: **Plants** native in the Old World tropics; **leaves** oblong to elliptic, to 10 cm. long, ciliate; **flowers** perfect, purple, orange, rose, or white, in dense chafy heads, subtended by 2 leafy bracts.

USE: Plants grown in flower borders or in the cutting garden for dried flower arrangements. The stems are cut before the flowers are fully open and hung upside down in a cool, airy place to dry.

CULTURE: Plants require full sun and a well-drained soil. Avoid overwatering. Propagation is by seeds started indoors in early April or direct seeded as soon as the soil can be worked in the spring.

CULTIVARS
'Buddy'. Flowers brilliant purple.
'Rubra'. Flowers red.   PLATE 112

Gypsophila L. (Baby's-breath)

CARYOPHYLLACEAE (Pink Family)

DESCRIPTION: A genus of 125 species of annual, biennial, or perennial herbs, or rarely subshrubs, native mostly in Eurasia, with 1 species in Egypt and 1 in Australia; **leaves** glaucous, glabrous, or glandular-hairy, opposite, linear-subulate, lanceolate, or spatulate; **flowers** white or pink, small, many, in cymes or panicles, with scarious bracts; calyx 5-toothed or 5-cleft; petals 5; stamens 10; styles mostly 2; **fruit** a 1-celled capsule, opening by 4 valves.

Gypsophila elegans Bieb. (Annual Baby's-breath). Annual to 50 cm. tall. July, August.

DESCRIPTION: **Plants** native in the southern Ukraine, Caucasus, eastern Turkey, and northern Iran; plants much-branched; **leaves** linear-lanceolate, to 5 cm. long; **flowers** white, on long pedicels, produced in a panicle of cymes.

USE: Plant toward the front of the flower border.

CULTURE: Plants require a well-drained soil and full sun. Propagation is by seeds sown directly where the plants are to bloom as early in the spring as the soil can be worked.

CULTIVARS
'Carmine'. Flowers carmine rose.
'Covent Garden'. Flowers large, white.
'Rose'. Flowers bright rose pink.

Gypsophila paniculata L. (Common Baby's-breath). Perennial to 1 m. tall. June-August.   PLATE 113

DESCRIPTION: **Plants** diffusely branched with stout rhizomes and deep tap-roots, native in central and eastern Europe to central Asia; **leaves** lanceolate, to 7.5 cm. long; **flowers** small, white, pink, or red, in diffusely branched panicles.

USE: Plant toward the back of the flower border.

CULTURE: Plants require a well-drained soil and full sun. Propagation is chiefly by division or cuttings. Double-flowered cultivars are grafted on seedling roots. Because of their taproots, plants should not be moved once they are established. Plants are short-lived in heavy soils.

CULTIVARS
'Bristol Fairy'. Flowers double, pure white.
'Flamingo'. Flowers double, pink.
'Pink Fairy'. Flowers full double, clear pink.

Gypsophila repens L. (Creeping Baby's-breath). Perennial to 25 cm. tall. June, July.

DESCRIPTION: **Plants** compact, spreading, native in the mountains of northwestern Spain to the Carpathians; **leaves** narrow, curved; **flowers** white, lilac, or pale purple, in small corymbs.

USE: A good rock garden plant.

CULTURE: Same as for *G. paniculata*.

CULTIVARS

'Alba'. Flowers white.

'Bodgeri'. Flowers double, pink.

'Rosea'. Flowers rose pink.

'Rosy Veil'. Flower double, pink.

Hedyotis L. (Bluets)

RUBIACEAE (Madder Family).

DESCRIPTION: A large genus of about 400 species of herbs or weak-stemmed shrubs, native of tropical, subtropical, or sometimes temperate regions; **plants** sometimes tufted, occasionally prostrate; **leaves** opposite, with stipules on the petioles; **flowers** usually solitary, sometimes in terminal or axillary cymes, usually 4-merous; corolla funnelform or salverform; **fruit** a capsule.

Hedyotis caerulea (L.) Hook. (Bluets, Quaker-ladies). Perennial to 15 cm. tall. June, July.

DESCRIPTION: **Plants** native from Wisconsin to Nova Scotia, south to Arkansas to Georgia; **leaves** oblanceolate, to 1.25 cm. long; **flowers** solitary, blue or white, with a yellow center; corolla salverform, to 1.25 cm. long.

USE: Plant in rock garden or in woodland wildflower garden.

CULTURE: Plants like a rich, well-drained soil, high in organic matter, and partial shade. Propagation is by division of plants in early spring or by seeds. Seeds should be sown in early May in a cold frame.

Hedyotis serpyllifolia — see *Hedyotis michauxii*

Hedyotis — other species

H. michauxii Fosb. (Creeping Bluets), native from Pennsylvania, south to Tennessee and Georgia, has creeping stems and small, deep blue or purple flowers in May and June.

H. purpurea (L.) Torr. (Purple Bluets), native from Michigan to New England, south to Texas and Alabama, produces its small, purple to lilac flowers in terminal cymes in June.

Helenium L. (Sneezeweed)

COMPOSITAE (Sunflower Family)

Helenium Tribe

DESCRIPTION: A genus of about 40 species of annual or perennial herbs, native to North and South America; **leaves** alternate, glandular-dotted, frequently clasping the stem at base; **flower** heads radiate or discoid, solitary or in peduncled cymes; involucral bracts in 2 rows, deflexed; receptacle convex to ovoid or globose, naked; disc flowers perfect, yellow, red brown, or red yellow; **achenes** turbinate or obpyramidal, 4- to 5-angled, with a pappus of 5 to 10 scarious, awn-tipped scales.

Helenium autumnale L. (Common Sneezeweed). Perennial to 1.5 m. tall. August, September.

DESCRIPTION: **Plants** with fibrous roots, branched, native from British Columbia to Quebec, south to Arizona and Florida; **stems** winged because of the clasping leaf bases; **leaves** linear-lanceolate to elliptic or ovate-lanceolate, to 15 cm. long, usually serrate, nearly glabrous; **flower** heads to 5 cm. across, radiate, solitary; disc flowers yellow; ray flowers also yellow.

USE: Plant in flower border for late summer bloom.

CULTURE: Heleniums are of easy culture in most any well-drained soil in full sun. Best success is obtained where liberal quantities of organic matter has been worked into the soil. Propagation is by seeds or by division. Seedlings started indoors in early April may bloom in late fall of the first year but the best bloom will be on established plants. Plant in spring and space plants about 30 cm. apart. The flowering season can be lengthened by removing the old bloom.

CULTIVARS

'Brilliant'. Ray flowers in a brilliant color range.
'Butterpat'. Ray flowers a golden yellow.   PLATE 114
'Chipperfield Orange'. Ray flowers orange yellow and red.
'Crimson Beauty'. Ray flowers crimson.
'Moerheim Beauty'. Ray flowers rich crimson red.
'Riverton Beauty'. Ray flowers gold with orange tint.

Helianthus L. (Sunflower)

COMPOSITAE (Sunflower Family)

Helianth Tribe

DESCRIPTION: A genus of about 150 species of coarse annual or perennial herbs, native in North and South America; **plants** often rhizomatous, with fibrous or fleshy, tuberous roots; **leaves** opposite near the base of the stem and often alternate above, simple; **flower** heads radiate, rarely discoid, usually solitary on long peduncles, or in corymbs; involucre mostly saucer-shaped to hemispherical; involucral bracts in 2 to 4 rows; receptacle flat to convex, scaly; disc flowers perfect; ray flowers in 1 row, pistillate, sterile, yellow; **achenes** laterally compressed with thin edges and a pappus that soon drops off.

Helianthus annuus L. (Common Sunflower). Annual to 3 m. tall. August, September.

DESCRIPTION: **Plants** coarse, rough-hairy, native in North America; **leaves** large, to 30 cm. long, ovate, truncate to cordate at base; **flower** heads large, to 30 cm. across; disc flowers red or purple; ray flowers orange yellow.

USE: Plant toward the back of the flower border.

CULTURE: The common sunflower is of easy culture in most soils in full sun. Propagation is by seeds sown directly where plants are to bloom.

CULTIVARS
'Autumn Beauty'. Flowering heads to 12 cm. across; ray flowers yellow, bronze, and red.
'Italian White'. Ray flowers white to cream colored.
'Teddy Bear'. Flowering heads fully double, golden yellow.   PLATE 115

Helianthus x *multiflorus* L. (Perennial Sunflower). Perennial to 2 m. tall. July-September.

DESCRIPTION: **Plants** of hybrid origin developed by crossing *H. annuus* x *H. decapetalus*; **stems** slightly hispid; **leaves** mostly alternate, ovate, to 25 cm. long; **flower** heads to 12 cm. across, single or double, with yellow ray flowers.

USE: Plant toward the back of the flower border.

CULTURE: Plants are of easy culture in most soils and full sun. Propagation is by seeds and by division in early spring.

CULTIVARS
'Flora Pleno'. Flowering heads double, bright yellow.
'Loddon Gold'. Flowering heads double, yellow.

Helichrysum Mill. (Everlasting)

COMPOSITAE (Sunflower Family)

Inula Tribe

DESCRIPTION: A large genus of nearly 500 species of annual or perennial herbs, subshrubs or shrubs, native in warmer regions, especially South Africa and Australia; **leaves** mostly alternate, rarely opposite, often downy or woolly; **flower** heads discoid, solitary or in terminal clusters; involucre hemispherical to cylindrical; involucral bracts overlapping in many rows, often petal-like, often brightly colored; receptacle naked; flowers all tubular, mostly perfect; **achenes** 5-angled to nearly cylindrical, with pappus of simple bristles.

Helichrysum bracteatum (Benten.) Andr. (Strawflower). Tender perennial grown as an annual to 1 m. tall. August, September.

DESCRIPTION: **Plants** branched above, native in Austrailia; **leaves** oblong-lanceolate, to 12 cm. long, green and glabrous above; **flower** heads to 6 cm. across; the inner involucral bracts are petal-like and of various colors including yellow, orange, red, and white.

USE: Strawflowers are commonly grown in the cutting garden for winter arrangements.

CULTURE: Plants require a well-drained soil and full sun. Propagation is by seeds started indoors. Transplant to the garden after danger of frost. Flowers are cut with long stems when fully open and dried in a well-ventilated room.

CULTIVARS

'Crimson Bikini'. Bracts crimson.
'Golden Bikini'. Bracts gold.
'Hot Bikini'. Bracts red.
'Pink Bikini'. Bracts pink.

Heliopsis Pers. (Oxeye)

COMPOSITAE (Sunflower Tribe)

Helianthus Tribe

DESCRIPTION: A small genus of 12 species of annual or perennial herbs, native in North America; **leaves** opposite, simple; **flower** heads radiate, solitary; involucral bracts in 1 or 2 rows, nearly equal; receptacle convex to conical, scaly; disc flowers perfect, yellow to purple or red; ray flowers pistillate, orange yellow to yellow or purple; **achenes** 4-sided or triangular with a pappus consisting of a few teeth or lacking.

Heliopsis helianthoides (L.) Sweet (Oxeye, False Sunflower). Short-lived perennial often grown as an annual, to 1.5 m. tall. July-September.

DESCRIPTION: **Plants** native from Michigan to New York, south to Mississippi and Georgia; **leaf** blades lanceolate-ovate to oblong-ovate, to 12 cm. long, serrate; **flower** heads to 12 cm. across; disc flowers brownish yellow; ray flowers yellow.

USE: An excellent border plant for late summer bloom.

CULTURE: Heliopsis thrives in any good garden soil in either full or partial shade. Propagation is mainly by division either in the fall or early in the spring. The species can be propagated from seeds but the seedlings will not bloom until the second year. Named cultivars must be vegetatively propagated.

CULTIVARS AND VARIETY

subspecies *scabra* (Dunal) T. R. Fisher. Differs from the species in having scabrous stems and leaves and by having ray flowers orange yellow. Many of the named cultivars are from this subspecies.   PLATE 116

'Gold Greenheart'. Flowering heads buttercup yellow; disc flowers green.

'Golden Plume'. Flowering heads fully double.

'Incomparabilis'. Flowering heads semi-double; ray flowers yellow.

'Patula'. Ray flowers golden yellow.

'Summer Sun'. Flowering heads double; ray flowers soft yellow.

Heliopsis scabra —see *Heliopsis helianthoides* subsp. *scabra*

Heliotropium L. (Heliotrope)

BORAGINACEAE (Borage Family)

DESCRIPTION: A genus of about 250 species of mostly hairy herbs, subshrubs, and shrubs of temperate and tropical climates; **leaves** simple, mostly alternate; **flowers** blue, purple, pink, and white, in cymes or sometimes axillary; calyx deeply 5-lobed; corolla 5-lobed; stamens 5, included in the corolla tube; **fruit** of 4 nutlets that separate or adhere in pairs.

Heliotropium arborescens L. (Heliotrope). Tender perennial grown as an annual. August, September.   PLATE 117

DESCRIPTION: **Plants** native in Peru; **leaves** elliptic or oblong-lanceolate, to 7.5 cm. long; **flowers** violet or purple, varying to white, fragrant, to 7 mm. long, in terminal cymes.

USE: Heliotrope has fragrant flowers and is often planted in the flower border. Commercially, the plant is grown for the perfume industry.

CULTURE: This plant is of easy culture in most soils. It thrives in full sun or light shade. Although a tender perennial, it is usually grown from seed started indoors. Seedlings should be pinched to produce a bushy plant. In greenhouses, plants are usually grown from cuttings.

CULTIVARS

'Marine'. Flowers a rich violet.

'Purple Bonnet'. Plants compact; flowers in rich shades of purple.

'Royal Fragrance'. Flowers dark purple.

Helipterum DC. (Everlasting)

COMPOSITAE (Sunflower Family)

Inula Tribe

DESCRIPTION: A genus of almost 90 species of annual or perennial herbs, subshrubs, or shrubs, native in South Africa, Australia, and Tasmania; **leaves** mostly alternate, entire; **flower** heads discoid, solitary, clustered, or corymbose; involucre broadly hemispherical, narrow-ovoid, or cylindrical; involucral bracts numerous, overlapping in several rows, scarious, often petal-like and brightly colored; receptacle flat, convex, or conical, naked; flowers all tubular, perfect or the outer row pistillate; **achenes** cylindrical, with a pappus of 1 row of plumose bristles.

Helipterum roseum (Hook.) Benth. (Rose Sunray). Annual to 60 cm. tall. July, August.

DESCRIPTION: **Plants** glabrous, native in western Australia; **leaves** linear to lanceolate, to 6 cm. long; **flower** heads solitary on long peduncles, to 5 cm. across; involucre hemispherical; involucral bracts petal-like, rose to white.

USE: Plants grown for dried flower arrangements. Plant either in rows in the cutting garden or in groups in the flower border.

CULTURE: Plants prefer a well-drained sandy soil and full sun. Seeds should be started indoors in early April or seeded directly where the plants are to bloom in early May. Space plants about a foot apart.

CULTIVAR

'Red Bonnie'. Involucral bracts large, red.

Helleborus L. (Hellebore)

RANUNCULACEAE (Buttercup Family)

DESCRIPTION: A genus of about 20 species of perennial herbs with stout roots, native in limestone soils of Europe and Asia; **leaves** mostly basal, palmately divided; **flowers** large, in cymes; sepals 5, green or petal-like; petals forming inconspicuous nectaries; stamens many; **fruit** of 3 to 10 sessile follicles.

Helleborus niger L. (Christmas Rose). Perennial to 30 cm. tall. April.   PLATE 118

DESCRIPTION: **Plants** native of Europe; **leaves** basal, evergreen; leaflets ovate-cuneate, slightly toothed; **flowers** solitary on red-spotted peduncles, white or sometimes suffused with pink, to 7.5 cm. across.

USE: Plant in woodland wildflower garden.

CULTURE: The hellebores grow best in a rich, moist soil high in organic matter. They require some shade. The plants are reported to be poisonous, but there are few records of humans being poisoned by hellebores. Propagation is by seeds or by division. Do not divide plants more often than once every 6 or 7 years.

Helleborus—other species

H. orientalis Lam. (Lenten Rose), native in Macedonia, Thrace, and Asia Minor, is similar to *H. niger* but less hardy. Sepals may be purple, pink, or green. A winter mulch is needed.

Hemerocallis L. (Daylily)

LILIACEAE (Lily Family)

DESCRIPTION: A small genus of about 15 species of clump-forming, perennial herbs, native from central Europe to China and Japan; **roots** are fibrous or sometimes fleshy; **leaves** basal, linear, keeled, often grasslike; **flowers** last only one day, are yellow, orange, red, or purple, borne in clusters on long scapes; perianth funnelform to campanulate with 6 segments; stamens 6, with versatile anthers; filaments inserted on the throat of the perianth; **fruit** a 3-valved capsule.

Hemerocallis aurantiaca Bak. (Orange Daylily). Perennial to 1 m. tall. July, August.

DESCRIPTION: **Plants** spreading by rhizomes, native in China; **leaves** linear, to 90 cm. long, sharply keeled; **flowers** orange, often flushed with purple, to 10 cm. across.

USE: Sometimes planted as a ground cover on steep banks.

CULTURE: This plant is of easy culture. It thrives on most soils in either full sun or partial shade. Propagation is largely by division in early spring.

Hemerocallis flava—see *Hemerocallis lilioasphodelus*

Hemerocallis fulva (L.) L. (Tawny Daylily). Perennial to 2 m. tall. July, August.

DESCRIPTION: **Plants** with spreading rhizomes and fleshy main roots, native in Europe and Asia, often naturalized in eastern United States; **leaves** linear, to 60 cm. long; **flowers** rusty orange to red, usually with darker stripes, to 8 cm. across.

USE: The species is used as a ground cover on slopes. Named cultivars are usually planted in the flower border.

CULTURE: Same as for *H. aurantiaca*.

CULTIVARS
'Flore Pleno'. Flowers double.
'Kwanzo'. Leaves striped with white; flowers double.
'Rosea'. Flowers rose red.

Hemerocallis lilioasphodelus L. (Lemon Daylily). Perennial to 1 m. tall. June, July.

DESCRIPTION: **Plants** spreading by rhizomes, native in eastern Siberia to Japan; **leaves** to 60 cm. long; **flowers** fragrant, yellow, to 10 cm. across.

USE: A good plant for the flower border.

CULTURE: Same as for *H. aurantiaca*.

CULTIVAR
'Rosea'. Flowers deep pink.

Hemerocallis—garden hybrids

Daylilies have been greatly improved in recent years by interspecies hybridization. Today, growers may choose from literally thousands of named cultivars. These differ in flower and plant size, color and time of bloom, and the substance of the flowers. The American Hemerocallis Society records all of the new cultivars, and regional chapters dispense information on the culture of daylilies. To obtain information on the best cultivars to plant, visit a public or private garden that features daylilies when the plants are in bloom, or visit a flower show featuring daylilies. Your state Horticultural Society can get you in touch with local growers.   PLATE 119

USE: One of our most popular border perennials. They are also used as cut flowers.

CULTURE: Daylilies are easy to grow. They thrive in any well-drained soil in either full sun or partial shade. Propagation is by division. This is best done in early spring, but with proper care, daylilies can be planted at almost any time during the growing season. Although each flower lasts for only one day, a succession of bloom will provide color in the border for about a month from a single plant. Since each cultivar has a slightly different blooming period, it is possible to have several months of continuous bloom by carefully selecting the cultivars. Most of the larger cultivars should be spaced about a meter apart.

CULTIVARS: There are thousands of named cultivars to choose from. The following are a few that are reasonably priced and readily available.

'Alpine Aire'. Plants 80 cm. tall; flowers midseason, to 15 cm. across, pink- to cream-colored, with a golden, ruffled edging.

'Aztec Pottery'. Plants to 70 cm. tall; flowers midseason, yellow with red center.

'Banana Sundae'. Plants to 75 cm. tall; flowers to 12 cm. across, early-midseason, banana yellow with darker center and ruffled edges.

'Bitsy'. A miniature to 45 cm. tall; flowers early, to 4 cm. across, lemon yellow with a green throat.

'Cartwheels'. Plants to 75 cm. tall; flowers midseason to late, deep golden yellow.

'Centennial Queen'. Plants to 90 cm. tall; flowers midseason, to 20 cm. across, bright yellow with tint of green in the throat.

'Chantilly Lace'. Plants to 75 cm. tall; flowers early to midseason, to 15 cm. across, shell pink with ruffled edges.

'Dewy Fresh'. Plants to 75 cm. tall; flowers midseason to late, light lemon yellow.

'Fancy Frills'. Plants to 85 cm. tall; flowers midseason, to 12 cm. across, medium yellow with a green throat and frilled edges.

'Hortensia'. A Stout Medal winner to 85 cm. tall; flowers midseason with repeat bloom, golden yellow, ruffled.

'Jubilee Pink'. Plants to 70 cm. tall; flowers midseason to late, deep pink.

'Klondike'. Plants to 1 m. tall; flowers late, large, light yellow.

'Navajo Pottery'. Plants to 70 cm. tall; flowers midseason, orange yellow with a red center.

'Peaches 'n Cream'. Plants to 95 cm. tall; flowers midseason, peach colored with pink blushes.

'Regalaire'. Plants to 80 cm. tall; flowers ruffled, red with a darker center.

'Royal Command'. Plants to 90 cm. tall; flowers early to midseason, bright red with a yellow throat.

'Step Forward'. Plants to 75 cm. tall; flowers early to midseason, pink blend with a deep red blotch in the throat.

'Taylor Russell'. Plants to 60 cm. tall; flowers midseason, soft pink with lavender overcast.

'Twinkling Star'. Plants to 45 cm. tall; flowers midseason, lilac pink with yellow throat.

'Wyandote'. Plants to 75 cm. tall; flowers midseason, bright red with narrow perianth segments.

'Young Love'. Plants to 90 cm. tall; flowers midseason, yellow tan-gold with a purple center.

Hepatica Mill. (Liverleaf)

RANUNCULACEAE (Buttercup Family)

DESCRIPTION: A genus of about 10 species of early, spring-flowering perennials, native in the northern hemisphere; **leaves** cordate, 3- to 5-lobed, evergreen, on long petioles; **flowers** white to purple or blue, solitary, on long scapes; involucre calyxlike, of 3 small bracts; sepals petal-like; petals lacking; **fruit** an achene.

Hepatica acutiloba DC. (Sharplobe Liverleaf). Perennial to 20 cm. tall. April, May. PLATE 120

DESCRIPTION: **Plants** native from Manitoba to Maine, south to Missouri and Georgia; **leaves** basal, 3-lobed, with acute lobes; **flowers** blue, pink, or white; involucral bracts narrow, pointed.

USE: Plant in woodland wildflower garden or in a shaded portion of the wildflower garden.

CULTURE: Plants like a well-drained soil high in organic matter and partial shade. Propagation is mainly by division in early spring. Plants can also be grown from seed planted in a cold frame in late summer. It takes longer for seedlings to reach a flowering size.

CULTIVARS
'Double'. Flowers with several rows of petal-like sepals.
'Millstream Pink'. Flowers pink.

Hepatica americana (DC.) Ker.-Gawl. (Roundlobe Liverleaf). Perennial to 15 cm. tall. April, May.

DESCRIPTION: **Plants** native on acid soils from Manitoba to Nova Scotia, south to Missouri and Florida; **leaves** oblate-reniform, 3-lobed, with rounded lobes; **flowers** blue to white, or rose-colored.

USE: Same as for *H. acutiloba*.

CULTURE: Same as for *H. acutiloba* except that plants require an acid soil.

CULTIVARS
'Alba'. Flowers white.
'Deep Blue'. Flowers deep blue.

Hepatica triloba —see *Hepatica americana*

Hesperis L. (Rocket)

CRUCIFERAE (Mustard Family)

DESCRIPTION: A genus of about 20 species of biennial or perennial herbs, native from the Mediterranean region to central Asia; **leaves** narrow, entire or toothed; **flowers** white to rose or purple in terminal paniculate racemes, often fragrant; sepals and petals 4; **fruit** an elongated silique.

Hesperis matronalis L. (Sweet Rocket, Dame's Rocket). Perennial, or sometimes biennial, to 1 m. tall. May, June.   PLATE 121

DESCRIPTION: **Plants** coarse, usually hairy, native in central and southern Europe, escaped from cultivation; **leaves** lanceolate to lanceolate-ovate, to 10 cm. long, toothed; **flowers** large, to 1 cm. across, lilac or light purple, occasionally white, fragrant, in terminal racemes; petals long-clawed.

USE: Plant in flower border or in woodland garden.

CULTURE: Plants thrive in sun or partial shade. The flowers are showy and sweetly fragrant. Propagation is by seeds sown in June. Once established, volunteer seedlings will furnish all of the plants needed. This plant can become a weed.

Heuchera L. (Alumroot)

SAXIFRAGACEAE (Saxifrage Family)

DESCRIPTION: A genus of about 50 species of perennial herbs of North America; basal **leaves** tufted, round-cordate or broadly 5- to 9-lobed, toothed, long-petioled; flowering scapes slender, overtopping the foliage; **flowers** small, green, white, red, or purple, in narrow panicles or racemes, 5-merous; **fruit** a capsule the inner side of 2 apical beaks.

Heuchera sanguinea Engelm. (Coralbells). Perennial to 60 cm. tall. June-September.   PLATE 122

DESCRIPTION: **Plants** native from Arizona to New Mexico, south to Mexico; **flowers** bright red, in loose panicles, campanulate; petals shorter than the calyx lobes.

USE: Plant toward the front of the border or in a rock garden. Flowers are excellent for cutting.

CULTURE: Coralbells thrive in any good garden soil that is well-drained and bloom best in full sun. Some of the named cultivars are of borderline hardiness, requiring winter protection. The species can be grown from seeds but most named cultivars are increased by division in early spring. Once established it is best to leave the plants alone except for weeding.

CULTIVARS

'Alba'. Flowers white.

'Coral Cloud'. Flowers vivid coral pink.

'Martin Bells'. Flowers coral red.

'Pleu de Feu'. Flowers deep pink.

Heuchera — other species

H. americana L. (Rock Geranium), native in the eastern United States, has greenish white flowers in June. A good rock garden species.

H. richardsonii R. Br., native from Saskatchewan to Manitoba, south to Minnesota and Indiana, has green flowers in June. It is sometimes planted in prairie gardens.

Heuchera — garden hybrids

In an attempt to obtain hardier plants, *H. sanquinea* has been crossed with *H. americana* and *H. richardsonii*. A number of promising seedlings have resulted but few of them are commercially available.

Hibiscus L. (Mallow)

MALVACEAE (Hollyhock Family)

DESCRIPTION: A genus of about 250 species of herbs, shrubs, and trees, native mostly in warm-temperate and tropical regions; **leaves** usually simple, mostly palmately veined and lobed or parted; **flowers** usually solitary in leaf axils, but sometimes in racemes, corymbs, and panicles; involucral bracts 4 to 20, separate, sometimes basally united to the calyx; calyx mostly bell-shaped, 5-lobed, sometimes prominently 10-veined; petals 5, mostly longer than the calyx lobes, white, yellow, red, purple, or rarely blue, generally with a basal maroon spot; stamens united in a tubular column, usually longer than the petals; style usually with 5 apical branches; **fruit** a 5-celled capsule.

Hibiscus moscheutos L. (Common Rose Mallow). Perennial to 2 m. tall. August, September.

DESCRIPTION: **Plants** native in bogs or marshes of the eastern United States;

leaves to 20 cm. long, lanceolate to broadly ovate, unlobed or shallowly 3- to 5-lobed, green above, white pubescent beneath; **flowers** white, pink, or rose, usually with crimson center, on long pedicels; involucral bracts mostly 10 to 14, lanceolate-linear, to 2.5 cm. long; calyx 2 to 4 cm. long, slightly enlarged; petals to 10 cm. long; **capsules** with a short beak.

USE: Plant toward the back of the flower border. The large flowers can be floated in water in a shallow container as table decorations.

CULTURE: Plants require a moisture retentive soil and full sun. Propagation is largely by seeds started early indoors. Choice selections can be increased by root divisions in early spring. Plants are slow to start growing in the spring. A winter protection is advisable.

CULTIVARS AND VARIETY

subspecies *palustris* (L.) R. T. Clausen. (Marsh Mallow). This subspecies is native in coastal marshes from Massachusetts to North Carolina and inland as fas as Indiana. This subspecies has been hybridized with other species to produce the beautiful garden hybrids.

Hibiscus —garden hybrids

H. moscheutos and its subspecies have been hybridized by crossing with *H. coccineus* and *H. militaris* to produce a series of beautiful garden hybrids with flowers up to 20 cm. across.

CULTIVARS

'Cotton Candy'. Flowers a clear satin pink.

'Dixie Belle'. Flowers very large, in a good color range.

'Red Shield'. Stems and leaves burgundy red.

'Southern Belle'. All-America Winner. Spectacular flowers to 20 cm. across, in white, pink, rose, carmine, and crimson colors, all with a red "eye." PLATE 123

Hosta Tratt. (Plantain Lily)

LILIACEAE (Lily Family)

DESCRIPTION: A genus of about 40 species of perennial herbs, with short rhizomes, native in Japan, China, and Korea; **plants** form large clumps; **leaves** basal, tufted, petioled; **flowers** white, blue, lilac, or violet, in terminal bracted, 1-sided racemes, which are usually taller than the leaves; perianth segments 6, united into a tube; stamens 6, curved; **fruit** a 3-valved capsule, with many winged seeds.

Hosta caerulea —see *Hosta ventricosa*

Hosta cathayana — see *Hosta lancifolia*

Hosta erronema — see *Hosta undulata* 'Erronema'

Hosta fortunei (Bak.) L. H. Bailey (Fortune's Plantain Lily). Perennial to 60 cm. tall. June, July.

DESCRIPTION: **Plants** native in Japan; **leaves** ovate, to 12 cm. long, with 8 to 10 veins on each side of the midrib, cordate, with a whitish bloom underneath; **flowers** funnelform, pale lilac to violet, to 4 cm. long; anthers purple.

USE: This species and other hosta species and named cultivars are widely planted as ground cover plants in shady areas.

CULTURE: Hostas prefer a moist soil high in organic matter and a shady location. Propagation is by division in early spring. Hostas have few insect or disease problems, but slugs can threaten the plants. Unfortunately the conditions that favor hostas also favor slugs. If these pests are present; use a slug bait containing Mesurol.

CULTIVARS AND VARIETY

'Aurea'. Leaves yellow in early spring, gradually turning a light green by summer.

'Aurea-maculata'. Leaves yellow in early spring, gradually turning light green.

'Marginata-albo'. Leaves green with a wide white margin.

var. *obscura* 'Aurea-marginata'. Leaves dark green with a deep yellow margin that holds color all season.

Hosta glauca — see *Hosta sieboldiana*

Hosta lancifolia Engl. (Narrow-leaved Plantain). Perennial to 60 cm. tall. July, August.

DESCRIPTION: **Plants** native in Japan; **leaves** ovate-lanceolate, to 12 cm. long, with 5 to 6 veins on each side of midrib, dark green, glossy, often long-pointed, on slender pedicels; **flowers** funnelform, dark violet, fading with age, to 5 cm. long; anthers dark violet.

USE: In addition to using this species as a ground cover, it is often used for edging.

CULTURE: Same as for *H. fortunei*. This species will take more sun than most of the other hostas.

CULTIVAR

'Albomarginata'. Leaves bordered with white.

Hosta plantaginea (Lam.) Asch. (Fragrant Plantain). Perennial to 75 cm. tall. August, September.

DESCRIPTION: **Plants** native in China and Japan; **leaves** ovate to cordate-ovate, to 25 cm. long, with 7 to 9 veins on each side of midrib, light green, glossy; **flowers** white, funnelform, fragrant, to 12 cm. long, in a short raceme.

USE: Same as for *H. fortunei*. This species is also grown for its showy fragrant flowers.

CULTURE: See *H. fortunei*.

CULTIVAR
'Grandiflora'. Flowers larger than in species, pure white.

Hosta sieboldiana (Lodd.) Engl. (Seersucker Plantain Lily). Perennial to 75 cm. tall. July, August.   PLATE 126

DESCRIPTION: **Plants** native in Japan; **leaves** ovate, cordate, to 35 cm. long, with about 12 veins on each side of midrib, usually very glaucous, rigid and very thick, short-pointed; **flowers** funnelform, pale lilac, to 4 cm. long, in a short, dense, 6- to 10-flowered raceme.

USE: See *H. fortunei*.

CULTURE: See *H. fortueni*.

CULTIVARS
'Aurea-marginata'. Leaves bordered with yellow. Also called 'Frances Williams'.
'Elegans'. Leaves very large, blue green, flowers nearly white.

Hosta subordata —see *Hosta plantaginea*

Hosta undulata (Otto & A. Dietr) L. H. Bailey (Wavyleaf Plantain Lily). Perennial to 1 m. tall. June, July.

DESCRIPTION: **Plants** presumably native in Japan but not known in the wilds; **leaves** elliptic to ovate, to about 15 cm. long, with about 10 veins on each side of midrib, striped lengthwise with cream or white, sharp-pointed, strongly wavy, abruptly narrowed to a winged petiole; **flowers** funnelform, pale lavender, to 5 cm. long; anthers violet.

USE: Same as for *H. fortunei*.

CULTURE: Same as for *H. fortunei*.

CULTIVARS
'Erronema'. Plants robust; leaves larger than in the species and less wavy, uniformly green.
'Univitata'. Leaves with a narrow, white central stripe.

Hosta — other species

H. crispula F. Mack, native in Japan but known only in cultivation, has ovate leaves with white margins.   PLATE 124

H. decorata L. H. Bailey (Blunt Plantain Lily), native home unknown, has ovate to elliptic leaves with white margins and winged petioles.

H. elata Hyl., native in Japan, has large, wavy leaves to 25 cm. long.

H. minor Nakai, native in Korea and Japan, is one of the smaller hostas with orbicular-ovate leaves with subcordate bases.

H. nakaiana F. Mack., native in Japan, has oblong-ovate leaves that are only 7.5 cm. long; flowers lilac to purple, to 5 cm. long, in capitate racemes, in July, often a repeat bloomer.

H. tardiflora (W. Irving) Stearn, native in Japan but known only in cultivation, is a small plant to 30 cm. tall, with lanceolate leaves to 15 cm. long. Leaf petioles are purple-spotted. Flowers are funnelform, dark purple, in dense racemes in August.

H. ventricosa Stern. (Blue Plantain Lily), native in eastern Asia, has large ovate-cordate leaves to 20 cm. long and winged petioles.

H. venusta, native in Japan and on the Cheju Island off Korea, is the smallest species, with leaves that are ovate to elliptic-ovate and only 5 cm. long.

Hosta — garden hybrids

Numerous interspecies hybrids have been developed and more appear on the market every year. Some of the named hybrids are eagerly purchased at high prices by hosta enthusiasts. Literally hundreds of named cultivars are on the market. To become acquainted with the various kinds, visit a grower of hostas or a public garden that features hostas. The University of Minnesota Landscape Arboretum has a fine collection. The following are but a few of the named cultivars.

CULTIVARS   PLATE 125

'August Moon'. Leaves large, yellow, holding color through growing season. Flowers pale lavender.

'Betsy King'. Plants medium-sized, with many deep purple flowers. PLATE 127

'Golden Anniversary'. Plants large, with pale lavender flowers. Leaves are yellow green in spring, turning a glossy green later.

'Gold Standard'. Plants medium-sized. Leaves green with a gold marbling throughout.

'Green Gold'. Plants medium-sized. Leaves dark green with margins that are first golden, then turning to a cream color. Flowers pale lavender.

'Krossa Regal'. Plants large, with blue green, wavy leaves of heavy substance. Flowers pale lavender on stalks up to 2 m. tall.

'Louisa'. Plants small, with white-margined leaves. Flowers white, on stalks to 30 cm. tall.

'Royal Standard'. Plants large, with leaves of a medium green color. Flowers white, slightly fragrant. Tolerates more light than others.   PLATE 128

'Ruffles'. Plants of medium size with dark green leaves with ruffled margins. Flowers large on tall, arching stalks.

'Sweet Susan'. Plants of medium size with many large, pale lavender, fragrant flowers.

'Wagon Gold'. Plants small, with bright yellow leaves that hold their color throughout the growing season. Flowers are lavender.

Houstonia—see *Hedyotis*

Hunnemannia Sweet.

PAPAVERACEAE (Poppy Family)

DESCRIPTION: A genus with but a single species of a glabrous, glaucous, perennial herb, native in Mexico; **leaves** ternately dissected; **flowers** yellow; sepals 2; petals 2; stamens 16 or more; **fruit** a linear capsule.

Hunnemannia fumariifolia Sweet (Mexican Tulip Poppy). Tender perennial grown as an annual to 60 cm. tall. July-October. PLATE 129

DESCRIPTION: **Plants** native in Mexico, to 60 cm. tall; **flowers** to 7.5 cm. across; **fruits** to 10 cm. long.

USE: Plant in flower border or rock garden. Flowers are attractive in flower arrangements.

CULTURE: Plants are of easy culture in almost any soil in full sun. The seeds can be sown directly as soon as the soil warms up in the spring or they can be started indoors in individual pots for earlier bloom. The plants resent root disturbance.

CULTIVAR

'Sunlite'. Flowers bright yellow.

Hyacinthus L. (Hyacinth)

LILIACEAE (Lily Family)

DESCRIPTION: A genus with but a single species of bulbous, perennial herbs, native in the Mediterranean region, Asia Minor, and Syria; bulbs tunicate;

leaves basal, narrow; **flowers** white, yellow, pink, red, or blue, in bracted, cylindrical racemes; perianth funnelform, with a cylindrical tube and 6 spreading or reflexed lobes; stamens 6, with versatile anthers; **fruit** a 3-celled capsule.

Hyacinthus orientalis L. (Dutch Hyacinth, Garden Hyacinth). Perennial to 30 cm. tall. May.   PLATE 130

DESCRIPTION: **Bulbs** with a purple or white tunic; **leaves** with upturned margins, to 30 cm. long; **flowers** fragrant, about 2.5 cm. long, sometimes double, nodding.

USE: Plant in rock garden, in flower border, or under shrubs. Also popular for winter forcing.

CULTURE: Plants require a deep, well-drained soil. Plant bulbs in late September or early October. Space the bulbs about 20 cm. apart and cover with about 15 cm. of soil. A winter mulch is needed. Plants may be short-lived.

CULTIVARS: Improvement of the hyacinth began in the 18th century. Today there are numerous named cultivars to choose from.
'Amethyst'. Flowers purple red.
'City of Harlem'. Flowers yellow.
'Delft Blue'. Flowers procelain blue.
'L 'Innocence'. Flowers white.
'Pink Pearl'. Flowers pink.
'Scarlet Perfection'. Flowers scarlet red.

Hymenocallis Salisb. (Spider Lily)

AMARYLLIDACEAE (Amaryllis Family)

DESCRIPTION: A genus of about 25 species of summer-flowering bulbous herbs, native in warmer parts of North and South America; **leaves** strap-shaped to linear; **flowers** white or yellow, mostly fragrant, in terminal umbels, subtended by 2 or more spathes; perianth tube variable in length with 6 narrow lobes; stamens 6, basally united into a cuplike crown or corona; ovary inferior, 3-celled; **fruit** a capsule.

Hymenocallis narcissiflora (Jacq.) Macbr. (Peruvian Daffodil). Tender perennial to 60 cm. tall. June-August.   PLATE 131

DESCRIPTION: **Plants** native in the mountains of Bolivia and Peru; **leaves** basal, strap-shaped, to 60 cm. long, petioled; **flowers** white; perianth tube to 10 cm. long, with lobes about as long; corona fringed, to 5 cm. long.

USE: Plant in clumps in the flower border.

CULTURE: Spider lilies like a well-drained soil high in organic matter. They are colorful when planted in clumps in full sun. Plant the bulbs about 10 cm. deep after the soil warms up in mid-May. The plants will start to bloom in about three weeks. The bulbs are tender and must be stored over winter in a warm room at a temperature of about 60° F. Cover the bulbs and roots with soil or sawdust to reduce moisture loss. They may fail to bloom if the storage temperature is too cool. Separate and plant the offsets from the bulbs to increase the number of plants.

CULTIVAR

'Sulphur Queen'. Flowers primrose yellow with a lighter colored throat.

Iberis L. (Candytuft)

CRUCIFERAE (Mustard Family)

DESCRIPTION: A genus of about 30 species of small, annual, or perennial herbs, sometimes woody at base and evergreen, native in central Europe and in the Mediterranean region; **leaves** narrow, entire or toothed, occasionally pinnatifid; **flowers** white, pink, red, or purple, in umbel-like clusters or in racemes that lengthen in fruit; sepals 4, petals 4, the 2 outer larger than the inner; **fruit** an orbicular silicle winged at the tip.

Iberis jucunda —see *Aethionema cordifolium*

Iberis sempervirens L. (Evergreen Candytuft). Perennial to 30 cm. tall. May.   PLATE 132

DESCRIPTION: **Plants** evergreen, native in southern Europe; **leaves** narrow-oblong, to 4 cm. long, blunt, entire; **flowers** white, in racemes that elongate in fruit.

USE: Plant in rock garden or use as a ground cover.

CULTURE: Plants require a well-drained soil and prefer full sun. Propagation is largely by cuttings rooted in June. They can also be increased by division or by seeds sown in spring.

CULTIVARS

'Autumn Snow'. Flowers white, in spring and fall.

'Little Gem'. Plants compact.

'Purity'. Flowers pure white.

'Snowflake'. Flowers large, pure white.

Iberis umbellata L. (Globe Candytuft). Annual to 40 cm. tall. June, July.

DESCRIPTION: **Plants** are native in the Mediterranean region; **leaves** lanceolate, to 8 cm. long, pointed, entire; **flowers** pink, violet, purple, and red, in a dense umble.

USE: Plant in rock garden or flower border.

CULTURE: Plants require a well-drained soil and full sun. Sow seeds directly outdoors in early May. Thin the plants to 25 cm. apart for best bloom. Seeds can be started indoors for earlier bloom but seedlings are sprawly and difficult to handle.

CULTIVAR

'Dwarf Fairy'. Plants compact; flowers in shades of pink, rose, carmine, crimson, lavender, purple, and white.

Iberis — other species

I. amara L. (Rocket Candytuft), native in western Europe, is an annual with white, fragrant flowers produced in racemes in June and July.

I. saxatilis L. (Rock Candytuft), native in southern Europe, is an evergreen subshrub, suitable for rock gardens. The white flowers are produced in terminal corymbs in May. Winter protection is needed.

Impatiens L. (Jewelweed, Touch-me-not)

BALSAMINACEAE (Balsam Family)

DESCRIPTION: A large genus of about 500 species of annual or perennial herbs, native mostly in the tropics and subtropics; **stems** mostly succulent and transparent; **leaves** simple; **flowers** solitary or variously clustered; sepals 3, rarely 5; the upper 2 small and green, the lower one petal-like, asymmetrically funnelform, usually with a long nectar-bearing spur; petals 5, the upper one (called the standard) flat or helmet-shaped, the lower 4 usually united in lateral pairs (called wings); stamens 5, united in a short tube near the top; ovary superior, 5-celled; **fruit** a 5-valved capsule, explosively dehiscent into 5 coiled valves.

Impatiens balsamina L. (Garden Balsam). Annual to 75 cm. tall. July, August.

DESCRIPTION: **Plants** native in India, China, and the Malay Penninsula; **leaves** alternate, to 15 cm. long, lanceolate, acuminate, deeply serrate; **flowers** white to yellow or dark red, often spotted, axillary and overtopped with foliage; **capsule** asymmetrically elliptic, to 2 cm. long.

USE: Plant in flower border.

CULTURE: The garden balsam likes a soil that is well-drained and high in organic matter. They will grow in full sun or partial shade. Propagation is by seeds started indoors in late March. It is best to grow seedlings in individual pots. Transplant to the garden after danger of frost has passed.

CULTIVARS

'Camelia'. Flowers double, resembling camelias.

'Royal'. Flowers double, in shades of salmon, cerise, mauve, white, pink, scarlet, purple, and red.

'Torch'. Flowers scarlet red.

Impatiens sultanii — see *Impatiens wallerana*

Impatiens wallerana Hook. (Patience Plant). Tender perennial grown as an annual to 1 m. tall. July-October.   PLATE 134

DESCRIPTION: **Plants** branched, native from Tanzania to Mozambique; **leaves** alternate, or upper leaves sometimes opposite, lanceolate-ovate to elliptic-oblong, up to 10 cm. long, acute to cuspidate, crenate-dentate; **flowers** solitary in leaf axils or in terminal racemes, to 5 cm. across, carmine, pink, reddish orange, purple, white, or bicolored; lower sepal to 5 cm. long with a slightly curved spur; **capsule** swollen, oblique-fusiform, to 2 cm. long, smooth.

USE: One of the best annuals for the shaded flower border or on the north side of buildings.

CULTURE: Plants thrive in most well-drained soils in partial shade. Start seeds indoors in late March or early April. Do not plant outdoors until all danger of frost has passed.

CULTIVARS AND STRAINS

'Blitz'. All-America Winner. Plants compact; leaves dark bronzy green; flowers reddish scarlet.

'Cherry Star'. Plants very compact; flowers cherry red with white star.

Futura (strain). Plants compact; flowers large, in bright shades of burgundy, coral, orange, pink, rose, red, and white.

Glitters (strain). Flowers in a wide color range.

'Orange Star'. Plants very compact; flowers large, dark orange with a white star.

Super Elfin (strain). Plants low, uniform; flowers in shades of fuchsia, orange, pink, salmon, scarlet, and white.

Twinkle (strain). Plants low; flowers in vibrant shades of fuchsia, rose, and red, striped with white.

Zigzag (strain). Plants with zigzag branches; flowers bicolored in soft shades of scarlet, orange, pink, rose, salmon, and purple.

Impatiens — other species

I. capensis Meerb. (Jewelweed, Touch-me-not), native in North America, has spotted orange yellow flowers. It is sometimes planted in moist sites in wild-flower gardens.

I. platypetala Lindl. (Java Snapweed), native in Java, has large purple, rose, pink, and orange flowers. 'Tangerine' has salmon orange flowers with a deep crimson center. 'Tangeglow' has very large tangerine orange flowers.   PLATE 133

Incarvillea Juss.

BIGNONIACEAE (Bignonia Family)

DESCRIPTION: A genus of about 14 species of annual or perennial herbs with tuberous **roots**, native in Asia; **leaves** pinnate or pinnatifid; **flowers** red, rose, pink, white, yellow, or purple, solitary or in terminal racemes or panicles; calyx 5-toothed or 5-lobed; corolla funnelform; stamens 4, inserted on the corolla tube, in 2 series of unequal length; **fruit** a capsule.

Incarvillea delavayi Bur. & Franch. (Hardy Gloxinia, Chinese Trumpet Flower). Perennial to 60 cm. tall. July, August.   PLATE 135

DESCRIPTION: **Plants** native in China; **leaves** basal, pinnate, 25 cm. long, with 6 to 11 pairs of lateral leaflets that are narrow-ovate to lanceolate, crenate; terminal leaflet elliptic or obovate, to 4 cm. long; **flowers** with a yellow and purple tube and purple lobes; to 8 cm. across, produced in a terminal raceme; **capsules** often winged.

USE: Plant in flower border.

CULTURE: Plants require a fertile, well-drained soil and full sun. Propagation is by seeds or by division of established plants. This beautiful perennial is of borderline hardiness and requires a winter mulch. I have seen it growing near Bagley, Minnesota.

Inula L. (Sunray)

COMPOSITAE (Sunflower Family)

Inula Tribe

DESCRIPTION: A genus of over 100 species of annual or perennial herbs, native in temperate and subtropical regions of the Old World; **stems** often glandular or hairy; **leaves** basal or alternate; **flower** heads radiate or discoid, solitary or in racemes, corymbs, or panicles; involucre hemispherical or campanulate; involucral bracts imbricate in several rows, the outer often herbaceous, the inner usually narrow and scarious; receptacle flat or convex, naked; disc flowers tubular, perfect, yellow with sagittate-tailed anthers; ray flowers pistillate, yellow or orange-yellow; **achenes** nearly cylindrical to 4- to 5-ribbed, with pappus of 1 row of capillary bristles.

Inula glandulosa —see *Inula orientalis*

Inula orientalis Lam. (Caucasian Inula). Perennial to 1.5 m. tall. July, August.

DESCRIPTION: **Plants** with spreading hairs, native in the Caucasus; basal **leaves** with petioles; stem leaves sessile, oblong, to 15 cm. long, nearly cordate, semiclasping, entire or with marginal glands; **flower** heads to 7 cm. across; ray flowers orange yellow.

USE: Planted in flower borders for their summer bloom.

CULTURE: Plants thrive in most soils in full sun. Propagation is by seeds or division. Root cuttings, planted in a sandy soil in a cold frame in October, will form new plants in the following spring.

Inula —other species

I. ensifolia L. (Swordleaf Sunray), native in Europe, has small, yellow flowering heads to 4 cm. across in July and August. It is a good rock garden plant. 'Golden Beauty' has golden yellow ray flowers.   PLATE 136

I. helenium L. (Elecampane), native in central Asia, is a tall plant with furrowed stems. The flowering heads are 8 cm. across, with yellow ray flowers in July and August.

Ipomoea L. (Morning-glory)

CONVOLVULACEAE (Morning-glory Family)

DESCRIPTION: A large genus of about 500 species of climbing, prostrate or erect, annual or perennial herbs, native in the tropics and warm-temperate regions; **leaves** alternate, entire, lobed or divided; **flowers** axillary, solitary or in few- to many-flowered clusters; corolla funnelform or campanulate, 5-lobed, with stripes; stamens on the corolla tube; **fruit** a 4- to 6-valved capsule.

Ipomoea purpurea (L.) Roth. (Common Morning-glory). Tender perennial grown as an annual to 5 m. tall. July-September.

DESCRIPTION: Hairy twining vines, native in tropical America; **leaves** broadly cordate-ovate, to 12 cm. long, entire; **flowers** purple, blue, or pink, to 7.5 cm. long.

USE: Plant on trellises or woven wire fences.

CULTURE: The plants are of easy culture in most any soil in full sun. The seeds can be seeded direct or started indoors in individual containers in early April. To increase germination, file through the hard seed coat to allow water to get through. Flowers open only in the morning and close when the sun gets high in the sky.

CULTIVARS

'Alba'. Flowers white.

'Huberi'. Leaves variegated with white; flowers pink to purple with white margins.

'Violacea'. Flowers violet purple, double.

Ipomoea tricolor Cav. (Common morning-glory). Tender perennial grown as an annual to 5 m. tall. July-September.

DESCRIPTION: Glabrous twining vines, native in tropical America; **leaves** orbicular or ovate, to 25 cm. across, cordate at base; **flowers** purplish blue with a white tube and red limbs, but variable in color in cultivars; corolla funnelform, to 10 cm. long.

USE: Same as for *I. purpurea.*

CULTURE: Same as for *I. purpurea.*

CULTIVARS

'Blue Star'. Flowers light sky blue with dark blue stripes.

'Cheerio'. Flowers scarlet red, day blooming.

'Early Call Rose'. All-America Winner. Flowers rich crimson carmine with a white throat.

'Heavenly Blue'. Flowers bright sky blue, to 12 cm. across.   PLATE 137

'Pearly Gates'. All-America Winner. Flowers white with a gold center.

'Scarlet O'Hara'. All-America Winner. Flowers crimson scarlet.

Ipomoea — other species.

I. alba L. (Moonflower), native in tropical America, is a tender perennial climber with milky juice. It is grown as an annual. The flowers are trumpet shaped, white, to 15 cm. across.

I. x *multifida* (Raf.) Shinn. (Cardinal Climber), a cross between *I. coccinea* and *I. quamoclit*, is a vigorous climber to 5 m. tall, with salverform flowers that are crimson with a white center from July to September.

I. quamoclit L. (Cypress Vine, Cardinal Climber), native in the American tropics, is a vigorous vine with pinnately cut leaves with threadlike segments. The flowers are trumpet-shaped, to 3 cm. across, in shades of white, rose, and scarlet from July to September.

Ipomopsis Michx.

POLEMONIACEA (Phlox Family)

DESCRIPTION: A genus of about 25 species of biennial or perennial herbs, native mostly in North America; **leaves** alternate, entire to pinnately dissected; **flowers** of various colors, in cymes or panicles subtended by a bract; calyx 5-lobed; corolla salverform or tubular; stamens 5; **fruit** a capsule.

Ipomopsis rubra (Nutt.) V.E. Grant (Scarlet Gilia, Standing Cypress). Tender perennial often grown as an annual to 2 m. tall. July, August. PLATE 138

DESCRIPTION: **Plants** native from Texas to South Carolina, south to Florida; **leaves** pinnately parted into filiform segments; **flowers** scarlet outside, yellow and dotted red inside in a narrow panicle.

USE: An attractive plant for the flower border.

CULTURE: Plants will grow in most soils in full sun. Although a perennial, this plant is usually grown as an annual by starting seeds indoors in early April. Space the plants about 30 cm. apart. Seeds can also be planted in a cold frame in July where the plants can be protected over winter before planting in the flower border.

Iris L. (Flag)

IRIDACEAE (Iris Family)

DESCRIPTION: A genus of over 200 species of rhizomatous or bulbous perennial herbs, native mostly in the North Temperate Zone; **leaves** mostly basal, 2-ranked, linear to sword-shaped; **flowers** in groups of 1 or more, borne on branched or unbranched scapes with 2 spathe valves, showy, in many colors; perianth tube of varying length; perianth segments 6, the outer 3 (falls) narrowed basally in a (haft), sometimes bearded, the inner 3 (standards) narrowed basally into a (claw), usually erect and arching, sometimes spreading or re-flexed; stamens borne at the base of the falls; style branches 3, bifid or crested, petal-like, colored, covering the stamens; **fruit** a leathery, 3- or 6-angled capsule.

Iris kaempferi Siebold (Japanese Iris). Perennial to 60 cm. tall. June, July. PLATE 139

DESCRIPTION: **Plants** rhizomatous, with branched flowering **stems**, native in Japan; **leaves** sword-shaped, to 60 cm. long, with a prominent midrib; **flowers** beardless, red purple; perianth tube to 2 cm. long; falls drooping, elliptic to obovate, to 7.5 cm. long, with yellow haft; standards narrowly oblanceolate, to 5 cm. long.

USE: Grown for their colorful flowers.

CULTURE: The Japanese iris requires a moist site and an acid soil. It is seldom planted except by iris enthusiasts. Propagation is by division. Winter protection using a mulch of marsh hay or clean straw is required.

CULTIVARS

'Azurea', Flowers blue.

'Eleanor Parry'. Flowers reddish purple.

'Gold Band'. Flowers pure white with a gold band on each segment of the perianth.

'Light in Opal'. Flowers soft rose pink.

'Nikko'. Flowers purple blue with deep purple veins.

'Purple and Gold'. Flowers velvety purple with golden throat.

'Reign of Glory'. Flowers silvery blue with blue stippling.

Iris sibirica L. (Siberian Iris). Perennial to 1 m. tall. June. PLATE 140

DESCRIPTION: **Plants** tufted, with short rhizomes, native in central Europe and Russia; **leaves** linear, to 75 cm. long; spathes 2- to 3-flowered with brown, scarious valves; **flowers** typically lilac blue or purple blue; perianth tube to 1.25 cm. long; falls beardless, reflexed, rounded-oblong, 2 cm. wide; standards broadly lanceolate, shorter than the falls.

USE: Popular in flower borders and for cut flowers.

CULTURE: Siberian iris are of easy culture, thriving in most soils in full sun. They grow best in moist soil and are often planted along streams. Propagation is by division in early spring. Clumps should be divided every 3 or 4 years. The plants become very matted and must be cut apart with a sharp knife or spade.

CULTIVARS

'Anniversary'. Plants 65 cm. tall; flowers white.

'Borbeleta'. Plants 90 cm. tall; flowers rich blue, with wavy petals.

'Early Bluebird'. Plants 80 cm. tall; flowers light blue, early.

'Ego'. Plants 65 cm. tall; flowers deep blue, ruffled.

'Pansy Purple'. Plants 80 cm. tall; flowers deep violet.

'Sky Wings'. Plants 85 cm. tall; flowers light blue and ivory in a beautiful color combination.

'Steve Varner'. Plants 80 cm. tall; flowers sky blue. One of the best.

Iris spuria L. (Butterfly Iris, Spuria Iris). Perennial to 1 m. tall. June, July.
PLATE 141

DESCRIPTION: **Plants** with short rhizomes, native in central and southern Europe, Algeria, and Iran; **leaves** linear, stiff, glaucous, to 30 cm. long; spathes 1- to 3-flowered; **flowers** beardless, blue purple to lilac; perianth tube to 2 cm. long; falls about 5 cm. long, orbicular, with a yellow ridge; standards oblanceolate, narrow, to 1.25 cm. wide.

CULTIVARS: The cultivars of *I. spuria* are becoming quite popular, since they lengthen the iris season.

USE: Plant toward the back of flower border. Flowers excellent for arrangements.

CULTURE: The spurias like a rich soil and plenty of moisture. Propagation is by division in early spring or fall.

CULTIVARS

'Baritone'. Plants 1.3 m. tall; flowers large, brown and yellow.

'Golden Lady'. Plants 1.3 m. tall; flowers light yellow.

'Highline Lavender'. Plants 1.2 m. tall; flowers lavender flushed with yellow.

'Imperial Night'. Plants 1.3 m. tall; flowers deep purple and bright yellow edged purple.

'Morning tide'. Plants to 1.2 m. tall; flowers white with light blue veins.

'Ruffled Canary'. Plants 90 cm. tall; flowers ruffled, white and yellow.

Iris — other species

I. cristata Ait., native from Maryland to Georgia and west to Oklahoma, is a popular rock garden plant only about 7.5 cm. tall, with a crest on the falls that is white and yellow and dotted with purple, in early May. 'Alba', with white flowers, and 'Abbey's Violet', with deep violet-blue flowers, are named cultivars.

I. missouriensis Nutt. (Western Blue Flag), native from British Columbia to South Dakota and south to Mexico, has beardless, white to lilac purple flowers in June. Sometimes planted in rock gardens and prairie gardens.

I. pseudoacorus L. (Yellow Flag), native in western Europe and northern Africa and naturalized elsewhere, has yellow flowers in June and is popular for planting in wet soil near streams or ponds.

I. pumila L. (Dwarf Iris), native in central Europe, southern Russia, and Asia Minor, is a popular rock garden plant with bearded flowers in shades of yellow, blue, and lilac, in May. There are numerous named cultivars.

I. versicolor L. (Blue Flag), native from Manitoba to Newfoundland, south to Minnesota and Virginia, has violet, blue violet, and red violet flowers that are beardless, in June. It likes moist soil and will even grow in shallow water.   PLATE 142

Iris — garden hybrids

The vast majority of all of the iris grown in gardens are of hybrid origin involving several species. The most popular group is the bearded iris. These have a fleshy, horizontally spreading rhizome that develops near the soil surface. Classification of these bearded iris is based on size. Tall Bearded Irises range in height from 45 cm. to over 1 m. in height and bloom in late May and early June. The Intermediate Bearded Irises range in height from 30 to 45 cm. The Dwarf Bearded Irises range in height from 7.5 cm. to 30 cm. and usually bloom in late April or early May.   PLATE 143

The bearded iris likes a well-drained soil and full sun. Propagation is by division of the fleshy rhizomes, usually done about 6 weeks after bloom or in late July or early August. The rhizomes have a dichotomous method of branching and grow outward from the center of the clump. Dig the plants carefully with a spading fork and pull apart the divisions. Cut back the tops to about 15 cm., making a clean cut at the base. Examine the divisions carefully for damage from the iris borer. Only healthy divisions should be replanted. Keep each variety separate and labeled. In replanting, make a V-shaped ridge with a square-nosed spade. Set the rhizome on the ridge with the roots spread out on either side. Cover with soil so the rhizome is just barely covered. Firm the soil, and water. If more than one rhizome is planted of each variety, space the rhizomes about 15 cm. apart in a circle with the growing points pointing outward. Keep the varieties separate, allowing enough space so the varieties do not grow together. Make a paper plan of your planting so you can check the identity of each variety if the label is lost.

Irises have their share of insect and disease problems. The iris borer is the most serious insect pest. The eggs are laid on the foliage and the young hatch out and feed on the leaves and then tunnel into the fleshy rhizome. A bacterial soft rot follows. Control is aimed at killing the young larvae before they enter the rhizome by using a good insecticide such as Malathion®.

A winter protection of marsh hay or clean straw should be applied in early November. Many of the new and better cultivars require such protection.

CULTIVARS: There are thousands of named iris cultivars and the number increases each year. Before buying new cultivars, become familiar with them by visiting a grower or public garden featuring iris when they are in bloom. Make a list of those cultivars that appeal to you. Talk with the grower to see what he would recommend. It is best to purchase rhizomes from a local source. You will get cultivars that have been tested for our climate, and the rhizomes will be fresher.

Ismene calathina — see *Hymenocallis narcissiflora*

Jeffersonia B. Barton (Twinleaf)

BERBERIDACEAE (Barberry Family)

DESCRIPTION: A small genus of only 2 species of perennial herbs, native to eastern North America and northeastern Asia; **leaves** basal, palmately veined or lobed; **flowers** white or blue, solitary, terminal on slender scapes; perianth of about 12 segments, the inner petal-like; stamens 6; ovary ovoid; **fruit** a leathery capsule.

Jeffersonia diphylla (L.) Pers. (American Twinleaf). Perennial to 45 cm. tall. April, May.   PLATE 144

DESCRIPTION: **Plants** native from Minnesota to New York, south to Alabama and Maryland; **leaf** blades to 15 cm. long and 12 cm. across, divided into 2 kidney-shaped, entire or lobed divisions, on long scapes; **flowers** white, to 2.5 cm. across; **capsule** dehiscent by a terminal lid.

USE: Plant in woodland wildflower garden.

CULTURE: Plants like partial shade and a soil that is well drained and high in organic matter. Propagation is by seeds sown as soon as ripe in summer in a sandy peat mixture in a cold frame or by division in September or early spring.

Jeffersonia dubia (Maxim.) Beth. & Hook. (Chinese Twinleaf). Perennial to 30 cm. tall. April, May.

DESCRIPTION: **Plants** native in eastern Asia; **leaf** blades orbicular to reniform, with a deep basal cleft, to 10 cm. across, on long petioles; **flowers** lavender blue, to 2.5 cm. across; **capsule** opening by a longitudinal slit.

USE: Same as for *J. diphylla.*

CULTURE: Same as for *J. diphylla.*

Kochia Roth.

CHENOPODIACEAE (Goosefoot Family)

DESCRIPTION: A genus of about 80 species of herbs or subshrubs, native in Eurasia; **leaves** alternate, narrow, entire; **flowers** small, axillary, solitary or clustered, perfect or pistillate; calyx 5-lobed; corolla none; stamens 5, exserted; ovary 1, with 2 stigmas; **fruit** a utricle, enveloped by the calyx, which develops wings.

Kochia scoparia forma *trichophylla* (Schmeiss) Schinz & Thall. (Summer Cypress, Burning Bush). Annual to 1.5 m. tall. Fall. PLATE 145

DESCRIPTION: **Plants** dense, globe-shaped or ellipsoid, native in Europe and Japan; **leaves** turning purplish red in September; **flowers** inconspicuous.

USE: Planted as a temporary hedge along driveways.

CULTURE: Plants are of easy culture in most soils in full sun. Start seeds indoors in early April. Space the plants about 30 cm. apart for a tight hedge. The fall color is a brilliant red.

Lamium L. (Dead Nettle)

LABIATAE (Mint Family)

DESCRIPTION: A genus of about 40 species of decumbent annual or perennial herbs, native in northern Africa, Europe, and Asia; **stems** square in cross section; **leaves** opposite, mostly toothed, lower leaves small, long petioled, middle leaves cordate, double-toothed; **flowers** in verticillasters formed in upper leaf axils; calyx tubular, 5-nerved, 5-toothed; corolla dilated at throat, 2-lipped, upper lip hooded, lower lip 3-lobed with middle lobe notched; stamens 4; **fruit** of 4 nutlets.

Lamium maculatum L. (Spotted Dead Nettle, Mountain Sage). Perennial to 60 cm. tall. June.

DESCRIPTION: **Plants** decumbent, sparsely to densely hairy, native in Europe and Asia, naturalized elsewhere; **leaves** ovate, crenate-dentate, often with whitish blotches bordering the midrib; **flowers** showy, pink, purple, or brownish purple, rarely white.

USE: Lamiums are sometimes planted as ground covers or in the prairie garden.

CULTURE: Plants are of easy culture in most soils. It is best to plant the lamiums where there will be good snow cover, as the plants are not very hardy. A winter mulch of hay or straw should be used in exposed sites. Propagation is by seeds started indoors or by spring division of established plants.

CULTIVARS

'Album'. Flowers creamy white.

'Aureum'. Leaves with yellow blotches along midrib.

'Beacon Silver'. Leaves variegated with silver green blotches; flowers pink.

'Chequers'. Flowers amethyst violet.

Lathyrus L. (Pea)

LEGUMINOSAE (Pea Family)

DESCRIPTION: A genus of over 100 species of herbs, native in the North Temperate Zone and in mountains of South America and Africa; **stems** winged or angular; **leaves** alternate, even-pinnate, the climbing species with usually branched tendrils; **flowers** showy, axillary, in racemes or solitary; calyx 5-lobed; petals 5, the upper petal (standard) broad, the 2 lateral petals (wings) clawed, and the two lower petals (keel) united to form a pouch that encloses the stamens and pistil; stamens 10, 9 united; pistil 1-celled; **fruit** a legume.

Lathyrus latifolius L. (Perennial Pea). Perennial vine to 2 m. tall. July, August.

DESCRIPTION: **Plants** climbing by tendrils, native in Europe, naturalized elsewhere; **leaflets** 2, opposite, with leaflike stipules; **flowers** several to many, in leaf axils, rose-colored or white, to 2.5 cm. across; **fruits** to 12 cm. long.

USE: Sometimes used as a ground cover on steep banks. They can also be grown on a trellis or fence.

CULTURE: The perennial pea is of easy culture. Propagation is by seeds sown directly where plants are to grow or by division in early spring.

CULTIVARS

'Albus'. Flowers white.

'Splendens'. Flowers dark purple and red.

'White Pearl'. Flowers large, white.

Lathyrus odoratus L. (Sweet Pea). Annual to 2 m. tall. June-August.
PLATE 146

DESCRIPTION: **Plants** mostly climbing, native in Italy; **leaflets** 2, opposite, elliptic, to 5 cm. long; **flowers** fragrant, showy, in many colors, 1 to 4 on long peduncles; **fruits** hairy, to 5 cm. long.

USE: Plant on trellis. This is an excellent cut flower.

CULTURE: The annual sweet pea is a difficult flower to grow where summers are hot; the plants prefer a cooler climate. I have seen beautiful sweet peas in Canada and along the North Shore of Lake Superior, and they thrive in the Pacific Northwest. Seeds must be planted early to get bloom before hot weather. The soil should be high in organic matter and kept moist. Earlier bloom can be fostered by starting seeds indoors in individual pots to reduce the shock of transplanting. Flowers should be picked to lengthen the flowering season.

CULTIVARS AND STRAINS

'Bijou'. Plants self-supporting; flowers heat resistant, in shades of scarlet, blue, white, cerise, and salmon pink.

Cuthbertson (strain). Plants climbing, heat resistant, in a brilliant color range.

'Galaxy'. Plants climbing; flowers in shades of blue, lavender, rose, salmon, scarlet, red, and white.

'Jet Set'. Plants self-supporting; flowers salmon, rose, crimson, and blue.

'Little Sweetheart'. Plants very dwarf; flowers in a good color range.

Spencer (strain). There are several Spencer strains, differing in size of flower and time of bloom. All are climbing types in a wide color range. A number of named cultivars are available.

Lavatera L. (Tree Mallow)

MALVACEAE (Mallow Family)

DESCRIPTION: A genus of about 20 species of herbs or shrubs, native mostly in the Mediterranean region; **leaves** palmately angled or lobed, with long petioles; **flowers** axillary or in terminal racemes; involucral bracts 3 to 9, united basally in a deep or shallow cup; petals 5, obcordate, white or rose-purple; **fruit** a schizocarp with 5 or more 1-seeded mericarps arranged in a whorl.

Lavatera trimestris L. (Herb Tree Mallow). Annual to 1 m. tall. July, August.   PLATE 147

DESCRIPTION: **Plants** branched, sparsely hairy; native in the Mediterranean region; **leaves** suborbicular, to 5 cm. long, palmately angled, on long petioles; **flowers** white, rose pink, or red, solitary in the axils of upper leaves, on elongated pedicels; calyx enlarges in fruit; petals obcordate, to 4 cm. long; **mericarps** 10 to 15, covered by the umbrellalike receptacle.

USE: Plant toward the back of the flower border.

CULTURE: Plants will grow in most garden soils in full sun. Seeds are planted directly where the plants are to bloom in early May. Thin the seedlings so the plants are about 30 cm. apart.

CULTIVARS

'Loveliness'. Flowers deep rose.

'Splendens'. Flowers rose red or white.

'Tanagra'. Flowers brilliant rose.

Leontopodium R. Br.

COMPOSITAE (Sunflower Family)

Inula Tribe

DESCRIPTION: A genus of about 25 species of tufted perennial herbs, native in the mountains of Europe and Asia; **leaves** mostly basal, entire; **flower** heads small, discoid, crowded into dense terminal cymes, subtended by bractlike leaves; involucral bracts overlapping, woolly, scarious-margined; flowers all tubular, imperfect, the outer ones usually pistillate; **achenes** nearly cylindrical, with pappus of deciduous bristles.

Leontopodium alpinum Cass. (Edelweiss). Perennial to 30 cm. tall. June.

DESCRIPTION: **Plants** native in the Pyrenees, Alps, and Carpathian Mountains of Europe; **leaves** linear to oblong-lanceolate, white-tomentose; bracts form a star up to 10 cm. across.

USE: Sometimes planted in rock gardens.

CULTURE: Edelweiss requires a deep sandy or gravelly soil with perfect drainage. Propagation is by seeds started indoors or seeded in a sandy soil in a cold frame. Plants can also be increased by careful division in September.

Leucojum L. (Snowflake)

AMARYLLIDACEAE (Amaryllis Family)

DESCRIPTION: A genus of 9 species of bulbous herbs, native in Europe and the western Mediterranean region; **leaves** basal; **flowers** nodding, solitary or in an umbel on a hollow scape and subtended by a spathe splitting along 1 side into 2 papery valves; perianth segments separate, white, tinged yellow, red, or green; ovary inferior; **fruit** a berry.

Leucojum vernum L. (Spring Snowflake). Perennial to 30 cm. tall. April, May.

DESCRIPTION: **Plants** native in central Europe; **leaves** to 22 cm. long; **flowers** solitary on short, nodding pedicels, white, tipped with green, to 2 cm. long.

USE: This is an attractive rock garden plant, or it can be planted under shrubs.

CULTURE: The spring snowflake likes a sandy loam soil in either sun or light shade. Heavy soils can be made suitable by the addition of compost. Late planted bulbs seldom bloom the first year, so plant the bulbs as soon as they can be purchased in late August or early September. Space the bulbs about 15 cm. apart and cover with 6 to 8 cm. of soil.

Leucojum—other species

L. aestivum L. (Summer Snowflake), native in central and southern Europe, blooms in June. Culture is the same as for *L. vernum*. 'Gravetye Giant' has larger flowers than the species.

L. autumnale L. (Autumn Snowflake), native in the Mediterranean region, has white flowers tinged with red in September and October.

Lewisia Pursh.

PORTULACACEAE (Purslane Family)

DESCRIPTION: A genus of about 20 species of fleshy perennial herbs, with thick starchy roots or corms, native to western North America; basal **leaves** in rosettes, stem leaves few; **flowers** white, rose, or red, solitary or in panicles; sepals 2 to 6; petals 4 to 18; stamens 5 to many; styles 3 to 8, united at the base; **fruit** a capsule opening by a lid.

Lewisia cotyledon (S. Wats.) B. L. Robinson. Perennial to 25 cm. tall. June.

DESCRIPTION: **Plants** evergreen, native in mountains of Oregon and California; **leaves** numerous, spatulate, to 7.5 cm. long, entire to wavy; **flowers** white with a red tinge or striped with red, produced in panicles on scapes to 25 cm. tall; petals 8 to 10, to 1 cm. long.

USE: Sometimes planted in rock or wall gardens.

CULTURE: Lewisias are difficult to grow, requiring perfect drainage and a soil that is free of lime. Propagation is by seeds started in sandy soil in a cold frame. When the seedlings are large enough, plant them in their permanent location. Because of their taproots, mature plants are difficult to transplant. The beautiful flowers make any special effort to grow this plant worth while.

VARIETY

var. *heckner* (C. V. Mort.) Munz. Leaves strongly toothed; flowers rose pink, to 4 cm. across.

Lewisia heckneri — see *Lewisia cotyledon* var. *heckneri*

Lewisia — other species

L. columbiana (J. T. Howell) B. L. Robinson, native in the mountains from British Columbia to California, has evergreen foliage and white or pink flowers, veined with red, in June. This is one of the easiest of the lewisias to grow.

L. rediviva Pursh. (Bitter Root), native from the Rocky Mountains west to the Pacific Ocean, has large, white- or rose-colored flowers in June.

Liatris Gaertn. (Blazing-star, Gay-feather)

COMPOSITAE (Sunflower Family)

Eupatorium Tribe

DESCRIPTION: A genus of about 40 species of perennial herbs, with corms, rhizomes, or an elongated root crown, native in North America; **leaves** alternate, simple, mostly linear to linear-lanceolate; entire, usually resin-dotted; **flower** heads discoid, in spikes, racemes, or panicles, the uppermost head always opening first; involucral bracts overlapping in several rows, lanceolate to orbicular, with scarious margins, ciliate or jagged; receptacle flat, naked; flowers all tubular, perfect, purple or rose purple, occasionally white; **achenes** cylindrical, usually 10-ribbed, with a pappus of 15 to 40 plumose or barbed bristles.

Liatris pycnostachya Michx. (Kansas Gay-feather). Perennial to 1.5 m. tall. July-September.

DESCRIPTION: **Plants** upright, usually hairy, native from South Dakota to Indiana, south to Texas and Florida; **leaves** linear, dotted; **flower** heads to 1 cm. across, in a dense spike to about 45 cm. long; involucre cylindrical to narrowly turbinate.

USE: Plant in flower border or in a prairie garden.

CULTURE: This is an easy plant to grow. It likes a fertile, well-drained soil and full sun. Propagation is by seeds or spring division. Start seeds in a cold frame in May. When seedlings are large enough, they can be lined out in a nursery row and moved to their permanent location the following spring.

CULTIVAR
'Alba'. Flowers white.

Liatris scariosa (L.) Willd. (Rattlesnake-master, Tall Gay-feather). Perennial to 1 m. tall. August, September.

DESCRIPTION: **Plants** upright, hairy, native in the mountains from Pennsylvania to Georgia; basal **leaves** lanceolate to narrowly ovate or obovate, to 25 cm. long; upper leaves oblanceolate, much shorter, sessile; **flower** heads to 2.5 cm. across, in racemes or panicles; involucre globose, with recurved bracts, the inner ones rounded and often purple at the tips.

USE: Same as for *L. pycnostachya*.

CULTURE: Same as for *L. pycnostachya*.

CULTIVARS
'September Glory'. Flowers deep purple.
'White Spires'. Flowers white.

Liatris spicata (L.) Willd. (Spike Gay-feather). Perennial to 1.5 m. tall. July-September.   PLATE 148

DESCRIPTION: **Plants** erect, nearly glabrous, native from Michigan to Long Island, south to Louisiana and Florida; **leaves** linear or linear-lanceolate, to 40 cm. long, reduced upward; **flower** heads about 1 cm. across, in dense spikes to 75 cm. long; involucre cylindrical to turbinate-campanulate, with bracts that are often purple with scarious margins.

USE: Same as for *L. pycnostachya*.

CULTURE: Same as for *L. pycnostachya*.

CULTIVARS
'Floristan White'. Flowers white.
'Kobold'. Flowers red purple.
'Silvertips'. Flowers lavender with silvery sheen.

Liatris — other species

L. aspera Michx., native from South Dakota to Ontario, south to Texas and South Carolina, is a tall plant to 2 m. tall and flowering heads to 2.5 cm. across, in tall spikes.

L. ligulistylis (A. Nels.) K. Schum. (Rocky Mountain Gay-feather), native from Alberta to Wisconsin, south to New Mexico, has flowering heads to 3 cm. across, in dense racemes.

Ligularia Cass. (Golden-ray)

COMPOSITAE (Sunflower Family)

Senecio Tribe

DESCRIPTION: A genus of about 100 coarse, showy perennial herbs, native in Europe and Asia; **leaves** basal and alternate with long petioles, broad; **flower** heads radiate, on short peduncles, arranged in racemes, corymbs, or panicles; involucral bracts broad, in 1 row; disc flowers several; ray flowers usually many, yellow or orange; **achenes** glabrous with pappus of rough hairs.

Ligularia clivorum —see *Ligularia dentata*

Ligularia dentata (A. Gray) Hara (Bigleaf Golden-ray). Perennial to 1 m. tall. July-September.

DESCRIPTION: **Plants** native in China and Japan; **leaves** orbicular-reniform, to 30 cm. long, cordate at base, dentate; **flower** heads to 12 cm. across, in corymbs; ray flowers 12 to 14, orange.

USE: Plant toward the back of the flower border or in a wildflower garden.

CULTURE: Plants prefer a rich, moist soil and either full sun or partial shade. Propagation is by seeds or by division of established plants in early spring.

CULTIVARS
'Desdemona'. Plants compact with purple stems and lower leaf surfaces.
'Greynog Gold'. Ray flowers yellow.
'Orange Queen'. Ray flowers deep orange.

Lilium L. (Lily)

LILIACEAE (Lily Family)

DESCRIPTION: A genus of over 80 species of perennial herbs, native in the North Temperate Zone; **plants** usually bulbous, sometimes stoloniferous or rhizomatous; **bulbs** scaly; **leaves** alternate or whorled, usually many; **flowers** solitary and terminal or several in terminal racemes, panicles, or umbels, white, yellow, orange, red, purple, or maroon, never blue, usually spotted inside; perianth funnelform, cup-shaped, or campanulate; perianth segments spreading or reflexed, each with a basal, nectar-bearing gland; stamens 6, with versatile anthers; **fruit** a 3-valved capsule.

Lilium canadense L. (Canada Lily). Perennial to 1.5 m. tall. July.   PLATE 149

DESCRIPTION: **Plants** native from Minnesota to Nova Scotia, south to Alabama; **leaves** lanceolate to oblanceolate, in whorls; **flowers** orange yellow to red, spotted with brown purple, nodding with recurved perianth segments borne in umbels from leaf axils.

USE: Useful for naturalizing.

CULTURE: The Canada lily is beautiful in roadside ditches and moist meadows, but it is short-lived under cultivation. It prefers a moist soil and full sun. Bulbs should be planted in early October.

Lilium candidum L. (Madonna Lily). Perennial to 2 m. tall. June, July.

DESCRIPTION: **Plants** native in the Balkans; basal **leaves** forming in the fall and persisting over winter, stem leaves alternate, oblanceolate, becoming smaller upward on the stem; **flowers** white, fragrant, campanulate with recurved perianth segments, borne in a raceme; anthers yellow.

USE: Sometimes planted in perennial borders.

CULTURE: A well-drained soil and full sun is best for this species. Unlike most lilies, the bulbs send up a rosette of leaves in the fall. If possible, plant bulbs in early September. Mosaic is a serious difficulty in cultivating the Madonna lily. If you have a mosaic problem, new plants should be grown from seed.

Lilium regale E. H. Wils. (Regal Lily). Perennial to 2 m. tall. July.   PLATE 151

DESCRIPTION: **Plants** native in western China; **leaves** alternate, many, to 12 cm. long; **flowers** funnelform, in umbels, lilac or purple outside, white inside.

USE: Plant in flower border.

CULTURE: Well-drained soil and full sun are preferred growing conditions. Plant bulbs about 15 cm. deep in early October.

Lilium speciosum Thunb. (Showy Japanese Lily). Perennial to 1.5 m. tall. August, September.

DESCRIPTION: **Plants** native in southern Japan; **leaves** alternate, broadly lanceolate or oblong, to 18 cm. long; **flowers** 1 to many in leafy panicles, nodding, fragrant, to 10 cm. across, white, suffused inside with rose and spotted with rose red; perianth segments strongly reflexed and wavy.

USE: A good species for the perennial border.

CULTURE: Plants require a well-drained soil and full sun. Plant bulbs 15 cm. deep in early October. Mulch newly planted bulbs about November 1.

CULTIVARS

'Album'. Flowers pure white.

'Garnet Red'. Flowers garnet red, with perianth segments edged with silver.

'Grand Commander'. Flowers crimson.

'Lucy Wilson'. Flowers pink, edged with white.

Lilium tigrinum — see *Lilium lancifolium*

Lilium — other species

Unless otherwise indicated, the following lilies bloom in July.

L. amabile Palib. (Korean Lily), native in Korea, has nodding, grenadine red flowers, spotted with black. Perianth segments reflexed.

L. auratum Lindl. (Gold-banded Lily), native in Japan, has large, fragrant, bowl-shaped, white flowers spotted with crimson. Perianth segments have yellow stripes or bands. Plants require a winter mulch. Specially treated bulbs are sometimes planted in the spring to avoid winter injury.

L. concolor Salisb. (Star Lily), native in China, has star-shaped, vermillion red flowers, to 5 cm. across, in umbrellalike racemes.

L. hansonii Leichtl. (Japanese Turk's-cap Lily), native in Japan, Korea, and Siberia, has leaves borne in whorls, and nodding, fragrant, orange yellow flowers spotted with purple brown, borne in loose racemes.

L. henryi Baker, native in central China, has orange flowers spotted with brown to 7.5 cm. across, in loose racemes. Perianth segments are strongly reflexed.

L. lancifolium Thunb. (Tiger Lily), native in Japan, Korea, and China, has turk's-cap-type, orange to salmon red flowers spotted with purple black, borne in racemes.

L. longiflorum Thunb. (Easter Lily), native in Japan, has several, trumpet-shaped, fragrant, white flowers in terminal clusters. This lily is sold as potted plants for Easter. After blooming, the bulbs can be planted outdoors where they will often bloom again in the fall. Plants should be mulched for winter protection.

L. martagon L. (Martagon Lily, Turk's-cap Lily), native in Europe and Asia, has numerous, nodding flowers in a raceme. The perianth segments are strongly reflexed and of various colors including purple, white, pink, dull red, or nearly black. Numerous cultivars have been named.

L. monodelphum Bieb. (Caucasian Lily), native in the northern Caucasus mountains, has numerous nodding flowers in a raceme. The perianth segments are golden yellow, sometimes spotted or tinged with purple, reflexed.

L. philadelphicum L. (Wood Lily), native from British Columbia to Quebec, south to New Mexico and Kentucky, has a few upfacing, saucer-shaped flowers to 10 cm. across, with perianth segments that are a vivid orange red with purple spots. In spite of its common name, it is seen more often in roadside ditches than in woods. PLATE 150

L. superbum L. (Turk's-cap Lily), native in wet soils from New Hampshire south to Alabama and Georgia, has nodding, orange scarlet flowers spotted with purple brown, in racemes or umbels. The perianth segments are strongly reflexed.

Lilium — garden hybrids

Hybrid lilies are much easier to grow than the species. Plant breeders, both amateur and professional, are engaged in lily breeding. As a result, hundreds of named cultivars are on the market and more appear each year. These lilies are mostly the results of interspecies crosses and combine the good qualities of the parent species.

USE: Garden lilies are excellent for cut flowers. For this purpose they are often planted in rows. More often, lilies are planted in the flower border. Allow at least a meter between plants. Several bulbs of each variety should be planted to produce a clump.

CULTURE: Most of the hybrid lilies prefer a well-drained, sandy loam soil in full sunlight. If you have a clay soil, work in plenty of organic matter. Propagation is by bulbs planted in the fall, in early October. Space the bulbs about 15 to 20 cm. apart and cover with 15 cm. of soil. Lilies have few insect problems. The virus disease called 'mosaic' can pose a threat to lilies: rogueing diseased plants is advised. Botrytis blight, a fungus disease, can cause premature defoliation and reduce the bloom. Good air circulation between the plants and using a preventive fungicidal spray will control Botrytis.

CULTIVARS: The following list has been prepared by one of our leading lily growers. All cultivars listed are readily available and moderate in price.

'Connecticut King'. Plants to 70 cm. tall; flowers saucer-shaped, upfacing, yellow blended with orange, spotless. PLATE 152

'Dawn Star'. Plants 80 cm. tall; flowers outfacing, light ivory yellow with darker edges, midseason. An excellent cultivar for cutting.

'Earl of Rochester'. Plants 1 m. tall; flowers upfacing, clear yellow, spotless, midseason.

'Orange Light'. Plants 1 m. tall; flowers a glowing orange. An excellent cut flower.   PLATE 153

'Ruby'. Plants 75 cm. tall; flowers upright, red, early.

'Sally'. Plants 1 m. tall; flowers downfacing, pink tan, late.

'Snow Lark'. Plants 65 cm. tall; flowers outfacing, white. This lily was the best in the 1980 London Lily Show. It is slightly more expensive but worth it.

Limonium Mill. (Statice, Sea Lavender)

PLUMBAGINACEAE (Leadwort Family)

DESCRIPTION: A genus of about 150 species of largely perennial herbs, widely distributed on all continents; **leaves** in basal rosettes, entire or pinnatifid; **flowers** small, white, yellow, rose, lavender, and blue, in loose panicles or spikes; calyx tubular, often colored; petals united only at base, clawed; stamens 5, borne at the base of the petals; **fruit** a capsule, enclosed in the persistent calyx.

Limonium caspium — see *Limonium bellidifolium*

Limonium reticulatum — see *Limonium bellidifolium*

Limonium sinuatum (L.) Mill. (Notchleaf Statice, Notchleaf Sea Lavender). Tender perennial grown as an annual to 75 cm. tall. June, July.

DESCRIPTION: **Plants** native in the Mediterranean region; **leaves** all basal, lyrate-pinnatifid, to 10 cm. long; **flowers** small, in corymbose panicles with winged branches; calyx funnelform, to 1.25 cm. long with blue violet lobes; corolla white, with lobes longer than the calyx lobes.

USE: This statice is sometimes planted in rock gardens and grown for winter bouquets.

CULTURE: Plants prefer a well-drained soil and full sun. Propagation is by seeds started in early spring or from cuttings taken in June and rooted in sand. A winter mulch is recommended.

CULTIVARS

'American Beauty'. Flowers rich deep rose.

'Apricot Beauty'. Flowers bicolor, in shades of peach, yellow, and chamois.

'Heavenly Blue'. Flowers sky blue.

'Iceberg'. Flowers white.

'Midnight Blue'. Flowers deep blue.

'Petite Bouquet'. Flowers rose and apricot with white and yellow centers.

Limonium – other species

L. bellidifolium (Gouan.) Dumort. (Caspian Sea Lavender), native in Europe and Asia, is suitable for planting in rock gardens. Flowers are produced in 2- to 3-flowered spikelets at the ends of a much-branched inflorescence. The corolla is pale blue or lilac and the calyx has white lobes.

L. bonduellii (Lestib.) O. Kuntze, native in Algeria, is grown for dried arrangements. The calyx and corolla are yellow.

L. latifolium (Sm.) O. Kuntze (Wideleaf Sea Lavender), native in Rumania, Bulgaria, and southern Russia, is also grown for dried arrangements. The flowers are small, in much-branched, globe-shaped inflorescences. The corollas are blue violet.

Linaria Mill (Toadflax)

SCROPHULARIACEAE (Figwort Family)

DESCRIPTION: A genus of about 100 species of annual and perennial herbs of temperate regions of the northern hemisphere; **leaves** opposite, whorled, or the upper alternate, entire, toothed or lobed; **flowers** yellow, blue, purple, or violet, in terminal racemes; calyx 5-parted; corolla 2-lipped, with a long spur at the base of the tube; stamens 4; **fruit** a capsule.

Linaria alpina (L.) Mill. (Alpine Toadflax). Perennial to 15 cm. tall. July, August.   PLATE 154

DESCRIPTION: **Plants** tufted, glaucous, native in the mountains of Europe; **leaves** linear or lanceolate, sessile; **flowers** blue or violet, with orange palates, and spurs as long as the corolla tube.

USE: The alpine toadflax is an excellent rock or wall garden plant.

CULTURE: Plants like a sandy, well-drained soil and full sun. Propagation is by seeds started in a cold frame in May. When the seedlings are large enough they are planted in their permanent location. Plants can also be increased by division in early spring.

Linaria – other species

L. bipartita (Venten.) Willd. (Cloven-lip Toadflax), native in Portugal and northern Africa, is an annual with violet purple flowers with orange palates.

L. genistifolia subspecies *dalmatica* (L.) Maire & Petitm., native from Italy to Russia, is a perennial with yellow flowers suitable for planting in the flower border.

L. maroccana Hook., native in Morocco, is an annual with violet purple flowers. A good plant for rock gardens and rock walls.

L. vulgaris Mill., native in Morocco but naturalized throughout all of North America, is a common roadside weed with yellow flowers with orange-bearded palates. This species is sometimes planted but it can become a weed.

Linnaea L. (Twinflower)

CAPRIFOLIACEAE (Honeysuckle Family)

DESCRIPTION: A single circumboreal species of trailing subshrubs; **leaves** opposite, simple, roundish; **flowers** nodding, campanulate, in pairs on slender peduncles; calyx and corolla 5-lobed; stamens 4; **fruit** an achene.

Linnaea borealis L. (Twinflower). Perennial to 15 cm. tall. June-August.   PLATE 155

DESCRIPTION: **Leaves** crenate, to 2.5 cm. long; **flowers** rose or white, fragrant.
USE: The twinflower is an interesting plant for a rock garden. It is also grown in the wildflower garden.
CULTURE: Plants require an acid, well-drained soil and partial shade. Acid peat should be used on nonacid soils. Propagation is by seeds, division, or cuttings taken in July and rooted in an acid sand-peat mixture. Early spring is the best time to divide established plants.

Linum L. (Flax)

LINACEAE (Flax Family)

DESCRIPTION: A genus of about 200 species of annual or perennial herbs or subshrubs, native to temperate and subtropical regions; **leaves** simple, usually alternate, narrow, entire; **flowers** red, yellow, blue, or white, in terminal or axillary racemes, corymbs, cymes, or panicles; sepals 5; petals 5, falling early; stamens 5, united at the base; pistil 1 with 5 styles; **fruit** a 5- or 10-celled capsule.

Linum grandiflorum Desf. (Flowering Flax). Annual to 60 cm. tall. June-August.

DESCRIPTION: **Plants** erect, glabrous, native in northern Africa; **leaves** linear-lanceolate to ovate-lanceolate, to 3 cm. long, acuminate, remotely ciliate;

flowers in shades of red to 4 cm. across, in loose panicles; sepals lanceolate-acuminate, to 1.25 cm. long.

USE: Plant in flower border or rock garden.

CULTURE: Plants like a well-drained soil and full sun. Propagation is by seeds sown directly where plants are to grow. Thin the plants to a spacing of about 20 cm.

CULTIVARS
'Caeruleum'. Flowers bluish purple.
'Roseum'. Flowers rose pink.
'Rubrum'. Flowers bright red.

Linum — other species

L. flavum L. (Golden Flax), native in central and southern Europe, is a perennial with yellow flowers suitable for planting in a large rock or wall garden.

L. narbonense L. (Narbonne Flax), native in the Mediterranean region, is a perennial with azure blue flowers with white centers. It is excellent for rock or wall gardens or in the front of the flower border. It blooms from June to August.

L. perenne L. (Perennial Flax), native in Europe, has large chicory blue flowers. 'Alba', with white flowers, and 'Heavenly Blue', with sky blue flowers, are named cultivars. The subspecies *alpinum* (Jacq.) Oeckend. is smaller and often planted in rock gardens.

Lithospermum L. (Puccoon)

BORAGINACEAE (Borage Family)

DESCRIPTION: A genus of about 40 hairy perennial herbs, native on all continents except Australia; **roots** commonly with a red or purple dye; **leaves** simple, alternate, sessile, entire; **flowers** yellow, orange, or white, in simple or branched cymes; calyx and corolla 5-lobed with glands in the throat; stamens 5, never exserted; **fruit** of 4 nutlets.

Lithospermum canescens (Michx.) Lehm. (Hoary Puccoon). Perennial to 45 cm. tall. April, May.   PLATE 156

DESCRIPTION: **Plants** native from Saskatchewan to Ontario, south to Texas and Georgia; **roots** with a red dye; **leaves** oblong or linear; **flowers** orange yellow, to 1.25 cm. long.

USE: Sometimes planted in rock gardens and prairie gardens.

CULTURE: The puccoons like a sandy soil and full sun. They can be propagated from seeds started in May in a cold frame or from cuttings taken from the new growth in spring. Mature plants have a taproot and are difficult to transplant.

Lobelia L.

LOBELIACEAE (Lobelia Family)

DESCRIPTION: A large genus of nearly 400 species of herbs, shrubs, and sometimes trees, native mostly in tropical and warm-temperate regions; **leaves** alternate, simple, **flowers** blue, violet, red, yellow, or white, mostly in bracted racemes; calyx 5-toothed; corolla 2-lipped, the upper lip with 2 distinct lobes, the lower larger and 3-cleft, with tube slit nearly to base; stamens 5; **fruit** a capsule.

Lobelia cardinalis L. (Cardinal Flower). Perennial to 1 m. tall. July-September.   PLATE 157

DESCRIPTION: **Plants** native in moist soils along streams from Minnesota to New Brunswick, south to Texas and Florida; **leaves** lanceolate to oblong, to 10 cm. long, often with a purplish cast; **flowers** scarlet, rarely pink or white, in bracted racemes; corolla to 4 cm. long; **capsule** subglobose, about 1 cm. across.

USE: Plant toward the back of the flower border or in the wildflower garden.

CULTURE: This native usually grows along the edges of streams and lakes. It prefers a moist soil high in organic matter. Propagation is by seeds started in May in a cold frame. When the seedlings are large enough they are moved to their permanent location. When conditions are favorable the plant reseeds itself.

CULTIVARS
'Alba'. Flowers white.
'Rosea'. Flowers pink.

Lobelia erinus L. (Edging Lobelia). Tender perennial grown as an annual, to 20 cm. tall. June-October.   PLATE 158

DESCRIPTION: **Plants** tufted, native in South Africa; **leaves** elliptic to obovate, becoming linear toward the top of the stem, to 2.5 cm. long, serrate; **flowers** blue or violet with yellow or white throat, in loose racemes; anthers blue.

USE: The edging lobelias are planted for mass effects toward the front of the flower border and for edging. They can also be grown in the rock garden.

CULTURE: Plants like a moist but well-drained soil. Propagation is by seeds started indoors in mid-March. Space the plants about 20 cm. apart.

CULTIVARS

'Blue Butterfly'. Flowers large, purple blue.

'Bright Eyes'. Flowers violet blue with white centers.

'Crystal Palace'. Flowers rich dark blue.

'Rosamond'. Flowers deep rosy red with white centers.

'Sapphire'. Flowers dark blue with white centers.

'White Lady'. Flowers sparkling white.

Lobelia — other species

L. siphilitica L. (Blue Lobelia), native from South Dakota to Maine, south to Kansas and North Carolina, is a coarse perennial with showy blue flowers. It blooms in August and September.   PLATE 159

Lobularia Desf.

CRUCIFERAE (Mustard Family)

DESCRIPTION: A small genus of 5 species of perennial or annual herbs, native in the Mediterranean region; **leaves** entire; **flowers** white; sepals and petals 4, entire; **fruit** a silicle, with valves slightly inflated.

Lobularia maritima (L.) Desv. (Sweet Alyssum). Tender perennial grown as an annual, to 1.5 cm. tall. June-October.   PLATE 160

DESCRIPTION: **Plants** sprawling, much branched, native in southern Europe; **leaves** linear to lanceolate; **flowers** small, mostly white, in flat-topped clusters.

USE: An excellent plant for edging and in rock gardens. It also can be planted for a temporary ground cover.

CULTURE: The sweet alyssum grows in any well-drained soil in full sun. Propagation is by seeds started either indoors in late March or by direct seeding. Late fall bloom can be improved by cutting off the faded flowers in August. Space the plants about 20 cm. apart.

CULTIVARS

'Carpet of Snow'. Flowers pure white.

'Rosy O'Day'. All-America Winner. Flowers deep rose.

'Royal Carpet'. All-America Winner. Flowers rich violet.

'Snow Drift'. Flowers white.

'Violet Queen'. Flowers reddish rose.

Lotus L.

LEGUMINOSAE (Pea Family)

DESCRIPTION: A genus of about 100 species of herbs or subshrubs, native mostly in temperate regions; **leaves** alternate, odd-pinnate; **flowers** in axillary umbels, pealike, with beaked keels; stamens 10, 9-united; **fruit** a narrow dehiscent legume.

Lotus corniculatus L. (Bird's-foot Trefoil). Perennial to 60 cm. tall. June-August.

DESCRIPTION: **Plants** often trailing, native in Europe and Asia, naturalized elsewhere; **leaves** trifoliate with obovate or oblanceolate leaflets; stipules large, resembling leaflets; **flowers** yellow, often tinged with red, in 3- to 6-flowered umbels on long peduncles; **fruits** to 2.5 cm. long.

USE: Sometimes used as a ground cover or in rock gardens.

CULTURE: Plants thrive in a well-drained soil and full sun. The species is grown from seeds sown directly in early May. The double-flowered 'Floro Plena' is propagated by cuttings. Individual plants may be short-lived but the species reseeds itself. This plant has escaped from cultivation and is common along roadsides and in lawns.

CULTIVAR
'Floro Pleno'. Flowers double.

Lunaria L. (Honesty, Money Plant)

CRUCIFERAE (Mustard Family)

DESCRIPTION: A small genus of erect biennial or perennial herbs, native in Europe; **leaves** simple, broad-toothed; **flowers** white to purple, in terminal racemes; sepals 4, petals 4, long-clawed; **fruit** a flat, oblong-elliptic to nearly orbicular silicle with a satiny, paper white spetum or partition.

Lunaria annua L. (Honesty, Silver-dollar, Money Plant). Biennial to 1 m. tall. May, June.

DESCRIPTION: **Plants** native in southern Europe, naturalized elsewhere, **leaves** ovate, coarsely toothed; **flowers** white or purple.

USE: Plants are grown for their seed pods that are used in dry flower arrangements.

CULTURE: Plants can be grown in poor soils either in sun or partial shade.

Seeds should be planted in May in a cold frame. Thin the seedlings and winter in the cold frame. Transplant in early spring. The stems are cut as soon as the fruits are mature and hung upside down in a dry, airy place to dry. The outer walls of the flat fruits are then removed, leaving the paper-white partitions. The plants sometimes self sow, but the seedlings are lacking in winter hardiness. Seeds started early indoors will sometimes flower and fruit the first year.

CULTIVARS

'Alba'. Flowers white.

'Variegata'. Leaves variegated with white.   PLATE 161

Lunaria biennis —see *Lunaria annua*

Lupinus L. (Lupine)

LEGUMINOSAE (Pea Family)

DESCRIPTION: A genus of about 200 species of annual or perennial herbs or subshrubs, native mainly in western North America; **leaves** alternate, palmately compound, with stipules united to the petioles; **flowers** in terminal spikes or racemes, showy, pealike, with erect standards with reflexed margins; stamens 10, united; **fruit** a flat legume, often constricted between seeds.

Lupinus hartwegii Lindl. (Hartweg Lupine). Annual to 90 cm. tall. July, August.

DESCRIPTION: **Plants** native in Mexico; **flowers** blue with partly rose-colored standards.

USE: Plant in flower border for mass effect.

CULTURE: Plants thrive in any good garden soil in either full sun or partial shade. Seeds can be planted directly where plants are to bloom and later thinned so plants are about 30 cm. apart. For earlier bloom, seeds can be started indoors in individual containers.

CULTIVAR

'Giant'. Flowers large, in shades of white, rosy mauve, and blue.

Lupinus perennis L. (Wild Lupine). Perennial to 60 cm. tall. May, June.   PLATE 162

DESCRIPTION: **Plants** native from Minnesota to Maine, south to Louisiana and Florida; **leaves** with 7 to 11 leaflets; **flowers** blue, rarely pink or white, in long racemes.

USE: Plant in flower border or in wildflower garden.

CULTURE: Soil should be well drained and on the acid side. Plants bloom either in full sun or in partial shade. Propagation is by seeds sown directly where plants are to bloom or in individual containers.

Lupinus — other species

L. polyphyllus Lindl. (Washington Lupine), native from British Columbia to California, has blue to red flowers and is one of the parents of garden hybrids.

L. subcarnosus Hook. (Texas Bluebonnet), native in Texas, is an annual with blue flowers that have a white or yellow spot on the standard and wings that are inflated in May.

Lupinus — garden hybrids

Lupines have been greatly improved by hybridization. The best known strain of garden hybrids is the Russell strain. These hybrids come in a variety of colors from white through lavender and pale blue to deep blue and purple, and from pale yellow through salmon pink, rose, apricot buff, to crimson. Numerous cultivars have been developed in Europe but in America most of the lupines are grown from seed. PLATE 163

Lychnis L. (Campion, Catchfly)

CARYOPHYLLACEAE (Pink Family)

DESCRIPTION: A genus of about 35 species of annual or perennial herbs, native in north temperate and arctic regions, **leaves** opposite; **flowers** in cymes, perfect or sometimes imperfect, scarlet or pink to purple; calyx 5-toothed, 10-veined, sometimes inflated; petals 5; stamens 10, **fruit** a 5-toothed capsule enclosed by the calyx.

Lychnis chalcedonica L. (Maltese Cross). Perennial to 60 cm. tall. June-September. PLATE 164

DESCRIPTION: **Plants** erect, hispid, native in Russia, sometimes escaped from cultivation; **leaves** ovate, pointed, stem leaves clasping; **flowers** vivid scarlet, to 2 cm. across, forming a cross, in 10- to 50-flowered terminal cymes.

USE: Sometimes planted in flower borders for their bright red flowers.

CULTURE: The Maltese cross will grow in most any soil that is well drained and in full sun. Propagation is by seeds or division. Seeds can be planted early indoors or in May in a cold frame or in a nursery row. As soon as the seedlings are large enough, transplant them to their permanent location. Divison should be done in early spring. Allow at least 30 cm. between plants.

CULTIVARS

'Alba'. Flowers white.

'Grandiflora'. Flowers large, flaming scarlet.

Lychnis coronaria (L.) Desr. (Rose Campion, Mullein Pink). Perennial or sometimes biennial, to 1 cm. tall. July. August.

DESCRIPTION: **Plants** densely white-woolly, native in northwestern Africa, southeastern Europe to central Asia; **leaves** ovate, to 10 cm. long; **flowers** pink to purple, rarely white, to 2 cm. across, in few-flowered cymes.

USE: Same as for *L. chalcedonica*.

CULTURE: Same as for *L. chalcedonica*.

Lychnis dioica—see *Silene dioica*

Lychnis viscaria L. (German Catchfly). Perennial to 1 m. tall. July, August. PLATE 165

DESCRIPTION: **Plants** native in Europe, central Asia, and Siberia; **leaves** linear to lanceolate, smooth; **flowers** purple, pink, or rarely white, in 3- to 6-flowered panicles; petals often emarginate.

USE: Same as for *L. chalcedonica*.

CULTURE: Same as for *L. chalcedonica*.

CULTIVARS

'Alba'. Flowers white.

'Flore Pleno'. Flowers double, rosy crimson.

'Splendens'. Flowers rosy pink.

Lychnis—other species

L. alpina L. (Arctic Campion), native in Europe and northeastern North America, has rosy purple flowers in June and July and is often planted in rock gardens.

L. coeli-rosa (L.) Desr. (Rose-of-heaven), native in the Mediterranean region, is an annual with rosy pink flowers.

L. flos-cuculi L. (Cuckoo Flower, Ragged Robin), native in Europe, has deep rosy red or white flowers. It is a hardy perennial suitable for the perennial border or rock garden.

L. x *haageana* Lam. (Haage Campion), a hybrid between *L. coronata* and *L. fulgens*, has showy flowers to 5 cm. across in shades of orange, red, scarlet, and crimson. It should be planted toward the front of the border.

Lycoris Herb.

AMARYLLIDACEAE (Amaryllis Family)

DESCRIPTION: A genus of about 10 species of bulbous herbs, native from China to Japan and Burma; **leaves** basal, strap-shaped, dying down in early summer; **flowers** showy in few-flowered umbels on a hollow scape; perianth segment, 6, separate or united into a short tube, red, pink, white, or yellow; ovary inferior; **fruit** a capsule.

Lycoris squamigera Maxim. (Magic Lily, Resurrection Lily). Perennial to 50 cm. tall. August.   PLATE 166

DESCRIPTION: **Plants** native in Japan; **leaves** narrow, basal, to 2.5 cm. wide, dying to the ground in late spring; **flowers** rose lilac or pink, to 7.5 cm. across.

USE: Plant toward the back of the flower border.

CULTURE: Plants require a well-drained soil and bloom best in full sun. Bulbs can be planted in the spring. Space the bulbs 15 cm. apart and cover with 10 cm. of soil. The plants develop strap-shaped leaves in the spring. These die down in July. In August the flowers appear and make a colorful display. The bulbs should be divided when the plants become crowded. A winter mulch should be used where snow cover is not dependable.

Lysichiton Schott. (Skunk Cabbage)

ARACEAE (Arum Family)

DESCRIPTION: A small genus of only 2 species of perennial herbs, native in wet, marshy soils in northeastern Asia and northwestern North America; **leaves** large, simple, arising from fleshy rhizomes; **flowers** small, imperfect, produced on a stout spadix, enclosed by a showy stalked spathe.

Lysichiton americanum Hult. & St. John (Yellow Skunk Cabbage). Perennial to 1 m. tall. April, May.   PLATE 167

DESCRIPTION: **Plants** native from Alaska to Montana, south to California; **leaves** basal, oblanceolate to elliptic; to 1 m. long and 30 cm. wide, narrowed to a winged petiole; **flowers** small, on a spadix enclosed by a yellow spathe.

USE: Plant along edges of streams and ponds.

CULTURE: Plants require a moist soil high in organic matter. Propagation is by division in September or early October. A winter mulch is needed where snow cover is light. Remove the mulch early before growth starts.

Lysichiton camtschatcense (L.) Schott. (White Skunk Cabbage). Perennial to 1 m. tall. April, May.

DESCRIPTION: **Plants** native in northern Japan and in Kamchatka, the Sakhalin Peninsula, and the Kurile Islands; plants similar to *L. americanum* except for the white spathes.

USE: Same as for *L. americanum*.

CULTURE: Same as for *L. americanum*.

Lysimachia L. (Loosestrife)

PRIMULACEAE (Primrose Family)

DESCRIPTION: A large genus of about 165 species of annual or perennial herbs widely distributed in temperate and subtropical regions; **stems** leafy; **leaves** simple, alternate, opposite, or whorled, often dotted with glands; **flowers** yellow or white, rarely pink, blue, or purple; calyx 5- to 6-parted; corolla rotate or campanulate, 5- to 7-parted; stamens 5 to 7, inserted in the corolla tube; **fruit** a 5-valved capsule.

Lysimachia nummularia L. (Moneywort, Creeping Charlie). Perennial creeper to 10 cm. tall. July, August.   PLATE 168

DESCRIPTION: **Plants** creeping, native in Europe, naturalized elsewhere; **leaves** opposite, nearly orbicular, to 2.5 cm. long; **flowers** yellow, solitary, in leaf axils.

USE: Sometimes planted as ground cover. It is also planted in hanging baskets and in window boxes.

CULTURE: Plants grow well on most soils in full sun or partial shade. A winter mulch is needed except where there is dependable snow cover. Propagation is by division at any time during the growing season.

CULTIVARS
'Aurea'. Foliage yellow.
'Grandiflora'. Flowers larger than in species.

Lysimachia punctata L. (Garden Loosestrife, Circle Flower). Perennial to 1 m. tall. July.

DESCRIPTION: **Plants** native in Europe, naturalized elsewhere; **leaves** mostly in whorls of 3 or 4, sometimes opposite, ovate-lanceolate; **flowers** yellow, in axillary whorls; petals margined with small glandular hairs.

USE: Sometimes planted in the perennial border. It is also useful for naturalizing along streams or at the edge of a pond.

CULTURE: Plants thrive in moist soils. Propagation is by division in spring or fall.

Lysimachia — other species

L. ciliata L., native from British Columbia to Nova Scotia, south to New Mexico and Florida, has opposite leaves and yellow flowers in July.

L. clethroides Duby. (Gooseneck Loosestrife), native in China and Japan, has white flowers in nodding racemes in August and September.

L. vulgaris L. (Garden Loosestrife), native in Eurasia and naturalized in America, is similar to *L. punctata* except the flowers are in leafy panicles. PLATE 169

Lythrum L. (Loosestrife)

LYTHRACEAE (Loosestrife Family)

DESCRIPTION: A genus of about 300 species of annual or perennial herbs, native in America, Europe, and Asia; **stems** 4-angled or winged; **leaves** mostly opposite, or alternate in the upper part of the plant; **flowers** purple to white, regular, solitary, paired in leaf axils, or in clusters in the axils of a terminal leafy inflorescence; petals 4 to 8; stamens 2 to 12, often unequal; **fruit** a 2-valved capsule.

Lythrum salicaria L. (Purple Loosestrife). Perennial to 2 m. tall. July-September.

DESCRIPTION: **Plants** more or less hairy, native in the Old World, naturalized elsewhere; **leaves** lanceolate, to 10 cm. long, cordate at base; **flowers** purple, often in whorled clusters in axils of leafy, interrupted, terminal spikes; appendages of calyx tube 2 or more times as long as the calyx lobes.

USE: A popular perennial for the border. It also grows well along streams or at the edge of pools.

CULTURE: Although native in wet soils, the plants grow well in any good garden soil. Propagation is by division in early spring. If only a few plants are needed, a portion of the plant can be removed without digging up the whole clump. The plants do not bloom well the first year after transplanting.

CULTIVARS

'Firecandle'. Flowers rose red.

'Happy'. Flowers dark pink.

'Robert'. Flowers rose red.

Lythrum virgatum (Wand Lythrum). Perennial to 2 m. tall. July-September.

DESCRIPTION: **Plants** smooth, native in Europe and Asia, naturalized in eastern United States; plants similar to *L. salicaria* except leaves narrower and lacking hairs, and **flowers** are mostly paired or clustered in open, leafy racemes with calyx appendages no longer than the calyx lobes.

USE: Same as for *L. salicaria*.

CULTURE: Same as for *L. salicaria*.

CULTIVARS

'Dropmore Purple'. Flowers purple.

'Morden Pink'. Flowers pink, sterile.

Lythrum — garden hybrids

Most of the garden hybrids have resulted from a cross between *L. virgatum* 'Morden Pink' x *L. alatum*, an American species.

CULTIVARS

'Columbia Pink'. Flowers pink.   PLATE 170

'Morden Gleam'. Flowers bright carmine.

'Morden Rose'. Flowers rose red on compact plants.

Machaeranthera Nees.

COMPOSITAE (Sunflower Family)

Aster Tribe

DESCRIPTION: A genus of about 25 species of annual, biennial, or perennial herbs or shrubs, native in western North America; **leaves** alternate, spiny, toothed to pinnately parted, rarely entire; **flower** heads usually radiate, solitary or in corymbs or panicles; involucre hemispherical to turbinate; involucral bracts in several rows; receptacle flat to slightly convex; disc flowers perfect, yellow; ray flowers pistillate, blue, purple, or white; **achenes** turbinate to linear, more or less compressed, with pappus of barbed hairs.

Machaeranthera tanacetifolia (HBK) Nees (Tahoka Daisy). Annual to 60 cm. tall. June-October.

DESCRIPTION: **Plants** native from Alberta to South Dakota, south to Mexico; **stems** leafy, nearly smooth; **leaves** pinnately parted, to 7.5 cm. long; **flower** heads to 6 cm. across; ray flowers violet blue or white.

USE: Plant toward the front of the flower border.

CULTURE: Easy to grow in most garden soils in full sun. Propagation is by seeds started indoors and transplanted to the garden after danger of frost. Space the plants about 30 cm. apart.

Macleaya R. Br.

PAPAVARACEAE (Poppy Family)

DESCRIPTION: A small genus of only 2 species of large, more or less glaucous perennial herbs, native in eastern Asia; **leaves** palmately veined and lobed; **flowers** small, many lacking petals, in showy panicles; **fruit** a capsule.

Macleaya cordata (Willd.) R. Br. (Plume Poppy, Tree Celandine). Perennial to 20 cm. tall. July, August.

DESCRIPTION: **Plants** with yellow sap, native in Japan and China; **leaves** to 20 cm. across, light green with dense, white, short pubescence underneath; **flowers** small, creamy white, in showy panicles; petals lacking; stamens 24 to 30; **capsule** with 4 to 6 seeds.

USE: Plant toward the back of the flower border.

CULTURE: Plants are of easy culture in any good garden soil in full sun. Propagation is by seeds or division of established plants in early spring. Plants come up early in the spring and are quite frost tender.

CULTIVAR
'Coral Plume'. Leaves silvery; flowers copper-colored.

Maianthemum Wiggers (False Lily-of-the-valley)

LILIACEAE (Lily Family)

DESCRIPTION: A small genus of low, perennial, rhizomatous, herbs, native in Europe, Asia, and North America; **leaves** 2 to 3, simple; **flowers** white, in terminal racemes; perianth segments 4, separate, spreading, stamens 4; **fruit** a berry.

Maianthemum canadense Desf. (False Lily-of-the-valley, Two-leaved Solomon's-seal). Perennial to 20 cm. tall. May, June.   PLATE 171

DESCRIPTION: **Plants** native from Northwest Territories to Ontario, south to South Dakota to North Carolina; **leaves** ovate-oblong, to 10 cm. long, subcordate with a narrow, V-shaped sinus.

USE: Plant in shaded portions of rock gardens or use as a ground cover in wildflower gardens.

CULTURE: Plants thrive in moist soil in organic matter in partial shade. Propagation is by seeds or more often by division of established plants in early spring or in September.

Malva L. (Mallow)

MALAVACEAE (Mallow Family)

DESCRIPTION: A genus of about 30 species of annual, biennial, or perennial herbs, native in Europe, North Africa, and temperate Asia; **leaves** mostly palmately angled, lobed, or dissected; **flowers** axillary, solitary, or in loose to dense clusters; involucral bracts 3, separate; petals white, pink, or purple; stamens united in a tubular column; **fruit** a discoid schizocarp with beakless mericarps.

Malva alcea L. (Hollyhock Mallow). Perennial to 1 m. tall. June-September.

DESCRIPTION: **Plants** native in Europe, naturalized elsewhere; **stems** stellate-pubescent; basal **leaves** reniform, shallowly 3-lobed, stem leaves divided into 3 to 7 pinnatifid segments; involucral bracts ovate; **flowers** axillary, white or rose mauve, to 5 cm. across, **mericarps** smooth.

USE: Plant in flower border or wildflower garden.

CULTURE: Mallows thrive in any good garden soil either in full sun or in partial shade. Plant seeds in a nursery row in May. When seedlings are large enough, transplant to their permanent location. Once established, plants should not be disturbed.

CULTIVAR

'Fastigiata'. Plant narrow, upright; flowers bright rose.

Malva moschata L. (Musk Mallow). Perennial to 1 m. tall. June-September.

DESCRIPTION: **Plants** branched, hairy, native to Europe and North Africa, naturalized elsewhere; **leaves** reniform and 3-lobed at base of the plant, stem leaves divided into 3 to 7 pinnatifid segments; **flowers** on slender pedicels, axillary, white or rose mauve, to 5 cm. across; **mericarps** hairy.

USE: Same as for *M. alcea.*

CULTURE: Same as for *M. alcea.*

Mammilaria vivipara — see *Coryphantha vivipara*

Martynia probosicidea — see *Proboscidea louisianica*

Matricaria capensis — see *Chrysanthemum parthenium*

Matthiola R. Br. (Stock)

CRUCIFERAE (Mustard Family)

DESCRIPTION: A genus of about 50 species of annual and perennial herbs or subshrubs, native mostly in southern Europe, northern Africa, and southwestern Asia; **stems** gray-pubescent with branched hairs; **leaves** elongated, entire, wavy, or pinnatifid; **flowers** lilac, purple, or white, in terminal racemes; sepals 4; petals 4, long-clawed; **fruit** a long, narrow silique.

Matthiola bicornis — see *Matthiola longipetala*

Matthiola incana (L.) R. Br. (Common Stock, Gillyflower). Tender perennial grown as an annual, to 75 cm. tall. June-September.

DESCRIPTION: **Plants** native in southern Europe; **leaves** oblong to oblanceolate, to 10 cm. long; **flowers** purple or red, varying to white, blue, and yellow in cultivated forms, fragrant, to 2.5 cm. across, often fully double.

USE: Grown for their sweet-scented flowers in the flower border or in rows for cutting.

CULTURE: Stocks dislike hot weather. They must be planted early to get bloom before hot weather. Seed should be started indoors in March and the seedlings transplanted to the border in early May. The flowers are especially fragrant in the evening.

CULTIVARS
'Dwarf Ten-week'. Flowers double, very fragrant.   PLATE 172
'Giant Imperial'. Flowers very large, in wide color range.
'Trisomic Seven Weeks'. Flowers very early, in wide color range.

Matthiola longipetala (Venten.) DC. (Evening Stock). Annual to 45 cm. tall.

DESCRIPTION: **Plants** native in southeastern Europe; **leaves** lanceolate or narrower, to 9 cm. long, entire with few teeth, lower leaves wavy, toothed or pinnatifid; **flowers** yellow, pink, or purple, very fragrant, opening in the evening; **siliques** cylindrical, terminated by 2 horns.

USE: Same as for *Matthiola incana*.

CULTURE: Same as for *Matthiola incana*.

VARIETY
subspecies *bicornis* (Sibth. & Sm.) P. W. Ball. Flowers pink or purple, very fragrant. This subspecies is planted more often than the species.

Mentha (Mint)

LABIATAE (Mint Family)

DESCRIPTION: A genus of about 25 species of erect or decumbent, aromatic, perennial herbs, native in temperate regions of the world; **stems** mostly square in cross section; **leaves** mostly opposite; **flowers** in dense, many-flowered verticillasters arranged in terminal spikes or heads; calyx tubular or campanulate, with 10 to 13 veins; corolla lavender or white with tube shorter than calyx and limb 4-lobed with upper lobe notched and larger than the lower; stamens 4, in 2 pairs, usually exserted; **fruit** of 4 smooth, netted, or tubercled nutlets.

Mentha x *piperita* L. (Peppermint). Perennnial to 1 m. tall. July, August.

DESCRIPTION: **Plants** of hybrid origin, resulting from a cross between *M. aquatica* x *M. spicata*; **leaves** petioled, lanceolate, to 6 cm. long, acute, serrate; **flowers** sterile, lilac pink; calyx tubular, smooth, with ciliate teeth.

USE: Sometimes planted in the flower border but more often in the herb garden.

CULTURE: Mints prefer a moist soil and full sun. Propagation is by seeds and division of established plants in early spring.

VARIETY
var. *citrata* J. F. Ehrh. (Lemon Mint). Leaves with a characteristic lemon odor when crushed.

Mentha — other species

M. requienii Benth. (Corsican Mint), native in Corsica, is the smallest mint, only 5 cm. tall. It is sometimes planted in rock gardens and between stepping stones. It requires winter protection.

M. spicata L. (Spearmint) is of unknown origin. It has showy flowers but is grown mostly for culinary use.

Mertensia Roth. (Bluebells)

BORAGINACEAE (Borage Family)

DESCRIPTION: A genus of about 40 species of perennial herbs, native in woods and thickets of Asia, Europe, and North America; **roots** mostly fleshy and tuberous; **leaves** simple, alternate, entire, often with transparent dots, petioled below, sessile above; **flowers** blue, purple, or white, in loose or congested bractless racemes or panicled cymes; calyx 5-lobed; corolla bell-shaped, 5-lobed, usually with crests in the throat; stamens 5; **fruit** of 4 erect, rough nutlets.

Mertensia virginica (L.) Pers. (Virginia Bluebells, Virginia Cowslip). Perennial to 60 cm. tall. May, June.   PLATE 173

DESCRIPTION: **Plants** glabrous, native from Wisconsin to New York, south to Kansas and Alabama; **leaves** elliptic to ovate, dying down after fruits mature; **flowers** blue to purple, rarely white, to 2.5 cm. long.

USE: Commonly planted under shrubs and in the shaded wildflower garden.

CULTURE: The Virginia bluebells prefer a sandy or peaty soil but will grow in most soils that have been enriched with organic matter. They like shade but they can be grown in full sun. They come up early and bloom before tree leaves are fully open. The leaves die down in midsummer. Propagation is by the fleshy tubers that are formed. Tubers should be planted in September.

CULTIVARS
'Alba'. Flowers white.
'Rubra'. Flowers pink.

Mimulus L. (Monkey Flower)

SCROPHULARIACEAE (Figwort Family)

DESCRIPTION: A genus of about 150 species of annual and perennial herbs or shrubs, native in South Africa, Asia, Australia, and in North and South

America; **plants** creeping to erect, smooth or hairy; often glandular-pubescent; **leaves** opposite, simple, entire or toothed; **flowers** yellow, orange, red, blue, violet, or purple, solitary, axillary or terminal, sometimes in spikelike racemes; calyx 5-angled, 5-toothed; corolla 2-lipped to nearly regular, upper lip 2-lobed, lower lip 3-lobed, throat open or closed by a palate; stamens 4; **fruit** a capsule.

Mimulus cardinalis Dougl. (Scarlet Monkey Flower). Perennial to 1 m. tall. July, August.

DESCRIPTION: **Plants** freely branched, sticky-pubescent, native from Oregon to Utah, south to Arizona and New Mexico; **leaves** obovate to oblong, to 12 cm. long, sessile; **flowers** scarlet to pale reddish yellow, to 5 cm. long; corolla strongly 2-lipped; stamens exserted.

USE: Plant toward the front of the flower border or along a stream or pool.

CULTURE: Monkey flowers prefer a rich, moist soil high in organic matter. In nature, they can be found near springs or streams. Propagation is by seeds started indoors in a sterilized mixture of equal parts leafmold, loam, and sand at a temperature of 60° F. They can also be propagated from cuttings or division.

Mimulus — other species

M. x *hybridus* Hort. resulted from a cross between *M. luteus* x *M. guttatus*. It is a large-flowered garden hybrid with flowers in various colors. 'Tigrinus' has striped and spotted flowers.

M. lewisii Pursh., native from Alaska to California and Colorado, has rose red to pink flowers.

M. moschatus Dougl. (Musk Plant), native from British Columbia to Montana and south to California, has yellow flowers, dotted with brown, and a musklike odor.   PLATE 174

M. ringens L. (Allegheny Monkey Flower), native from Manitoba to Nova Scotia and south to Texas and Virginia, has blue to violet blue, rarely pink or white flowers.

Mirabilis L. (Umbrellawort)

NYCTAGINACEAE (Four-o'clock Family)

DESCRIPTION: A genus of about 60 species of annual or perennial herbs, native in subtropical America and Australia; **roots** often tuberous; **leaves** opposite; **flowers** 1 to several within calyxlike, more or less deeply 5-lobed involucres, in axillary corymbs or panicles; calyx corollalike, funnelform to tubular, campanulate, or rotate; stamens 3 to 5; **fruit** an ellipsoid to globose achene.

Mirabilis jalapa L. (Four-o'clock). Tender perennial grown as an annual, to 1 m. tall. August, September.   PLATE 175

DESCRIPTION: **Plants** native in tropical America; **leaves** ovate, petioled; **flowers** red, pink, yellow, or white, often striped and mottled, to 3.5 cm. across.

USE: Plant toward the back of the flower border or use as a summer hedge along a driveway.

CULTURE: Plants thrive on most soils in full sun. The flowers open only in late afternoon and evening. Propagation is by seeds started indoors or by direct seeding. Space the plants about 30 cm. apart.

CULTIVARS

'Jingles'. Flower striped and flecked with white, yellow, gold, orange, and red combinations.

'Pygmy'. Plants compact; flowers in a wide color range.

Mitchella L. (Partridgeberry)

RUBIACEAE (Madder Family)

DESCRIPTION: A small genus of 2 evergreen perennial herbs, native in eastern North America and eastern Asia; **stems** trailing, rooting, to 30 cm. long; **leaves** opposite with minute stipules on the petioles; **flowers** white, in axillary or terminal pairs; corolla funnelform with 4 short lobes; **fruit** a red, rarely white, berry.

Mitchella repens L. (Partridgeberry). Perennial to 5 cm. tall. May-July.

DESCRIPTION: **Plants** native from Minnesota to Nova Scotia, south to Mexico and Florida; **leaves** orbicular-ovate, to 2 cm. long, often with white lines; **flowers** white; **fruits** red, to 1 cm. across.

USE: A useful plant in rock gardens and wildflower gardens. It is also an excellent plant in terrariums.

CULTURE: The partridgeberry requires a well-drained acid soil that is high in organic matter. It prefers partial shade. Propagation is by seeds sown as soon as ripe in a sandy-peat soil or by division in early spring.

Mitella L. (Bishop's-cap, Miterwort)

SAXIFRAGACEAE (Saxifrage Family)

DESCRIPTION: A genus of about 12 species of rhizomatous herbs, native in North America and northeastern Asia; **leaves** mostly basal, cordate, long-petioled; **flowers** small, in simple racemes; calyx tube saucer-shaped with 5 lobes; petals 5, pinnately cut; stamens 5 or 10; ovary mostly inferior; **fruit** a capsule with an apical lid.

Mitella diphylla L. (Bishop's-cap, Miterwort). Perennial to 45 cm. tall. May, June.   PLATE 176

DESCRIPTION: **Plants** native from Minnesota to Quebec, south to Missouri and Virginia; **leaves** 1 pair, cordate, sessile or nearly so; **flowers** white, 7 mm. across.

USE: Plant in rock garden or use as a ground cover in the wildflower garden.

CULTURE: The mitellas like an acid soil in organic matter and partial shade. Propagation is by seeds sown as soon as ripe in a peaty soil mix or by spring divison.

Mollucella L.

LABIATAE (Mint Family)

DESCRIPTION: A genus of 4 species of glabrous, annual herbs, native from the Mediterranean region to northwestern India; **stems** mostly square in cross section; **leaves** opposite, crenate, petioled; **flowers** in axillary, many-flowered verticillasters; calyx inconspicuous, campanulate, 5- to 10-veined, 5- to 10-toothed, with teeth mucronulate to spiny, corolla inconspicuous, 2-lipped; stamens 4, in pairs; **fruit** of 4, 3-angled, smooth nutlets.

Mollucella laevis L. (Bells-of-Ireland, Shellflower). Annual to 90 cm. tall. July, August.

DESCRIPTION: **Plants** native in Asia Minor; **leaves** ovate-triangular, to 5 cm. long; **flowers** inconspicuous, in many flowered verticillasters; calyx conspicuous, cup-shaped, green, surrounded by inflated bractlets to 2 cm. long and pointed.

USE: Plant in flower border or in a row for cutting.

CULTURE: Plant in full sun in any good, well-drained soil. Although attractive in the garden, the bells of Ireland are grown primarily for dried flower arrangements. The inflated green calyces are quite showy when dried. Propagation is by seeds started indoors in late March. Space the plants about 30 cm. apart in the garden.

Monarda L. (Bergamont, Bee Balm)

LABIATAE (MINT FAMILY)

DESCRIPTION: A genus of about 12 species of annual or perennial herbs, native in North America; **stems** mostly square in cross section; **leaves** opposite, entire, or toothed; **flowers** in many-flowered verticillasters, subtended by many, often leafy bracts; calyx tubular, 15-veined, 5-lobed, with tube often hairy inside; corolla tube longer than the calyx, with 2-lipped limb; with the upper lip erect and often notched and the lower lip spreading, 3-lobed; fertile stamens 2, exserted, with 2-celled anthers; **fruit** of 4 smooth nutlets.

Monarda didyma L. (Bee Balm, Oswego Tea). Perennial to 1 m. tall. July, August.

DESCRIPTION: **Plants** native in rich woods from New England south to Tennessee and Georgia; **leaves** ovate-acuminate, to 10 cm. long, serrate-dentate, with distinct petioles; **flowers** vivid scarlet red, to 3 cm. long, in terminal, headlike verticillasters.

USE: Plant toward the back of the flower border.

CULTURE: Monardas tolerate some shade but do best in full sun. The soil should be fertile and well drained. Powdery mildew can be a serious problem in late summer. A suitable fungicide may be needed to keep the mildew under control. Propagation is by division of established plants in early spring.

CULTIVARS
'Adam'. Flowers cerise red.
'Cambridge Scarlet'. Flowers bright crimson.   PLATE 177
'Croftway Pink'. Flowers pink.
'Mahogany'. Flowers deep red brown.
'Salmon Queen'. Flowers salmon pink.
'Snow Queen'. Flowers white.
'Violet Queen'. Flowers violet.

Monarda — other species

M. fistulosa L. (Wild Bergamot), native from British Columbia to Quebec and south to Arizona and Georgia, has bright lavender flowers.

M. punctata L. (Dotted Mint, Horsemint), native from Minnesota to Vermont and south to Texas and Florida, has yellow flowers spotted with purple in 2 or more headlike verticillasters. Plants usually grow in open woods in sandy soils.

Montebretia crocosmiiflora — see *Crocosmia* x *crocosmiiflora*

Muscari Mill. (Grape Hyacinth)

LILIACEAE (Lily Family)

DESCRIPTION: A genus of about 40 species of bulbous, spring-flowering herbs, native in the Mediterranean region and southwestern Asia; **bulbs** tunicate; **leaves** all basal; **flowers** urn-shaped to subglobose, usually constricted at the apex, blue, white, olive, or rarely yellow, nodding, in terminal, bracted racemes; perianth with 6 reflexed, toothlike lobes; stamens 6, with filaments arising from the middle of the perianth tube; **fruit** a 3-angled capsule.

Muscari armeniacum Leichtl. (Armenian Grape Hyacinth). Perennial to 20 cm. tall. April, May.

DESCRIPTION: **Plants** native in northeastern Asia Minor; **leaves** linear, to 30 cm. long, appearing in the fall; **flowers** oblong, to 8 mm. long, deep violet with white teeth.

USE: Grape hyacinths are best planted under shrubs or trees, on grassy slopes or other half-wild places. The stringy leaves present an untidy appearance in more formal places.

CULTURE: Grape hyacinths thrive in any well-drained soil of average fertility. Plant the bulbs as soon as they can be purchased, preferably in September. Space the bulbs about 10 cm. apart and cover with 5 cm. of soil.

CULTIVARS
'Blue Spike'. Flowers bright blue.
'Cantab'. Flowers cambridge blue.
'Heavenly Blue'. Flowers bright blue.

Muscari botryoides (L.) Mill. (Common Grape Hyacinth). Perennial to 30 cm. tall. April, May.

DESCRIPTION: **Plants** native in central and southern Europe to the Caucasus; **leaves** linear, to 30 cm. long; **flowers** globose, blue, with white teeth, about 4 mm. long, in a dense raceme.

USE: Same as for *M. armeniacum*.

CULTURE: Same as for *M. armeniacum*.

CULTIVARS
'Album'. Flowers white.   PLATE 178

'Caeruleum'. Flowers bright blue.
'Carneum'. Flowers flesh-colored.

Myosotis L. (Foreget-me-not)

BORAGINACEAE (Borage Family)

DESCRIPTION: A genus of about 50 species of annual, biennial, or perennial herbs, native in the temperate zones of all continents; **leaves** simple, entire; with basal leaves petioled and stem leaves sessile; **flowers** pink, blue, or white, solitary or in terminal cymes; calyx 5-lobed; corolla salverform, 5-lobed, with scales in the throat; stamens 5; **fruit** of 4 smooth, shiny nutlets.

Myosotis alpestris — see *Myosotis sylvatica*

Myosotis oblongata — see *Myosotis sylvatica*

Myosotis palustris — see *Myosotis scorpioides*

Myosotis scorpioides L. (True Forget-me-not). Perennial to 45 cm. tall. May, June.   PLATE 179

DESCRIPTION: Creeping, rhizomatous **plants** with angled stems, native in Europe and Asia, naturalized elsewhere; **leaves** oblong-lanceolate or oblanceolate; **flowers** bright blue with yellow, pink, or white centers. to 6 cm. across.

USE: Good for naturalizing along streams or pools.

CULTURE: Forget-me-nots are easy to grow in any moist soil either in sun or partial shade. Propagation is by seeds sown directly where the plants are to grow or by spring division. Volunteer seedlings can be a nuisance in rock gardens or flower borders.

CULTIVARS
'Indigo Compacta'. Plants compact; flowers rich blue.
'Semperflorens'. Flowers rich blue with yellow centers.

Myosotis sylvatica Hoffm. (Woodland Forget-me-not). Annual or biennial to 60 cm. tall. May, June.

DESCRIPTION: **Plants** erect, hairy, native in Europe and Asia; naturalized elsewhere; **leaves** oblong-linear to oblong-lanceolate; **flowers** blue with yellow eye, varying pink or white, to 8 mm. across. Seeds or plants sold as *M. alpestris* usually belong to this species.

USE: Sometimes planted in rock gardens but self spreading can cause the plants to stray.

CULTURE: Plants do best in semi-shaded, moist sites. Propagation is by seeds sown directly where plants are to grow, or volunteer seedlings can be transplanted.

CULTIVARS
'Alba'. Flowers white.
'Blue Ball'. Plants compact; flowers rich indigo blue.
'Fischeri'. Flowers bluish pink.
'Rosea'. Flowers rose-colored.

Narcissus L. (Daffodil)

AMARYLLIDACEAE (Amaryllis Family)

DESCRIPTION: A genus of 20 species of spring-flowering herbs with tunicate **bulbs**, native to Europe and northern Africa; **leaves** basal; **flowers** 1 or several on a scape, subtended by a 1-valved spathe; perianth yellow or white, generally salverform, with a long and tubular or short and ringlike corona (crown); ovary inferior; **fruit** a capsule.

Narcissus bulbocodium L. (Hoop-petticoat Daffodil). Perennial to 30 cm. tall. May, June.   PLATE 180

DESCRIPTION: **Plants** native in Spain, Portugal, and southern France; outer bulb coat white to maroon; **leaves** very slender, nearly cylindrical, to 40 cm. long; **flowers** solitary, bright yellow, with narrow perianth segments and corona 2.5 cm. long; stamens more than half as long as the corona.

USE: Plant in a rock garden or in daffodil collections.

CULTURE: Plants require a well-drained soil. Plant bulbs in September or early October.

CULTIVAR AND VARIETY
var. *conspicua* (Haw.) Barb. Flowers larger than in species.
'Tenuifolius'. Corona 6-lobed.

Narcissus cyclamineus DC. Perennial to 30 cm. tall. May, June.

DESCRIPTION: **Plants** native in Spain and Portugal; **leaves** narrowly linear, keeled; **flowers** solitary, to 4.5 cm. long, deep yellow, drooping; perianth tube very short, with reflexed segments; corona wavy-edged, as long as the segments; stamens half as long as the corona.

USE: Same as for *N. bulbocodium*.

CULTURE: Same as for *N. bulbocodium*.

CULTIVARS

'February Gold'. Flowers molten yellow.

'Peeping Tom'. Flowers golden yellow.

'Tete-a-tete'. Flowers yellow.

Narcissus jonquilla L. (Jonquil). Perennial to 45 cm. tall. May, June.

DESCRIPTION: **Plants** native in southern Europe and Algeria; **leaves** narrow, rushlike, to 45 cm. long; **flowers** 2 to 6, yellow, fragrant; perianth tube 2.5 cm. long; corona wavy-edged, much less than half as long as the segments.

USE: Same as for *N. bulbocodium*.

CULTURE: Same as for *N. bulbocodium*.

Narcissus poeticus L. (Poet's Narcissus). Perennial to 45 cm. tall. May, June.

DESCRIPTION: **Plants** native in France and Greece; **leaves** narrow, to 45 cm. long; **flowers** mostly solitary, white, very fragrant; perianth tube to 2.5 cm. long; corona very short, with wavy red edge, much shorter than the segments.

USE: Same as for *N. bulbocodium*.

CULTURE: Same as for *N. bulbocodium*.

Narcissus tazetta L. (Polyanthus Narcissus). Perennial to 45 cm. tall. May, June.

DESCRIPTION: **Plants** native in the Mediterranean region; **leaves** strap-shaped, to 2 cm. wide; **flowers** 4 to 8, white, fragrant; perianth tube to 2.5 cm. long, with obovate segments; corona light yellow, much shorter than the segments.

USE: Planted mainly for winter forcing.

CULTURE: Plants can be forced without the necessity of a cool period for rooting. Potted bulbs can be forced at ordinary room temperatures.

CULTIVAR

'Paper White'. Flowers pure white. Commonly planted for indoor forcing.

Narcissus triandrus L. (Angel's-tears). Perennial to 30 cm. tall. May, June.

DESCRIPTION: **Plants** native in Spain; **leaves** narrow, rushlike; **flowers** 1 to 6, pure white to pale yellow; perianth tube to 2 cm. long; corona entire, cuplike, white or yellow, half as long as the segments or more.

USE: Same as for *N. bulbocodium*.

CULTURE: Same as for *N. bulbocodium*.

CULTIVARS

'Albus'. Flowers white.

'Concolor'. Flowers yellow.

Narcissus — other species

N. x *incomparabilis* Mill., a natural hybrid between *N. poeticus* and *N. pseudonarcissus* is native from Spain to the Tyrol mountains. It has solitary yellow flowers with perianth tube to 2 cm. long, and a wavy-edged corona about half as long as the segments.

N. juncifolia Lag., native in Spain and southern France, has rushlike leaves and bright yellow flowers with perianth tube about 1.25 cm. long with overlapping lobes, and a wavy-edged corona of darker yellow color.

L. pseudonarcissus L. (Daffodil, Trumpet Narcissus), native in Europe, has solitary yellow flowers with greenish perianth tube to 2.5 cm. long, and a corona to 5 cm. long.

Narcissus — garden hybrids   PLATES 181, 182

Most of the cultivated daffodils are of hybrid origin. Thousands of named cultivars exist, and new ones appear each year. These hybrids are the result of interspecies hybridization. The Royal Horticultural Society recognizes 11 divisions as follows:

1. Trumpet Narcissi. Flowers solitary; corona as long as the segments or longer.
2. Large-cupped Narcissi. Flowers solitary; corona 1/3 to nearly as long as the segments.
3. Small-cupped Narcissi. Flowers solitary; corona less than 1/3 as long as the segments.
4. Double Narcissi. Flowers double.
5. Triandrus Narcissi. Flowers with characteristics of *N. triandrus*.
6. Cyclamineus Narcissi. Flowers with characteristics of *N. cyclamineus*.
7. Jonquilla Narcissi. Flowers with characteristics of *N. jonquilla*.
8. Tazetta Narcissi. Flowers with characteristics of *N. tazetta*.
9. Poeticus Narcissi. Flowers with characteristics of *N. poeticus*.
10. Species and natural hybrids.
11. Miscellaneous Narcissi. All that do not fit one of the above groups.
    The above classification is followed by most American growers.

USE: Daffodils are planted in flower borders and used for naturalizing under trees and shrubs.

CULTURE: The main prerequisite for growing daffodils is a well-drained soil. They bloom best where they receive good light but they can be grown in partial shade. Propagation is by bulbs. Plant the bulbs 15 to 20 cm. deep as early in the fall as possible, preferably by early October to allow time for root development. If the bulbs must be planted later than this, mulch to allow more time for root development. Work a fertilizer high in phosphorus into the soil before planting. After the daffodils bloom, allow the foliage to die down naturally before removing. When the plants become crowded it is best to divide the bulbs and replant.

CULTIVARS: Because there are so many named cultivars offered, it is difficult to single out a few that are best. The best thing to do is to study the various catalogs that have colored illustrations, and visit public and private gardens that have daffodil displays. Your state and regional daffodil society probably features a spring flower show where the newer cultivars can be seen.

Nelumbium —see *Nelumbo*

Nelumbium luteum —see *Nelumbo lutea*

Nelumbium nelumbo —see *Nelumbo nucifera*

Nelumbo Adans. (Lotus, Water Lotus)

NYMPHACEAE (Water Lily Family)

DESCRIPTION: A genus of 2 species of aquatic species of herbs, with thickened rhizomes rooted in the mud, native in Asia and North America; **leaves** nearly orbicular, concave, peltate, usually pushed above the water by long petioles; **flowers** solitary, large, showy, mostly overtopping the leaves; sepals 4 or 5; petals and stamens many, attached at the base of an obconical, flat-topped receptacle in which many 1-ovuled carpels are embedded.

Nelumbo lutea (Willd.) Pers. (American Lotus). Perennial to 2 m. tall. July, August. PLATE 183

DESCRIPTION: **Plants** native from Minnesota to southern Ontario, south to Texas and Florida; **leaves** circular, mostly above the water, to 60 cm. wide, entire, bluish green; **flowers** pale yellow, to 25 cm. across.

USE: The native American lotus is difficult to grow. It is best to enjoy it where it is growing naturally.

CULTURE: The American lotus grows in lakes and rivers with a solid bottom where the large, fleshy rhizomes can anchor themselves. The water should not freeze to the bottom.

CULTIVAR

'Flavescens'. Flowers numerous, smaller, with a red spot in the center.

Nelumbo nucifera Gaertn. (Sacred Lotus, East Indian Lotus). Perennial to 2 m. tall. July-September.   PLATE 184

DESCRIPTION: Plants native from southern Asia to Australia; leaves glaucous, to 90 cm. across, with often wavy margins; flowers very fragrant, pink, rose, or sometimes white.

USE: The sacred lotus needs a large pool or pond to show it off to advantage.

CULTURE: The sacred lotus is planted in tubs in a mixture of 2 parts soil and 1 part manure. The tubs are then put in the pond or pool so the surface of the soil will be covered with about 30 cm. of water. The rhizomes should be covered with about 10 cm. of soil. Planting is done in the spring in mid-May. The rhizomes cannot stand freezing so the tubs must be stored over winter in a frost free storage cellar at a temperature of 35 to 45° F. Plants can also be grown from seeds planted in sand in water.

CULTIVARS

'Alba Grandiflora'. Flowers large, white.

'Alba Striata'. Sepals white, edged with rose carmine.

'Rosea Plena'. Flowers double, rose pink, to 40 cm. across.

Nemesia Venten

SCROPHULARIACEAE (Figwort Family)

DESCRIPTION: A genus of about 50 species of tender annual or perennial herbs and subshrubs, native mostly in South Africa; leaves opposite; flowers of various colors, in terminal racemes or solitary in leaf axils; calyx 5-lobed; corolla 2-lipped, with a short tube and a sac or spur at the base and a palate in the throat; stamens 4; fruit a capsule.

Nemesia strumosa Benth. Annual to 60 cm. tall. June to September.

DESCRIPTION: Plants native in South Africa; leaves opposite, lanceolate to linear, toothed, sessile; flowers white or in shades of yellow and purple, often marked with purple.

USE: Nemesias are attractive border plants where summers are cool. They are also grown as house plants for winter bloom.

CULTURE: Nemesias like a deep, fertile soil high in organic matter. Seeds can be started indoors and seedlings transplanted to the border after danger of frost. The plants dislike hot summers.

CULTIVARS

'Grandiflora'. Flowers larger than in species, in shades of white, yellow, orange, pink, crimson, rose, etc.

'Nana Compacta'. Plants dwarf; flowers pink or red.

Nemophila Nutt.

HYDROPHYLLACEAE (Waterleaf Family)

DESCRIPTION: A genus of 11 species of annual herbs, native in North America; **stems** slightly succulent and brittle; **leaves** opposite or alternate, usually pinnatifid; **flowers** blue or white, usually solitary, rarely in racemelike cymes; calyx 5-parted, with 5 spreading or reflexed appendages in each sinus; corolla campanulate to rotate, 5-lobed; stamens 5; **fruit** a 1-celled capsule.

Nemophila insignis — see *Nemophila menziessi*

Nemophila menziesii Hook & Arn. (Baby-blue-eyes). Annual to 30 cm. tall. June-August.   PLATE 185

DESCRIPTION: **Plants** native in California; **stems** procumbent, obscurely winged or angled; **leaves** alternate, to 5 cm. long, pinnatifid with 9 to 11 segments; **flowers** bright blue with white centers, to 4 cm. across, usually solitary.

USE: Plant toward the front of the flower border or in the rock garden.

CULTURE: Plants prefer a sandy loam soil in full sun or partial shade. The seedlings are difficult to transplant so it is best to sow the seeds directly where the plants are to grow. Thin the plants to about 30 cm. apart. This plant dislikes heat and blooms best where summers are cool.

CULTIVARS

'Alba'. Flowers white.

'Marginata'. Flowers blue, with white margins.

Nepeta L. (Catmint)

LABIATAE (Mint Family)

DESCRIPTION: A genus of about 250 species of mostly perennial herbs, native in Europe, Asia, and northern Africa; **stems** mostly square in cross section; **leaves** opposite, usually petioled; **flowers** irregular, in verticillasters; calyx tubular, 5-toothed; corolla tube dilated, with a 2-lipped limb, upper lip 2-lobed, lower lip 3-lobed; stamens 4, in 2 pairs; **fruit** of 4 smooth, obovoid nutlets.

Nepeta mussinii K. Spring. (Mauve Catmint). Perennial to 30 cm. tall. May to September.

DESCRIPTION: **Plants** with short-pubescent, decumbent **stems**, native in Iran and the Caucasus; **leaves** ovate-cordate, crenate, to 25 cm. long; **flowers** blue, in a loose terminal raceme.

USE: Plant in flower border or in rock garden.

CULTURE: The catmint likes a well-drained soil. Propagation is by spring division or from rooted cuttings taken in June.

Nepeta — other species

N. cataria L. (Catnip), native in Europe and naturalized elsewhere, has leaves that are gray underneath. The flowers are small, white with pale purple spots, in loose spikes. Cats are attracted by the odor. 'Citrioides' is a lemon-scented cultivar.

N. x faessenii Bergmans, a sterile hybrid between *N. mussinii* x *N. nepetella*, has violet blue flowers from June to August. It makes an attractive ground cover about 60 cm. tall. This hybrid species is often confused in the trade with *N. mussinii*.

Nicotiana L. (Tobacco)

SOLANACEAE (Potato Family)

DESCRIPTION: A genus of about 70 species of annual or perennial herbs, rarely shrubs, native in tropical and subtropical regions of America and Australia; **stems** usually sticky-hairy; **leaves** alternate, simple, entire, rarely wavy-margined; **flowers** fragrant, white, yellow, purple, or red, in terminal panicles or 1-sided cymes; calyx tubular-campanulate, 5-lobed, persistent; corolla salverform with long tube and 5-lobed limb; stamens 5; **fruit** a capsule.

Nicotiana alata Link & Otto (Flowering Tobacco). Annual to 1 m. tall. July-September.

DESCRIPTION: **Plants** native in South America; **stems** viscid; **leaves** ovate to elliptic, to 25 cm. long, decurrent at the base; **flowers** chalky white inside, greenish outside (variously colored in named cultivars), opening in the evening, in few-flowered terminal racemes; corolla tube to 10 cm. long; stamens with purple anthers.

USE: Plant in the flower border.

CULTURE: The flowering tobacco thrives in any good garden soil in full sun. Start the seeds indoors in early April and transplant the seedlings to the border after danger of frost. Space the plants about 30 cm. apart. The flowers open in the evening and give off a delightful fragrance.

CULTIVARS

'Affinis'. Flowers pure white, fragrant.

'Lime Sherbet'. Flowers lime green, with star-shaped corolla lobes.

'Nicki Red'. All-America Winner. Day-blooming; crimson red flowers. PLATE 186

'Sensation'. Day-blooming flowers in shades of white, pink, rose, red, mauve, wine, and purple.

Nierembergia (Ruiz & Pav.) Cupflower

SOLANACEAE (Potato Family)

DESCRIPTION: A genus of 30 species of glabrous perennial herbs and subshrubs, native from Mexico to Chile and Argentina; **leaves** alternate, simple, entire; **flowers** axillary, solitary, or in cymes; calyx tubular to campanulate, deeply 5-lobed; corolla pale violet to blue or white, salverform to cup-shaped, with a 5-lobed limb; fertile stamens 4, borne on the corolla; staminode 1; **fruit** a 2-valved capsule.

Nierembergia hippomanica Miers. (Cupflower). Tender perennial grown as an annual, to 30 cm. tall. June-September.

DESCRIPTION: **Plants** native in Argentina; **leaves** linear-spatulate, to 2 cm. long; **flowers** axillary, violet, to 2 cm. across.

USE: This is an excellent plant for edging, for rock gardens, or for mass effect in the border.

CULTURE: Cupflowers like a rich soil that is well-drained and full sun. Start seeds indoors in late March. Space plants about 20 cm. apart in the garden.

CULTIVAR

'Purple Robe'. Flowers rich violet blue. PLATE 187

Nigella L. (Fennel Flower)

RANUNCULACEAE (Buttercup Family)

DESCRIPTION: A genus of about 20 species of annual herbs, native in the Mediterranean region and western Asia; **leaves** 2- to 3-pinnate into linear or filiform leaflets; **flowers** mostly solitary, showy, white, blue, or yellow; sepals 5, petal-like; petals 5, 2- lipped; with a hollow, nectariferous claw; **fruit** of 2 to 14 more or less united follicles.

Nigella damascena L. (Love-in-a-mist). Annual to 45 cm. tall. July-September.

DESCRIPTION: **Plants** native in southern Europe and northern Africa; **leaves** palmately parted with filiform segments; **flowers** white to light blue, to 4 cm. across, with a large, finely divided involucre.

USE: Plant toward the front of the border.

CULTURE: Nigellas are grown for their finely cut foliage and their colorful flowers. Plants are difficult to transplant so it is best to sow the seeds directly where the plants are to bloom in any good garden soil. Seedlings must be thinned to about 20 cm. apart. The most common cause of failure is the failure to thin the seedlings.

CULTIVARS
'Miss Jeckyll'. Flowers white or bright blue.
'Persian Jewels'. Flowers in shades of white, pink, red, and purple.

Nymphaea L. (Water Lily)

NYMPHAEACEAE (Water Lily Family)

DESCRIPTION: A genus of 35 species of aquatic perennial herbs with stout, horizontal or erect rhizomes, native in most countries; **leaves** simple, commonly nearly orbicular with a sinus reaching nearly to the petiole, with long petioles that permit the leaf blade to float on the surface of the water; **flowers** showy, floating on or standing above the water surface, opening during the daytime, or in some tropical species opening only at night; sepals 4; petals many, united to the ovary; stamens many; carpels many; **fruit** subglobose, many-seeded, depressed and saucerlike at the tip, maturing under water.

Nymphaea odorata Ait. (Fragrant White Water Lily). Perennial. July, August.

DESCRIPTION: **Plants** native in the eastern United States; **leaves** to 25 cm. across, dull green above, purplish beneath; **flowers** fragrant, white, to 12 cm. across, opening in the morning, lasting for 3 days.

USE: Sometimes planted in natural or man-made ponds.

CULTURE: Rhizomes can be planted in the mud at the bottom of the pond in early spring.

Nymphaea tuberosa Paine (Magnolia Water Lily). Perennial. July, August. PLATE 188

DESCRIPTION: **Plants** native in eastern United States; **leaves** to 35 cm. across, green beneath; **flowers** pure white, to 20 cm. across, with little or no fragrance, opening shortly after noon.

USE: Same as for *N. odorata*.

CULTURE: Same as for *N. odorata*.

Nymphaea — garden hybrids

Hybrid water lilies are classified as hardy or tropical. The hardy cultivars can be left in the pond or pool over winter if the water is deep enough to prevent freezing of the rhizomes. The tropical water lilies are tender and must be wintered indoors. Propagation is mainly by division of the rhizomes. The rhizomes are usually planted in tubs in a mixture of 2 parts soil and 1 part manure. The rhizomes should be covered with 10 cm. of soil. Submerge the container so the top of the soil will be 30 cm. below the water surface. Winter storage should be in a cool cellar with a temperature of 40° F.

CULTIVARS

Hardy water lilies:
'Chromatella'. Flowers yellow.
'Lustrous'. Flowers rose pink, with yellow stamens.
'Marliac Rose'. Flowers deep pink.
'Marliac White'. Flowers white with a flush of pink.

Tropical water lilies: PLATE 189
'Bagdad'. Flowers wisteria blue.
'Blue Beauty'. Flowers blue.
'Director George T. Moore'. Flowers deep purple blue.
'Golden West'. Flowers peach pink.
'Mrs. C. W. Ward'. Flowers deep rosy pink.
'Talisman'. Flowers yellow overlaid with pink.

Nymphoides J. Hill (Floating-heart)

GENTIANACEAE (Gentian Family)

DESCRIPTION: A genus of about 20 species of aquatic, perennial herbs of wide distribution; **leaves** simple, deeply cordate, short-petioled, floating; **flowers** in dense axillary umbels, 5-merous; corolla deeply parted, stamens borne on corolla tube; **fruit** a capsule.

Nymphoides indica (Thwaites) O. Kuntze (Water Snowflake). Tender perennial plants. June-September.   PLATE 190

DESCRIPTION: **Plants** native in the tropics; **leaves** floating, orbicular, to 20 cm. across, deeply cordate at the base; **flowers** white with yellow centers and lobes that are fringed and 1 cm. long.

USE: Plant in shallow ponds or pools.

CULTURE: Same as for tropical hybrid water lilies.

CULTIVAR

'Variegata'. Leaves green and bronze.

Ocimum L. (Basil)

LABIATAE (Mint Family)

DESCRIPTION: A genus of about 150 species of herbs or shrubs, native in warm or tropical regions, chiefly in Africa; **stems** square in cross section; **leaves** opposite, usually toothed; **flowers** small, in 6- to 10-flowered verticillasters arranged in terminal racemes or panicles; calyx campanulate, 2-lipped, lower lip with 4 pointed teeth; corolla 2-lipped, upper lip 4-lobed, lower lip concave; stamens 4, in 2 pairs; **fruit** of 4 nutlets.

Ocimum basilicum L. (Common Basil, Sweet Basil). Annual to 60 cm. tall. July, August.

DESCRIPTION: **Plants** native in the Old World; **leaves** ovate-elliptic, to 12 cm. long, tapering at base; **flowers** small, white or purple.

USE: Basils are usually grown for their fragrant foliage and for culinary use. A few, with colored foliage, are grown as ornamentals in the flower border.

CULTURE: Basils like a well-drained soil and full sun. Propagation is by seeds started indoors in early April. Space the plants about 30 cm. apart in the flower border.

CULTIVARS

'Citriodorum'. Leaves lemon-scented.

'Dark Opal'. All-America Winner. Leaves dark purplish brown; flowers purplish pink.   PLATE 191

Oenothera L. (Evening Primrose)

ONAGRACEAE (Evening Primrose Family)

DESCRIPTION: A genus of about 80 species of annual, biennial, and perennial herbs of wide distribution in the Western Hemisphere; **plants** stemless, decumbent, or upright; **leaves** alternate, simple, entire to pinnatifid; **flowers** solitary and axillary to racemose or paniculate, 4-merous, calyx tube usually long; corolla with 4 separate petals; stamens usually 8, with anthers attached near the center; ovary inferior, cylindrical or clavate, sometimes winged; **fruit** a capsule.

Oenothera fruticosa L. (Sundrops). Perennial to 60 cm. tall. May-July.

DESCRIPTION: **Plants** mat-forming by rhizomes, native in eastern United States; basal **leaves** oblanceolate, to 7.5 cm. long, stem leaves lanceolate, smaller; **flowers** yellow, axillary, to 2.5 cm. across, opening in the daytime; **fruits** club-shaped.

USE: Plant toward the front of the flower border or use in a rock garden.

CULTURE: Plant in well-drained soil that is moisture retentive in full sun. Water if the plants show signs of wilting. Propagation is usually by division in early spring.

Oenothera fruticosa var. *youngii* — see *Oenothera tetragona*

Oenothera glauca — see *Oenothera tetragona* var. *fraseri*

Oenothera macrocarpa — see *Oenothera missouriensis*

Oenothera missouriensis Sims. (Ozark Gumbo Lily). Perennial to 35 cm. tall. May, June.   PLATE 192

DESCRIPTION: **Plants** with a deep taproot, native from Kansas and Missouri, south to Texas; **leaves** in a basal rosette, lanceolate, to 10 cm. long, entire, petioled; **flowers** few, yellow, often with a reddish cast, to 10 cm. across; **capsule** 4-winged, to 7.5 cm. long.

USE: Plant toward front of border or in rock garden.

Oenothera — other species

O. biennis L. (Common Evening Primrose), native in eastern North America, is a rather coarse biennial with yellow flowers in elongated terminal racemes. It is a common roadside plant and is sometimes planted in prairie gardens.

O. caespitosa Nutt. (Tufted Gumbo Lily), native in the Rocky Mountains and adjoining plains, has large, white, fragrant flowers in May and June. It is a good rock garden plant.

O. tetragona Roth. (Sundrops), native in the eastern United States, is similar to *O. fruticosa*. The flowers are smaller and the fruits are less club-shaped. The var. *fraseri* (Pursh.) Munta has smooth leaves.

Omphalodes Mill. (Navelwort)

BORAGINACEAE (Borage Family)

DESCRIPTION: A genus of about 24 species of annual or perennial herbs, native in Europe, Asia, and Mexico; **leaves** simple, alternate, basal leaves long-petioled, stem leaves few; **flowers** white or blue, in loose racemes; calyx 5-cleft; corolla 5-lobed, with short tube and with scales in the throat; stamens 5; **fruit** of 4 horizontal nutlets.

Omphalodes cappadocica (Willd.) DC. (Navelwort). Perennial to 25 cm. tall. May, June. PLATE 193

DESCRIPTION: **Plants** low, spreading, native in Asia Minor; **leaves** ovate, to 10 cm. long, cordate; **flowers** blue, with white centers, in loose racemes.

USE: Plant in rock gardens or use as a ground cover.

CULTURE: Plants prefer a light, well-drained soil and partial shade. Some winter protection is needed. Propagation is by seed started in May in a cold frame. When seedlings are large enough, they can be transplanted to their permanent location. Division of established plants in early spring is another method of propagation.

Omphalodes—other species

O. linifolia (L.) Moench., native in Spain and Portugal, is an annual 30 cm. tall, with white flowers in July and August.

O. luciliae Boiss., native in Greece and Asia Minor, is a lovely perennial rock garden plant with lavender blue flowers in June and July.

O. verna Moench. (Creeping Forget-me-not), native in Europe, makes an attractive ground cover with small blue flowers in May.

Opuntia Mill. (Prickly Pear Cactus)

CACTACEAE (Cactus Family)

DESCRIPTION: A genus of about 300 species of prostrate to upright, jointed cacti, native in dry regions in North and South America; **stems** mostly branched; joints usually flattened and commonly obovate, or cylindrical to globose; **leaves** cylindrical to conical, soon deciduous; spines naked or sheathed, rarely lacking, produced on areoles; **flowers** sesile, showy, commonly yellow; perianth tube scarely exceeding the inferior ovary, with segments separate, mostly spreading; stamens many, shorter than the perianth segments; **fruit** a dry or fleshy berry.

Opuntia humifusa (Raf.) Raf. (Common Prickly Pear Cactus). Perennial to 20 cm. tall. June, July.   PLATE 194

DESCRIPTION: **Plants** native from Montana to Massachusetts, south to Texas and Florida; **stems** prostrate and spreading, with fibrous roots; joints flattened, nearly orbicular, to 15 cm. across; aerioles remote, spineless, or those on the edge spiny; spines brown, to 2 m. long; **flowers** yellow, to 10 cm. across; **fruits** obovoid, green to purple, to 5 cm. long.

USE: Plant in sunny rock garden.

CULTURE: Opuntias require a well-drained soil, preferably a sandy loam. They require full sun. Although they are desert plants, they do require ample moisture during the growing season. Propagation is by seeds or division. Each fleshy joint will root when placed in contact with moist soil. Because of the spines, it is best to wear leather gloves when working around these cacti.

Opuntia vulgaris — see *Opuntia humifusa*

Opuntia — other species

O. fragilis (Nutt.) Haw. (Brittle Prickly Pear Cactus), native from British Columbia to Manitoba, south to Arizona and Texas, has smaller, ovoid to subglobose joints, and small yellow flowers in June.

O. polyacantha Haw. (Plains Prickly Pear Cactus), native from Washington to Alberta, south to Arizona and Texas, has spiny stems and showy, yellow flowers in June.

Orchis L.

ORCHIDACEAE (Orchid Family)

DESCRIPTION: A genus of about 50 terrestrial herbs with tuberous roots or rhizomes, native in Eurasia and North America; **stems** leafy; **leaves** 1 or more; **flowers** few to many in congested or loose racemes; sepals separate, spreading, nearly equal; petals similar but smaller, meeting with the upper sepal to form a hood over the column; lip simple, more or less 3-lobed, united with the lower part of the column, extending at the base into a prominent spur; column short.

Orchis spectabilis L. (Showy Orchid). Perennial to 20 cm. tall. May, June.   PLATE 195

DESCRIPTION: **Plants** native in rich woods from Minnesota to New Brunswick, south to Arkansas to Georgia; **leaves** basal, oblong-ovate, to 15 cm. long;

flowers showy, pink to mauve, rarely white, in 2- to 15-flowered racemes; lip white, entire, orbicular-ovate, to 2 m. long.

USE: The showy orchid is a good plant for the wildflower garden.

CULTURE: Plants require light shade and a soil that is high in organic matter. Propagation is by division of established plants. This orchid is protected by law. Do not dig native plants.

Orchis — other species

O. rotundifolia Banks (Small Round-leaved Orchid), native in moist woods from the Yukon to Greenland, south to British Columbia and New York, has a single basal leaf and small flowers that are white, spotted with purple.

Ornithogalum L.

LILIACEAE (Lily Family)

DESCRIPTION: A genus of about 100 species of scapose, bulbous herbs, native in Africa, Europe, and western Asia; **bulbs** tunicate; **leaves** basal; **flowers** white, greenish white, or yellow to orange red, in racemes, corymbs, or umbels; perianth segments 6, separate; stamens 6 with versatile anthers; **fruit** a 3-angled capsule.

Ornithogalum umbellatum L. (Star-of-Bethlehem). Perennial to 30 cm. tall. May, June.

DESCRIPTION: **Plants** native in Europe and northern Africa; **leaves** basal, linear, to 30 cm. long, with a white midrib; **flowers** white, to 2.5 cm. across, in 5- to 20-flowered corymbose racemes.

USE: Plant in shady rock gardens or under trees.

CULTURE: The star-of-Bethlehem prefers light shade and a well-drained soil. It forms a carpet of starry flowers in May and June when planted under trees at the edge of woods. Plant the bulbs in September or early October. Space the bulbs 15 cm. apart and cover with 5 cm. of soil. The plant reseeds itself.

Oxalis L. (Wood Sorrel)

OXALIDACEAE (Oxalis Family)

DESCRIPTION: A large genus with about 800 species of annual or perennial herbs, native on all continents; **plants** often bulbous, tuberous, or rhizomatous; **leaves** alternate, cloverlike, usually with 3 leaflets, often closing at night;

flowers in most colors except blue, in 1- to several-flowered umbellate cymes; sepals and petals cohering at the base; stamens 10, in 2 series; **fruit** a capsule.

Oxalis violacea L. (Violet Wood Sorrel). Perennial to 25 cm. tall. April-June.   PLATE 196

DESCRIPTION: **Plants** native from Montana to Maine, south to Texas and Florida; **bulbs** brown, scaly; **leaflets** 3, obreniform, to 2.5 cm. wide; **flowers** violet to rose purple, seldom white, in 3- to 10-flowered umbels.

USE: Plant in rock garden or wildflower garden.

CULTURE: The violet wood sorrel prefers a soil high in organic matter and partial shade. Propagation is by bulbs or seeds. The seeds can be started indoors in March.

Oxalis — other species

O. deppei Lodd. (Good-luck Plant), native in Mexico, is a tender perennial that is often grown as a house plant. Bulbs can be planted outdoors in the spring and dug in the fall. The flowers are red in May and June.

O. lasiandra Zucc. (Primrose Oxalis) is another tender perennial with crimson flowers.

Pachysandra Michx. (Spurge)

BUXACEAE (Boxwood Family)

DESCRIPTION: A genus of 5 species of monoecious, perennial herbs or subshrubs, native in eastern Asia and North America; **leaves** simple, often crowded at the ends of branches; **flowers** in erect, terminal spikes, with the staminate ones above the pistillate; petals lacking; staminate flowers with 4 stamens opposite the sepals; pistillate flowers with 4 to 6 sepals; **fruit** a 3-beaked capsule or sometimes a drupe.

Pachysandra terminalis Siebold & Zucc. (Japanese Spruge). Evergreen perennial to 30 cm. tall. June.   PLATE 197

DESCRIPTION: **Plants** prostrate, native in Japan; **leaves** obovate, to 10 cm. long, toothed above the middle, wedge-shaped; **flowers** white, in terminal spikes.

USE: Plant as a ground cover in shade.

CULTURE: The Japanese spurge thrives in most soils if planted in the shade and where the plants will have a good winter snow cover. Propagation is by rooted cuttings taken in June or July, by spring division, and by seeds. Seeds should be started in a cold frame in May. Space plants 30 cm. apart.

CULTIVARS

'Green Carpet'. Leaves bright emerald green.

'Silver Edge'. Leaves with a silver edge.

Pachysandra — other species

P. procumbens Michx. (Allehany Spurge), native from Kentucky south to Louisiana and Florida, makes an attractive ground cover in the woodland garden. The leaves are a dull green and the flowers are green to purple in June.

Paeonia L. (Peony)

PAEONIACEAE (Peony Family)

DESCRIPTION: A genus of about 30 species of coarse perennial herbs or shrubs, native in north termperate regions of Eurasia and western North America; herbaceous species rhizomatous or with tuberous **roots**; **leaves** alternate, large, compound; **flowers** 1 to few at the ends of arching stems; petals typically 5 to 10, purple, red, pink, yellow, or white; stamens many, often petal-like; pistils 2 to 8; **fruit** of horizontally spreading follicles.

Paeonia lactiflora Pall. (Chinese Peony). Perennial to 90 cm. tall. June.

DESCRIPTION: **Plants** stout, mound-shaped, smooth, native in Tibet, China, and Siberia; **leaves** 2-ternate; leaflets elliptic to lanceolate, entire or occasionally lobed; **flowers** to 10 cm. across, fragrant, typically white, but often in shades of pink or red.

USE: Plant in flower border.

CULTURE: See culture under garden hybrids.

Peonia officinalis L. Perennial to 60 cm. tall. June.

DESCRIPTION: **Plants** native from France to Hungary and Albania; **leaves** 2-ternate; leaflets more or less deeply cut into narrow elliptic segments, to 10 cm. long, smooth above, hairy beneath; **flowers** red, to 12 cm. across; filaments red; follicles 2 or 3.

USE: Plant in flower border.

CULTURE: See culture under garden hybrids.

Paeonia —other species

P. anomala L., native from the Ural Mountains to Siberia and central Asia, has bright crimson flowers and is one of the first peonies to bloom, often being in bloom for Memorial Day.

P. tenuifolia L. (Fernleaf Peony), native in southwestern Europe to the Caucasus, has finely divided leaves and deep crimson flowers in late May. 'Plena' has double flowers.

Paeonia —garden hybrids

Most of the peonies grown are of hybrid origin with *P. lactiflora* as one of the parents. Hundreds of named cultivars are on the market and new ones are produced each year.

USE: Peonies are best grown either in rows or in a mixed flower border.

CULTURE: Peonies grow in most garden soils but they prefer a well-drained clay loam soil. They are heavy feeders and flowering is improved by a fall application of well-rotted manure and a spring application of a complete fertilizer high in phosphorus. Plants should be clean cultivated or mulched to control weeds. Some means of support may be needed to keep the flowers from falling over; peony rings on wire stakes are available for this purpose. After flowering, remove the faded flowers to prevent fruiting and seed production. For show purposes, lateral flower buds should be removed, allowing only 1 flower to develop per stem.

Propagation of peonies is by division. September is the best time to divide. Carefully lift the plant, using a spading fork, and shake or wash the soil from the roots. With a sharp knife or spade, cut the clump into 1-rooted sections. Each division should have 3 to 5 buds or "eyes." Before replanting, prepare the soil by working in organic matter and either bone meal or fertilizer high in phosphorus to a depth of at least 30 cm. Plant the roots vertically with the buds about 5 cm. below the soil surface. It usually takes at least 2 years after transplanting to get good bloom. Peonies are long-lived and should not be disturbed if they are growing and flowering satisfactorily.

Peonies are relatively free from insect and disease problems. Botrytis blight causes a wilting of flowering stems and the flowers fail to open. This disease is most prevalent in cool, humid weather. To prevent spread, cut off and destroy all diseased stems and drench the plants and soil with a good fungicide.

CULTIVARS AND CLASSIFICATION: Peonies are classified into 5 groups, according to the structure of the flowers. These groups are:

Double. Flowers with 5 or more basal or true petals and a mound of petal-like
　　stamens and carpels.

Semi-double. Flowers with 5 or more basal or true petals and one or more rows of petal-like stamens and a center of stamens and carpels.

Japanese. Flowers with 5 or more true petals and a center of staminodes that produce no pollen.

Anemone. Flowers with 5 or more true petals and a center of petal-like stamens that may be of the same color or a different color from the petals.

Single. Flowers with 5 or more true petals and a center of normal stamens and carpels.

So many named cultivars exist that it is difficult to single out a few that are best. Visit a public garden featuring peonies or a flower show at peony time. The following are good cultivars that are available at a reasonable price:

'Bonanza'. A nonfading deep red double.

'Coral Charm'. An early semi-double with a coral peach color.

'Cytheria'. A semi-double with bright pink flowers.

'Dolorodell'. A large-flowered double with cameo pink flowers.

'Festiva Maxima'. A double with white flowers with red flecks. This cultivar is over 100 years old.

'Gay Paree'. A Japanese with cerise and white flowers.

'Kansas'. A tall double with light red flowers.

'Krinkled White'. A single with dainty white flowers.

'Miss America'. The best semi-double with white petals and a yellow center.

'Pillow Talk'. A double with light pink flowers.

'Princess Margaret'. A double with dark pink flowers.

'Red Charm'. An early double red.

'Sea Shell'. A single with soft warm pink flowers.   PLATE 198

Papaver L. (Poppy)

PAPAVARACEAE (Poppy Family)

DESCRIPTION: A genus of about 50 species of annual or perennial herbs with milky sap, native mostly in the Old World, but a few species native in western North America; **leaves** lobed or dissected; **flowers** showy, nodding in bud, solitary on long stalks; sepals 2, early deciduous; petals 4, crumpled in bud, red, white, violet, or yellow; stamens many; **fruit** a subcylindrical to nearly globose capsule, opening by a terminal pore.

Papaver alpinum — see *Papaver burseri*

Papaver nudicaule L. (Iceland Poppy). Biennial to 30 cm. tall. May, June.   PLATE 199

DESCRIPTION: **Plants** native in arctic regions of North America, south to Colorado and in Eurasia; **leaves** mostly basal, petioled, pinnately lobed or cleft; **flowers** white, orange, or red, fragrant, to 7.5 cm. across; **capsules** often hairy.

USE: Plant in flower border.

CULTURE: The Iceland poppy can be grown on any well-drained soil in full sun. This poppy is a true biennial. Plant seeds in May or June in individual pots in a cold frame. Because the seeds are very small, it is difficult to plant a single seed. Thin the seedlings while small to a single plant per pot. Transplant to the border in September, being careful not to disturb the roots. A new supply of seedlings should be grown each year. Plants deteriorate in hot humid weather and should be removed.

CULTIVARS

'Champagne Bubbles'. Flowers very large, in wide color range.
'Golden Monarch'. Flowers golden yellow.
'Sparkling Bubbles'. Flowers in shades of yellow, rose, orange, and scarlet.
'Summer Promise'. Flowers in bright colors.

Papaver orientale L. (Oriental Poppy). Perennial to 1 m. tall. May, June.

DESCRIPTION: **Plants** robust, hairy, native in southwestern Asia, sometimes naturalized elsewhere; **leaves** pinnately dissected with lanceolate segments; **flowers** red, sometimes orange or pink, sometimes double, to 10 cm. across.

USE: Plant in the flower border.

CULTURE: The Oriental poppy thrives in ordinary well-drained soil in full sun. Once established, the plants should not be disturbed. Propagation is by root cuttings taken in summer as soon as the foliage dies down. Pieces of the fleshy root 7 to 10 cm. long should be planted in a sandy soil in a cold frame. The roots should be placed horizontally and covered with 5 cm. of the sandy soil. Keep the frame closed for a few weeks while new roots are forming. The cuttings will be well rooted by spring and the plants can be transplanted to their permanent location in May. The Oriental poppies are good companion plants for irises and lupines.

CULTIVARS: Numerous cultivars have been named. These must be vegetatively propagated.   PLATE 200

'Allegro'. Flowers single, dazzling scarlet.
'Beauty of Livermore'. Flowers crimson.

'Carmine'. Flowers dark cardinal red, spotted black.
'Curlilocks'. Flowers shocking pink.
'Queen Alexandria'. Flowers rosy salmon.
'Snow Queen'. Flowers white.

Papaver rhoeas L. (Corn Poppy, Shirley Poppy). Annual to 90 cm. tall. June, July.

DESCRIPTION: **Plants** erect, branched, with bristly hairs, native in Europe and Asia, naturalized elsewhere; **leaves** irregularly pinnate, to 15 cm. long; **flowers** to 5 cm. across, on long stems, cinnabar red, deep purple, scarlet, or white, single or double.

USE: Plant in sunny flower border.

CULTURE: As with most poppies, the Shirley poppy is difficult to transplant. It is best to sow the seeds directly where the plants are to bloom in late April or early May. Thin the plants to about 20 cm. These plants dislike hot, humid weather and should be removed from the border after they finish flowering.

CULTIVARS
'Flander's Field'. Flowers single orange scarlet.
'Sweet Briar'. Flowers double, deep rose pink.

Papaver — other species

P. burseri Crantz, (Mountain Poppy), native in the mountains of central Europe, has white flowers to 2 cm. across. This is a good poppy for rock gardens.

P. somniferum L. (Opium Poppy), native in southeastern Europe and western Asia, is the source of opium. The flowers are often double, white, pink, red, or purple, with a dark spot at the base of each petal. Seeds are seldom sold by seed companies because of the narcotic properties but some gardeners save their own seed. Like the Shirley poppy, it is an annual.

Pardanthus chinensis — see *Belamcanda chinensis*

Pelargonium L'Her. (Geranium)

GERANIACEAE (Geranium Family)

DESCRIPTION: A large genus of about 280 species of annual or perennial herbs or shrubs, mostly native in South Africa; **leaves** entire, lobed, or dissected, with usually prominent stipules; **flowers** irregular, 1- to many-flowered umbels borne terminal, axillary, or opposite the leaves; calyx with a spur united to the pedicel, 5-lobed; petals 5, rarely 4 or 2, the upper pair usually larger; stamens 10, only 5 to 7 with fertile anthers; **fruit** 5-valved, the valves coiling upward as they dehisce.

Pelargonium x *hortorum* L. H. Bailey (Bedding Geranium). Tender perennial to 60 cm. tall. June-October.

DESCRIPTION: **Plants** of hybrid origin involving *P. inquinans, P. zonale,* and other species; **leaves** rounded or reniform, cordate at base, scalloped and crenate-toothed, often zoned or variegated, to 12 cm. across; **flowers** red, pink, salmon, or white, in dense umbels; calyx spur elongate.

USE: Plant in window boxes or containers for summer bloom on a patio or plant in the flower border for a mass effect.

CULTURE: The bedding geraniums like a well-drained soil and full sun. Propagation is by rooted cuttings or from seed. In recent years, most seed companies have been selling geranium seeds. These seed strains are improving and now produce uniform seedlings of good flower color. Seeds must be started in January or February to have seedlings of flowering size to plant in the garden about Memorial Day. Most garden centers feature geranium plants.

CULTIVARS: Many florists feature named cultivars that must be vegetatively propagated. The following are seed propagated: PLATE 201
Flash Series. Plants compact; umbels globe-shaped.
    'Fire Flash'. Flowers fiery vermillion red.
    'Red Express'. Flowers red, semi-double.
    'Salmon Flash'. Flowers deep salmon.
Jolly Series. Umbels large, to 12 cm. across.
    'Jolly Apple Blossom'. Flowers apple-blossom pink.
    'Jolly Red Giant'. Flowers glowing red.
    'Jolly Red Wink'. Flowers red with white centers.
Ringo Series. Leaves zoned; flowers very early.
    'Heidi'. Flowers bicolor, rosy salmon with white centers.
    'Ice Queen'. Flowers white.
    'Rosita'. Flowers rose pink, large.
Sprinter Series. Plants compact; umbels flat on top.
    'Sprinter Deep Rose'. Flowers deep red.
    'Sprinter Salmon'. Flowers orange salmon.
    'Sprinter Scarlet'. All-America Winner. Flowers dazzling scarlet.

Pelargonium peltatum (L.) L'Her. (Ivy Geranium). Tender perennial to 90 cm. tall. June-October.

DESCRIPTION: **Plants** trailing or climbing, native in South Africa; **leaves** peltate, broadly ovate, shallowly 5-angled or 5-lobed, sometimes zoned with red, to 7.5 cm. across; **flowers** rose carmine, varying to white, with dark veins on upper petals, in 5- to 7-flowered umbels; upper petals much larger than the lower.

USE: Ivy geraniums are often used in hanging baskets and patio containers.

CULTURE: Ivy geraniums bloom best where summers are cool. They are popular in Europe in window boxes. Culture is the same as for *P.* x *hortorum*.

Pelargonium —other species

Numerous species and named cultivars of hybrid origin are grown for specific purposes. There are a large number of scented-leaved geraniums, usually grown as pot plants and sometimes planted outdoors in the herb garden in the summer.

Pentstemon Mitch. (Beard-tongue)

SCROPHULARIACEAE (Figwort Family)

DESCRIPTION: A genus of about 250 species of perennial herbs or shrubs, native mostly in western North America; **leaves** opposite, rarely in whorls of 3 or the upper leaves alternate, sessile above and petioled below; **flowers** scarlet purple, blue, or yellow, solitary or in terminal racemes or panicles; calyx 5-parted; corolla tubular, 2-lipped; fertile stamens 4; staminode 1; **fruit** a many-seeded capsule.

Pentstemon barbatus (Cav.) Roth. (Beardlip Beard-tongue). Perennial to 1 m. tall. July, August.

DESCRIPTION: A glabrous, glaucous perennial, native from Utah to Mexico; basal **leaves** oblong to ovate, stem leaves linear to lanceolate, entire; **flowers** red, to 2 cm. long, strongly 2-lipped, lower lip yellow-bearded; staminode smooth.

USE: Plant in flower border.

CULTURE: Plants thrive in any well-drained soil in sun or light shade. Propagation is largely by seeds started in July in a cold frame. Cuttings can also be taken from side shoots in September and rooted in a cold frame.

CULTIVARS   PLATE 202
'Elfin Pink'. Flowers clear pink.
'Pink Beauty'. Flowers shell pink.
'Prairie Dusk'. Flowers rose purple.
'Prairie Fire'. Flowers fiery red.

Pentstemon grandiflorus Nutt. (Shell-leaf Beard-tongue). Usually a biennial to 1 m. tall. May, June.

DESCRIPTION: **Plants** glabrous and glaucous, native from North Dakota to

Illinois, south to Wyoming and Texas; **leaves** entire, thick, fleshy, obovate at base of plant, elliptic to round-ovate and clasping on the stems; **flowers** lilac or blue lavender, to 5 cm. long, very showy; staminode hooked, minutely bearded at apex.

USE: Plant in flower border or in prairie garden.

CULTURE: Same as for *P. barbatus*. Being a biennial, new plants must be started each year.

CULTIVAR
'Albus'. Flowers white.

Pentstemon — other species

Many native species in the western states are suitable for the rock garden or for the wildflower garden. They hybridize readily and volunteer seedlings are not like their parents.

P. caespitosus Nutt. (Mat Beard-tongue), native in Wyoming, Utah, and Colorado, is a low, creeping plant with blue flowers, suitable for a rock garden.

P. cardwellii T. J. Howell (Cardwell Beard-tongue), native in Washington and Oregon, has bright purple flowers about 4 cm. long on short plants 25 cm. tall. This is a good rock garden plant.

P. digitalis Nutt., native from South Dakota to Maine and south to Texas, has white to pink flowers about 2.5 cm. long.

P. newberryi A. Gray (Mountain-pride, Newberry Beard-tongue), native in northern California and neighboring Nevada, is a charming rock garden plant with rose red flowers.

P. pinifolius Greene, native from New Mexico to Mexico, is another rock garden species with needlelike leaves and scarlet flowers from June to September.

Pentstemon — garden hybrids

These have been developed largely in England and Europe. *P. hartwegii* and *P. cobaea*, both American species, were used in their development. Although perennial, they are usually grown as annuals from seed planted indoors in February. Plants have showy flowers in a wide range of colors. Named cultivars must be propagated by cuttings but there are several seed propagated strains. Giant Floradale and Hyacinth-flowered are 2 such strains.

CULTIVARS
'Bashful'. Flowers orange red.
'C. V. Crystal'. Flowers pure white.
'Rose Elf'. Flowers coral pink.

Petalostemon Michx. (Prairie Clover)

LEGUMINOSAE (Pea Family)

DESCRIPTION: A genus of about 40 species of glandular-dotted perennial herbs, native in North America; **leaves** alternate, crowded, odd-pinnate; **flowers** in dense heads or spikes, with 4 petals united basally to the stamen tube and the standard separate; **fruit** a short, indehiscent legume, included in the calyx.

Petalostemon candidum (Willd.) Michx. (White Prairie Clover). Perennial to 75 cm. tall. June, July.

DESCRIPTION: **Plants** native from Saskatchewan to Manitoba, south to Arizona and Mississippii; **leaflets** 7 to 9, linear or oblong; **flowers** white in oblong spikes to 7.5 cm. long.

USE: Sometimes planted in the flower garden but more often in the prairie garden.

CULTURE: Plants grow in any well-drained soil in full sun. Propagation is by direct seeding in early spring. Plants develop a taproot, which makes transplanting difficult.

Petalostemon purpureum (Venten.) Rydb. (Purple Prairie Clover). Perennial to 90 cm. tall. June, July.   PLATE 203

DESCRIPTION: **Plants** native from Saskatchewan to Indiana, south to New Mexico and Texas; **leaflets** 3 to 5, linear, to 2 cm. long; **flowers** violet to crimson, in dense spikes to 5 cm. long.

USE: Same as for *P. candidum.*

CULTURE: Same as for *P. candidum.*

Petrorhagia (Ser.) Link.

CARYOPHYLLACEAE (Pink Family)

DESCRIPTION: A genus of about 25 species of annual or perennial herbs, native from the Canary Islands through the Mediterranean region to Kashmir; **leaves** opposite, awl-shaped to oblong; **flowers** small, in clusters, heads, or solitary; calyx 5-toothed; corolla of 5 entire or bifid petals; stamens 10; ovary 1-celled, with 2 styles; **fruit** a capsule, dehiscent by 4 teeth.

Petrorhagia saxifraga (L.) Link (Coat Flower, Tunic Flower). Perennial to 10 cm. tall. June-July.

DESCRIPTION: **Plants** native in central and southern Europe, east to central

Asia; **stems** creeping, woody at base; **leaves** linear-lanceolate, setose-serrate; **flowers** white or pink; calyx pubescent; petals about 8 mm. long.

USE: Plant in rock garden or toward the front of the flower border.

CULTURE: The plants require full sun and a well-drained soil. Propagation is by seeds or by spring division. Double-flowered cultivars must be vegetatively propagated.

CULTIVARS

'Alba'. Flowers white.

'Pleniflora Rosea'. Flowers double pink. The plant called Lady Mary is probably this cultivar.

'Rosea'. Flowers rose pink.

Petunia Juss.

SOLANACEAE (Potato Family)

DESCRIPTION: A genus of about 30 species of mostly sticky-pubescent, annual or perennial herbs, native in tropical and subtropical South America; **leaves** alternate, simple, entire; **flowers** solitary, axillary, violet to white, or pale yellow, blue, pink, and red in cultivated forms, funnelform or salverform; stamens borne on the corolla, 4 fertile, 1 smaller and rudimentary; **fruit** a 2-celled capsule with many seeds.

Petunia x *hybrida* Hort. (Common Garden Petunia). Tender perennial grown as an annual to 30 cm. tall. June-October.

DESCRIPTION: The garden petunia is a complex hybrid involving at least 3 species: *P. axillaris*, *P. inflata*, and *P. violacea*; **leaves** variable; **flowers** up to 12 cm. across, in various colors; corolla funnelform.

USE: Petunias are one of the most popular of all bedding plants. They are planted in flower borders, window boxes, and patio containers.

CULTURE: Plants do best in a well-drained soil and in full sun. The seeds should be started indoors in late March or early April. Plants can also be purchased from any garden center. Space the plants about 30 cm. apart. Petunias have few pests or insects. Aster yellows sometimes affects plants in August, causing a stunting of the plants and deformed flowers. Control of the 6-spotted leaf hopper will help to prevent infection.

CULTIVARS: Garden petunias are classified as Multifloras or Grandifloras. The Multifloras have many flowers in a riot of colors and are about 7 cm. across. Grandifloras have fewer but larger flowers to 10 or more cm. across. Double and single forms occur in each class. There are literally hundreds of named cultivars to choose from; the following are but a few.

Multiflora Petunias   PLATE 205
  'Apple Tart'. Flowers double, rich scarlet red.
  'Commanche'. All-America Winner. Flowers single, scarlet red.
  'Peach Tart'. Flowers double, clear salmon.
  'Summer Sun'. Flowers single, deep yellow.
  'White Delight'. Flowers double, pure white.

Grandiflora Petunias
  'Apple Blossom'. All-America Winner. Flowers fringed, salmon pink.
  'Blushing Maid'. All-America Winner. Flowers double, salmon pink. PLATE 204
  'Glacier'. Flowers single, white.
  'Pink Cascade'. Flowers single, rich pink.
  'Salmon Bouquet'. Flowers double, light salmon pink.

Phaseolus L. (Bean)

LEGUMINOSAE (Pea Family)

DESCRIPTION: A genus of about 20 species of mostly climbing herbs, native in the warm temperate to the tropical regions of the New World; **leaves** alternate, trifoliate; **flowers** clustered or in racemes, pealike, with orbicular standard and a spreading or somewhat contorted beaked keel; stamens 10, 9 united and 1 separate; **fruit** a flat, dehiscent legume.

Phaseolus coccineus L. (Scarlet Runner Bean). Tender perennial grown as an annual, to 3 m. tall. July-September.   PLATE 206

DESCRIPTION: Tall twining vines, native in tropical America; **leaflets** broadly ovate, to 12 cm. long; **flowers** clustered, bright scarlet, to 2.5 cm. long; **fruit** an edible, flat legume to 30 cm. long; seeds broad, to 2.5 cm. long, black, mottled red.

USE: Plant on a trellis for summer bloom.

CULTURE: A rich, well-drained soil and full sun are required. The seeds should be planted about May 20.

CULTIVAR
'Albus'. Flowers and seeds white.

Phlox L.

POLEMONIACEAE (Phlox Family)

DESCRIPTION: A genus of about 60 species of erect, diffuse, or cespitose annual or perennial herbs, native mostly in North America; **leaves** opposite or the uppermost sometimes alternate, simple; **flowers** blue, purple, crimson, pink, or white, solitary or in terminal cymes or panicles; calyx 5-cleft; corolla salverform, 5-lobed; stamen 5, unequal in length, inserted on the corolla tube; **fruit** a 3-valved capsule, rupturing the calyx at maturity.

Phlox amoena — see *Phlox* x *procumbens*

Phlox borealis Wherry (Arctic Phlox). Perennial to 10 cm. tall. May.

DESCRIPTION: **Plants** creeping, native in Alaska; **leaves** linear, to 10 cm. long, dark green, nearly evergreen; **flowers** lilac, lavender, or rarely white.

USE: Plant in rock gardens or use as a ground cover.

CULTURE: The arctic phox grows best in a rich, well-drained soil. It blooms best in full sun. The dense, matlike growth crowds out most weeds except grasses. The nearly evergreen foliage stays dark green from early spring to winter. Propagation is by division or rooted cuttings. Plants spaced 30 cm. apart will fill in during a single growing season.

Phlox decussata — see *Phlox paniculata*

Phlox divaricata L. (Blue Phlox, Wild Sweet William). Perennial to 45 cm. tall. May, June.   PLATE 207

DESCRIPTION: **Plants** spreading, sometimes decumbent and rooting at the nodes, native from Minnesota to Quebec, south to Texas and Georgia; **leaves** elliptic, ovate to oblong, to 5 cm. long; **flowers** pale violet blue to lavender, to 4 cm. across, with notched corolla lobes.

USE: Plant in woodland wildflower garden.

CULTURE: The blue phlox does best in light shade and a moist soil high in organic matter. Propagation is by seeds and division.

CULTIVARS
'Alba'. Flowers white.
'Canadensis'. Flowers bright blue.
'Laphamii'. Flowers rich blue violet.
'Springtime'. Flowers deep lavender pink.

Phlox drummondii Hook. (Annual Phlox). Annual to 50 cm. tall. June-October.

DESCRIPTION: **Plants** sprawling, native in south-central Texas; **leaves** ovate to lanceolate, to 7.5 cm. long, upper leaves alternate; **flowers** rose red, varying to white, buff, pink, red, and purple, to 2.5 cm. across, in dense cymes.

USE: Plant in rock gardens and toward the front of the flower border.

CULTURE: Plants prefer a rich, well-drained soil and full sun. Propagation is by seeds started indoors in early April or seeds can be sown in early May directly where plants are to grow. Space plants about 20 cm. apart.

CULTIVAR AND STRAINS

Dwarf Beauty (strain). Plants compact, free-flowering, in blue, crimson, pink, and white.

Fordhook (strain). Flowers round-petaled, in wide color range and in large clusters.

'Twinkle'. All-America Winner. Flowers fantastically fringed and artfully star-shaped, in a good color range.   PLATE 208

Phlox paniculata L. (Garden Phlox). Perennial to 2 m. tall. July-September.

DESCRIPTION: **Plants** clump-forming, native from Illinois to New York, south to Arkansas and Georgia; **leaves** elliptic to elliptic-lanceolate or ovate, to 15 cm. long; **flowers** pink purple, varying to white, salmon, scarlet, lilac, and purple in cultivars, to 2.5 cm. across, in large terminal panicles.

USE: Plant toward the back of the flower border.

CULTURE: Plants grow best in a rich well-drained soil in full sun. Keep the soil moist. Propagation of named cultivars is by spring division and by root cuttings. Foliage diseases can threaten the plants, but good air circulation between plants helps to reduce disease. Remove faded flowers before they produce seeds. Volunteer seedlings revert to a magenta-colored flower.

CULTIVARS: Numerous cultivars have been named. The following are but a few.   PLATE 209

'Blue Ice'. Flowers blue with a pink eye.

'Dresden China'. Flowers shell pink with a darker eye.

'Mt. Fujiyama'. Flowers clear white.

'Orange Perfection'. Flowers luminous orange.

'Starfire'. Flowers brilliant red.

Phlox subulata L. (Moss Phlox). Perennial to 15 cm. tall. May, June.

DESCRIPTION: **Plants** mat-forming, native from Michigan to New York, south to Maryland; **leaves** linear to awl-shaped, to 2.5 cm. long, crowded, nearly evergreen; **flowers** red purple, violet purple, pink, and white, to 2 cm. across, with corolla lobes shallowly notched.

USE: Plant in rock garden or use as a ground cover.

CULTURE: Plants like full sun and a rich, well-drained soil. Weeds can cause serious difficulties. The growth is not dense enough to crowd out weeds and the spreading growth habit makes weeding difficult. Winter injury can also be a problem in open winters.

CULTIVARS

'Atropurpurea'. Flowers carmine red.
'Emerald Blue'. Flowers pale to medium blue.
'Emerald Pink'. Flowers pink.
'Scarlet Flame'. Flowers bright scarlet.
'White Delight'. Flowers pure white.

Phlox — other species

P. bifida L. (Sand Phlox), native from Michigan south to Arkansas and Tennessee, has flowers that are lavender or rarely lilac, with deeply notched petals in May.

P. carolina L. (Thick-leaf Phlox), native from Missouri to North Carolina and south to Mississippi and Florida, is an upright perennial to 1 m. tall. with purple, pink, or white flowers from June to August. 'Miss Lingard', with white flowers, and 'Rosalinda', with amaranth pink flowers, are named cultivars.

P. douglasii Hook. (Douglas Phlox), native from Michigan to Quebec and south to California and Nevada, is a low, creeping phlox with lavender, pink, or white flowers in May. 'Rosea', with rose-colored flowers, and 'Snow Queen', with white flowers, are named cultivars.

P. pilosa L. (Prairie Phlox), native from Minnesota to Connecticut and south to Texas and Florida, has attractive purple to pink, rarely white, flowers to 2 cm. across in June. It is sometimes planted in prairie gardens.

P. x procumbens Lehm. is a hybrid resulting from a cross between *P. stolonifera* and *P. subulata*. It is a creeping plant with purple flowers. Plants sold as *P. amoena* are often this hybrid.

P. stolonifera Sims. (Creeping Phlox), native from Pennsylvania to Georgia, has purple or violet flowers to 2.5 cm. across. 'Blue Ridge', with shiny blue flowers, 'Ariane', with pure white flowers, and 'Violet Queen', with dark violet flowers, are named cultivars.

Physalis L. (Ground Cherry, Husk Tomato)

SOLANACEAE (Potato Family)

DESCRIPTION: A genus of about 80 species of annual or perennial herbs, native chiefly in the Americas; **leaves** alternate, simple, petioled, variously lobed and often soft to the touch; **flowers** mostly solitary in leaf axils; calyx 5-toothed, enlarging and becoming bladderlike in fruit, with 10 prominent veins; corolla usually yellow, sometimes blue or white with dark spots in the center; stamens 5; **fruit** a green or yellow berry enclosed by the inflated calyx.

Physalis alkekengi L. (Chinese-lantern). Tender perennial grown as an annual, to 60 cm. tall. August, September.

DESCRIPTION: **Plants** rhizomatous, native from southern Europe to Japan; **leaves** simple, ovate-rhombic, to 8 cm. long, entire or wavy; **flowers** nodding; calyx vermillion red; corolla white, rotate; 5-lobed; **fruit** a red berry surrounded by the inflated calyx.

USE: Plant in flower border or in cutting garden.

CULTURE: Plants prefer a rich, well-drained soil and full sun. Start the seeds indoors in late March and transplant seedlings to the garden after danger of frost. Space the plants about 30 cm. apart.

CULTIVARS
'Gigantea'. Fruits larger than in species.
'Pygmaea'. Plants dwarf.

Physalis franchettii — see *Physalis alkekengi*

Physostegia Benth. (False Dragonhead)

LABIATAE (Mint Family)

DESCRIPTION: A genus of about 15 species of perennial herbs, native in North America; **stems** mostly square in cross section; **leaves** opposite, often toothed; **flowers** showy, in solitary or panicled leaflets spikes; calyx tubular or campanulate, 10-veined, slightly inflated in fruit; corolla white, purple, red, or pink, with tube much longer than the calyx and 2-lipped limb, upper lip erect, entire, lower lip 3-lobed; stamens 4, in 2 pairs; **fruit** of 4 smooth nutlets.

Physostegia virginiana (L.) Benth. (Obedient Plant, False Dragonhead). Perennial to 1 m. tall. July-September.   PLATE 210

DESCRIPTION: **Plants** rhizomatous, native from Minnesota to New Brunswick, south to Missouri to South Carolina; **leaves** lanceolate, to 12 cm. long, acute, sharply serrate; **flowers** to 3 cm. long, showy, rose purple, inflated at the mouth.

USE: Plant in wildflower garden or in flower border.

CULTURE: Plants prefer a moist soil and light shade although they can be grown in full sun. Propagation is largely by division of established plants in early spring.

CULTIVARS
'Alba'. Flowers white.
'Bouquet Rose'. Flowers rose-colored.
'Summer Snow'. Flowers pure white.
'Vivid'. Flowers deep pink.

Platycodon A. DC. (Balloon Flower)

CAMPANULACEAE (Bellflower Family)

DESCRIPTION: A small genus with but a single species of perennial herbs, native in eastern Asia; **flowers** inflated in bud, balloonlike; stamens with dilated filaments; **fruit** a capsule opening at the apex.

Platycodon grandiflorus (Jacq.) A. DC. (Balloon Flower). Perennial to 75 cm. tall. July, August. PLATE 211

DESCRIPTION: **Plants** erect, smooth, branched above, native in eastern Asia; **leaves** ovate to ovate-lanceolate to 7.5 cm. long, sharply toothed, glaucous-blue beneath; **flowers** inflated, balloonlike in bud, pale blue, lilac, or white, solitary and terminal on side branches; corolla broadly bell-shaped to nearly spherical.

USE: Plant in flower border. Dwarf cultivars are also planted in rock gardens.

CULTURE: Plants prefer a well-drained soil and either full sun or light shade. Propagation is by seeds started indoors in early April or planted in a cold frame in early May. When large enough, the seedlings are transplanted in their permanent location. Once established, the plants should not be moved.

CULTIVARS AND VARIETY
var. *mariesii* (Hort.) Nichols (Dwarf Balloon Flower). Plants compact, to 30 cm. tall. A good rock garden plant.
'Double Blue'. Flowers double, in exotic shades of blue with darker veins.
'Shell Pink'. Flowers soft shell pink.

Podophyllum L. (Mayapple)

BERBERIDACEAE (Barberry Family)

DESCRIPTION: A genus of 2 species of rhizomatous perennial herbs, native in North America and Asia; basal **leaves** large, peltate, solitary, lobed; leaves on flowering stems paired, palmately lobed; **flowers** solitary in leaf axils, waxy; sepals 6; petals 6 or 9; stamens as many as or twice as many as petals; **fruit** a fleshy, ellipsoid berry.

Podophyllum peltatum L. (Mayapple, Mandrake). Perennial to 45 cm. tall. May, June.   PLATE 212

DESCRIPTION: **Plants** native from Minnesota to Quebec, south to Texas and Florida; **leaves** 5- to 9-lobed, to 30 cm. across; **flowers** white, to 5 cm. across; stamens 12 to 18; **fruits** yellow or rarely red, 5 cm. long with edible flesh.

USE: Plant in woodland wildflower garden.

CULTURE: Mayapples like a shaded area and a soil that is high in organic matter. Propagation is by seeds or by spring division of established plants. The seeds should be planted in a nursery row or cold frame in May. Once established, the plants should not be disturbed.

Polemonium L. (Jacob's-ladder)

POLEMONIACEAE (Phlox Family)

DESCRIPTION: A genus of about 25 species of decumbent annual or rhizomatous perennial herbs, native in Europe, Asia, and the Americas; **leaves** alternate, pinnate; **flowers** blue, purple, yellow, and white, solitary to capitate in terminal or axillary cymes; calyx enlarging with the fruit; corolla campanulate to funnelform; stamens equal; **fruit** a 3-celled capsule.

Polemonium caeruleum L. (Greek Valerian, Jacob's-ladder). Perennial to 90 cm. tall. June, July.

DESCRIPTION: **Plants** native in Europe and Asia; **leaflets** 19 to 27, lanceolate to elliptic; **flowers** blue, to 2.5 cm. across; stamens longer than the corolla.

USE: Plant in wildflower garden or in rock garden.

CULTURE: Plants prefer light shade and a moist, well-drained soil high in organic matter. Propagation is by spring division or by seeds. Volunteer seedlings can be moved in early spring. Space the plants about 30 cm. apart.

CULTIVARS

'Album'. Flowers white.

'Blue Pearl'. Flowers light cobalt blue with yellow centers.

Polemonium reptans L. (Creeping Jacob's-ladder). Perennial to 60 cm. tall. May, June.   PLATE 213

DESCRIPTION: **Plants** tufted, native from Minnesota to New Hampshire, south to Oklahoma and Georgia; **leaflets** 7 to 19, ovate to lanceolate, to 5 cm. long; **flowers** blue, to 2 cm. long; **fruits** on a stalk.

USE: Same as for *P. caeruleum*.

CULTURE: Same as for *P. caeruleum*.

CULTIVAR

'Album'. Flowers white.

Polianthes L.

AGAVACEAE (Agave Family)

DESCRIPTION: A genus of about 12 species of tuberous rooted herbs, native in Mexico; **leaves** grasslike, mostly basal; **flowers** red or white, in terminal racemes or spikes; perianth tubular, 6-lobed, stamens 6, ovary inferior, 3-celled; **fruit** a capsule.

Polianthes tuberosa L. (Tuberose). Tender perennial to 1 m. tall. August, September.

DESCRIPTION: **Plants** probably native in Mexico but unknown in the wild form; **leaves** linear, 45 cm. long, clasping the stem; **flowers** waxy white, to 6 cm. long, in terminal racemes, very fragrant.

USE: Tuberoses can be planted in clumps in the flower border or in rows in the cutting garden.

CULTURE: Tuberoses like a warm, well-drained soil and a sunny location. The tuberous roots are dug in the fall and stored over winter in a dry place at about 60° F. The tubers can be planted outdoors after danger of frost. Earlier bloom can be had if the tubers are potted up and started indoors in early April. Space the plants about 20 cm. apart.

CULTIVARS

'Excelsior Double Pearl'. Flowers double.

'Mexican'. Flowers single.

Polygonatum Mill. (Solomon's-seal)

LILIACEAE (Lily Family)

DESCRIPTION: A genus of about 30 species of rhizomatous perennial herbs, native in north temperate regions; **rhizomes** horizontal, much-jointed; **stems** erect to arching; **leaves** alternate, opposite, or whorled; **flowers** green to yellow, axillary, solitary, or in clusters; perianth cylindrical, 6-lobed; stamens 6, borne on the perianth tube; **fruit** a blue black berry.

Polygonatum commutatum (Schult.) A. Dietr. (Great Solomon's-seal). Perennial to 1.8 m. tall. May, June.

PLATE 214

DESCRIPTION: **Plants** with arching stems, native from Manitoba to New Hampshire, south to Mexico and Georgia; **leaves** alternate, ovate-lanceolate to ovate, to 18 cm. long, smooth; **flowers** greenish white, to 2 cm. long, on 2- to 10-flowered axillary peduncles.

USE: Plant in a shady wildflower garden in front of shrubs or in a mass planting.

CULTURE: Plants like a rich, moist soil high in organic matter and light shade. Propagation is by division, either in the fall or early in the spring.

CULTIVARS: Some authors consider this species to be a tetraploid form of *P. bilflorum.*
'Variegatum'. Leaves soft green with cream edges.

Polygonatum — other species

P. biflorum (Walt.) Elliott (Small Soloman's-seal), native from North Dakota to Massachusetts, south to New Mexico and Florida, is similar to *P. commutatum* except for its smaller size; it is only about half as tall.

P. multiflorum (L.) All. (Eurasian Solomon's-seal), native in Europe and Asia, has larger and whiter flowers than the American species. Use and culture is the same.

Polygonum L. (Knotweed, Fleece Flower)

POLYGONACEAE (Buckwheat Family)

DESCRIPTION: A large genus of about 150 species of annual or perennial herbs of wide distribution, sometimes twining or aquatic; **stems** appear to be jointed; **leaves** alternate, simple, entire, variously shaped, with stipular sheaths; **flowers** small but often showy in racemes, spikes, or heads; sepals 5, petal-like; stamens 8; **fruit** a small, 3-angled achene, partly or completely enclosed by the sepals.

Polygonum capitatum Buch.-Ham. (Pinkhead Knotweed). Tender perennial grown as an annual, to 25 cm. tall. August, September.

DESCRIPTION: **Plants** trailing, native in the Himalayas; leaves elliptic, to 4 cm. long; **flowers** pink or white, bell-shaped, to 3 mm. long, in dense heads to 2 cm. across.

USE: Use as a temporary ground cover.

CULTURE: This annual is of easy culture, thriving in most soils. It is propagated by seeds that can be sown directly where plants are to grow or started indoors for earlier bloom. Volunteer seedlings can pose a problem.

CULTIVAR

'Magic Carpet'. Flowers rose pink.

Polygonum cuspidatum var. *compactum* (Hook.) L. H. Bailey (Japanese Fleece Flower). Perennial to 60 cm. tall. August. September. PLATE 215

DESCRIPTION: **Plants** native in Japan; **leaves** elliptic to nearly orbicular, abruptly pointed; **flowers** with sepals enlarging over the fruits and turning red, in axillary, panicled racemes.

USE: This variety is often planted as a ground cover.

CULTURE: Plants thrive on any good garden soil. Propagation is by division or by rooted cuttings. Plants spread by underground rhizomes and can be very invasive. Plant only where its spread can be controlled by effective barriers. This is the plant often sold as *P. reynoutria*.

Polygonum reynoutria — see *Polygonum cuspidatum* var. *compactum*

Polygonum — other species

P. affine D. Don. (Himalayan Fleece Flower), native in the Himalayan Mountains, makes an attractive ground cover with bright rose-colored flowers in dense, upright spikes in August and September.

P. aubertii L. (Silver Lace Vine), native in western China and Tibet, is a popular vine with fragrant, white flowers in loose panicles in July and August. Some winter protection is needed.

P. cuspidatum Siebold & Zucc. (Mexican Bamboo), native in Japan, is a coarse perennial with large leaves and jointed stems. It is planted for its bold foliage, but it can be invasive.

Pontederia L. (Pickerel Weed)

PONTEDERIACEAE (Pickerel Weed Family)

DESCRIPTION: A genus of only a few species of aquatic, perennial herbs, native in North and South America; **leaves** thick, parallel-veined, long-petioled; **flowers** blue, in spikes, **fruit** an achene.

Pontederia cordata L. (Pickerel Weed). Perennial to 1 m. tall. July, August.

DESCRIPTION: **Plants** native from Minnesota to Nova Scotia, south to Texas and South Carolina; **leaves** narrowly ovate, cordate at base, to 25 cm. long on long petioles; **flowers** blue, in spikes; upper lobes of perianth segments with 2 yellow spots.

USE: Plant in shallow pools or streams.

CULTURE: Plants require wet soil. It is usually planted in mud in shallow pools not over 30 cm. deep. Once established, do not disturb. Propagation is by division of the rhizomes in early spring.

Portulaca L. (Moss Rose, Purslane)

PORTULACEAE (Purslane Family)

DESCRIPTION: A genus of over 100 species of fleshy and trailing, mostly annual herbs, widely distributed in warm countries; **leaves** alternate, sometimes cylindrical and fleshy, the upper forming an involucre below the flowers; **flowers** often showy and variously colored; calyx 2-cleft; petals 4 to 6, usually 5, stamens 8 or more; **fruit** a capsule opening by a lid.

Portulaca grandiflora Hook. (Moss Rose, Rose Moss). Annual to 30 cm. tall. July-September. PLATE 216

DESCRIPTION: **Plants** trailing, native in Brazil; **leaves** alternate, cylindrical, fleshy, to 2.5 cm. long; **flowers** solitary, rose, yellow, red, or white, often striped, to 3 cm. across.

USE: Plant in rock garden or sunny border.

CULTURE: Plants thrive in well-drained soil and full sun. Seeds can be sown directly where plants are to bloom or seeds can be started indoors for earlier bloom. Space the plants about 20 cm. apart. Flowers close at night or in cloudy weather.

CULTIVARS

'Magic Carpet'. Flowers double, in a blend of pink, red, salmon, orange, yellow, and white.

'Sun Kiss'. Flowers double and ruffled, in many colors.

'Sunnyside'. Flowers large, double, in a blend of colors.

Potentilla L. (Cinquefoil)

ROSACEAE (Rose Family)

DESCRIPTION: A large genus of about 500 species of annual or perennial herbs, rarely shrubs, native in north temperate and arctic regions; **leaves** alternate, palmately or pinnately compound; **flowers** yellow, white, or red, solitary or in cymes; sepals 5, with alternating bractlets; petals 5, stamens and pistils many; **fruit** an achene.

Potentilla nepalensis Hook. (Nepal Cinquefoil). Perennial to 45 cm. tall. July-September.

DESCRIPTION: **Plants** spreading, hairy, native in the Himalayas; **leaves** palmate with 5 leaflets that are obovate-oblong to oblanceolate, to 6 cm. long, coarsely toothed; **flowers** rose red, to 2.5 cm. across, in forked panicles.

USE: Plant in flower border.

CULTURE: Plants like full sun and a well-drained soil. The species can be propagated by seeds started indoors in March. The named cultivars are vegetatively propagated by division. Space the plants about 30 cm. apart.

CULTIVARS

'Miss Willmott'. Flowers carmine rose, with darker centers.   PLATE 217

'Roxana'. Plants semi-prostrate; flowers orange scarlet.

Potentilla tridentata Ait. (Wineleaf Cinquefoil, Three-toothed Cinquefoil). Perennial to 30 cm. tall. June-August.

DESCRIPTION: **Plants** spreading, native from Minnesota to Greenland, south to Iowa and Georgia; **leaves** palmate, with 3 leaflets, each leathery, semi-evergreen, often turning red in the fall, cuneate-oblong, 3- to 5-toothed, nearly smooth; **flowers** small, white, in stiff cymes.

USE: Plant in rock gardens or use as a ground cover.

CULTURE: Plants require a well-drained soil and full sun. Propagation is chiefly by division of established plants in early spring. Space the plants about 30 cm. apart.

Potentilla — other species

P. alba L. (White Cinquefoil), native in central Europe, has silky leaves and large white flowers. It is often planted in rock gardens.

P. atrosanguinea Wall. (Himalayan Cinquefoil), native in the Himalayas, has large dark purplish red flowers in panicled cymes. 'W. Rollison' has bright orange flowers, and 'Yellow Queen' has double yellow flowers with a red center.

P. aurea L. (Golden Cinquefoil), native in Europe, has showy yellow flowers on low plants 30 cm. tall.

P. fragiformis Willd. (Strawberry Cinquefoil), native in northeastern Asia, has showy yellow flowers. This is a good ground cover plant.

P. palustris (L.) Scop. (Marsh Cinquefoil), native from Manitoba to Quebec, south to California and New Jersey, has red to purple flowers and is suitable for planting in wet soils near a pool or stream.

P. reptans L. (Creeping Cinquefoil), native in Europe and Asia, is a good ground cover plant with yellow flowers. 'Flore Plena' has double flowers.

Potentilla —garden hybrids

A number of garden hybrids of unknown parentage have been introduced.
USE: Plant in flower border.
CULTURE: Plants are of easy culture in any well-drained garden soil in full sun. Propagation is by spring division of established plants.
CULTIVARS
'Firedance'. Flowers rose red with yellow edges, to 5 cm. across.
'Glory of Nancy'. Flowers orange crimson.
'Lady Rolleston'. Flowers orange, to 5 cm. across.
'Yellow Queen'. Flowers lemon yellow.

Primula L. (Primrose)

PRIMULACEAE (Primrose Family)   PLATE 220

DESCRIPTION: A large genus of about 400 species of usually scapose perennial herbs, native in temperate zones; **leaves** basal, simple; **flowers** in many colors, in heads, umbels, or sometimes in superimposed whorls; calyx 5-toothed; corolla funnelform or salverform, the tube longer than the calyx, the lobes entire or 2-lobed; stamens 5; **fruit** a 5- to 10-valved capsule.

Primula acaulis —see *Primula vulgaris*

Primula cashmeriana —see *Primula denticulata*

Primula denticulata Sm. (Himalayan Primrose). Perennial to 30 cm. tall. April, May.   PLATE 219

DESCRIPTION: **Plants** cespitose, native in the Himalayas; **leaves** oblong to oblanceolate, to 15 cm. long, tapering to a long petiole; **flowers** purple or pinkish purple with a yellow eye, rarely white, to 1.25 cm. across, in dense spikelike heads.

USE: Plant in rock garden or in moist soil near a pool.

CULTURE: Primulas prefer a moist soil high in organic matter. They will grow in full sun or in light shade. Plants should be watered during dry periods. Propagation is by seeds planted as soon as ripe. Start the seeds in a cold frame and transplant in the early spring. Volunteer seedlings can also be transplanted.

CULTIVARS
'Alba'. Flowers white.
'Insarich Crimson'. Flowers crimson.
'Rubin'. Flowers ruby red.

Primula x *polyantha* Hort. (Polyanthus Primrose). Perennial to 30 cm. tall. April, May.

DESCRIPTION: **Plants** of hybrid origin involving *P. elatior*, *P. veris*, and *P. vulgaris*; **leaves** obovate, tapering at base to a winged petiole; **flowers** large, showy, in many colors.

USE: Same as for *P. denticulata*.

CULTURE: Same as for *P. denticulata*. Winter protection is needed.

CULTIVARS AND STRAINS: Numerous cultivars and seed strains are on the market. Plants are of borderline hardiness. It is best to grow the seedlings in a cold frame where they can be protected over winter. Plants can be moved to their permanent location in early spring.
'Blue Beauties'. Flowers violet blue with a golden eye.
Pacific Giants (strain). Flowers very large, to 6 cm. across.
'Rainbow'. Flowers in many bright shades.

Primula — other species

P. auricula L. (Auricula Primrose), native in the European Alps, has large flowers in many colors and leaves that are quite thick. It is a good rock garden species.

P. cortusoides L. (Orange-eye Primrose), native in western Siberia, is a very hardy species with rose-colored flowers in many-flowered umbels. PLATE 218

P. frondosa Janka (Balkan Rose Primrose), native in the Balkans, has rose lilac to reddish purple flowers with yellow eyes.

P. japonica A. Gray (Japanese Primrose), native in Japan, has purplish red flowers in superimposed whorls.

P. sieboldii E. Morr. (Siebold Primrose), native in Japan and northeastern Asia, has large, white, rose, or purple flowers with white centers, to 4 cm. across.

P. vulgaris Huds. (English Primrose), native in Europe, has yellow, purple, or blue flowers. It requires winter protection.

Proboscidea J. C. Keller (Unicorn Flower)

MARTYNIACEAE (Martynia Family)

DESCRIPTION: A genus of 9 species of sticky-pubescent herbs, native in America; **leaves** large, long-petioled; **flowers** large, purple, in loose, axillary racemes; calyx 5-lobed, spathelike; corolla 5-lobed; stamens 4; **fruit** a 2-valved capsule with fleshy exterior and woody interior, terminating in a long curved beak that splits lengthwise.

Proboscidea louisianica (Mill.) Thell. (Common Unicorn Flower). Annual to 90 cm. tall and 1.6 m. wide. July-September.

DESCRIPTION: **Plants** clammy, spreading, native from Indiana to Delaware, south to New Mexico and Texas; **leaves** nearly orbicular to ovate-cordate, to 30 cm. across, wavy-margined; **flowers** creamy white to violet or light red, blotched with purple, to 5 cm. long.

USE: This plant is grown mainly as a novelty. Because of its coarse texture, it is best grown in the vegetable garden.

CULTURE: Plants thrive in any well-drained soil. Propagation is by seeds started indoors in early April. Transplant seedlings in the garden about June 1. Space the plants 1.5 m. apart.

Prunella L. (Self-heal)

LABIATAE (Mint Family)

DESCRIPTION: A genus of about 7 species of perennial herbs, native in Asia, Europe, northwestern Africa, and North America; **stems** square in cross section; **leaves** opposite, simple; **flowers** in 6-flowered verticillasters arranged in a dense, terminal, cylindrical spike; calyx tubular-campanulate, 2-lipped; upper lip 3-toothed, lower lip 2-toothed; corolla tube longer than the calyx, obconical, with 2-lipped limb, the upper lip hooded; stamens 4, in 2 pairs with append-aged filaments; **fruit** of 4 oblong, smooth nutlets.

Prunella x *webbiana* Hort. (Webb Self-heal). Perennial to 60 cm. tall. June-October.

DESCRIPTION: **Plants** possibly of hybrid or garden origin with *P. grandiflora* as one of the parents; **leaves** blunt; **flowers** bright purple.

USE: Plant in the rock garden or flower border.

CULTURE: Plants like a well-drained soil and partial shade. Propagation is by division of established plants.

CULTIVARS
'Loveliness'. Flowers lilac-colored.
'Pink Loveliness'. Flowers pink.
'Rotkappchen'. Flowers nearly red.
'White Loveliness'. Flowers white.

Prunella — other species

P. grandiflora (L.) Scholl. (Bigflower Self-heal), native in Europe, has spikes of deep purple flowers.

P. vulgaris L. (Common Self-heal), native in Eurasia, has deep violet blue flowers. It is sometimes planted in rock gardens but it can escape and become a weed in the lawn.

Pulmonaria L. (Lungwort)

BORAGINACEAE (Borage Family)

DESCRIPTION: A genus of about 12 species of hairy, spring-flowering, perennial herbs of Europe and Asia; **plants** with creeping rhizomes; basal **leaves** simple, green or white-spotted, long-petioled, stem leaves few, alternate; **flowers** blue, purple, pink, or white, in bracted, terminal, forked cymes; calyx 5-lobed; corolla 5-lobed, with a tuft of hairs in the throat; stamens 5, included; **fruit** of 4 smooth nutlets.

Pulmonaria saccharata Mill. (Bethlehem Sage). Perennial to 30 cm. tall. May, June.

DESCRIPTION: **Plants** setose-hairy, native in Europe; **leaves** white-spotted, basal leaves elliptic, narrowed to a petiole, pointed, stem leaves ovate-oblong, petioled or sessile; **flowers** white or reddish violet, to 2.5 cm. long.

USE: Plant toward the front of the flower border, in a rock garden, or wild-flower garden.

CULTURE: The plants prefer a moist soil and light shade. Propagation is mainly by spring division. Plants must be watered during dry spells.

CULTIVARS

'Alba'. Flowers white.

'Bowles Red'. Flowers burnt orange red.

'Mrs. Moon'. Leaves spotted; flowers blue, pink in bud.   PLATE 221

'Pink Dawn'. Flowers rose pink.

Pulmonaria — other species

P. angustifolia L. (Blue Lungwort), native in Europe, has plain green leaves and blue flowers.

P. officinalis L. (Common Lungwort, Jerusalem Cowslip), native in Europe, has white-spotted leaves and rose violet, blue, or red flowers.

Pulsatilla patens —see *Anemone patens*

Pulsatilla vulgaris —see *Anemone pulsatilla*

Puschkinia Adams.

LILIACEAE (Lily Family)

DESCRIPTION: A small genus of 2 species of spring-flowering, bulbous perennial herbs, native to Asia Minor and the Caucasus; **leaves** basal; **flowers** white or blue, in a raceme on a scape; perianth segments 6, united into a short tube; stamens 6, filaments united into a cuplike crown; **fruit** a 3-valved capsule.

Puschkinia libanatica —see *Puschkinia scillioides* var. *libanatica*

Puschkinia scilloides Adams. (Squill Puschkinia). Perennial to 15 cm. tall. April, May.   PLATE 222

DESCRIPTION: **Plants** native in Asia Minor and the Caucasus; **leaves** linear, strap-shaped; **flowers** blue, 1.25 cm. long, in upright racemes.

USE: Plant under shrubs or in rock gardens.

CULTURE: Plants thrive in most soils. Plant bulbs in October about 5 cm. deep and 15 cm. apart. Dig and divide the bulbs when the plants become crowded.

VARIETY

var. *libanatica* (Zucc.) Boiss. Flowers smaller than in the species.

Pyrethrum coccineum —see *Chrysanthemum coccineum*

Pyrola L. (Shinleaf, Wintergreen)

PYROLACEAE (Wintergreen Family)

DESCRIPTION: A genus of about 12 species of evergreen, perennial herbs with underground, scaly **rhizomes**, native in temperate regions of the northern hemisphere; **leaves** basal, simple; **flowers** white, green, pink, or purple, in terminal scapose racemes; calyx 5-parted; petals 5; stamens 10; **fruit** a 5-valved capsule.

Pyrola rotundifolia L. (Wild Lily-of-the-valley, European Pyrola). Perennial to 30 cm. tall. June, July.

DESCRIPTION: **Plants** native in Europe and in North America; **leaf** blades nearly round, to 5 cm. across, thick and leathery, glossy; **flowers** white, fragrant, spirally arranged; calyx lobes oblong; petals thick and waxy.

USE: Plant in rock garden or in the wildflower garden.

CULTURE: Partial shade and an acid soil are required. The soil should be moist and high in organic matter. Propagation is chiefly by division in early spring. The seeds can also be planted in an acid soil high in organic matter in a cold frame as soon as ripe.

VARIETY

var. *americana* (Sweet) Fern. Differs from the species in being larger.

Pyrola —other species

P. asarifolia Michx. (Pink Pyrola), native from British Columbia to New Brunswick, south to New Mexico and Indiana, has kidney-shaped leaves and pale pink flowers.

P. elliptica Nutt. (Waxflower, Shinleaf), native in Japan and North America, has elliptic leaves and creamy white flowers.

Quamoclit pennata —see *Ipomoea quamoclit*

Quamoclit sloteri —see *Ipomoea* x *multifida*

Ranunculus L. (Buttercup, Crowfoot)

RANUNCULACEAE (Buttercup Family)

DESCRIPTION: A large genus of about 250 species of widely distributed herbs; **leaves** alternate, simple, or compound; **flowers** yellow, white, or red; sepals and petals mostly 5; petals often falling early; stamens many; **fruit** a head of achenes.

Ranunculus acris L. (Common Buttercup, Tall Buttercup). Perennial to 90 cm. tall. June, July.

DESCRIPTION: **Plants** branched, native in Europe, naturalized elsewhere; **leaves** orbicular, palmately 2- to 7-lobed, with lobes cut into 3-toothed segments; **flowers** yellow, to 2.5 cm. across.

USE: Plant in flower border or naturalize along a stream or near a pool.

CULTURE: Buttercups like a moist soil and full sun. Propagation is by division or by seeds started in a nursery row in May. The double-flowered form must be vegetatively propagated.

CULTIVAR

'Flore Pleno'. Flowers fully double. Planted more often than the species.

PLATE 223

Ranunculus asiaticus L. (Persian Buttercup). Tender perennial to 45 cm. tall. May, June.

DESCRIPTION: **Plants** hairy, tuberous rooted, native in southeastern Europe and southwestern Asia; **leaves** 2- to 3-ternate with segments deeply trifid; **flowers** variously colored, to 4 cm. across and often fully double.

USE: Plant in flower border.

CULTURE: The Persian buttercup likes a moist soil high in organic matter. It is best to dig the tuberous roots in the fall and store them in a cool, dry place over winter. In mid-March the tubers can be potted and then transplanted to the garden in early May.

CULTIVAR

'Telecote Giants'. Flowers double or semi-double, in shades of yellow, gold, red, orange, and pink.

Ranunculus — other species

R. aconitifolius L. (Aconite Buttercup), native in the mountains of central Europe, has tuberous roots and large white flowers and red buds. 'Flore Pleno' has double flowers.

R. montanus Willd. (Mountain Buttercup), native from the Pyrenees to the Caucasus, is a good rock garden plant with yellow flowers, blooming from May to July.

Ratibida Raf. (Prairie Coneflower)

COMPOSITAE (Sunflower Family)

Helianthus Tribe

DESCRIPTION: A genus of 5 biennial or perennial herbs, native in North America; **leaves** alternate, pinnatifid; **flower** heads radiate, solitary on long peduncles; involucral bracts in 1 row, green; receptacle globe-shaped to columnar, scaly; disc flowers brown; ray flowers drooping, yellow or purple; **achenes** compressed.

Ratibida columnaris —see *Ratibida columnifera*

Ratibida columnifera (Nutt.) Woot. & Standl. (Prairie Coneflower). Perennial to 1 m. tall. July, August.   PLATE 224

DESCRIPTION: **Plants** branching from the base, native from British Columbia to Minnesota, south to Mexico and Texas; **leaves** with linear to narrowly lanceolate, entire, leaf segments; ray **flowers** to 2 cm. long.

USE: Plant toward the back of the flower border or use in prairie gardens.

CULTURE: Plants like a well-drained soil and full sun. Propagation is usually by seeds planted in May in a nursery row or sown directly where plants are to grow. Mature plants are difficult to transplant.

Ratibida pinnata (Venten.) Barnh. (Prairie Coneflower). Perennial to 1 m. tall. July, August.

DESCRIPTION: **Plants** branched, native from Minnesota to Ontario, south to Oklahoma and Georgia; **leaf** segments lanceolate, serrate; ray **flowers** yellow to 5 cm. long.

USE: Same as for *R. columnifera*.

CULTURE: Same as for *R. columnifera*.

Reseda L. (Mignonette)

RESEDACEAE (Migonette Family)

DESCRIPTION: A genus of about 60 species of herbs, native mostly in the Mediterranean region; **leaves** alternate, simple, or pinnate; **flowers** small, in terminal spikelike racemes, usually perfect; sepals 4 to 7; petals 4 to 7, unequal, cleft; stamens 7 to 40, more or less united and crowded on 1 side of the flower; carpels 3 to 6, united below; **fruit** a 1-celled capsule opening at the top.

Reseda odorata L. (Common Mignonette). Annual to 30 cm. tall. July-September.

DESCRIPTION: **Plants** with decumbent stems, native in northern Africa; **leaves** simple, elliptic to spatulate, often 3-lobed, to 7.5 cm. long; **flowers** small, yellowish white, in dense terminal racemes, very fragrant.

USE: Plant in the flower border.

CULTURE: The plants are grown for their fragrant flowers. They like a well-drained soil and full sun. Propagation is by seeds sown directly where the plants are to bloom as soon as the soil can be worked in the spring. Thin the seedlings to about 15 cm. apart.

CULTIVARS
'Grandiflora'. Flowers larger than in the species.
'Machet'. Flowers red.

Rhodanthe roseum — see *Helipterum roseum*

Ricinus L. (Castor Bean)

EUPHORBIACEAE (Spurge Family)

DESCRIPTION: A genus of one monoecious species of herbs with watery sap, native in tropical Africa but naturalized elsewhere; **leaves** alternate, simple, palmately veined and lobed, peltate, on long petioles; **flowers** in panicles with pistillate ones above the staminate; **fruit** a capsule.

Ricinus communis L. (Castor Bean). Annual to 5 m. tall. August, September.   PLATE 225

DESCRIPTION: **Plants** coarse, native in tropical Africa; **leaves** 5- to 11-lobed, to 90 cm. across; **flowers** small with petals lacking; **seeds** to 1 cm. long.

USE: Plant as a bold accent plant toward the back of the flower border.

CULTURE: Plants thrive in any well-drained soil either in full sun or in partial shade. Propagation is by seeds sown directly in the border or started indoors in individual pots in early April. Plants are frost tender so do not set plants outdoors until danger of frost has passed or about Memorial Day. The seeds are poisonous and should not be eaten.

CULTIVARS
'Red Spire'. Stems red; leaves bronzy green.
'Scarlet Queen'. Leaves maroon; flowers orange scarlet.
'Zanzibarensis'. Leaves bright green with white veins.

Rudbeckia L. (Coneflower)

COMPOSITAE (Sunflower Family)

Helianthus Tribe

DESCRIPTION: A genus of about 25 species of annual, biennial, and perennial herbs, native in North America; **leaves** alternate, simple, pinnatifid, or rarely compound; **flower** heads usually radiate and showy; receptacle hemispherical to columnar, scaly; disc flowers perfect; ray flowers yellow to redbrown; **achenes** 4-angled with a short crown for a pappus or pappus lacking.

Rudbeckia hirta L. (Black-eyed Susan). Short-lived perennial usually grown as an annual, to 90 cm. tall. July-September.

DESCRIPTION: **Plants** hairy, native from British Columbia to Newfoundland, south to Mexico and Florida; **leaves** simple, the lower petioled, the upper sessile, oblanceolate to elliptic; **flower** heads to 10 cm. across; disc flowers brown purple; ray flowers orange or orange yellow; pappus lacking.

USE: Plant in the flower border for a mass effect.

CULTURE: Plants thrive in any well-drained soil in full sun. Propagation is by seed sown directly where the plants are to bloom or started indoors in early April. Volunteer seedlings can be transplanted in early spring.

CULTIVARS: Most of the cultivars are known as Gloriosa Daisies. PLATE 226
'Double Gold'. All-America Winner. Heads double or semi-double; ray flowers golden yellow.
'Golden Daisy'. Ray flowers golden yellow, darker at base.
'Goldquelle'. Heads semi-double; ray flowers yellow.
'Marmalade'. All-America Winner. Ray flowers golden orange.
'White Lustre'. Ray flowers white.

Rudbeckia purpurea — see *Echinacea purpurea*

Rudbeckia — other species

R. fulgida Ait. (Orange Coneflower), native from Illinois to New Jersey, south to Alabama, has orange yellow ray flowers and a crown for a pappus.

R. laciniata L. (Cutleaf Coneflower), native from Montana to Quebec, south to Arizona and Florida, is a tall plant to 3 m. tall and has greenish yellow ray flowers. The double-flowered form 'Hortensis' is the old-fashioned Golden Glow found in many old gardens.

Sagittaria L. (Arrowhead)

ALISMATACEAE (Water Plantain Family)

DESCRIPTION: A genus of about 20 species of monoecious, stoloniferous, often tuber-bearing, perennial herbs, native in bogs and aquatic habitats in America; **leaves** either under water and reduced to narrow phyllodes, or rising above water and then with elliptic, lanceolate, or ovate, often sagittate leaf blades; **flowers** white, in scapose racemes or panicles, with the pistillate flowers below the staminate; sepals 3, green; petals 3, white, deciduous; stamens 7 to many; carpels many; **fruit** a head of flattened, winged, beaked achenes.

Sagittaria latifolia Willd. (Arrowhead, Duck Potato). Perennial to 1 m. tall. June-September. PLATE 227

DESCRIPTION: **Plants** tuber-bearing, native in North America; **leaves** mostly triangular, arrow-shaped at base; **flowers** white, in terminal panicles.
USE: Plant near pools or streams.
CULTURE: Plants require a wet soil or shallow water with a mud bottom. Propagation is mainly by division of tubers in early spring. Plant tubers in the wet soil or in the mud at the bottom of a pool or stream. The tubers are edible and were used as food by the American Indians. They also are an important food for ducks.

Sagittaria — other species

S. sagittifolia L. (Old World Arrowhead, Swamp Potato), native in Eurasia, is similar to *S. latifolia* but has smaller flowers with purple spots at the base of the petals. 'Flore Pleno' is a double-flowered cultivar.

Salpiglossis Ruiz & Pav.

SOLANACEAE (Potato Family)

DESCRIPTION: A genus of 5 species of erect, viscid-pubescent annual, biennial, or perennial herbs, native in Chile; **leaves** alternate, simple; **flowers** solitary, showy, borne in leaf axils or opposite the leaves; calyx tubular, 5-lobed;

corolla funnelform, with a wide throat and 5-lobed limb, often colorfully striped or veined; stamens 4, in 2 pairs; staminode 1; **fruit** an oblong, 2-valved capsule.

Salpiglossis sinuata Ruiz & Pav. (Painted Tongue). Annual to 75 cm. tall. July-September.

DESCRIPTION: **Plants** native in Chile; **leaves** elliptic or narrowly oblong, to 10 cm. long, sinuate-toothed or pinnatifid; **flowers** dull to bright yellow or dark purple to scarlet or nearly blue, to 5 cm. across.

USE: The painted tongue is a colorful plant in the border.

CULTURE: The plants like a well-drained soil and full sun. Seeds are started indoors in early April or they may be planted in the border in early May. Space the plants about 20 cm. apart. Staking is required in a windy location. Plants do not bloom well in hot weather.

CULTIVARS
'Bolero'. Flowers velvety, in shades of gold, rose, red, crimson, and blue.
PLATE 228

'Splash'. Plants compact, free-flowering.

Salvia L. (Sage)

LABIATAE (Mint Family)

DESCRIPTION: A large genus of over 750 species of herbs, subshrubs, and shrubs of worldwide distribution; **stems** mostly square in cross section; **leaves** opposite simple, pinnatifid, or rarely pinnately compound; **flowers** in axillary, 2- to many-flowered verticillasters; calyx 2-lipped with unequal teeth; corolla 2-lipped; stamens 2, each with 1 fertile cell; **fruit** of 4 ovid, 3-angled nutlets.

Salvia farinacea Benth. (Mealy-cup Sage). Tender perennial grown as an annual to 90 cm. tall. July-October.   PLATE 229

DESCRIPTION: **Plants** native in New Mexico; **leaves** ovate-lanceolate to ovate, to 7.5 cm. long, coarsely and irregularly serrate; **flowers** violet-blue, in interrupted spikes; floral bracts small, green, early deciduous; calyx densely white- to purple-tomentose; corolla to 1.5 cm. long.

USE: Plant in flower border.

CULTURE: Plants thrive in well-drained soil and full sun. Propagation is by seed started indoors in early April. Space the plants about 30 cm. apart.

CULTIVARS
'Blue Bedder'. Flowers wedgewood blue.

'Catima'. Flowers dark blue.
'Regal Purple'. Flowers violet blue.
'White Bedder'. Flowers creamy white.

Salvia haematodes —see *Salvia pratensis*

Salvia splendens F. Sellow (Scarlet Sage). Tender perennial grown as an annual, to 60 cm. tall. July-September.

DESCRIPTION: **Plants** glabrous, native in southern Brazil; **leaves** ovate, to 8 cm. long, acuminate, crenate-serrate; **flowers** mostly scarlet, in racemes with red, deciduous bracts; calyx campanulate, red; corolla to 4 cm. long, scarlet, with lower lip much reduced.

USE: Same as for *S. farinacea*.

CULTURE: Same as for *S. farinacea*.

CULTIVARS
'America'. Plants 45 cm. tall; flowers vivid red.
'Blaze of Fire'. Plants 35 cm. tall; flowers brilliant scarlet.   PLATE 230
'Pink Sundae'. Plants 35 cm. tall; flowers rose pink.
'Purple Blaze'. Plants 40 cm. tall; flowers deep purple.
'St. John's Fire'. Plants 25 cm. tall; flowers brilliant scarlet.
'White Fire'. Plants 35 cm. tall; flowers creamy white.

Salvia x *superba* Stapf. (Garden Sage). Perennial to 1 m. tall. June-September.   PLATE 231

DESCRIPTION: Sterile hybrids between *S.* x *sylvestris* x *S. villicaulis*; **stems** woody at base; **leaves** ovate-oblong, to 7.5 cm. long, crenulate, gray green; **flowers** violet purple, in dense spikes with red purple bracts.

USE: Plant in groups in the flower border.

CULTURE: Plants like a well-drained soil and full sun. Propagation is mainly by division of established plants in early spring. Space plants 30 cm. apart.

CULTIVARS
'Blue Queen'. Plants compact; flowers deep blue.
'Compacta'. Flowers violet blue on compact plants.
'East Friesland'. Flowers intense violet blue.
'Purple Spires'. Plants compact; flowers purple, in dense spikes.

Salvia — other species

S. azurea var. grandiflora Benth., native from Nebraska to Minnesota, south to Texas and Kentucky, is a perennial with blue flowers. Plant northern strains.

S. coccinea Juss. (Texas Sage, Scarlet Sage), native in the southern states and tropical America, is a tender perennial grown as an annual. It has deep scarlet flowers in July and August.

S. officinalis L. (Common Garden Sage), native in Spain and Asia Minor, is a tender perennial grown as an annual. It is grown mostly for culinary use. Named cultivars include 'Purpurascens' with reddish purple leaves and 'Tricolor' with variegated white and green leaves edged or tipped with purple.

S. patens Cav. (Gentian Sage), native in the mountains of Mexico, is a tender perennial grown as an annual with large, intense blue flowers to 7 cm. long.

Sanguinaria L. (Bloodroot)

PAPAVARACEAE (Poppy Family)

DESCRIPTION: A genus with but a single species of perennial herbs, native in woodlands of eastern North America; **plants** with a red sap and a stout, fleshy rhizome; **leaves** solitary, petioled, lobed; **flowers** terminating a scape; sepals 2, deciduous; petals 8 to 16; stamens many; **fruit** an ellipsoidal capsule.

Sanguinaria canadensis L. (Bloodroot, Red Puccoon). Perennial to 20 cm. tall. April, May.   PLATES 232 AND 233

DESCRIPTION: **Plants** native from Manitoba to Nova Scotia, south to Oklahoma and Florida; **leaves** palmately lobed, to 20 cm. across; **flowers** white, sometimes tinged with pink, to 5 cm. across; **capsule** to 2 cm. long.

USE: Plant in the rock garden or in the wildflower garden.

CULTURE: Bloodroots are among the most beautiful of our spring-blooming wildflowers. The double-flowered form is most beautiful. They thrive in well-drained soils high in organic matter and in partial shade. Propagation is by division of the fleshy rhizomes in the fall or early spring. Once established, the plants should not be disturbed. The species can also be increased by seeds sown as soon as ripe.

Sanvitalia Lam.

COMPOSITAE (Sunflower Family)

Helianthus Tribe

DESCRIPTION: A genus of 7 species of annual or perennial herbs or shrubs, native mostly in the southwestern United States, Mexico, and Central America; **leaves** opposite, simple, hairy, the lower petioled, the upper sessile; their bases united and sheathing the stem; **flower** heads radiate, terminal; involucral bracts overlapping in 2 to 3 rows; receptacle hemispherical to conical, scaly, the scales acuminate-cuspidate or rounded at the apex; disc flowers brown or purple; ray flowers pistillate, white to pale yellow or orange; **achenes** 3- to 4-angled or winged.

Sanvitalia procumbens Lam. (Trailing Sanvitalia, Tufted Sanvitalia). Annual to 15 cm. tall. July-October.

DESCRIPTION: **Plants** procumbent, much-branched, native in Mexico and Guatemala; **leaves** broadly lanceolate to broadly ovate, to 6 cm. long; **flower** heads 2 cm. across; ray flowers yellow to orange.

USE: Plant as ground cover, in the rock garden, or plant in masses toward the front of the flower border.

CULTURE: Plants grow best in a sandy loam soil and in full sun. Propagation is by seeds started indoors about April 1. Space the plants about 15 cm. apart. Seeds can also be direct seeded in early May. Thin the seedlings to 15 cm. apart.

CULTIVAR

'Gold Braid'. Flowers yellow.   PLATE 234

Saponaria L. (Soapwort)

CARYOPHYLLACEAE (Pink Family)

DESCRIPTION: A genus of about 30 species of annual, biennial, or perennial herbs, native in Eurasia, chiefly in the Mediterranean region; **leaves** opposite; **flowers** white, pink, or red, in cymes, heads, or panicles; calyx cylindrical or oblong, 5-toothed; petals 5, clawed, with conical scales at junction of claw and blade, entire or emarginate; stamens 10; **fruit** a 4-toothed capsule; **seeds** flat, kidney-shaped.

Saponaria ocymoides L. (Rock Soapwort). Perennial to 25 cm. tall. July-September.

DESCRIPTION: **Plants** procumbent to ascending, much-branched, native in southern Europe; **leaves** spatulate or elliptic to ovate-lanceolate, to 2.5 cm. long; **flowers** purple, in loose cymes; calyx glandular-hairy.

USE: Plant in the rock garden or toward the front of the flower border.

CULTURE: Plants thrive in any well-drained soil and in full sun. Propagation is either by seeds or by spring division of established plants. Space the plants about 20 cm. apart.

CULTIVARS

'Alba'. Flowers white.
'Rubra'. Flowers deep red.
'Splendens'. Flowers deep rose.   PLATE 235

Saponaria — other species

S. officinalis L. (Bouncing Bet), native in Europe and Asia and naturalized elsewhere, has white to pink flowers in July and August. The species spreads rapidly and can become a weed.

S. x *olivana* Wocke, a cross between *S. caespitosa* and *S. pumla*, has rosy red flowers in June.

Sarracenia L. (Pitcher Plant)

SARRACENIACEAE (Pitcher Plant Family)

DESCRIPTION: A genus of 8 species of rhizomatous, carnivorous perennial herbs of boggy soils in eastern North America; **leaves** clustered in rosettes, erect, tubular, or trumpet-shaped, with a keel or wing on 1 side and terminated by a lid; **flowers** nodding, solitary or erect naked stems, regular, perfect; sepals and petals 5; stamens many; style expanded at the apex into an umbrellalike cap; **fruit** a capsule.

Sarracenia flava L. (Yellow Pitcher Plant). Perennial to 1 m. tall. May, June.

DESCRIPTION: **Plants** native from Virginia south to Alabama and Florida; **leaves** are erect, trumpet-shaped, yellowish green with a crimson throat, the lid erect with reflexed margins; **flowers** solitary, yellow, to 10 cm. across, very showy.

USE: Plant in wet, boggy soil near a pool or stream.

CULTURE: The pitcher plant requires an acid, boggy soil. Unless one has a natural bog, it is necessary to create an artificial bog by using black plastic under a layer of acid peat. The hollow leaves of the pitcher plant catch insects and obtain their nitrogen by digesting them. The plants are of interest at all seasons but especially in bloom. Propagation is chiefly by spring division. Seed propagation is possible. Scatter the seeds, when ripe, around established plants. Some winter protection is needed.

Sarracenia purpurea L. (Common Pitcher Plant). Perennial to 40 cm. tall. June, July.   PLATE 236

DESCRIPTION: **Plants** native from Saskatchewan to Labrador, south to Alabama and Florida; **leaves** evergreen, spreading, to 30 cm. long, slender below, swollen above, green, variegated, or suffused with red purple, lid erect; **flowers** purple or greenish purple, to 6 cm. across.

USE: Same as for *S. flava.*

CULTURE: Same as for *S. flava* except that no winter protection is required.

Saxifraga L. (Saxifrage)

SAXIFRAGACEAE (Saxifrage Family)

DESCRIPTION: A genus of about 300 species of annual, biennial, or perennial herbs, native in rocky soils in temperate, subarctic, and alpine regions of the world; **leaves** usually basal and clustered, stem leaves, when present, smaller and alternate; **flowers** white, pink, purple, or yellow, in racemes, panicles, or cymes, 5-merous; calyx free or adhering to the base of the ovary, 5-cleft or 5-parted; petals entire, commonly deciduous; ovary superior or partly inferior; **fruit** a bilobed capsule or 2 nearly separate follicles.

Saxifraga aizoon — see *Saxifraga paniculata*

Saxifraga cordifolia — see *Bergenia cordifolia*

Saxifraga paniculata Mill. (Aizoon Saxifrage). Perennial to 30 cm. tall. July.

DESCRIPTION: **Plants** tufted, native in arctic North America, Europe, and Asia; **leaves** narrow-spatulate, to 3 cm. long, in basal rosettes; **flowers** creamy white, marked with purple, to 1.25 cm. across, in panicles.

USE: Plant in a rock garden or wildflower garden.

CULTURE: Plants like a well-drained soil that is high in organic matter. If your soil is a heavy clay, use a mixture of garden soil, sand, leaf mold, and crushed rock. The species can be increased by seeds, but named cultivars must be vegetatively propagated by early spring division or by rooted cuttings.

CULTIVARS
'Alba'. Flowers white.
'Balcana'. Flowers white with red spots.
'Lutea'. Flowers yellow.
'Rosea'. Flowers light pink.

Saxifraga — other species

S. cotyledon L. (Jungfrau Saxifrage), native in the mountains of Europe, has fragrant white flowers veined with pink, to 2 cm. across.

S. umbrosa L. (London-pride Saxifrage), native in Europe, has white flowers sprinkled with red in May and June.

Saxifraga — garden hybrids

A few garden hybrids of mixed parentage have been introduced.
'Four Winds'. A mossy saxifrage with masses of pink cup-shaped flowers in May.
'Kinscote White'. A mossy saxifrage with white flowers. This hybrid was developed in England.

Scabiosa L. (Pincushion, Scabious)

DIPSACACEAE (Teasel Family)

DESCRIPTION: A genus of about 80 species of annual or perennial herbs, native in Europe, Asia, and Africa, but mainly in the Mediterranean region; **leaves** opposite, entire or dissected; **flowers** white, yellow, rose, or blue, in long-stemmed, involucrate heads, subtended by receptacular bracts; calyx cup-shaped, with 5 bristly teeth, enveloped by a cup-shaped involucel; corolla with 4 to 5 nearly equal lobes, or sometimes 2-lipped, with marginal corollas usually larger; stamens 4 or rarely 2; **fruit** an achene crowned with a persistent calyx.

Scabiosa atropurpurea L. (Sweet Scabious). Annual to 60 cm. tall. June-September.

DESCRIPTION: **Plants** erect, native in southern Europe; basal **leaves** oblong-spatulate to lyrate, coarsely toothed, stem leaves pinnatifid; **flowers** dark purple, rose, lilac, or white, in ovate to oblong heads to 5 cm. across.

USE: Plant in flower border for mass effect.

CULTURE: The scabiosa grows best in a rich, well-drained soil. Propagation is by seeds started indoors in early April. Space the plants 30 cm. apart.

CULTIVARS

'Dwarf Double'. Plants compact; flowers in dense round heads, in shades of blue, white, rose, and lavender.

'Giant Imperial'. Flowers in fully double, ball-shaped heads to 7.5 cm. across, in shades of blue, white, rose, pink, salmon, crimson, and lavender.

Scabiosa caucasica Bieb. (Perennial Scabious, Bluebonnet). Perennial to 60 cm. tall. June-September.   PLATE 237

DESCRIPTION: **Plants** native in the Caucasus; basal **leaves** lanceolate-linear, glaucous, stem leaves divided; **flowers** light blue, in flat heads to 7.5 cm. across; involucre covered with gray hairs.

USE: Same as for *S. atropurpurea*.

CULTURE: Soil requirements same as for *S. atropurpurea*. Propagation of named cultivars is by spring division.

CULTIVARS

'Alba'. Flowers white.

'Black Knight'. Flowers dark red.

'Blue Perfection'. Flowers lavender blue.

'House's Giant'. Flowers in shades of azure to deep blue.

Scilla L. (Squill)

LILIACEAE (Lily Family)

DESCRIPTION: A genus of about 85 species of bulbous, perennial herbs, native in Africa, Europe, and Asia; **bulbs** tunicate; **leaves** basal; **flowers** blue to purple or white, subtended by a bract, in few- to many-flowered, terminal racemes; perianth segments 6, prominently 1-veined; stamens 6, with filaments arising from the perianth segments; **fruit** a 3-lobed or 3-angled capsule.

Scilla campanulata —see *Endymion hispanicus*

Scilla hispanica —see *Endymion hispanicus*

Scilla sibirica And. (Siberian Squill). Perennial to 15 cm. tall. April, May.   PLATE 238

DESCRIPTION: **Plants** native in Russia; **leaves** 2 to 5, strap-shaped, to 15 cm. long, ascending; **flowers** deep blue, rotate, to 1.25 cm. across, in bracted 1- to 3-flowered racemes; anthers violet.

USE: Plant in rock garden, under shrubs or trees, or in the lawn.

CULTURE: Squills are easy to grow in most soils. They multiply rapidly by bulb division and by reseeding. Bulbs should be planted in September or as soon as they can be purchased. Cover the bulbs with 5 to 10 cm. of soil and space the bulbs 15 cm. apart. If squills are planted in the lawn, the first mowing in the spring should be delayed until the leaves of the squill die down.

CULTIVARS
'Spring Beauty'. Flowers deep blue.
'Tubergeniana'. Flowers silvery white with bluish tinge.
'White Triumphator'. Flowers white.

Scilla — other species

S. numidica Poir, native of North Africa, is a summer-flowering species with many small, rose-colored flowers in dense racemes in August. The foliage comes up in the spring and dies down before the flower stems appear.

S. scilloides (Lindl.) Druce (Chinese Squill), native in eastern Asia, has small rosy purple flowers in dense racemes.

S. tubergeniana J. M. C. Hoog, native in northern Iran, has large, nearly white flowers with a blue dorsal stripe on each perianth segment.

Scutellaria L. (Skullcap)

LABIATAE (Mint Family)

DESCRIPTION: A genus of about 300 species of rhizomatous, perennial herbs of wide distribution; **stems** mostly square in cross section; **leaves** opposite, simple; **flowers** in remote pairs or in dense paniculate racemes; calyx campanulate, 2-lipped, lips entire with a crestlike projection on the back of the upper lip; corolla tube long, curved upwards, glabrous inside, with 2-lipped limb; stamens 4 with hairy anthers; **fruit** of 4 nutlets.

Scutellaria indica L. (Skullcap). Perennial to 30 cm. tall. June, July.

DESCRIPTION: **Plants** procumbent, native in China and Japan; **leaves** ovate, to 2.5 cm. long, crenate-serrate, petioled; **flowers** blue, in dense racemes.

USE: Plant in flower border, rock garden, or wildflower garden.

CULTURE: Plants like a well-drained soil and full sun. Propagation is by seeds started in May in a cold frame or nursery row or by division of established plants in early spring.

VARIETY
var. *parvifolia* (Mak.) Mak. Flowers lilac to blue. A popular rock garden plant.

Scutellaria japonica —see *Scutellaria indica* var. *parvifolia*

Scutellaria —other species

S. *alpina* L., native in the mountains of Europe and Siberia, has purple flowers. It is a popular rock garden plant.

S. *scordiifolia* Fisch., native in Europe and Asia, has blue, axillary flowers.

Sedum L. (Stonecrop)

CRASSULACEAE (Orpine Family)

DESCRIPTION: A large genus of about 600 species of succulent, perennial herbs or subshrubs, native in north temperate regions and in the mountains of the tropics; **leaves** mostly alternate, often small and overlapping, mostly sessile; **flowers** 5-merous, in terminal cymes; sepals separate, sometimes spurred; petals separate or united at base, commonly yellow or white; stamens usually 10; **fruit** of follicles.

Sedum acre L. (Golden-carpet, Gold Moss). Perennial to 12 cm. tall. June, July.

DESCRIPTION: **Plants** creeping, mat-forming, native in northern Africa, Europe, western Asia, naturalized elsewhere; **leaves** triangular-ovate, to 5 mm. long; **flowers** bright yellow, to 1.25 cm. across.

USE: The creeping sedums are popular rock garden and ground cover plants. They can also be planted in wall gardens.

CULTURE: Plant in well-drained soil and full sun. Propagation is by seeds or, more commonly, by division or rooted cuttings.

CULTIVAR
'Aureum'. Leaves yellow.

Sedum album L. (White Stonecrop). Perennial to 20 cm. tall. June, July.

DESCRIPTION: **Plants** mat-forming, native in Europe, western Asia, and northern Africa; **leaves** alternate, linear-oblong to obovate, to 1.5 cm. long, cylindrical or nearly so; **flowers** white, to 1 cm. across.

USE: Same as for S. *acre*.

CULTURE: Same as for S. *acre*.

CULTIVARS
'Chloroticum'. Leaves yellowish green.

'Murale Nigra'. Leaves purple; flowers pink.

'Purpureum'. Leaves purple.

Sedum kamtschaticum Fisch. & C. A. Mey. (Orange Stonecrop). Perennial to 30 cm. tall. June, July.

DESCRIPTION: **Plants** mat-forming, native in eastern Asia; **leaves** linear to spatulate, to 5 cm. long, toothed at apex; **flowers** yellow, to 2 cm. across; stamens as long as the petals.

USE: Same as for *S. acre*.

CULTURE: Same as for *S. acre*.

CULTIVAR AND VARIETIES

subspecies *middendorfianum* (Maxim.) R. T. Clausen. Stamens shorter than the petals.

'Variegatum'. Leaves variegated.

subspecies *ellacambianum* (Praeg.) R. T. Clausen. Leaves light green, crenate; flowers 1 cm. wide.

Sedum spectabile Boreau (Showy Stonecrop). Perennial to 60 cm. tall. July-September.

DESCRIPTION: **Plants** with tuberous roots, native in China and Korea; **leaves** opposite or in 3s or 4s, obovate, to 7 cm. long, toothed, glaucous; **flowers** pink, to 1 cm. across, in flat-topped cymes; stamens longer than the petals.

USE: Plant in flower border.

CULTURE: Plant in well-drained soil in full sun. Propagation is largely by division of established plants in early spring. Seedlings may volunteer but these should be rogued out, especially if you are growing named cultivars.

CULTIVARS

'Album'. Flowers white.

'Brilliant'. Flowers rose pink.   PLATE 239

'Indian Chief'. Flowers bronze rose, turning brick red.

'Meteor'. Flowers carmine red.

'Stardust'. Flowers ivory white.

'Variegatum'. Leaves variegated with white.

Sedum spurium Bieb. (Tworow Stonecrop). Perennial to 20 cm. tall. June, July.

DESCRIPTION: **Plants** mat-forming, native in Europe; **leaves** obovate-cuneate, to 2.5 cm. long, crenate-serrate toward the apex; **flowers** pink to purple, 1 cm. long, in dense cymes.

USE: Same as for *S. acre*.

CULTURE: Same as for *S. acre*.

CULTIVARS

'Album'. Flowers white.

'Bronze Carpet'. Leaves bronze; flowers pink.

'Dragon's Blood'. Flowers wine red. PLATE 240

Sedum — other species

S. anacampseros L. (Evergreen Orpine, Shy Stonecrop), native in southern Europe, has dull purple flowers on creeping stems.

S. brevifolium DC., native in southwestern Europe and northwestern Africa, has white flowers on creeping plants.

S. ewersii Ledeb, native from the Himalayas to Mongolia, has pink flowers on creeping plants.

S. hispanicum L. (Spanish Stonecrop), native in southeastern Europe, has yellow flowers on short-lived plants.

S. maximum Suter, native in Europe and the Caucasus, is an upright plant to 60 cm. tall, with greenish flowers. 'Atropurpureum' has purple leaves and stems.

S. reflexum L. (Jenny Stonecrop), native in Europe, has golden yellow flowers on creeping plants. 'Cristatum' has crested flowers resembling a cockscomb, and 'Sea Gold' has gold-tipped leaves.

S. sieboldii Sweet. (Siebold Stonecrop), native in Japan, has pink flowers on low, arching stems in September and October. 'Variegatum' has leaves variegated with yellow blotches.

S. telephium L. (Live-forever Stonecrop), native from eastern Europe to Japan, is an upright plant to 60 cm. tall with red to purple flowers in August and September. 'Autumn Joy' has rusty brown flowers.

Senecio L. (Groundsel)

COMPOSITAE (Sunflower Family)

Senecio Tribe

DESCRIPTION: A very large genus of nearly 3,000 species of annual or perennial herbs or shrubs, native in all parts of the world; **leaves** alternate or all basal; **flowers** usually yellow, sometimes in shades of orange, blue, or purple, in usually radiate, sometimes discoid heads that are either solitary or clustered; involucral bracts in one row; **achenes** mostly cylindrical, ribbed, with a pappus of soft white bristles.

Senecio cineraria DC. (Dusty-miller, Silver Groundsel). Tender perennial grown as an annual, to 75 cm. tall. July-September.   PLATE 241

DESCRIPTION: **Plants** with white, woolly hairs, native in the Mediterranean region; **leaves** pinnately cut into oblong, blunt segments, covered with silvery hairs, becoming green on the upper surface; **flower** heads to 4 cm. across in compound terminal corymbs; ray flowers yellow or cream-colored.

USE: Use for edging flower beds or in masses in the border for color contrast.

CULTURE: Plants thrive in any well-drained soil in full sun. Propagation is by seeds started indoors in early April. Space the plants about 20 cm. apart.

CULTIVARS
'Diamond'. Leaves finely cut and silvery white.
'Silver Dust'. Leaves finely cut and silvery white.
'Silver Queen'. Leaves very lacy, silvery white.

Senecio clivorum — see *Ligularia dentata*

Senecio — other species

S. aureus L. (Golden Groundsel, Golden Ragwort), native from Newfoundland south to Texas and Florida, has yellow flower heads to 2 cm. across in terminal corymbs.

S. x *hybridus* (Willd.) Regal (Cineraria), developed in England by crossing *S. cruentus*, *S. heritieri*, and other species, is a popular florist's pot plant with large, colorful flower heads in white, pink, red, purple, violet, and blue colors. Plants are often purchased in bloom and displayed on patios. Plants dislike heat and need lots of water.

S. vira-vira Hieron (Dusty-miller), native in Argentina, is grown for its silvery leaves that are pinnately dissected. The flower heads are white, discoid, without ray flowers. 'Frosty' is a named cultivar with silvery white leaves.

Sieversia reptans — see *Geum reptans*

Sieversia triflora — see *Geum triflorum*

Silene L. (Catchfly, Campion)

CARYOPHYLLACEAE (Pink Family)

DESCRIPTION: A genus of 500 species of annual, biennial, or perennial herbs, or sometimes subshrubs, widely distributed in the northern hemisphere; **leaves** opposite, without stipules; **flowers** white, pink, or red, solitary or in cymes or panicles; calyx tubular, 5-toothed, 10- to 60-veined; petals 5, mostly 2-lobed or emarginate, with scales usually present at the juncture of blade and claw; stamens 10; **fruit** a capsule, dehiscent by terminal teeth.

Silene alpestris—see *Silene quadrifolia*

Silene virginica L. (Fire Pink). Perennial to 90 cm. tall. May-September.

DESCRIPTION: **Plants** native from Minnesota to New Jersey, south to Oklahoma to Georgia; **leaves** oblanceolate, to 10 cm. long, with ciliate petioles; **flowers** scarlet, in 7- to 10-flowered inflorescences; calyx 2 cm. long, hairy; petals 2-lobed.

USE: Plant in a rock garden, flower border, or wildflower garden.

CULTURE: Plants like a well-drained soil high in organic matter and light shade. Propagation is by seeds or by spring division.

Silene—other species

S. acaulis L. (Cushion Pink, Moss Campion), native in the mountains of Eurasia and North America, has pink or purple flowers and is sometimes planted in rock gardens.

S. armeria L. (Garden Catchfly), native in Europe, has pink flowers in flat-topped cymes.

S. dioica (L.) Clairv. (Red Campion), native in Europe, has reddish purple flowers with inflated calyces. 'Flore Pleno' has double flowers.

S. keiskei Miq., native in central Japan, has pink flowers in few-flowered cymes. An excellent rock garden plant.   PLATE 242

S. quadrifida (L.) L. (Alpine Campion), native in the Alps, has large, white flowers. 'Flore Pleno' has double flowers.

S. schafta C. C. Gmel. (Moss Campion), native in the Caucasus, is an attractive rock garden plant with pink or purple flowers in August and September.

Sisyrinchium L. (Blue-eyed Grass)

IRIDACEAE (Iris Family)

DESCRIPTION: A genus of about 75 species of clump-forming perennial herbs, native in North America; **rhizomes** very short or none; **leaves** grasslike, linear or cylindrical; **flowers** blue, yellow, or white, in terminal, solitary or in fascicled clusters, each cluster subtended by a spathe; perianth rotate or campanulate, with 6 nearly equal segments; stamens 3, awl-shaped; **fruit** a 3-valved capsule.

Sisyrinchium angustifolium Mill. (Common Blue-eyed Grass). Perennial to 50 cm. tall. May, June.   PLATE 243

DESCRIPTION: **Plants** with forked, broadly winged stems, native from Manitoba to Newfoundland, south to Indiana and Virginia; **leaves** mostly basal, grasslike, dark green; **flowers** pale blue to violet, to 1.25 cm. across, in terminal clusters.

USE: Plant in a rock garden or in a prairie garden.

CULTURE: Plants require a well-drained soil high in organic matter. They should not be disturbed once they become established. Add compost around the plants in the spring and water during dry periods. Propagation is chiefly by spring division.

CULTIVAR
'Album'. Flowers white.

Sisyrinchium — other species

S. campestre Biekn., native from Manitoba to Illinois, south to Texas and Louisiana, has light blue to white flowers.

S. montanum Greene, native from British Columbia to Quebec, south to Colorado and New York, has bluish violet flowers.

Smilacina Desf. (False Solomon's-seal, Spikenard)

LILIACEAE (Lily Family)

DESCRIPTION: A genus of about 25 species of rhizomatous, perennial herbs, native in North America and Asia; **stems** leafy, unbranched, usually arching; **leaves** alternate; **flowers** white, pink, or purple, in terminal racemes or panicles; perianth segments 6, separate; stamens 6; **fruit** a berry.

Smilacina racemosa (L.) Desf. (False Spikenard, False Solomon's-seal). Perennial to 90 cm. tall. May, June.   PLATE 244

DESCRIPTION: **Plants** finely hairy, native from British Columbia to Nova Scotia, south to Arizona and Georgia; **leaves** short-petioled, elliptic to lanceolate-ovate, to 15 cm. long; **flowers** white, in terminal panicles; **fruits** red, sometimes spotted purple.

USE: A good plant for the wildflower garden.

CULTURE: Plants prefer a soil high in organic matter and light shade. Propagation is largely by spring division. They spread by underground rhizomes.

Smilacina — other species

S. stellata (L.) Desf. (Small Solomon's-seal, Star-flowered Lily-of-the-valley), has the same distribution as *S. racemosa*. It differs in being smaller with small, star-shaped white flowers.

S. trifolia (L.) Desf. (Labrador Solomon's-seal), native in the northern United States, Canada, and Siberia, has smaller leaves and bright red fruits.

Solidago L. (Goldenrod)

COMPOSITAE (Sunflower Family)

Aster Tribe

DESCRIPTION: A genus of about 130 species of summer- and autumn-flowering perennial herbs, native chiefly in North America; **stems** upright from a rhizome or root crown; **leaves** alternate, simple, entire or toothed; **flower** heads small, radiate, in racemes, corymbs, or panicles; involucre cylindrical to campanulate; receptacle flat or slightly convex, naked, pitted; disc flowers perfect, yellow; ray flowers yellow, pistillate; **achenes** angled or nearly cylindrical, with pappus of many capillary bristles.

Solidago nemoralis Ait. (Gray Goldenrod). Perennial to 1 m. tall. August-October.

DESCRIPTION: **Plants** native from Alberta to Nova Scotia, south to Texas and Kentucky; basal **leaves** oblanceolate to spatulate-obovate, petioled, reduced upward; **flower** heads in panicles with 1-sided, recurved bracts.

USE: Plant in perennial flower border or in a prairie garden.

CULTURE: Goldenrods are of easy culture and thrive in most garden soils in full sun. The flowers have been falsely accused of causing hay fever. Actually, the goldenrod pollen is insect transmitted and not carried in the air. What happens is that the fluffy flowers catch and hold ragweed pollen, the real culprit in causing hay fever. Propagation is by seeds or by division of established plants in early spring.

Solidago —garden hybrids

Several species have been involved in developing garden hybrids.
'Cloth of Gold'. Ray flowers primrose yellow.
'Golden Mosa'. Ray flowers lemon yellow.   PLATE 245
'Peter Pan'. Flowering heads well above the leaves.

Spiraea palmata —see *Filipendula purpurea*

Stachys L. (Hedge Nettle, Betony)

LABIATAE (Mint Family)

DESCRIPTION: A genus of about 300 species of herbs and subshrubs of temperate and subtropical regions; **stems** mostly square in cross section; **leaves** opposite, entire or toothed; **flowers** small, in 2- to many-flowered verticillasters arranged in terminal spikelike to headlike inflorescences; calyx tubular-campanulate, 5- to 10-veined; 5-toothed; corolla purple, red, pink, yellow, or white, with a cylindrical tube and a 2-lipped limb, with upper lip often concave and 2-lobed and lower lip 3-lobed; stamens 4, in 2 pairs; **fruit** of 4 ovoid nutlets.

Stachys byzantina C. Koch (Woolly Betony, Lamb's-ears). Perennial to 80 cm. tall. July-September.

DESCRIPTION: **Plants** erect, white woolly-hairy, native in Turkey and southwestern Asia; **leaves** oblong-spatulate, tapering at the base, dense white-woolly; **flowers** pink or purple, to 2.5 cm. long; calyx to 1.25 cm. long; corolla densely white-tomentose.

USE: Plant toward the front of the flower border or use as an edging plant.

CULTURE: Plants require a well-drained soil and full sun. Propagation is by seeds or by spring division. Space the plants 30 cm. apart. Some winter protection is needed in the form of a mulch of hay or clean straw in early November.

CULTIVAR
'Silver Carpet'. Leaves especially white.   PLATE 246

Stachys lanata —see *Stachys byzantina*

Stachys—other species

S. *grandiflora* (Willd.) Benth. (Big Betony), native in the Caucasus, has large, violet-colored flowers in several verticillasters in July and August.

S. *officinalis* (L.) Trevisan (Betony), native in Europe and Asia, has reddish purple, rarely pink or white flowers in May and June.

Statice bonduellii—see *Limonium bonduellii*

Statice caespitosa—see *Armeria juniperifolia*

Statice latifolia—see *Limonium latifolium*

Statice sinuata—see *Limonium sinuatum*

Steironema ciliatum—see *Lysimachia ciliata*

Stokesia L'Her (Stokes's Aster)

COMPOSITAE (Sunflower Family)

Vernonia Tribe

DESCRIPTION: A genus of a single species of perennial herbs, native in North America; **leaves** alternate; **flower** heads large, many-flowered; involucral bracts in several rows, the intermediate ones spinulose-pectinate; receptacle naked; disc flowers tubular, ray flowers 5-lobed; **achenes** 3- to 4-angled, with pappus of 4 to 5 deciduous awns.

Stokesia cyanea—see *Stokesia laevis*

Stokesia laevis (J. Hill.) Greene (Stokes's Aster). Perennial to 60 cm. tall. July-September.

DESCRIPTION: **Plants** with woolly stems, native from South Carolina to Louisiana and Florida; **leaves** alternate, oblong-lanceolate, to 20 cm. long, spiny-toothed toward the base; **flowers** lavender-blue, in large flowering heads to 10 cm. across.

USE: Plant in flower border.

CULTURE: Plants require a rich, loamy soil and full sun. Propagation is by seeds planted in a cold frame in May or by spring division of established plants.

Some winter protection in the form of marsh hay or clean straw is needed. Evergreen boughs put over the plants in November could also be used.

CULTIVARS

'Alba'. Ray flowers white.

'Blue Danube'. Ray flowers light blue.

'Rosea'. Ray flowers rose-colored.

Symplocarpus Salisb. (Skunk Cabbage)

ARACEAE (Arum Family)

DESCRIPTION: A genus with but a single species of perennial herbs of swamps and wet woods, with a disagreeable skunklike odor, native in North America and Asia; **leaves** large, arising from a stout vertical rhizome; spathe inflated, enclosing a spherical spadix; **flowers** perfect with a 4-parted perianth; stamens 4; **fruits** 1-seeded, embedded in the spongy spadix.

Symplocarpus foetidus (L.) Salisb. (Skunk Cabbage). Perennial to 45 cm. tall. April, May.   PLATE 247

DESCRIPTION: **Plants** native from Minnesota to Nova Scotia, south to Texas and Florida; **leaves** basal, ovate-cordate, to 45 cm. long, entire; **flowers** small, perfect, on a spherical spadix enclosed by a purple-brown spadix, mottled with greenish yellow.

USE: Plant near a stream or pond in wet soil.

CULTURE: Plants require a wet soil with water moving through the soil. Propagation is by seeds planted as soon as ripe or by spring division of established plants. This interesting plant should not be planted unless you have the right conditions.

Tagetes L. (Marigold)

COMPOSITAE (Sunflower Family)

Helenium Tribe

DESCRIPTION: A genus of about 30 species of strongly scented annual or perennial herbs, native in North and South America; **leaves** mostly opposite, simple or more often pinnatifid or pinnate, gland-dotted; **flower** heads solitary or in cymose clusters; involucre campanulate or cylindrical, with bracts in 1 row; ray flowers yellow, orange, or red brown; **achenes** elongate, with pappus of 3 to 10 scales.

Tagetes erecta L. (American Marigold, Aztec Marigold, African Marigold). Annual to 90 cm. tall. June-October.

DESCRIPTION: **Plants** stout, native in Mexico and Central America; **leaves** pinnate; **flower** heads solitary, to 12 cm. across, on a pedicel that enlarges upward; ray flowers 5 to 8 in wild forms or many and often 2-lipped or quilled in cultivated forms, light yellow to orange.

USE: Plant toward the back of the flower border. Flowers are good for cutting.

CULTURE: Marigolds are among the most popular annuals for adding color to the border and for cutting. They require full sun and a well-drained soil. Propagation is by seeds started indoors in early April, or the seeds can be sown directly where the plants are to bloom in early May. Spacing of the plants can vary from 20 to 40 cm. depending on the vigor and size of the mature plants. Marigolds have few insect or disease problems. The "aster yellows" disease, spread by the 6-spotted leaf hopper, is the most common disease, causing a stunting and a yellowing of the foliage. Affected plants produce few flower heads that open fully. Control of the 6-spotted leaf hopper is necessary to prevent this disease.

CULTIVARS: These cultivars are often called African Marigolds in many seed catalogs, even though they are of American origin. There are hundreds of named cultivars and more appear each year. Many of the newer cultivars are F_1 hybrids.

'Alaska'. Ray flowers primrose yellow.
'First Lady'. All-America Winner. Ray flowers light yellow.   PLATE 248
'Glitters'. All-America Winner. Chrysanthem-flowered, canary yellow.
'Golden Hawaii'. Ray flowers rich golden orange.
'Showboat'. All-America Winner. Ray flowers rich yellow.

Tagetes patula L. (French Marigold). Annual to 45 cm. tall. June-October.

DESCRIPTION: **Plants** branched, native in Mexico and Guatemala; **leaves** pinnate; **flower** heads solitary, to 5 cm. across, on long peduncles; involucre campanulate; ray flowers few to many, yellow, orange, red brown, or bicolored.

USE: Plant in flower border or use for edging.

CULTURE: Same as for *T. erectum*.

CULTIVARS: Hundreds of cultivars have been named and more appear each year.

'Bolero'. Fully double; ray flowers rich gold and mahogany.
'Golden Boy'. Fully double with crested centers; ray flowers golden.

'Harmony Boy'. Similar to 'Golden Boy' but ray flowers mahogany red.
'Janie'. All-America Winner. Fully double, crested; ray flowers golden orange.
'Naughty Marietta'. All-America Winner. Heads single, ray flowers golden yellow splashed with maroon.   PLATE 249

Tagetes signata — see *Tagetes tenuifolia*

Tagetes tenuifolia Cav. (Signet Marigold). Annual to 60 cm. tall. June-October.

DESCRIPTION: **Plants** with slender stems, native in Mexico and Central America; **leaves** pinnate, with narrow linear-lanceolate leaflets; **flower** heads, solitary but numerous on slender peduncles, to 2.5 cm. across; involucre cylindric-campanulate; ray flowers few, yellow.

USE: Same as for *T. erectum.*

CULTURE: Same as for *T. erectum.*

CULTIVARS
'Golden Gem'. Plants dwarf with lacy leaves; ray flowers golden orange.
'Lemon Gem'. Same but with lemon yellow flowers.   PLATE 250
'Little Giant'. Ray flowers golden orange with purple blotch.

Tagetes — garden hybrids

T. erecta and *T. patula* have been crossed to produce sterile triploid hybrids.
'Ginger Snap'. Ray flowers spicy russet red.
'Legal Gold'. Ray flowers pure gold with red base.
'Showboat'. Ray flowers bright yellow.
'Tiger'. Ray flowers orange.

Tanacetum L. (Tansy)

COMPOSITAE (Sunflower Family)

Anthemis Tribe

DESCRIPTION: A genus of about 50 species of aromatic annual or perennial herbs or sometimes subshrubs, native in Europe and Asia; **leaves** alternate, entire or 1- to 3-pinnatifid; **flower** heads solitary or in corymbs or heads, radiate or discoid; involucral bracts in 2 or 3 rows, usually scarious; receptacle flat to low-conical, naked; disc flowers tubular, perfect, yellow; ray flowers, when present, yellow, pistillate; **achenes** 5-angled.

Tanacetum vulgare L. (Common Tansy). Perennial to 1 m. tall. August-October.

DESCRIPTION: **Plants** coarse, aromatic, rhizomatous, native in Europe and Asia, widely naturalized; **leaves** with deeply incised leaflets; **flower** heads numerous, to 8 mm. across, in flat-topped corymbs; ray flowers lacking, disc flowers tubular, golden yellow.

USE: Sometimes grown in flower border.

CULTURE: Tansy is easy to grow in any well-drained soil. They were more popular in old-fashioned gardens than they are today. Escaped plants can often be seen growing along the side of the road. The flower stems are often cut and the flowers dried for winter bouquets. Propagation is usually by spring division.

Thalictrum L. (Meadow Rue)

RANUNCULACEAE (Buttercup Family)

DESCRIPTION: A genus of about 100 species of perennial herbs, native in north temperate regions of the world; **leaves** ternately compound; **flowers** small, in panicles, racemes, or corymbs; sepals 4 or 5, deciduous; petals lacking; stamens many, sometimes colored and showy; pistils few; **fruit** a ribbed or winged achene.

Thalictrum aquilegifolium L. (Columbine Meadow Rue). Perennial to 1 m. tall. May, June.

DESCRIPTION: **Plants** glaucous, native in Europe and Asia; **leaflets** orbicular or oblong; **flowers** dioecious; stamens purple or pink, much longer than the white sepals; **achenes** 3-winged.

USE: Plant toward the back of the flower border or in the wildflower garden.

CULTURE: The meadow rues are easy to grow in any well-drained soil, either in full sun or partial shade. Propagation is by seeds or spring division. Space the plants about 30 cm. apart.

CULTIVARS
'Album'. Flowers white.
'Roseum'. Flowers lilac rose.

Thalictrum — other species

T. dasycarpum Fisch. & Ave-Lall. (Purple Meadow Rue), native from Alberta to Ontario, south to Arizona and Ohio, has purple stamens. Plant toward the back of the border.

T. dioicum L. (Early Meadow Rue), native from North Dakota to Quebec, south to Missouri and Georgia, has purple flowers in May.

T. dipterocarpum Franch. (Yunnan Meadow Rue), native in western China, has rose violet flowers on tall plants.

T. minus L., native in Europe, has fernlike foliage and is an attractive rock garden plant.

T. polygamum Muhlemb. (Tall Meadow Rue), native from Ontario to Newfoundland, south to Tennessee and Georgia, has white flowers in July and August.

Thermopsis R. Br. (False Lupine)

LEGUMINOSAE (Pea Family)

DESCRIPTION: A genus of about 20 species of herbs, native in North America and northeastern Asia; **leaves** compound with 3 palmately arranged leaflets and 2 leaflike stipules; **flowers** pealike, in racemes; stamens 10, separate; **fruit** a narrow, flat legume.

Thermopsis caroliniana M. A. Curtis (Carolina False Lupine). Perennial to 1 m. tall. June, July.   PLATE 251

DESCRIPTION: **Plants** native from North Carolina to Georgia; **leaflets** ovate to obovate, to 7.5 cm. long; **flowers** yellow, in dense, terminal racemes to 25 cm. long.

USE: Plant toward the back of the flower border.

CULTURE: The false lupines like a well-drained soil and full sun. Propagation is mainly by seeds started indoors in April or planted outdoors in a nursery row in May. Plants develop a taproot so they should be transplanted to their permanent location while small. Old plants can be divided in early spring but the plants are slow to recover and may not stand the shock of transplanting.

Thermopsis lanceolata — see *Thermopsis lupinoides*

Thermopsis lupinoides (L.) Link (Lanceleaf False Lupine). Perennial to 30 cm. tall. June, July.

DESCRIPTION: **Plants** native in Siberia and Alaska; **leaflets** ovate-lanceolate, to 4 cm. long; **flowers** yellow; **fruit** strongly recurved, to 5 cm. long.

USE: Same as for *T. caroliniana*.

CULTURE: Same as for *T. caroliniana*.

Thumbergia Retz.

ACANTHACEAE (Acanthus Family)

DESCRIPTION: A genus of about 100 species of erect or climbing herbs or subshrubs, native in warm parts of central and southern Africa, Madagascar, and Asia; **leaves** opposite; **flowers** blue, yellow, orange, or white, usually solitary, subtended by 2 large bracts; calyx small, ringlike; corolla large, tubular, with 5 nearly equal lobes and tube curved and swollen on one side; stamens 4, borne near the base of the tube; **fruit** a spherical capsule that is beaked above.

Thunbergia alata Bojer (Black-eyed Susan Vine). Tender perennial grown as an annual, to 1.5 cm. tall. July-September.   PLATE 252

DESCRIPTION: A twining vine native in tropical Africa; **leaves** triangular-ovate, to 7.5 cm. long, toothed, with winged petioles; **flowers** salverform, cream-colored with a dark purple throat or white with a dark center or orange yellow with a darker center.

USE: Plant at the base of a low trellis or fence.

CULTURE: Plants like a rich, well-drained soil and partial shade. Propagation is by seeds sown indoors in early April. Transplant in the garden after danger of frost.

CULTIVARS

'Angel Wings'. Flowers large, pure white.

'Suzie'. Flowers in clear colors of orange, yellow, and white with black centers.

'White Wings'. Flowers pure white with a chartreuse throat.

Thymus L. (Thyme)

LABIATAE (Mint Family)

DESCRIPTION: A genus of over 300 species of aromatic shrubs or perennial herbs of Europe and Asia; **stems** usually prostrate or creeping, square in cross section; **leaves** opposite, small, entire; **flowers** small, in 1- to many-flowered verticillasters, often crowded in a terminal head; calyx cylindrical to campanulate, 10- to 13-veined, usually 2-lipped, with straight tube and hairy throat; corolla with a straight tube, hairy throat, and a 2-lipped limb; stamens 4, usually exserted; **fruit** of 4 glabrous nutlets.

Thymus x *citriodorus* (Pers.) Schreb. (Lemon Thyme). Perennial to 30 cm. tall. June, July.   PLATE 253

DESCRIPTION: **Plants** much-branched, lemon-scented, of hybrid origin developed by crossing *T. pulegeoides* x *T. vulgaris*; **leaves** narrowly rhombic-ovate to lanceolate, to 1 cm. long, revolute, glabrous; **flowers** pale lilac in oblong heads.

USE: Plant in rock garden or use as ground cover. Also planted for culinary use.

CULTURE: Thymes require a well-drained soil and prefer light shade, although they will grow in full sun. Propagation is by spring division or by seeds sown directly where the plants are to grow. Winter protection is required unless they are planted where they will have good snow cover.

CULTIVARS
'Argenteus'. Leaves variegated white.
'Aureus'. Leaves golden.
'Gold Edge'. Leaves with a golden edge.
'Silver Queen'. Leaves with a silver edge.

Thymus lanuginosus —see *Thymus pseudolanuginosus*

Thymus praecox subspecies *arcticus* (E. Durand) Jalas (Mother-of-thyme). Perennial to 10 cm. tall. June, July.

DESCRIPTION: **Plants** creeping, hairy, native in Greenland and Scandinavia, south to Spain; **leaves** nearly leathery, obovate, densely glandular-dotted, to 6 mm. long; **flowers** rose purple, in hemispherical clusters to 1.25 cm. across.

USE: Same as for *T.* x *citriodorus.*
CULTURE: Same as for *T.* x *citriodorus.*
CULTIVARS
'Albus'. Flowers white.
'Aureus'. New leaves yellow.
'Carneus'. Flowers flesh-colored.
'Coccineus'. Flowers crimson.
'Roseus'. Flowers pink.
'Splendens'. Flowers red.

Thymus serpyllum —see *Thymus praecox* subspecies *arcticus*

Thymus —other species

T. herba-barona Loisel. (Caraway Thyme), native in Corsica and Sardinia, is a subshrub with rose colored flowers and leaves that have the odor of caraway when crushed. It is sometimes planted in rock gardens. It needs winter protection.

T. pseudolanuginosus Ronn. (Woolly Thyme), native home unknown, has pale pink flowers and woolly leaves. Plant in crevices in flagstone walks and terraces.

T. vulgaris L. (Garden Thyme), native near the Mediterranean Sea, has white to lilac-colored flowers and hairy leaves. 'Aureus' has yellow leaves. PLATE 254

Tiarella L. (False Miterwort)

SAXIFRAGACEAE (Saxifrage Family)

DESCRIPTION: A genus of 6 species of rhizomatous herbs, native in North America and Asia; **leaves** mostly basal, cordate and palmately lobed or trifoliate; **flowers** small, white or red, in simple or branched racemes; calyx campanulate, 5-lobed, united at base to ovary; petals 5; stamens 10, **fruit** a capsule.

Tiarella cordifolia L. (Foamflower). Perennial to 30 cm. tall. May, June. PLATE 255

DESCRIPTION: **Plants** rhizomatous; mat-forming, native from Ontario to Nova Scotia, south to Alabama and Georgia; **leaves** to 10 cm. long, dentate, with long petioles; **flowers** white or red, small, in simple racemes; calyx lobes triangular.

USE: Plant as ground cover in a shady wildflower garden or rock garden.

CULTURE: Plants require a moist, acid soil high in organic matter. Propagation is mainly by spring division.

Tigridia Juss. (Tiger Flower, Shellflower)

IRIDACEAE (Iris Family)

DESCRIPTION: A genus of about 27 species of bulbous, perennial herbs, native in Mexico, south to Chile; **stems** simple or forked, cylindrical; **leaves** few, linear to sword-shaped; **flowers** in many colors, lasting for a single day but produced in succession, erect or nodding; perianth segments 6, campanulate or cup-shaped, spreading or reflexed; stamens 3 with filaments united to form a tube; **fruit** a 3-valved capsule.

Tigridia pavonia (L.) DC. (Tiger Flower, Mexican Shellflower). Tender perennial. July-September.

DESCRIPTION: **Plants** native in Mexico and Guatemala; **leaves** linear to linear-lanceolate, to 45 cm. long; **flowers** red, spotted with yellow and purple, to 15 cm. across.

USE: Plant in the flower border.

CULTURE: The culture is essentially the same as described for gladiolus. Plant in a well-drained soil in full sun. Propagation is by bulbs planted in mid-May. Space the bulbs 15 cm. apart and cover with 7.5 cm. of soil. Dig the bulbs after the foliage dies down in the fall and store in a frost-free room over winter. The flowers last only a single day.

CULTIVARS

'Alba'. Flowers white with red spots.

'Canariensis'. Flowers pale yellow with red spots.

'Red Giant'. Flowers scarlet with yellow centers.

Tithonia Desf. (Mexican Sunflower)

COMPOSITAE (Sunflower Family)

Helianthus Tribe

DESCRIPTION: A genus of 10 species of stout annual or perennial herbs or shrubs, native in Mexico and Central America; **leaves** alternate or occasionally opposite on lower part of stems, coarsely toothed to deeply lobed; **flower** heads radiate, usually solitary on long, hollow peduncles; involucre broadly campanulate to hemispherical, with involucral bracts in 2 to 5 rows; receptacle hollow, scaly; disc flowers perfect, yellow; ray flowers golden yellow to orange; **achenes** 4-angled, with pappus of 1 or 2 persistent, scalelike awns and several separate to united scales, sometimes lacking.

Tithonia rotundifolia (Mill.) S. F. Blake (Mexican Sunflower). Annual to 2 m. tall. July-September.

DESCRIPTION: **Plants** robust, native in Mexico and Central America; **leaves** ovate to triangular, to 30 cm. long, cordate, with serrate to crenate margins; **flower** heads orange scarlet, to 7.5 cm. across.

USE: Plant toward the back of the flower border.

CULTURE: Plants like a moist, well-drained soil and full sun. Propagation is by seeds started indoors in early April. Space the plants 60 cm. apart in the garden in late May. The flowers are showy and are good for cutting.

CULTIVAR

'Torch'. All-America Winner. Flowering heads fiery orange red.   PLATE 256

Torenia L. (Wishbone Flower)

SCROPHULARIACEAE (Figwort Family)

DESCRIPTION: A genus of about 40 species of annual or perennial herbs, native in tropical and subtropical regions of Asia and Africa; **stems** freely branching, prostrate to erect, 4-angled; **leaves** opposite; simple; **flowers** of various colors, axillary or in few-flowered racemes; calyx tutular, pleated or 3- to 5-winged, enlarging in fruit; corolla cylindrical, 2-lipped; stamens 4; **fruit** a capsule.

Torenia fournieri Linden (Wishbone Flower, Bluewings). Annual to 30 cm. tall. July-October.

DESCRIPTION: **Plants** native in Vietnam; **leaves** dentate, to 5 cm. long; **flowers** pale violet, yellow on the outside, upper lip with 3 purplish blue lobes and a yellow blotch at the base.

USE: Plant toward the front of the flower border.

CULTURE: Torenias like a cool, moist soil and partial shade. They dislike hot, dry weather. Start seeds indoors in early April. Transplant the seedlings to the garden in late May. Space the plants about 30 cm. apart.

CULTIVARS

'Bicolor'. Flowers blue and white.
'Compacta'. Plants very compact, 20 cm. tall.
'Grandiflora'. Flowers larger than in species.

Trachymene Rudge

UMBELLIFERAE (Parsley Family)

DESCRIPTION: A genus of about 12 species of herbs, native in Australia and South Pacific Islands; **leaves** mostly ternately compound; **flowers** white or blue, in simple umbels subtended by lanceolate bracts; **fruits** flattened.

Trachymene coerulea R. C. Grah. (Blue Lace Flower). Annual to 60 cm. tall. July-September.

DESCRIPTION: **Plants** native in Australia; **leaves** ternately or biternately compound into narrow segments; **flowers** light blue, in simple, long-peduncled umbels to 7.5 cm. across.

USE: Plant toward the front of the flower border.

CULTURE: Plants like a cool, well-drained soil and full sun. They grow best in climates where the summers are cool. They dislike hot, humid weather. Start the seeds indoors in early April or sow them directly in the flower border in early May. Space the plants about 20 cm. apart.

Tradescantia L. (Spiderwort)

COMMELINACEAE (Spiderwort Family)

DESCRIPTION: A genus of about 20 species of perennial herbs, native in North and South America; **stems** erect or trailing; **flowers** blue, rose, purple, or white, in axillary or terminal clusters, each cluster subtended by paired leaf-like bracts or by a single bract; sepals and petals 3, separate; stamens 6, with usually hairy filaments; **fruit** a capsule.

Tradescantia x *andersoniana* W. Ludw. & Rohw. (Garden Spiderwort). Perennial to 90 cm. tall. July-September.

DESCRIPTION: A garden hybrid resulting from crosses between *T. ohioensis* x *T. subaspera* x *T. virginiana*; **stems** erect; **leaves** linear-lanceolate, to 30 cm. long; **flowers** showy, in various colors, to 2.5 cm. across.

USE: Plant in a prairie or wildflower garden.

CULTURE: Plants prefer a moist soil and thrive in either full sun or partial shade. One fault is that the stems are weak and tend to fall over after blooming, presenting an untidy appearance in the flower border. Propagation is usually by division of established plants in early spring.

CULTIVARS
'Alba'. Flowers white.
'Bluestone'. Flowers solid blue.
'Iris Prtichard'. Flowers white, flushed with blue.
'J. C. Weguelin'. Flowers pale blue.
'Pauline'. Flowers orchid pink.
'Purple Dome'. Flowers brilliant purple.
'Red Cloud'. Flowers bright rose red.   PLATE 257

Tradescantia — other species

T. bracteata Small., native from Minnesota to Texas, has rose or rarely blue flowers.

T. virginiana L. (Common Spiderwort), native from Minnesota to Maine, south to Missouri and Georgia, has violet purple flowers. Cultivars sold under this name probably belong to *T.* x *andersoniana*.

Trillium L. (Wake-robin)

LILIACEAE (Lily Family)

DESCRIPTION: A genus of about 30 species of spring-flowering woodland herbs with short, bulbous rootstocks, native in North America, the Himalayas, and eastern Asia; **stems** simple; **leaves** 3, in a terminal whorl, subtending a single flower; **flowers** solitary, sessile or peduncled; sepals 3, green; petals 3, white, yellow, green, pink, or purple, separate; stamens 6; **fruit** a 3-celled berry.

Trillium grandiflorum (Michx.) Salisb. (Showy Trillium). Perennial to 50 cm. tall. May.   PLATE 259

DESCRIPTION: **Plants** native in hardwood forests from Minnesota to Quebec, south to Missouri and Georgia; **leaves** broadly ovate to rhombic, to 12 cm. long; **flowers** white, fading to rosy pink, to 7.5 cm. across.

USE: Plant in wildflower garden or in rock garden.

CULTURE: Trilliums like a well-drained soil high in organic matter and shade. They increase slowly but once established, they live for a long time. Propagation is largely by division in late summer after the foliage dies down. Seeds can also be planted, but it takes several years for plants grown from seed to bloom.

CULTIVARS: Several double-flowered forms are in cultivation. So far as I know, these have never been given cultivar names.   PLATE 260

Trillium luteum — see *Trillium viride* var. *luteum*

Trillium stylosum — see *Trillium catesbaei*

Trillium — other species

T. catesbaei Elliott (Rosy Wake-robin), native from North Carolina south to Alabama and Georgia, has pink or rose flowers on nodding peduncles.

T. cernuum L. (Nodding Trillium), native from Saskatchewan to Newfoundland, south to Alabama and Georgia, has nodding white or pink flowers.

T. erectum L. (Purple Trillium, Stinking Benjamin), native from Ontario to Quebec, south to Illinois and Georgia, has ill-scented brownish purple, rarely white, yellow, or green flowers.   PLATE 258

T. nivale Ridd. (Snow Trillium, Dwarf White Trillium), native from Minnesota to Pennsylvania, south to Nebraska and Missouri, is the earliest and the smallest trillium with white flowers. They are only about 15 cm. tall.   PLATE 261

T. recurvatum L. (Purple Trillium, Prairie Trillium), native from Nebraska to Michigan, south to Mississippi and Alabama, has brownish purple flowers with reflexed sepals.

T. sessile L. (Toad Trillium, Toadshade), native from Missouri to New York, south to Arkansas and Georgia, has mottled leaves and flowers that are brownish purple, maroon, or yellowish green and that are unstalked.

T. undulatum Willd. (Painted Trillium), native from Manitoba and Quebec, south to Tennessee and Georgia, has white flowers with purple veins. It is perhaps the most beautiful of all the trilliums but the most difficult to grow. It requires an acid soil.

T. viride (L.) Beck. (Wood Trillium), native from Kansas to Illinois, south to Oklahoma and Arkansas, has sessile, green flowers and mottled leaves. *T. viride* var. *luteum* (Muhlenb.) Gleason has yellow flowers.   PLATE 262

Tritonia crocosmiiflora — see *Corcosmia crocosmiiflora*

Trollius L. (Globeflower)

RANUNCULACEAE (Buttercup Family)

DESCRIPTION: A genus of about 20 species of perennial herbs, native mostly in swampy or wet soils in the North Temperate regions of the world; **leaves** palmately lobed or divided; **flowers** usually solitary; sepals 5 to 15, petal-like; petals 5 or more, often small; stamens many; **fruit** of many follicles.

Trollius europaeus L. (Common Globeflower). Perennial to 60 cm. tall. May, June.   PLATE 263

DESCRIPTION: **Plants** with unbranched stems, native in Europe and arctic America; basal **leaves** petioled, 3- to 5-lobed, stem leaves sessile, 3-lobed; **flowers** yellow, more or less globular, to 2.5 cm. across.

USE: Plant in flower border, around pools, or for cut flowers.

CULTURE: Globeflowers like a rich, moist soil and full sun. Propagation is by division in early spring or by seeds sown as soon as ripe in a cold frame. The seeds are slow to germinate and may take a year or longer to come up.

CULTIVARS
'Lemon Queen'. Flowers soft lemon yellow.
'Miss Mary Russell'. Leaves finely cut, lacy.
'Pritchard's Giant'. Flowers very large, golden yellow.
'Superbus'. Flowers lemon yellow.

Trollius — other species

T. asiaticus L., native in Asia, has orange flowers that are smaller than those of *T. europaeus*. 'Byrne's Giant' has deep lemon yellow flowers.

T. chinensis Bunge (Chinese Globeflower), native in northern China, has golden yellow flowers on long peduncles. 'Golden Queen' has deep orange flowers.

Tropaeolum L. (Nasturtium)

TROPAEOLACEAE (Nasturtium Family)

DESCRIPTION: A genus of about 20 species of annual or perennial herbs with an acrid, watery sap, spreading or climbing by means of coiled petioles. sometimes with tuberous **roots**, native in the mountains from Mexico to Chile; **leaves** alternate, usually simple, entire or lobed, peltate, usually long-petioled; **flowers** showy, mostly orange, yellow, or red; stamens 8, in 2 whorls; **fruit** wrinkled, 3-lobed, separating into 3, 1-seeded sections.

Tropaeolum majus L. (Garden Nasturtium). Tender perennial grown as an annual. July-October. PLATE 264

DESCRIPTION: **Plants** sprawling, succulent, native in the Andes of South America; **leaves** orbicular or reniform, to 15 cm. across, mostly entire; **flowers** yellow, orange, or red, sometimes striped or spotted, to 6 cm. across.

USE: Plant in flower border.

CULTURE: Plants bloom best on rather poor soil in full sun. In rich soil the plants are inclined to be vegetative. Plants dislike hot, humid weather and do best where the summers are cool. Seeds can be started indoors in early April, or they can be planted where the plants are to grow in early May.

CULTIVARS

'Cherry Rose'. Plants compact; flowers double, cherry rose.

'Cherry Scarlet'. Plants compact; flowers double, cherry scarlet.

'Double Gleam'. All-America Winner. Flowers double or semi-double in a fine color range.

'Whirlybird'. Flowers spurless, upfacing, in shades of rose, gold, and scarlet.

Tropaeolum peregrinum (Canary-bird Vine, Canary Creeper). Annual to 3 m. or more. August-October. PLATE 265

DESCRIPTION: **Plants** climbing, native in Peru and Ecuador; **leaves** deeply 5-lobed with long petioles; **flowers** canary-yellow, to 2.5 cm. across; upper petals erect and fimbriate, the spur green and curved.

USE: Plant at base of a trellis or fence.

CULTURE: This vine is easy to grow in most any soil and in full sun. The yellow, canary-colored flowers are quite showy. Seeds can be started indoors in early April or sown directly in early May.

Tulipa L. (Tulip)

LILIACEAE (Lily Family)

DESCRIPTION: A genus of about 100 species of hardy spring-flowering bulbous perennial herbs, native in temperate areas of Europe and Asia; **bulbs** tunicate with tunics of various textures; **leaves** mostly basal, a few on flowering stems; **flowers** campanulate to rotate, in most colors except blue, usually solitary, perianth segments 6, separate; stamens 6; **fruit** a 3-valved capsule with many flat seeds.

Tulipa fosterana W. Irving (Foster Tulip). Perennial to 25 cm. tall. April, May.

DESCRIPTION: **Plants** native in Turkestan; tunic of bulb silky-hairy inside; **leaves** 3 or 4, broadly ovate, to 20 cm. long; **flowers** opening flat, to 10 cm. across, brilliant scarlet with yellow-margined black basal blotch; stamens black.

USE: Plant in the rock garden, in the foundation planting, or in the flower border.

CULTURE: Tulips are easily grown in any well-drained soil. They bloom best in full sun but they will tolerate light shade. Propagation is by bulbs planted in October or early November. Plant the bulbs 15 to 20 cm. deep and about 15 cm. apart. Do not remove the foliage in the spring until the leaves turn yellow and die down.

CULTIVAR
'Red Emperor'. Flowers vermillion scarlet.

Tulipa kaufmanniana Regel. (Water-lily Tulip). Perennial to 20 cm. tall. April, May.

DESCRIPTION: **Plants** native in Turkestan; tunic papery, sparsely hairy inside; **leaves** 3 to 5, broadly oblong, to 25 cm. long; **flowers** white, pink, scarlet, yellow, with yellow basal blotch and carmine veins inside, to 7.5 cm. across; stamens yellow.

USE: Same as for *T. fosterana*.

CULTURE: Same as for *T. fosterana*.
CULTIVARS
'Ancilla'. Flowers pure white with red rim.
'Fritz Kreisler'. Flowers salmon pink.
'Hearts Delight'. Flowers pale rose.
'Scarlet'. Flowers scarlet with yellow basal blotch.

Tulipa—other species

T. chrysantha Boiss. (Golden Tulip), native in Iran and northwestern India, has bright yellow flowers stained red inside.

T. clusiana DC. (Lady Tulip), native in Iran and Afghanistan, has bulbs with a leathery tunic, white or yellow flowers with a carmine blotch at the base of each perianth segment, and purple stamens.

T. greigii Regel. (Greig Tulip), native in Turkestan, has bulbs with a membranous tunic, and orange scarlet flowers with a yellow-bordered black blotch inside, and mottled leaves.

T. praestans Hort. (Leather-bulb Tulip), native in central Asia, has bulbs with a leathery tunic and brick red flowers with purple anthers.

Tulipa—garden hybrids   PLATE 266

Numerous species have been used in developing modern tulips. These tulips are classified as follows:
Early—flowering in April.
   1. Single Early. Plants to 40 cm. tall; flowers single.
   2. Double Early. Plants to 40 cm. tall; flowers double.
Midseason—flowering in late April or early May.
   3. Mendel. Plants to 50 cm. tall; flowers single.
   4. Triumph. Plants more than 50 cm. tall; flowers single.
   5. Darwin Hybrids. Flowers single, resulting from a cross between the Darwin tulips and *T. kosteriana*.
Late—flowering in mid or late May.
   6. Darwin. Plants tall; flowers single, rectangular outline at base.
   7. Lily-flowered. Flowers single, with pointed, reflexed perianth segments.
   8. Cottage. Flowers single, often long and egg-shaped.
   9. Rembrandt. Flowers striped or marked with brown, bronze, black, red, pink, or purple on a red, white, or yellow ground color.
10. Parrot. Flowers with laciniate perianth segments.
11. Double Late. Flowers fully double, peony-flowered.

Species—wild species and their cultivars and those hybrids in which the wild species is evident.

12. Kaufmanniana. Leaves often mottled; flowers large, very early.
13. Fosteriana. Leaves often mottled or striped; flowers large, early.
14. Greigii. Leaves mottled or striped; flowers later than the Kaufmannianas.
15. Other species. Species other than the above.

USE: Tulips are widely planted in the flower border, the cutting garden, or in foundation plantings. They are also planted in formally designed beds, especially in parks and public grounds.

CULTURE: Tulips like a well-drained soil and full sun. They will tolerate light shade but they cannot compete with the roots of trees and shrubs. Propagation is by bulbs. These should be planted preferably in October. If it is necessary to plant the bulbs later, the soil should be mulched to allow time for root development before the ground freezes. Space the bulbs about 15 cm. apart and 15 to 20 cm. deep. It is best to plant the bulbs in groups in the border with each group of uniform color. The longevity of tulips depends on soil drainage and the depth of planting: when the bulbs are planted too shallow, they have a tendency to divide and many small bulbs result that are too small to bloom. Some growers lift their bulbs after the foliage dies down and replant them in the fall. The bulbs should be stored over summer in a well-ventilated room. If you leave the bulbs in the soil all summer as most gardeners do, the tops should be allowed to die down before they are removed. Annual flowers can be planted between the tulip plants so the area will have summer bloom.

In preparing the soil for tulips, work in a complete fertilizer such as a 5-10-5 or bone meal. This should be applied at the rate of about 2 pounds per 100 square feet. Avoid using fresh animal manures. Compost and well-decayed manure can be safely used.

CULTIVARS: There are thousands of named cultivars to choose from. Descriptions are given in catalogs and bulb displays in garden centers. Display gardens can also be visited when the tulips are in bloom to aid in the selection of cultivars.

Tunica saxifraga—see *Petrorhagia saxifraga*

Uvularia L. (Merrybells, Bellwort)

LILIACEAE (Lily Family)

DESCRIPTION: A genus of 5 species of rhizomatous, perennial herbs, native in North America; **stems** simple or branched, leafy; **leaves** alternate, sessile or perfoliate; **flowers** campanulate, yellow, nodding, usually solitary, perianth segments 6, separate; stamens 6; **fruits** a 3-lobed or 3-winged capsule.

Uvularia grandiflora Sm. (Big Merrybells). Perennial to 75 cm. tall. April, May.   PLATE 267

DESCRIPTION: **Plants** native from Minnesota to Quebec, south to Okalahoma and Tennessee; **leaves** oblong to lanceolate-ovate, perfoliate, to 12 cm. long; **flowers** lemon yellow to 5 cm. long, with perianth segments smooth on the inside.

USE: Bellworts are attractive when planted in a shady wildflower garden.

CULTURE: Plants like a soil high in organic matter. The soil should be kept moist during the summer. Propagation is either by seeds or by spring division. Plant the seeds in a soil high in organic matter.

Uvularia —other species

U. perfoliata L. (Straw Bellwort, Wood Merrybells), native from Minnesota to Quebec and south to Louisiana and Florida, differs from *U. grandiflora* by having the perianth segments glandular-papillose on the inside.

U. sessilifolia L. (Wild Oats), native from South Dakota to New Brunswick and south to Arkansas and Alabama, has greenish yellow flowers and leaves that are sessile.

Valeriana L. (Valerian)

VALERIANACEAE (Valerian Family)

DESCRIPTION: A genus of about 200 species of perennial herbs, subshrubs, or shrubs, with thickened, strong-smelling taproots or rhizomes, native in all countries except Australia; **leaves** opposite, simple, pinnatifid, or compound, often in basal rosettes; **flowers** small, white, pink, rose, or yellow, in clustered or panicled cymes, perfect or imperfect; calyx inrolled at first, becoming pappuslike in fruit; corolla rotate, funnelform or sometimes campanulate; stamens usually 3; ovary inferior; **fruit** an achene crowned by a persistent calyx.

Valeriana officinalis L. (Garden Heliotrope). Perennial to 1 m. tall. May-August.

DESCRIPTION: **Plants** native in Europe and western Asia, naturalized elsewhere; **leaves** pinnatifid with 7 to 10 pairs of oblong-ovate to lanceolate segments; **flowers** white, pink, or lavender in paniculate cymes, very fragrant; corolla funnelform, slightly saccate at base.

USE: Plant as a background plant in the border. The flowers are good for cutting.

CULTURE: Plants like a moist soil and full sun. Propagation is by seeds started in May in a cold frame or by spring division.

CULTIVARS
'Alba'. Flowers white.
'Coccinea'. Flowers deep red.

Valeriana supina L. (Austrian Valerian). Perennial to 15 cm. tall. May-August.

DESCRIPTION: **Plants** cespitose, native in central Europe; **leaves** simple, obovate to lanceolate, to 2 cm. long, entire, ciliate; **flowers** pink, fragrant.

USE: Plant in a rock garden.

CULTURE: Same as for *V. officinalis.*

Verbascum L. (Mullein)

SCROPHULARIACEAE (Figwort Family)

DESCRIPTION: A genus of about 250 species of hardy, mostly biennial herbs, native in Asia and Europe, chiefly in the Mediterranean region; **stems** erect from a basal rosette of leaves; **leaves** alternate, simple, sometimes pinnatifid; **flowers** mostly yellow, sometimes tawny, red, blue, or purple, rarely white, in spikes, racemes, or panicles; calyx deeply 5-parted; corolla rotate, deeply 5-lobed, with a short tube; stamens 5; **fruit** a capsule.

Verbascum phoeniceum L. (Purple Mullein). Perennial to 1 m. tall. May-August.

DESCRIPTION: **Plants** erect, native in southern Europe and Asia; **leaves** glabrous above, hairy beneath, toothed; **flowers** purple or red, in dense racemes.

USE: Plant toward the back of the flower border.

CULTURE: The purple mullein is grown for its colorful flowers. It grows in any well-drained soil in full sun. Propagation is chiefly by spring division. It can also be grown from seeds planted in May in nursery rows. Space the plants about 30 cm. apart. Volunteer seedlings can be transplanted in early spring.

Verbascum —garden hybrids

V. phoenicium has been crossed with other species to produce several named cultivars.
'Golden Bush'. Flowers yellow.
'Pink Domina'. Flowers rose pink.

Verbena L. (Vervain)

VERBENACEAE (Vervain Family)

DESCRIPTION: A genus of about 200 species of usually hairy, erect or decumbent to prostrate, annual or perennial herbs or subshrubs, native mostly in the tropics or subtropics of North and South America; **stems** often 4-angled; **leaves** opposite, rarely whorled or alternate, toothed, parted, or dissected, rarely entire; **flowers** of various colors, in spikes, the spikes terminal or rarely axillary, solitary, or sometimes in corymbs or broad panicles, mostly bracted; calyx 5-lobed, 5-ribbed; corolla salverform or funnelform, somewhat 2-lipped; stamens 4, rarely 2; **fruit** dry, enclosed in the persistent calyx, separating into 4 nutlets at maturity.

Verbena x *hybrida* Voss (Garden Verbena). Tender perennial grown as an annual, to 60 cm. tall. June-October.

DESCRIPTION: **Plants** decumbent with creeping stems of hybrid origin from crosses between *V. peruviana* and other species; **leaves** oblong to oblong-ovate, to 10 cm. long, obtusely dentate or somewhat lobed basally, with short-margined petioles; **flowers** pink, red, white, yellow, blue, purple, or variegated, in flat heads.

USE: Plant toward the front of the flower border or in the rock garden.

CULTURE: Plants like a well-drained soil in full sun. Propagation is by seeds started indoors in April. Seedlings are transplanted to the garden after danger of frost has passed. Space the plants about 30 cm. apart.

CULTIVARS
'Amethyst'. Flowers mid-blue.
'Blaze'. All-America Winner. Flowers bright scarlet.
'Crystal'. Flowers pure white.
'Ruffled Pink'. Flowers semi-double, ruffled, salmon pink.
'Sangria'. All-America Winner. Flowers velvety, wine red with white centers.
'Sparkle'. Flowers in a rich range of colors.   PLATE 268
'Springtime'. Flowers in shades of scarlet, pink, rose, blue, maroon, purple, and white, mostly with white centers.

Verbena — other species.

V. bipinnatifolia Nutt. (Dakota Vervain), native in South Dakota and south to Arizona and Alabama, has prostrate stems and small, lilac purple flowers. Sometimes planted in prairie gardens.

V. hastata L. (Blue Vervain), native from British Columbia to Nova Scotia and south to Arizona, has erect stems and small blue flowers. Sometimes planted in prairie gardens.

V. rigida K. Spreng. (Vervain), native in southern Brazil and Argentina, is a tender perennial grown as an annual. It is a spreading plant with spikes of bright reddish violet flowers all summer.

Veronica L. (Speedwell)

SCROPHULARIACEAE (Figwort Family)

DESCRIPTION: A genus of about 250 species of annual or perennial herbs in North Temperate regions; **plants** prostrate to erect; **leaves** usually opposite, rarely whorled or alternate, simple, entire or toothed; **flowers** small, white, rose, purple, or blue, in axillary or terminal spikes, racemes, or corymbs, sometimes solitary; calyx 4- to 5-parted; corolla rotate; stamens 2; **fruit** a flattened, notched capsule.

Veronica incana L. (Woolly Speedwell). Perennial to 60 cm. tall. May, June.

DESCRIPTION: **Plants** white-woolly, native in northern Asia and U.S.S.R.; **leaves** oblong to lanceolate, to 7.5 cm. long, obtusely crenate, petioled; **flowers** blue, in terminal racemes.

USE: Plant in masses in the flower border or in a rock garden.

CULTURE: Plants thrive in any well-drained soil in full sun. Propagation is by early spring division or by seeds started in May in a cold frame or nursery row. Space the plants about 30 cm. apart.

CULTIVARS
'Nana'. Plants compact; flowers in blue spikes.
'Rosea'. Flowers dark, rose purple.

Veronica latifolia var. *prostrata* — see *Veronica prostrata*

Veronica maritima — see *Veronica longifolia*

Veronica ruprestris — see *Veronica prostrata*

Veronica spicata L. (Spike Speedwell). Perennial to 15 cm. tall. June-August.

DESCRIPTION: **Plants** native to northern Europe and Asia; **stems** erect or ascending; **leaves** oblong to lanceolate, to 5 cm. long, toothed; **flowers** blue or pink, in dense spikelike racemes.

USE: Same as for *V. incana*.

CULTURE: Same as for *V. incana*.

CULTIVARS

'Barcarole'. Flowers rose pink.

'Blue Peter'. Flowers navy blue.

'Icicle'. Flowers pure white.

'Nana'. Flowers in miniature spikes, cobalt blue.

Veronica — other species

V. alpina L. (Alpine Speedwell), native in Europe, Asia and northwestern North America, has dark blue or violet flowers in dense racemes. A good rock garden plant.

V. latifolia L. (Hungarian Speedwell), native in Europe, has blue, rose, or white flowers in axillary racemes. 'Crater Lake Blue' has gentian blue flowers in tall spikes.

V. longifolia L., native in Europe, is a tall species with many lilac-colored flowers in dense racemes from July to frost. 'Blue Giantess' has deep blue flowers.

V. pectinata L. (Comb Speedwell), native in Asia Minor, is a low, creeping plant with deep blue flowers with white centers. 'Rosea' has rose-colored flowers.

V. prostrata L. (Hungarian Speedwell), native in Europe, has deep blue flowers in terminal racemes in May and June. 'Heavenly Blue' has sapphire blue flowers and 'Mrs. Holt' has bright pink flowers.

V. repens Loisel. (Creeping Speedwell), native in Corsica and Spain, has small, pale blue flowers in May.

Veronica — garden hybrids

A number of garden hybrids have been introduced. These involve crosses between *V. spicata* and other species. Some of the cultivars listed under *V. spicata* may be of hybrid origin. Most of these hybrids bloom from June to August.

CULTIVARS
'Blue Charm'. Flowers blue on mound-shaped plants.
'Blue Giant'. Flowers deep blue.
'Lavender Charm'. Flowers lavender blue.
'Minuet'. Leaves silvery gray; flowers soft pink.   PLATE 269
'Sarabande'. Leaves gray; flowers deep violet blue.

Vinca L. (Periwinkle)

APOCYNACEAE (Dogbane Family)

DESCRIPTION: A genus of about 12 species of trailing, mostly evergreen herbs or subshrubs, native in Europe; **leaves** opposite, entire; **flowers** axillary, solitary, 5-merous, perfect; corolla more or less funnelform; stamens attached at the middle of the corolla tube; **fruit** a pair of spreading, cylindrical follicles.

Vinca minor L. (Common Periwinkle, Myrtle). Perennial to 10 cm. tall. April, May.

DESCRIPTION: **Plants** with creeping stems, native in Europe; **leaves** oblong to ovate, to 5 cm. long, tapered at both ends; **flowers** lilac blue, to 2 cm. across, with tube 6 mm. long and obtuse-truncate lobes.

USE: Plant as ground cover in sheltered locations that will have good snow cover.

CULTURE: The plants will grow in most soils. They are shade tolerant and form an attractive evergreen ground cover under trees. They must have winter protection in the form of a mulch or snow cover. Propagation is chiefly by division or by rooted cuttings. Space the plants 30 cm. apart in early spring.

CULTIVARS
'Alba'. Flowers white.
'Bowlesii'. Flowers dark blue.
'Miss Jeckyll's White'. Leaves very small; flowers white.

Vinca rosea — see *Catharanthus roseus*

Vinca — other species

V. herbacea Wald St. & Kit. (Herbaceous Periwinkle), native in eastern Europe and Asia Minor, has deciduous leaves and blue flowers. This is the hardiest of the periwinkles and requires no winter protection.

V. *major* L. (Bigleaf Periwinkle), native in Europe, has larger leaves and flowers than V. *minor*. It is tender and must be wintered in a greenhouse or in the home as a house plant. It is popular for window boxes and hanging baskets. 'Variegata' has leaves margined with white or yellow. 'Morning Glory' has blue purple flowers and 'Pink Carousel' has pink flowers.

Viola L. (Violet)

VIOLACEAE (Violet Family)

DESCRIPTION: A large genus of about 500 species of annual or perennial herbs of wide distribution in temperate regions; **plants** stemless or with leafy stems; **leaves** with persistent and often leaflike stipules; **flowers** often of 2 kinds, those that open early in the spring that are showy and sterile, and those that bloom in summer that are nonshowy, closed, and self-pollinated, producing many seeds; showy flowers 5-merous, nodding, the lower petal spurred, the other 4 in 2 unlike pairs; **fruit** a capsule, opening into 3 boat-shaped, keeled valves.

Viola cornuta L. (Horned Violet, Tufted Pansy). Perennial to 30 cm. tall. June-September.

DESCRIPTION: **Plants** tufted, native in Spain and Pyrenes; **leaves** ovate, wavy-toothed, with large triangular stipules; **flowers** violet (various colors in named cultivars), with a slender spur as long as the sepals.

USE: Plant in flower border or rock garden.

CULTURE: Plant in moist but well-drained soil in full sun or partial shade. The species can be propagated by seeds but the named cultivars are propagated by division. Volunteer seedlings are common.

CULTIVARS

'Alba'. Flowers white.

'Blue Elf'. Flowers small, blue.

'Lutea Splendens'. Flowers bright yellow.

'Purple Glory'. Flowers deep purple with yellow eye.

Viola odorata L. (Sweet Violet). Perennial to 20 cm. tall. May, June.

DESCRIPTION: **Plants** tufted, native in Europe and Africa. naturalized around farmsteads; **leaves** cordate-ovate to reniform, toothed; **flowers** fragrant, deep violet (various colors in named cultivars), to 2 cm. across, with a short, nearly straight spur.

USE: Plant in rock garden or wildflower garden.

CULTURE: Same as for *V. cornuta*.

CULTIVARS

'Queen Charlotte'. Flowers large, deep blue.

'Red Giant'. Flowers red violet.

'The Czar'. Flowers long-peduncled, bright blue.

'White Czar'. Flowers long-peduncled, white.

Viola papilionacea—see *Viola sororia*

Viola tricolor L. (Johnny-jump-up, Viola), Short-lived perennial to 30 cm. tall. June-September.

DESCRIPTION: **Plants** native in Europe, naturalized; **leaves** ovate to lanceolate, wedge-shaped at the base, crenate, with large leaflike stipules; **flowers** variously colored, to 2 cm. across.

USE: Plant in rock garden or flower border.

CULTURE: Same as for *V. cornuta*.

CULTIVARS

'Monarch'. Flowers large, in a wide range of self colors, bicolors, and picotees. Heat resistant.

'Yellow Prince'. Flowers bright yellow.

Viola x *wittrockiana* Gams. (Garden Pansy). Tender perennial grown as an annual to 20 cm. tall. June-September.

DESCRIPTION: **Plants** of hybrid origin, involving crosses between *V. tricolor*, *V. lutea*, and *V. altaica*; **leaves** ovate and subcordate or lanceolate-elliptic and wedge-shaped at base; **flowers** rounded in outline, to 12 cm. across, in various colors and patterns.

USE: Plant in flower border as an edging or for mass effect toward the front of the border.

CULTURE: Pansies bloom best in full sun but they will tolerate some shade. They like a cool soil and bloom best in cool weather. Propagation is by seeds started indoors in February or March. Space the plants about 20 cm. apart. They are frost hardy and can be planted outdoors in early May. Plants live over winter when there is ample snow cover.

CULTIVARS AND STRAINS

Color Festival (strain). Early flowering in a bright color range.

'Golden Chief'. Flowers pure gold.

'Imperial Blue'. All-America Winner. Flowers light blue with a bluish violet face and a gold eye.   PLATE 272

Majestic Giants (strain). All-America Winner. Flowers large, to 10 cm. across, in wide color range and handsome faces.

'Orange Prince'. All-America Winner. Flowers medium-sized, glowing apricot orange with mahogany faces.

Super Swiss Giants (strain). Plants compact, early flowering; flowers large, velvety, in wide color range with contrasted faces.

Viola — other species

V. blanda Willd. (Sweet White Violet), native from Minnesota to Quebec and south to Louisiana and Georgia, has fragrant white flowers in May.

V. canadensis L. (Tall White Violet), native from Alberta to New Brunswick and south to New Mexico and South Carolina, has leafy stems and white flowers with yellow centers in May and June.

V. cucullata Ait. (Marsh Blue Violet), native from Ontario to Newfoundland and south to Missouri and Georgia, is stemless with violet-colored flowers with a darker throat and a white spot at the base. 'Freckles' has creamy white flowers speckled with tiny purple markings. 'Priceana' has deep blue flowers with white margins.

V. pedata L. (Bird's-foot Violet), native in sandy soils in full sun from Minnesota to Maine and south to Missouri and North Carolina, has deeply divided leaves with narrow lobes and large lilac-colored flowers to 2 cm. across in May and early June. 'Bicolor' has blue and purple flowers and blooms again in the fall.   PLATE 270

V. pubescens Ait. (Downy Yellow Violet), native from North Dakota to Nova Scotia and south to Oklahoma and Georgia, has yellow flowers with purple brown markings near the base in May.   PLATE 271

V. sororia Willd. (Woolly Blue Violet), native from Minnesota to Quebec and south to Oklahoma and North Carolina, has dark blue or purple flowers and woolly leaves in May.

Waldsteinia Willd. (Barren Strawberry)

ROSACEAE (Rose Family)

DESCRIPTION: A genus of a few species of strawberrylike perennial herbs with creeping stolons, native in the North Temperate regions of the world; **leaves** mostly basal, 3- to 5-lobed or divided; **flowers** yellow, on bracted scapes about as long as the leaves; sepals 5, alternating with 5 bracteoles; petals 5; stamens many; **fruit** of 2 to 6 achenes, each with a slender, deciduous style.

Waldsteinia fragarioides (Michx.) Tratt. (Barren Strawberry). Perennial to 20 cm. tall. April, May.   PLATE 273

DESCRIPTION: **Plants** with shallow, creeping rhizomes, native from Minnesota to New Brunswick, south to Missouri and Georgia; **leaves** trifoliate with broadly wedge-shaped leaflets, to 5 cm. long, toothed near apex; **flowers** yellow, to 2 cm. across, on several-flowered scapes.

USE: Plant for ground cover or in a rock garden or a wall garden.

CULTURE: Plants grow in most soils and full sun. Propagation is by division in early spring.

Waldsteinia ternata (Steph.) Fritsch. Perennial to 20 cm. tall. April, May.

DESCRIPTION: **Plants** native from central Europe to Siberia or Japan; **leaflets** 3, on short pedicles, to 3 cm. long, evergreen, toothed to lobed; **flowers** yellow, to 2 cm. across.

USE: Same as for *W. fragarioides*.

CULTURE: Same as for *W. fragarioides*.

Waldsteinia trifolia — see *Waldsteinia ternata*

Yucca L.

AGAVACEAE (Agave Family)

DESCRIPTION: A genus of about 40 species of stemless or shrublike plants, native mostly in warmer parts of North America; **leaves** stiff, swordlike; **flowers** white or violet, in racemes or panicles; perianth of 6 separate or partly united segments; stamens 6; ovary superior, 3-celled; **fruit** a dry or fleshy capsule — if fleshy, the capsule does not open.

Yucca filamentosa L. (Adam's-needle). Perennial to 3 m. tall. June.   PLATE 274

DESCRIPTION: **Plants** nearly stemless, native from Kentucky to Maryland, south to Georgia; **leaves** swordlike, to 75 cm. long and 2.5 cm. wide, abruptly narrowed at the apex to a stout spine, margins with long, curly threads; **flowers** nearly white, to 5 cm. across, in tall panicles to 2 m. long; **fruit** a dry, dehiscent capsule.

USE: Plant toward the back of the flower border.

CULTURE: Yuccas require a well-drained soil and full sun. The Adam's-needle is of borderline hardiness. A good snow cover helps to reduce winter injury. Because of their size it is difficult to provide winter protection. Propagation is by spring division or by seeds. It takes a number of years for plants grown from seed to reach a flowering size. Many plants sold as *Y. filamentosa* may actually be *Y. smalliana*. Space plants about 1 m. apart.

CULTIVARS
'Bright Edge'. Flowers creamy white.
'Bright Sword'. Leaves with yellow stripes.

Yucca glauca Nutt. (Soapweed). Perennial to 1 m. tall. June.

DESCRIPTION: **Plants** clump-forming, native from Wyoming to North Dakota, south to Arizona and Texas; **leaves** linear, to 75 cm. long and 1 cm. wide, pale green, with thread-bearing margins; **flowers** fragrant, greenish white, often tinged with rosy brown, to 5 cm. across, in upright racemes; **fruit** a dehiscent capsule to 6 cm. long.

USE: Same as for *Y. filamentosa*.

CULTURE: Same as for *Y. filamentosa*. This is the hardiest species of yucca, but the plants are slow to come into bloom.

CULTIVAR
'Rosea'. Flowers tinted rose outside.

Yucca smalliana Fern. (Adam's-needle). Perennial to 3 m. tall. June.

DESCRIPTION: **Plants** stemless, native from South Carolina south to Mississippi and Florida; **leaves** firm, erect, and spreading, tapering at both ends, margins with curly fibers; **flowers** white, in tall panicles.

USE: Same as for *Y. filamentosa*.

CULTURE: Same as for *Y. filamentosa*.

Zantedeschia K. Spreng. (Calla Lily)

ARACEAE (Arum Family)

DESCRIPTION: A genus of 6 species of stemless herbs with thick bulblike rhizomes, native in South Africa; **leaves** large, entire, on long petioles; **flowers** monoecious, borne on a fleshy spadix enclosed by a showy spathe that is expanded above; perianth lacking.

Zantedeschia elliottiana (W. Wats.) Engl. (Golden Calla). Tender perennial to 75 cm. tall. July, August.

DESCRIPTION: **Plants** rhizomatous, stemless, native in South Africa; **leaves** ovate, to 30 cm. long, cordate or sagittate at base, white spotted, on long petioles to 60 cm. long; **flowering** spathe yellow inside, greenish yellow outside, with a flaring and recurved blade, to 15 cm. long.

USE: Plant in moist soil around a pool.

CULTURE: Calla lilies must have moist soil. They will tolerate some shade but bloom best in full sun. Propagation is by division of the tuberous rhizomes. The rhizomes are potted in early April and the plants set out in the garden after danger of frost has passed. The tubers must be dug in the fall and stored over winter in a frost free place.

Zinnia L.

COMPOSITAE (Sunflower Family)

Helianthus Tribe

DESCRIPTION: A genus of about 17 species of annual or perennial herbs or subshrubs, native in the southwestern United States, Mexico, and South America; **leaves** opposite, entire, usually sessile; **flower** heads radiate, showy, solitary and terminal on hollow peduncles; receptacles scaly; ray flowers brightly colored, persistent; **achenes** compressed, with pappus of awns, or lacking.

Zinnia angustifolia HBK (Oblongleaf Zinnia). Annual to 45 cm. tall. June-October.

DESCRIPTION: **Plants** erect, native in Mexico; **leaves** linear to linear-lanceolate, to 6 cm. long; **flower** heads to 4 cm. across; disc flowers black purple, ray flowers 7 to 9, 1 cm. long, bright orange with a central yellow stripe.

USE: Plant toward the front of the flower border.

CULTURE: Plants thrive in most garden soils in full sun. Propagation is by seeds started indoors in early April or seeded directly where plants are to grow. Powdery mildew can be a problem in the fall. Avoid watering in the evening.

CULTIVAR

'Classic'. Ray flowers golden orange.

Zinnia elegans Jacq. (Common Zinnia). Annual to 90 cm. tall. June-October.

DESCRIPTION: **Plants** native in Mexico; **leaves** ovate, lanceolate, or oblong, to 12 cm. long; **flower** heads variable, up to 12 cm. across; disc flowers yellow to purple, when present, ray flowers 8 to 20, spatulate and usually red in the wild type, but often numerous and variously colored in named cultivars.

USE: This is one of the most popular and colorful of all garden flowers. Plant in the flower border for a mass color effect. Flowers are excellent for cutting. Smaller cultivars can be planted in a rock garden to provide summer color.

CULTURE: Plants are easy to grow in any well-drained soil but they bloom best in full sun. Seeds can be started indoors in early April or they can be direct seeded in early May. Space the plants 20 to 30 cm. apart depending on the mature size. Powdery mildew is about the only disease that threatens the plants, and it comes late in the summer. It can be controlled with a good fungicide but good air circulation and watering before evening will usually be sufficient.

CULTIVARS: Hundreds of named cultivars have been introduced, ranging in size from small-flowered dwarf plants to tall plants up to 1 m. tall and flowering heads up to 12 cm. across. Many of these named cultivars have received the coveted All-America award. The following are but a few of those receiving such recognition.

'Bonanza'. Flowering heads golden orange.
'Carved Ivory'. Flowering heads to 12 cm. across, ivory white.
'Cherry Button's'. Flowering heads small, cherry red.
'Cherry Ruffles'. Flowering heads deep scarlet red.
'Firecracker'. Flowering heads rich red.
'Flame'. Flowering heads a vibrant fiery red.
'Red Man'. Flowering heads deep scarlet.
'Rosy Future'. Flowering heads rose pink.
'Scarlet Ruffles'. Flowering heads deep scarlet red.
'Thumbelina'. Flowering heads small, to 3 cm. across, in wide color range.
'Wild Cherry'. Flowering heads very large, vibrant cherry rose.
'Yellow Ruffles'. Flowering heads vibrant golden yellow.

Zinnia haageana Rege. (Mexican Zinnia). Annual to 60 cm. tall. June-October.

DESCRIPTION: **Plants** native in Mexico; **leaves** lanceolate, to 7.5 cm. long, sessile; **flower** heads to 5 cm. across; disc flowers orange, ray flowers 8 to 9, orange in wild types but more numerous and often bicolored in cultivated types.

USE: Same as for *Z. elegans*.

CULTURE: Same as for *Z. elegans*.

CULTIVARS

'Chippendale'. Flowering heads daisylike, with yellow ray flowers and red disc flowers.   PLATE 276

'Old Mexico'. All-America Winner. Flowering heads fully double, to 6 cm. across, with deep mahogany red ray flowers, edged with bright gold. Mildew resistant.

'Persian Carpet'. All-America Winner. Flowering heads double or semi-double, to 4 cm. across, in a good color range; ray flowers tipped with a contrasting color.

Zinnia linearis — see *Zinnia angustifolia*

Glossary

GLOSSARY

Acaulescent. Apparently without a stem, the leaves and flowers arising near the surface of the ground.

Achene. A dry, indehiscent fruit with a thin wall and a single seed.

Acuminate. Tapering to a slender point.

Acute. Forming an acute angle at base or apex.

Aggregate. A fruit made up of an aggregation of several pistils from the same flower.

Alternate. Situated singly at each node, as leaves on a stem or flowers along an axis.

Androecium. The stamens in a single flower considered collectively.

Annual. Plant that grows from seed to maturity and dies in a single growing season.

Annular. In the form of a ring.

Annulus. Literally, a ring, as the fleshy corona or rim of the corolla in members of the milkweed family.

Anther. The pollen-bearing portion of the stamen, composed of two pollen sacs.

Apetalous. Without petals.

Apiculate. Ending abruptly in a small, usually sharp tip.

Asymmetric. Not symmetric, as in flowers in which the petals are not all alike.

Auricle. An ear-shaped lobe or appendage, as the projections at the base of some leaves or petals.

Awn. A slender terminal bristle.

Axil. The upper angle that a lateral organ such as a leaf petiole forms with the stem.

Axillary. Located in or arising from an axil.

Berry. A fleshy fruit developed from a single ovary and usually containing several seeds embedded in a fleshy pulp.

Biennial. Living two years only and blooming the second year.

Bifid. Two-cleft at the apex.

Bipinnate. Twice pinnate as in compound leaves.

Blade. The expanded terminal part of a flat organ, as leaf, petal, or sepal, in contrast to the narrowed basal portion.

Bract. A modified leaf from the axil of which a flower or flower cluster arises.

Bractlet. A secondary or very small bract.

Bulb. A short, vertical, underground stem for food storage on which fleshy, modified leaf bases are attached.

Bulblet. A small bulb, often formed in leaf axils or in other unusual places.

Bullate. Blistered or puckered.

Calyx. The outer whorl of modified leaves in a flower, called sepals; usually green.

Campanulate. Bell-shaped, usually descriptive of a corolla or calyx.

Capillary. Hairlike, very slender.

Capitate. Headlike; in a head.

Capsule. A dry, dehiscent fruit formed from a multicarpelled ovary and usually containing many seeds.

Carpel. A modified floral leaf that forms a simple pistil or part of a compound pistil.

Cespitose. Growing in dense tufts; usually applied only to plants of small size.

Ciliate. With marginal hairs.

Clavate. Club-shaped, gradually increasing in diameter toward the summit.

Cleistogamous. Descriptive of a flower that does not open.

Column. The structure formed by the fusion of the style and stamens in the orchid family.

Compound. Referring to leaves made up of two or more leaflets or ovaries made up of two or more carpels.

Cordate. Heart-shaped.

Corm. A short, vertical, underground storage or reproductive organ, consisting mainly of a thickened stem portion with scalelike leaves.

Corolla. The second whorl of leaves in a flower, called petals; usually large and showy.

Corona. A structure exhibited in some plants between the corolla and the stamens and often simulating an additional part of the perianth. It may arise from the corolla in the genus *Narcissus* or from the stamen in the genus *Asclepias*.

Corymb. A type of a raceme in which the axis is relatively short and the lower pedicels are relatively long, thus producing a flat-topped inflorescence.

Crenate. Leaf margins that are toothed with rounded, shallow teeth.

Cuneate. Wedge-shaped.

Cuspidate. With a sharp, abrupt, and often rigid point.

Cyathium. A type of inflorescence found in the genus *Euphorbia.* Male and female flowers are produced in a cup-shaped involucre.

Cyme. A convex or flat-topped flower cluster in which the central flower opens first.

Deciduous. Falling after the completion of its normal function; refers to leaves and floral parts.

Decumbent. Prostrate at base, erect or ascending elsewhere.

Dehiscent. Opening, as in an anther to discharge pollen, or in a fruit to discharge seeds.

Dentate. Toothed along the margins, the apex of each tooth sharp and pointing outward.

Dioecious. Bearing staminate and pistillate flowers on separate plants.

Disc. The central part of the head of the composit family, composed of tubular flowers.

Dissected. Deeply divided into many slender segments.

Drupe. A fruit with a fleshy exocarp and a hard or bony endocarp that encloses the seed or seeds.

Drupelet. A small drupe.

Ellipsoid. Shaped more or less like a football.

Emarginate. Notched at the apex.

Entire. With a continuous unbroken margin.

Epigynous. A flower in which the basal parts of the perianth adhere to the ovary; the perianth and stamens then appear to rise from the summit of the inferior ovary.

Epiphyte. A plant with no connection with the soil, growing on another plant but not deriving its food or water from it.

Evergreen. Remaining green all winter.

Exserted. Projecting out or beyond; often referring to stamens or styles that project beyond the perianth.

Fall. One of the parts of the outer whorl of the perianth in *Iris* and other related genera, often broader than those of the inner whorl and often drooping or deflexed.

Filament. The basal stalklike portion of the stamen below the anthers.

Fimbriate. Fringed.

Follicle. A dry dehiscent fruit developed from a simple ovary and splitting along a single suture.

Fruit. A ripened ovary, together with such parts of the plant that are regularly associated with it.

Fusiform. Descriptive of a solid body that is thick in the middle and tapers to both ends.

Gibbous. Swollen or protuberant on one side and commonly toward the base.

Glabrous. Smooth, without pubescence.

Glaucous. Covered with a powdery bloom that is bluish white or bluish gray.

Gynoecium. The pistil or pistils of a single flower considered collectively.

Hastate. Having two divergent basal lobes.

Head. A dense flower cluster, composed of sessile or nearly sessile flowers crowded on a short axis.

Herb. A plant that dies to the ground each fall.

Herbaceous. Dying back to the ground at the end of the growing season; leaf-like in color or texture.

Hirsute. Pubescent with spreading hairs.

Hispid. Pubescent with stiff spreading hairs.

Hypogynous. Borne on the receptacle or under the ovary; refers to sepals, petals, and stamens in flowers having a superior ovary.

Imbricate. Overlapping like shingles on a roof.

Incised. Deeply and irregularly cut.

Indehiscent. Not opening at maturity, usually applied to fruit.

Inferior. Descriptive of an ovary that adheres to the lower parts of the perianth and therefore appears to be located below the other floral parts.

Inflorescence. A complete flower cluster, including the axis and bracts.

Involucre. A set of bracts closely associated with each other and subtending an inflorescence.

Involute. Rolled inward so the lower side of the organ is exposed.

Irregular. Descriptive of a flower in which the members of one or more sets of organs differ among themselves in size, shape, or structure.

Keel. A sharp or conspicuous longitudinal ridge; also the two lower united petals in the pea family.

Labellum. The lip of the flower in the orchid family.

Laciniate. Deeply cut into narrow segments.

Lanceolate. Shaped like a lance head, much longer than wide and widest below the center.

Leaflet. A single element of a compound leaf.

Legume. A dry dehiscent fruit derived from a simple ovary and usually opening along two sutures.

Limb. The upper, more or less widened portion of the corolla or calyx in flowers where the petals or sepals are fused to form a tube.

Linear. Narrow and elongate with nearly parallel sides.

Loment. A fruit in the pea family in which the fruit is constricted between the seeds, with the one-seeded segments separating at maturity.

Lyrate. Pinnately lobed, with the terminal lobe the largest.

Mericarp. One of the segments into which the mature fruits in the carrot and mallow families split at maturity.

-merous. A suffix referring to the parts in each circle of floral organs, usually with a numerical prefix.

Monoecious. A plant bearing both staminate and pistillate flowers but not perfect ones.

Node. A point on the stem from which leaves or branches arise.

Nutlet. A small nut, differing from an achene by its thicker wall.

Ob-. A prefix, signifying in a reverse direction.

Oblique. Slanting, with unequal sides, as in the leaves of begonia.

Oblong. Descriptive of a leaf or fruit that is wider than linear with nearly parallel sides.

Obtuse. Blunt.

Orbicular. Essentially circular.

Ovary. The basal, usually expanded portion of the pistil in which the seeds develop.

Ovate. Descriptive of a flat structure that is broader than lanceolate and widest below the center.

Ovule. A reproductive organ within the ovary that develops into a seed after fertilization.

Palate. An elevated portion of the lower lip of the corolla, wholly or partly closing the throat.

Palmate. With three or more lobes or veins arising from one point.

Panicle. A compound or branched inflorescence that is usually longer than wide.

Pappus. An outgrowth of hairs, scales, or bristles from the summit of the achene in many species in the composit family.

Parasite. A plant that derives its food and water from another plant to which it is attached.

Pectinate. Comblike.

Pedicel. The stalk of a single flower in an inflorescence.

Peduncle. The portion of a stem that bears a solitary flower or an inflorescence, that is either leafless or with bracts.

Peltate. A more or less rounded leaf with the petiole attached near the center of the undersurface.

Pendent. Drooping or hanging downward.

Perfect. Descriptive of a flower having both stamens and pistils.

Perianth. The calyx and corolla considered together, or either of them if the other is lacking.

Pericarp. The outer wall of a fruit.

Petal. A separate segment of the corolla.

Petiole. The basal stalklike portion of a leaf.

Petiolule. The stalk of a leaflet of a compound leaf.

pH. Measure of acidity. A pH of 7 is neutral. A pH above 7 is alkaline whereas a pH below 7 is acid.

Phyllode. An expanded bladeless petiole.

Pinnate. Having branches, lobes, leaflets, or veins on two sides of a rachis.

Pinnatifid. With lobes or divisions pinnately arranged.

Pistil. The central organ of a flower, composed of ovary, style, and stigma.

Pistillate. Having a pistil; usually applied to flowers that lack stamens.

Plumose. Feathery; usually applied to a feathery style, with dense pubescence.

Procumbent. Prostrate or trailing, but not rooting at the nodes.

Pseudo. False.

Pubescent. Bearing hairs on the surface.

Raceme. A type of inflorescence with an unbranched axis and flowers borne along the axis on short pedicels. The lowest flowers open first.

Rachis. The axis of an inflorescence or a compound leaf.

Ray. A branch of an umbel or umbel-like inflorescence; a corolla of a ray flower in the composit family.

Receptacle. The end of the pedicel or peduncle that bears the floral organs.

Regular. Describing a flower in which the members of each circle of parts are similar in size and shape.

Reniform. Kidney-shaped; wider than long, rounded in outline, and with a wide basal sinus.

Rhizome. An underground stem, usually horizontal and often fleshy, with roots on the undersurface.

Rosette. A cluster of basal leaves crowded on short internodes.

Saccate. Saclike or dilated.

Sagittate. Arrow-shaped with two basal lobes.

Salverform. Descriptive of a fused corolla that is tubular at base with a widely spreading limb.

Samara. A dry, indehiscent, usually one-seeded fruit with a well-developed wing.

Saprophyte. A plant without green color that derives its food and water from dead organic matter in the soil.

Scape. A peduncle with one or more flowers arising directly from the ground or from a very short stem.

Scarious. Thin and chaffy in texture and not green.

Schizocarp. A dry, dehiscent fruit that splits into mericarps at maturity; mostly in the carrot family.

Sepal. One segment of the calyx.

Serrate. Toothed along the margin, with the apex of each tooth pointed and directed forward.

Serrulate. Diminutive of serrate.

Setose. Beset with bristles.

Sheath. An organ that wholly or partly surrounds another organ at the base, as when the base of the leaf partially surrounds the stem.

Silicle. A short silique.

Silique. A special type of capsule found in the mustard family, in which the two valves separate from a thin longitudinal partition called the replum.

Simple. Descriptive of a pistil developed from a single carpel or a leaf with the blade in one piece.

Sinuate. Having a wavy margin.

Solitary. Occurring singly as a solitary flower.

Spadix. A form of a spike or head with a thick or fleshy axis.

Spathe. A large, usually solitary bract subtending and often enclosing an inflorescence.

Spatulate. Shaped like a spatula, maintaining its width or somewhat broadened toward the rounded summit.

Spike. An elongate inflorescence with sessile or nearly sessile flowers. The oldest flowers are near the base as in a raceme.

Stamen. A member of the third set of floral organs, typically composed of the anther and filament.

Staminode. A sterile structure formed in place of a normal stamen.

Standard. The uppermost petal in flowers of the pea family.

Stellate. Star-shaped; a term usually applied to branched hairs.

Stigma. The terminal portion of the pistil modified for the reception and germination of pollen.

Stipules. A pair of small structures at the base of the petiole in certain leaves, varying from minute to leaflike.

Stolon. A horizontal branch arising at or near the base of a plant and taking root and developing new plants at the nodes or at the tip.

Style. The more or less elongated portion of the pistil between the ovary and the stigma.

Sub-. A prefix meaning more or less or somewhat.

Succulent. Fleshy and juicy.

Tendril. A portion of a stem or leaf modified to serve as a holdfast organ.

Tepal. A sepal or a petal. A term applied when the sepals and petals look alike in undifferentiated perianths.

Ternate. In threes.

Tetraploids. Plants with twice the normal number of chromosomes.

Truncate. With the base or apex straight or nearly so, as if cut off.

Tuber. A thickened portion of a rhizome used for food storage and also for propagation.

Tubercle. A small tuberlike structure, usually distinct in color texture from the organ on which it is borne.

Tunicate. Describing a bulb in which the leaf bases form concentric rings.

Turbinate. Top-shaped.

Umbel. A type of racemose inflorescence with short internodes and long pedicles, forming usually a flat-topped inflorescence. In a compound umbel, the pedicels are again umbellately branched at the summit.

Undulate. Wavy-margined.

Utricle. A small, thin-walled, one-seeded, more or less inflated fruit.

Versatile. Attached by the back and freely movable.

Verticillaster. A type of inflorescence found in the mint family where the flowers form in axillary whorls.

Woolly. With long, soft, often matted hairs.

Index of Common Names

INDEX OF COMMON NAMES